The
KURDS

The
KURDS

A PEOPLE IN SEARCH OF
THEIR HOMELAND

Kevin McKiernan

St. Martin's Press
New York

www.stmartins.com

Library of Congress Cataloging-in-Publication Data

McKiernan, Kevin.
 The Kurds : a people in search of their homeland / Kevin McKiernan.
  p. cm.
 ISBN 0-312-32546-0
 EAN 978-0-312-32546-6
 1. Kurds—Ethnic identity. 2. Kurds—Iraq. 3. Kurds—Turkey. 4. McKiernan, Kevin. I. Title.

DS59.K86M427 2006
956'.00491597—dc22   2005044673

First Edition: March 2006

10   9   8   7   6   5   4   3   2   1

For Catalina

Contents

BOOK III

War in Iraq

BOOK IV

Victory

Acknowledgments

Over the last fifteen years of traveling in the Middle East, I've met countless Kurds, who have invited me into their homes and, often, their lives. I had the privilege of listening to their stories and sharing in their dreams, and for that I will always be grateful.

Timothy Wager of the Sandra Dijkstra Literary Agency proposed that I write a book on the Kurds, after reading one of my news dispatches from Iraq. Without his interest and the fierce and unwavering support of Sandy Dijkstra, the project would likely have remained on my ever-lengthening list of "things to do in the future." Of the many family, friends, and supporters who encouraged me during the course of this long undertaking, I would like to thank Catherine Boyer, Caitrin McKiernan, Seamus McKiernan, Ethna McKiernan, Mike Brabeck, Ted Elbert, and Haskell Wexler for their generosity in reviewing the manuscript and providing valuable feedback. I am particularly indebted to John Tirman, David Mc-Dowall, E. Roger Owens, and Studs Terkel for offering key advice and insight on particular chapters in the book, to Rashid Karadaghi for his good humor in correcting my Kurdish vocabulary, and to Matt Coffman, my assistant, for his tireless work in the early stages of the project, even when research requests may have seemed arcane or trivial. I am grateful to several journalists for help in my original reporting, in particular to Jessica Lutz, both for her encyclopedic knowledge of Turkey and for the principled example she set for the rest of us in struggling to report both sides of the Turkish-Kurdish conflict. I would also like to acknowledge the kind assistance of the Fund for Santa Barbara, the Samuel Rubin Foundation, Rita Taggert, Leinie Bard, and Archie Bard.

I want to express my keen appreciation to Michael Flamini, Katherine Tiernan, Frances Sayers, Bob Berkel, and the editors at St. Martin's Press for their encouragement as well as their patience. And I want to thank Ruby, my mother-in-law, who passed away at age eighty-eight just as this book was going to press, for helping me keep some perspective during the last two years, inquiring each evening when I came from my office—often with a straight face—"Can you tell me one thing of importance you accomplished today?" Finally, I express my gratitude to my father, who died last year at the age of eighty-nine, for his love and support, and for teaching me the meaning of respect.

BOOK I

The Stage Is Set

.

1

Viva la Fiesta

A man who has been bitten by a snake
will always be afraid of rope.

—KURDISH PROVERB

Beginning

As bulldozers unearthed the corpses of fifty-four men executed in 1983 by
Saddam Hussein's troops, several Kurds from a nearby refugee camp stared at
the remains with curiosity. "They are just skeletons in uniforms," said one refugee.

The hands of many of the captives had been tied, noted another refugee, re-
marking that the killings must have been hasty: Loaded ammunition clips
clung to their belts and one of the dead wore a canteen that was still full, eight
years later. Someone unhooked it from the skeleton's belt and emptied the water into the grave. Nevertheless, what stuck in the minds of the Kurds, traumatized victims of a genocidal campaign largely unknown in the West at the time,
was the sight of the watches, inexpensive ones, on the wrists of two of the corpses.
The brand name was Orient, and the watches were still ticking. One witness told
me calmly, "Everyone here was surprised that watches could last so long underground."

Watches ticking on the wrists of skeletons. Husbands and sons disappearing.
Millions of refugees fleeing for the mountains in winter lest they, too, "disappear." Such searing images were my introduction to the Kurds when I arrived in
northern Iraq in 1991, at the end of the first Gulf War. The White House had exhorted the Iraqis to rise up against Saddam Hussein. The Kurds did rebel, but
without aid from Washington, they were savagely crushed, and one and one-half
million starving refugees were driven into the mountains of Iran and Turkey. I
followed their story in all three countries, and then I saw it fall out of the news.
That was a dozen years before a U.S. invasion would topple Hussein, bringing
Shiite Arabs and minority Kurds to power in Baghdad and setting the stage for
the Transitional National Assembly's selection of Kurdish leader Jalal Talabani as
president of Iraq.

By 1991, I had seen my share of conflict as a journalist, beginning as a public radio reporter in the 1970s, when I covered the FBI-Indian wars in South Dakota. Since then, I had been a witness to war in Central America, Africa, and the Middle East. Despite the horrors I had seen elsewhere, I was unprepared for the scale of devastation visited upon the Kurds. By the time I arrived in Iraq, one hundred eighty thousand Kurds were dead or missing, according to human rights monitors, and nearly four thousand villages had been destroyed in a brutal campaign of ethnic cleansing. Tens of thousands of Kurdish refugees still remained in the mountains, most of them living in tents in the snow or under plastic tarps, still terrified that Hussein's troops—who were regrouping after their retreat from Kuwait—would return.

Before long, many of the Kurdish refugees I met would be inching their way home, putting the nightmare of Iraqi domination behind them, trying to piece together a future. For the remainder of the decade, Iraqi Kurds would occupy a mini-enclave in northern Iraq, protected by allied overflights but mostly forgotten by the world. After a quarter century of forced relocation to "modern villages," mass murder, and widespread disappearances, they suddenly found themselves in the throes of a fragile liberation. For the first time, the Iraqi Kurds could travel and associate freely, share information, trace missing relatives, and rebuild villages. Sporadic fighting remained between Iraqi soldiers and the Kurdish *peshmerga* (those who face death). But each day, despite the misgivings of neighboring Turkey, Iran, and Syria, and even the United States, the Kurds of Iraq were moving closer to autonomy, if not eventual independence. Despite betrayals by friends and allies, something in their spirit, if not their luck, seemed to be changing.

I didn't realize it at first, but the Kurds are the largest ethnic group in the world without their own state. Like many first-time visitors, I would learn that "Kurdistan" was an ethnic mosaic of shifting tribal alliances that had been divided historically among the Ottoman, Persian, and Russian empires. It had never been a unified nation, but the territory of the Kurds inside the Ottoman empire, a politically and linguistically diverse area, had been carved up after World War I, the land parceled out to Iraq, Turkey, and Syria (at this point, the borders of Kurdish areas in Iran and the Soviet Union already existed). At the time, I had little sense of the Kurdish dream of reunification or of the regional powers that manipulated internal divisions among the Kurds to deny them that dream. To appreciate the complex and interwoven world of a divided people, I needed to follow the story beyond Iraq, across illusory borders to neighboring countries—especially to Turkey, which is home to a majority of the world's Kurds. It was only after more than a dozen trips to these Kurdistans, some of the visits lasting months, that I began to realize that what had occurred in this seemingly remote land had important connections to the West, especially to the United States.

As the Kurds emerged from the shadow of history, and I pursued their multi-layered story, two insights slowly came into focus. I began to realize that the local repression of the Kurds in the Middle East had been—and was being—carried out with international assistance, primarily through the supply of weapons, and, accordingly, that war crimes trials for individuals such as the "Butcher of Baghdad" would accomplish little more than revenge if the important lessons of this collusion were ignored. The other realization was the striking relevance of *American* history, a parallel that gradually illuminated each successive journey. As I pushed deeper into Kurdistan, I was struck by the fact that the Kurdish story mirrored key aspects of the conflict over land, language, and identity I had encountered at home as a young American reporter in Indian Country.

In 1991 I certainly had no idea of what lay ahead. Little could I imagine that I was embarking on an odyssey that would take years and that would bring me face-to-face with the ongoing struggle of Kurds in Iraq and Iran, a hidden war in Turkey, where I'd see Kurdish refugees driven from their homes by U.S. weapons, guerrilla safe houses in Syria and Lebanon, backpacking trips behind army lines, and more than a few scrapes with hostile soldiers. I had little inkling of future regime change in Baghdad or of a post-Saddam era in which the Kurds' old fear of dictatorship would be replaced by heady nationalism. Finally, like many others, I could not have predicted the U.S. occupation misfortune or the ferocity of an insurgency that would threaten Iraq's unity, inadvertently propelling the Kurds toward autonomy and homeland.

Hometown Pageantry

It was a hot afternoon in August, a few months after the toppling of Saddam Hussein, and Santa Barbara's Fiesta parade was about to begin. By now, rodeo riders were kicking up dust at the Earl Warren Showgrounds, the barbeque grills on East Beach were smoking, and bars all over the resort town were coming alive with mariachi music. The sidewalks in front of the Paseo Nuevo mall were packed. Onlookers yelled, "Viva la Fiesta!" and playfully cracked each other with *cascarónes*, colored eggs filled with confetti. As the crowds jockeyed for position, politicians waved flat-brimmed flamenco hats from motorized floats, and little girls in ruffled dance dresses, *trajes flamencas*, twirled in the street.

In another clash of culture and politics, a small group of Chumash Indians hoisted placards protesting the enslavement of native tribes in the late 1700s, the period when Spain built a Catholic mission and a military garrison in Santa Barbara. Such counterdemonstrations took place every summer. For most parade watchers, the protests were a harmless sideshow, almost a part of the festivities. If there were contradictions, the noisy hoopla seemed to drown them out. Old Spanish Days was as close as Santa Barbara came to a sanctioned, citywide bash.

Now in its seventy-ninth year, the fiesta had become an annual tourism bonanza for local merchants, a hybrid ethnic event promoted by the city council and the chamber of commerce. The war in Iraq seemed over. It was carnival time in Santa Barbara.

The Kurdish Driver

Among the thousands attending the festivities was Karzan Mahmoud, my Kurdish driver from northern Iraq. I watched Karzan slip into the middle of State Street, awkwardly clutching a Kodak camera in his left hand. He was trying to take photos of the deputy sheriffs passing on horseback. The deputies were decked out in cowboy boots and hats, wore pearl-handled revolvers in holsters, and carried rifles in leather cases by their silver-colored saddles. Karzan's right hand, mangled in a terrorist attack in Iraq, lay stiffly at his side, but that crisis was largely behind him now and he seemed delighted by the spectacle. He had seen cowboys and horses in the black-and-white westerns on Iraqi TV. Now he was in California, in a western of his own. "Karzan big man," he said jokingly in his much-improved English.

Karzan's camera was a gift from my high school friend, Mike Brabeck, the Boston physician who arranged the U.S. surgeries for Karzan's wounds. The young Kurd, looking much older than his twenty-five years, had been shot the year before in an assassination attempt on the Kurdish prime minister. Hit by twenty-three bullets in less than a minute, Karzan knew it was a wonder he'd survived. For the last few months, thanks to Dr. Brabeck, Massachusetts surgeons had been operating to repair the damage. Recently, the *Boston Globe* had published a dramatic account of his recovery, complete with before and after photos. Karzan had twenty copies of the *Globe* story packed away in his suitcase, ready to give his friends back home.

I had met Karzan in northern Iraq in February 2002, when I was on assignment for ABC News. It was more than a year before the Iraq war. I was the only American reporter in Kurdistan, and the Iraqi Kurds had rolled out the red carpet. Barham Salih, the prime minister of the Patriotic Union of Kurdistan (PUK), one of the two major Kurdish factions, assigned Karzan as my driver, and the PM sent along a couple of bodyguards with AK-47s to look after me. He was worried, he said, that I'd be a target of an al-Qaeda–linked group called Ansar al-Islam.

As it turned out, the target was the prime minister himself. Only a month after my visit, heavily armed assassins attacked Salih's home. Salih escaped injury, but five of his bodyguards—all Karzan's friends—were killed in a ferocious firefight on the prime minister's doorstep. Karzan and three other members of the security detail were wounded. Moments after hearing the news, the mother of one of the slain guards collapsed from a heart attack and died.

. . .

The assault in northern Iraq took place just a few weeks after Danny Pearl, the *Wall Street Journal* reporter, was beheaded in Pakistan. When I learned about Pearl's murder, I was in northern Syria, the Kurdish part of the country. At the time, I was staying in a cheap hotel near the Tigris River, preparing to cross quietly into Iraqi Kurdistan. I had rented a $12 room, a cold and filthy cubicle with SWETH—a misspelling of "suite"—hand printed on the door. It was a Friday morning, and I'd just been awakened by the drone from the loudspeakers mounted on a minaret of a mosque near the hotel. The *muezzin* was calling the faithful to prayer.

I heard a series of loud explosions, and I quickly made my way to the lobby, a dingy room partially lit by the glow of a black-and-white television. The desk clerk was friendly and he told me not to worry. It was noisy, he said, because it was *al-Adha*, the holy day that celebrates the story of Abraham, the father of Islam, the prophet revered by both Muslims and Jews. He explained that Abraham had been instructed by God to show his loyalty by sacrificing his firstborn son. At the last minute, an angel had substituted a sheep, and the child was spared. That was why Muslims were celebrating with fireworks and why at that moment, the clerk said, two million Muslims were making the annual pilgrimage to Mecca.

News was blaring in the background. The clerk pointed to the TV screen. The Arab news station al-Jazeera, was replaying a tape of kidnappers pointing a gun at Pearl's head. The scene was followed by footage of the reporter's pregnant wife, who was anxiously awaiting word of his fate.

The Kurdish prime minister said he was worried I'd become another Danny Pearl. The concern was understandable. Three months earlier, only weeks after the September 11 attacks in the United States, Bush administration officials had quietly alerted Kurdish leaders to their plans for "regime change" in Iraq. But the hopes of the Kurds for U.S. intervention had been dashed before, and Kurdish leaders were keenly aware that an American casualty in Iraq could lessen the public's appetite for war. The killing of a journalist, an American visitor under the protection of the Kurds, might be front-page news. It could hurt the war effort.

Compared to the wealth of tragedies incurred by the Kurds, the loss of a visiting reporter seemed insignificant. However, the Kurds had a history of multiple betrayals, and with fresh interest in their cause emanating from Washington, they were hypersensitive to minor shifts in American public opinion. The U.S. appetite for foreign adventures was fickle enough, without the preventable death of an American making it go sour one more time. Besides, I was a familiar face in Kurdistan, with more than a dozen visits since 1991. I knew the prime minister was looking out for my welfare.

I first met Salih in the mid-1990s, when he represented the PUK in

Washington. It was a challenging time for all the Kurds, a period of intense but mostly unrewarded effort to attract world recognition. The rebellion in Turkey, the longest Kurdish uprising in history, had been virtually ignored by the U.S. media. The struggle of the Kurds of Syria and Iran had received even less coverage in the Western press. The Kurds of Iraq had managed to gain some notice after the Gulf War in 1991, only to sink back into oblivion for the remainder of the decade. They were stuck in their powerless enclave, surrounded by Saddam Hussein's army on one side and hostile neighbors Syria, Turkey, and Iran on the other sides. The U.S. air cover, initiated in 1991, had given them an opportunity to transcend internal differences, which had plagued their independence movement for a quarter century. Instead of unifying for strength against their common enemies, however, Iraqi Kurds in the mid-1990s were killing each other over profits from oil smuggling. Landlocked, with no seaport or airport, struggling to govern a "rump state," they were beholden to the interests of outside powers and riven by factionalism, greed, and shortsightedness. They seemed to be at another dead end, and it looked as if they had blown their chance. Some critics were writing them off as one of history's losers.

On balance, they were now better off than before Saddam had crushed their uprising in 1991. After that short-lived rebellion, the allies had set up a safety zone in northern Iraq, giving the Kurds a piece of territory about twice the size of the state of Massachusetts—a no-fly zone, with protection by coalition jets. But on the ground, in some places only a matter of minutes away, Hussein's army was still a menace. The wily despot had survived the Kuwait war, just as he had survived the 1970s, when the Nixon administration paid the Kurds to rebel in Iraq only to broker a secret deal with Saddam that sold them out. Despite more than a decade of protection by the West, Kurdish leaders in 2002 were wary of another betrayal.

Factionalism

The issue of oil has played a key role in Kurdish history since the 1920s, when the British made their first oil strikes in northern Iraq. When I visited in 2002, one of the most intractable issues between the Kurdish factions was the exclusive control by the Kurdish Democratic Party (KDP) of transit fees on Iraqi oil shipments bound for Turkey—fees the United States estimated to be one million dollars per day. However, with active encouragement by Washington officials, the quarrelsome parties were meeting regularly to iron out their differences—enough, at least, to accommodate U.S. plans for war.

With the threat from Saddam still alive, Kurdish fence-mending was reminiscent of the need for strategic alliances in American history. What Benjamin Franklin said about the bickering American colonists now applied to the Kurds: They had better hang together or they might hang *separately*. As long as the factions fought each other and Saddam clung to power, they would remain impotent, their long-term interests sidelined. For the time being at least, the United States was supplying the glue—President Bush's hints of regime change—and the two Kurdish parties looked as if they would stick together.

Even if the administration was right that Saddam Hussein had stockpiled weapons of mass destruction, and even if a U.S. attack provoked him into using the weapons on the nearby Kurds, Kurdish leaders believed the risk was worth it. The war offered a once-in-a-lifetime gamble to advance from fear and obscurity to freedom and recognition. With a rare opportunity to ride on the coattails of Uncle Sam, Kurdish leaders were not talking about seemingly theoretical problems: potential damage to the prestige of the security council, the danger of preemption as a precedent for settling future disputes among hostile nations, or the prospect of a U.S. invasion reenergizing al-Qaeda. Others could worry about international consequences. The Kurds had been victims too long. The war was their chance.

Ancient Times

There was a time when the Kurds were powerful and prominent. Most scholars trace the beginnings of Kurdish civilization to pre-Christian times. Some archaeologists point to what they believe are references to the Kurds in Sumerian inscriptions dating to 2,000 B.C., which were discovered in present-day Turkey, near Lake Van. Others refer to writings by the Greek historian Xenophon in the fourth century B.C., which describe a disobedient tribe of fighters, the likely ancestors of the Kurds, who made a living hell for the Greek army. According to Xenophon's *Anabasis (Retreat of the Ten Thousand)*, "They dwelt up among the mountains, were a warlike people, and were not subjects of the king."

Indian Renaissance

Some Kurds believe they are indigenous to the Middle East, an original people akin to native tribes in the Americas. Regardless of their respective origins, there are parallels between the groups as perennial underdogs with a history of conflict—much of it rooted in culture and ethnicity.

American Indians, militarily conquered in the nineteenth century, saw a reawakening of spirit and confidence in the 1970s. The period was marked by a revival of native language and religion in the Americas, but it was a bloody time as well, especially on the Pine Ridge Indian Reservation in South Dakota. My own baptism by fire came in 1973, during the U.S. government's long siege of Wounded Knee, the site of the famous 1890 massacre. I saw Indians shot to death during the ten-week standoff at Wounded Knee; and I was nearly shot myself. Wounded Knee was followed by three years of civil war on the reservation, where I saw both Indians and FBI agents killed by gunfire. The bitter war between the so-called traditionalist and assimilated factions was similar in some ways to the internecine conflict that has plagued the Kurds for generations.

I wondered then what it was that was worth *dying* for. Was it land or language, or identity or sovereignty, or a combination of them all? Later, when I met the Kurds, brushing up against a struggle that also had triggered genocide, some of the same questions resurfaced.

Like all analogies, the Indian-Kurd parallel went flat when pushed to the extreme. Native American groups, for example, were fiercely proud of their *tribal* characteristics, while some Iraqi Kurds today—despite distinct family communities and separate dialects from other Kurds—find the word "tribal" unsophisticated, even offensive. Yet, there were valid parallels, not the least of which were the ancient—albeit disputed—origins for both civilizations. Remains found recently on islands off the coast of my hometown of Santa Barbara, California, for example, suggest that the native presence in North America could be more than ten thousand years old—a claim that, if true, might challenge or at least alter the long-held theory of an "ice bridge" from Siberia to North America.

The Kurds—or their forebears—might be almost as old.

Medes

Many Kurds today maintain they are descended from the Medes, the nomadic tribes that lived between the Persian Gulf and the Caspian Sea centuries before the birth of Christ. The Medes were mentioned in texts of the ancient Assyrians in the ninth century B.C. The first legendary Median king was Deioces, who was crowned in the year 728 B.C. By 612 B.C., the Medes had become powerful enough to attack and overrun Nineveh, the Assyrian capital, located in modern-day Iraq. At its height, the empire of the Medes reached from Asia Minor to Central Asia.

The Kurds well may have *mixed* origins. Most scholars maintain that there is no pure race, that every culture has a composite past as well as a salvation history—whether it be the fabled founding of Rome by Romulus and Remus or the legendary chopping down of the famous cherry tree by George Washington. It is not surprising that the Medes figure prominently in modern-day accounts of Kurdish history, especially in political ones. The name of MED TV, the television station of the Kurdistan Workers' Party (PKK), the Kurdish separatists in Turkey, is a case in point. I first encountered MED TV in the 1990s, when I traveled with PKK rebels in southeastern Turkey. Theirs was an old-fashioned war, and PKK guerrillas used mules to transport heavy weapons up and down the mountain trails. However, one of the animals carried a high-tech satellite dish, which was used to capture broadcasts from the MED TV station in Belgium, two thousand miles away. The PKK anthem sung by the rebels and featured on MED TV contained the words, "We are the *sons of the Medes*. . . . Our god is Kurdistan." During my trip, I met several women guerrillas with the nom de guerre Medea. By that point, the Kurdish uprising had already taken more than thirty thousand lives, most of them Kurds. One guerrilla claimed the costly rebellion was a matter of self-defense. "This is the land of the Medes," she told me. "This is our *home*."

While modern scholarship differs about their origins, it is safe to say that the Kurds come from an Indo-European tribe that was first noticed in the Zagros Mountains, near the present-day borders of Iraq, Iran, and Turkey, sometime between 4,000 and 700 B.C. The Kurds lived in the Fertile Crescent between the Tigris and Euphrates Rivers in early Mesopotamia, the so-called cradle of civilization. Their story, by whatever account, is ancient history.

Today, twenty-five to thirty million Kurds live in the Middle East. The number does not include the millions of Kurds who fled the Middle East for political or economic reasons during the twentieth century. The exodus started at the end of World War I, and the process intensified near the end of the century, largely due to conflict in Iraq and Turkey. Today, the far-flung Kurdish diaspora is heaviest in Western Europe and Scandinavia, but it extends to Australia, Canada, the United States, and other countries. After World War I, the United States and its European allies pledged to give the Kurds a homeland. Instead, the West reneged on the promise, spawning generations of resistance fighters—"terrorists" in the eyes of their respective governments in Iraq, Turkey, Iran, and Syria.

Betrayal and a Place of Their Own

In the decades following World War I, the Kurds were both targeted and betrayed by world powers. Enforcing its postwar mandate on Iraq in the 1920s, Britain ordered the Royal Air Force (RAF) to bomb Kurdish rebels and other dissident tribesmen. Widespread resistance to occupation continued on and off for more than a decade, much of it in mountainous areas of northern Iraq. In one incident in 1930, British troops fired directly into Kurdish protesters in the city of Sulaimaniah, killing dozens. Meanwhile, Kurdish unrest in neighboring Turkey led to major uprisings in 1925 and 1938. Turkish troops crushed the rebellions and executed dozens of Kurdish leaders in public hangings.

In the 1940s, as the British-supported Iraqi army put down a large rebellion in Iraq, the Kurds in Iran managed to get political support from the Soviets to establish their own republic. But it soon became clear that Iranian Kurds were just pawns in a postwar chess game. After only nine months, the Soviets withdrew their patronage, partly in exchange for access to Iranian oil. Some leaders of the short-lived Kurdish republic were executed; others took refuge in the Soviet Union. After the briefest appearance on the world stage, the Kurdish movement slipped back into the shadows.

In 1958, the Iraqi monarchy was overthrown, raising hopes that Kurds and Arabs might live together in a new and unified country. Dissident Kurds were invited to return to Iraq, and a new constitution was drafted explicitly mentioning the Kurds for the first time. The rapprochement was short-lived, however, and in 1961 Kurdish rebels took up arms once again, reviving their struggle against the central government. In the 1970s, the Kurds were led to believe that America was behind them after U.S. Secretary of State Henry Kissinger secretly channeled U.S. funds to rebel bases in Iraq. The real U.S. agenda, though, was to get land concessions from Iraq for the Shah of Iran, who was a friend of Kissinger's. When that was accomplished, Kurdish military locations were disclosed, and rebel resistance collapsed within days. The Kurds had been tricked.

In the 1980s, the Kurds watched in horror as the United States and its allies armed Saddam Hussein. As America and Europe looked away, the Iraqi dictator killed Kurdish civilians, some of them with chemical weapons supplied by the West. Iraq's invasion of Kuwait in 1990 triggered the first Gulf War, a conflict that raised—but soon dashed—the hopes of the Kurds. After massive U.S. aerial and ground attacks in 1991, Iraqi forces retreated, paving the way for an allied march to Baghdad. Before the war, President George H. W. Bush had branded Saddam "worse than Hitler," but the American president had no international mandate to overthrow the Iraqi regime and, had he attempted to so, it is likely that Syria and Saudi Arabia would have dropped out of the coalition. Fearing repercussions from the allies, as well as U.S. domestic political fallout from extended involvement in Iraq, Bush declined to enlarge the conflict. Instead, the president exhorted the Kurds and others to rise up against the Iraqi dictator. When they did, however, the United States stood to the side, allowing Saddam to crush the rebellion with Russian-made helicopter gunships returned to the Iraqi army under the generous American terms of surrender. The president's decision forced almost two million Kurds to flee for safety to the mountains of Iran and Turkey, one of the largest migrations in modern history. Tens of thousands of hapless refugees died trying to escape the Iraqi army. Once again, the Kurds found themselves alone and abandoned.

Among the refugees in 1991 was my friend Karzan (then thirteen years old), his parents, and siblings. As his family hurried on foot to cross the Iranian frontier, Karzan's sister—a toddler at the time—was struck by a car driven by a panicked Kurd who was also trying to escape. The child sustained permanent head injuries. A decade later, al-Qaeda would become a major threat to the Kurds. As his now-teenage brain-damaged sister struggled, Karzan would be shot by terrorists, bringing new heartache to the family.

In the mid-1990s, under the Clinton administration, CIA agents based themselves in Kurdish territory and recruited both Kurds and Arabs for a new revolt against the Baghdad government. But once again, there was no U.S. follow-through. The Kurds saw American resolve aborted by half-hearted commitment and, seemingly, by fear of another entanglement abroad. In northern Iraq, where the most pressing issue was fear of renewed attack by Saddam's troops, hundreds of Kurds were captured and executed, thousands more forced to flee. Another uprising had failed.

To the Forefront

It was August 2003, and I was back home after seven months in Iraq. The war launched the previous March had come—but it hadn't gone. No one could dispute that the regime had been overthrown, or that thousands of Iraqi troops and civilians and hundreds of allied soldiers were dead, or that U.S. and British forces occupied the country. However, Saddam was a still a fugitive, saboteurs were setting off bombs and blowing up oil pipelines, guerrillas were attacking U.S. forces, and the Shiites, who made up the majority of the Iraqi population, were demonstrating in the streets with signs that said YANKEE GO HOME. Widespread looting, while characterized by U.S. Secretary of Defense Donald Rumsfeld as "untidiness" at the end of a dictatorship, in fact had gutted the country's infrastructure. The administration continued to dismiss resistance to the occupation as the work of ragtag ex-Ba'athists—"dead enders" in Rumsfeld's words—but a far broader discontent had begun to emerge.

Clearly, the "shock and awe" phase of the war had overwhelmed Iraqi resistance, but the failure to plan for what came next threatened to become a major foreign policy disaster. Three months earlier, the president had landed on an aircraft carrier near San Diego to declare "mission accomplished" in Iraq. Now, though, the temperature in Baghdad was 120 degrees Fahrenheit, and the United States still couldn't get the water or electricity to work.

By contrast, the Kurds of northern Iraq were polishing an experiment in democratic self-rule that they had begun in 1991. The chaos in the rest of Iraq only made them appear more civilized. While a nasty conflict still lingered between the Kurds, Arabs, and the Turkmen in the oil-rich city of Kirkuk, the bulk of Kurdistan was still the safest part of postwar Iraq. Compared to the rest of the country, the Kurds were beginning to look like winners.

And here was Karzan, my bodyguard and driver, eight thousand miles and eleven time zones from home in Iraq, cavorting at a fiesta in Santa Barbara. Here was a Kurd who had beaten some long odds: He had survived a well-planned terrorist attack in the Middle East, and then strangers in Boston, Massachusetts—a city and state he'd never heard of—had offered, without charge, to rebuild his life. It had been an improbable journey from the get-go, beginning with the challenge of an Iraqi citizen snagging a U.S. visa in the wake of the events of September 11.

When he'd first asked for help, I'd given the scheme little chance of success. Now he was my houseguest—the young man who'd been wounded twenty-three times defending a Kurdish prime minister—a tourist limping around Old Spanish Days, dodging horse traffic with a smile on his face. Here was Karzan, whose family story embodied much of the recent and tragic history of the Kurds, wearing a Mexican sombrero to shade him from the California sun, prancing around with a camera, mimicking the photojournalists he'd seen documenting his own culture.

Karzan looked right at home with the crowds lining the parade route, but his getup gave me an excuse to tease him about his arrival in America. A few months earlier, he'd briefly been detained at JFK after steel surgical pins in his leg triggered metal detectors in the airport. Now he was in Santa Barbara, a Middle Eastern tourist in the time of Homeland Security. I mentioned the proximity of the Mexican border to Karzan and I described the familiar green vans of the U.S. Immigration Services, which were known to cruise our local streets. I playfully adjusted his borrowed sombrero. With the black humor we had come to enjoy in a growing friendship, I reminded him that mistakes could happen.

What a sight he was, this optimistic Kurd at a party celebrating Spain's influence in California two centuries before. With all those contradictions, the bad luck of Kurdish history and his own troubles back home, he could be vulnerable. It would be a pity, I warned him jokingly, if he got picked up by the U.S. Border Patrol and deported to Tijuana.

2

1991: Secret Nation or Forgotten Enclave?

When you lose a language, you lose a culture, intellectual wealth,
a work of art. It's like dropping a bomb on a museum, the Louvre.

—PROFESSOR KENNETH HALE, LINGUIST

For it hath alwayes bene the use of the conqueror to despise the
language of the conquered, and to force him by all meanes to learne his.

—EDMUND SPENSER

1991 Emergency Airlift

Had it not been for a telephone call near the end of the Persian Gulf War in 1991, I might never have met the Kurds or been tempted to try to unravel their hidden, often tangled, story. The call was from Direct Relief International (DRI), a nonprofit organization in Santa Barbara, asking me to travel to Iran. For almost half a century, DRI had collected medical supplies for refugees around the world. Over the years, I had escorted DRI shipments to El Salvador, Cuba, Jordan, and other countries.

The Iraqi army had just been driven from Kuwait. Saddam Hussein's forces were attacking a group called the Kurds, and they were fleeing from Iraq in huge numbers. DRI was organizing an airlift to Kurdish refugee camps in western Iran. Could I accompany a couple of tons of supplies? Iran was a closed society at the time, off limits to most journalists. An estimated 1.5 million Kurdish refugees were already in Iran, but the government was restricting foreign press, and most journalists were flocking to Turkey, where a relatively smaller number of refugees—an estimated five hundred thousand—had fled. The trip offered unique access, and I didn't hesitate to accept, even if my motives were mixed.

Gaining admission to Iran could be tricky, but DRI's track record would help. In 1989, the agency had responded to a massive earthquake in Iran, sending tons of supplies for relief. These days, Direct Relief was one of the few U.S.-based agencies welcome in the country. Another advantage was the fact that I had an Irish passport. Considering the frosty relations between Tehran and Washington, a non-U.S. passport could make it easier to get the necessary visa.

Back in 1991 I may have fancied myself a world traveler, but the truth was that I knew little or nothing about the Kurds. To prepare me for the trip, DRI set up a crash course with the only Iraqi Kurd in town, a postdoctoral student at the University of California, Santa Barbara (UCSB). His name was Rashid Karadaghi. Twenty years earlier, he had emigrated from a Kurdish city in Iraq, a place called Sulaimaniah. To get my visa, I had to be in Washington, D.C., the next day to meet the "Iranian Interest Section"—which turned out to be just two Iranians with one briefcase, some letterhead in Farsi, and a portable machine for visa embossing—in a back room at the embassy of Algeria (a country that maintained diplomatic relations with Iran). There wasn't much time. Rashid had forty-five minutes to clue me in on the geopolitical history of the Kurds in Iran, Iraq, Syria, and Turkey and the crimes of the dictator Saddam Hussein in Iraq.

Freedom Fighter Armed with a Dictionary

Rashid lived in the student ghetto near UCSB, in a one-room cottage where the floor was littered with scraps of paper, old texts, and scrolls of words. Recently, he had earned his Ph.D. in American literature, and now he paid the rent by teaching English composition courses at the university. The cluttered floor space, though, was a mirror of his true passion. Rashid was in the process of writing a comprehensive Kurdish-English dictionary, a drawn-out endeavor that would become his life's work. He had been at it for more than twenty years, and now he had reached page 4,112 in the giant manuscript, having just added "domino effect," a term he had heard on a talk show on his car radio. He had recorded a staggering 60,000 entries by longhand, telling me proudly, "You know, Samuel Johnson's *Dictionary* only had 42,000 entries!"

Rashid was thousands of miles from Sulaimaniah, the place he still called home. He had been gone for a generation, but he had held on to his culture by devoting himself to the preservation of the Kurdish language. By now, he'd become an American citizen, but his life's focus was identity, not just nationalism. "The Kurdish language," he insisted, "makes us who we are." Rashid explained that Kurdish was an Indo-European language closely related to Farsi, the mother tongue of Iran. There were two primary branches, Sorani and Kermanji, each of which was distinct enough to give a speaker of the other dialect occasional difficulty in following a conversation. The subdialects of Kurdish include Zaza, Leki, Gurani, and Kirmanshahi. Rashid spoke Sorani, the language of the eastern part of Iraq's Kurdish region (Sorani is also the dialect spoken by many of Iran's seven million Kurdish citizens).

Rashid reminded me of my own roots. My mother and father were born in the United States, but three of my grandparents were Irish immigrants. When I was young, my father made a living as a college professor, but his real dream was to create an Irish-American cultural institute, one devoted to Irish heritage, art, music, and the Irish language. He finally realized the dream, and he became a speaker and writer of Irish. He was convinced, as he often said, that "What is bred in the bone will out." Despite his American citizenship, he became a leader in Ireland in the movement to revive and preserve the Irish language. In the United States, he founded an international institute with members from eighty-nine countries, established a prominent Celtic library, taught Irish literature courses on a university campus, and became an invited guest at the White House. He had a doctorate in American literature, but he rejected the argument that assimilation required the erasure of heritage and identity.

My father's work resonated strongly with me in the 1970s, when as a young man I went to South Dakota to report on Americans Indians. There, I encountered people who had lost their original tongue—the Lakota language—and now were trying to learn it from their elders, the "keepers of the flame." The teachers on the Rosebud and Pine Ridge Indian Reservations were old traditionalists like Fools Crow, Black Elk, and Crow Dog. They talked of their forebears—and of history in general—in the *present* tense, noting how the legendary Chief Sitting Bull, a speaker of Lakota, often had reminded his followers, "If someone loses something and goes back and carefully looks for it, he will find it."

On the surface, Rashid's Kurdish-English dictionary idea wasn't a revolutionary concept, not when you consider how expression and sentence patterns are rooted in self-conception and how oppressors across the ages have targeted native languages and tried to eliminate them. Still, in his own way he struck me as a fighter, every bit as much a Kurdish patriot as the *peshmerga* I would soon meet in the Middle East, the men with the sun-hardened faces holding AK-47s in their mountain bunkers. "They can confiscate your land and they can take your cattle away, too," Rashid said, "but as long as you have your language, you are a people."

When it came to briefing me, Rashid had his work cut out for him. The rapid onslaught of information about the Kurdish history, politics, and culture seemed overwhelming. Halfway through the compressed tutorial, I tried to recite what I'd just learned about Turks, Kurds, Syrian Kurdistan, Iranian Kurdistan, Turkish Kurdistan, and so on. But I'd become tongue-tied. "So you people," I stammered foolishly, "do you people speak *Turdish*?"

Iran on an Irish Passport

The Irish passport was a legacy of my grandparents, who'd come to America in steerage at the end of the nineteenth century. They were failed tenant farmers with one-way tickets to a new world. They hardly could have guessed that one day the U.S. Congress would recognize dual citizenship, making me and my children eligible for one of their travel documents.

I can't say the passport has saved my life, but at times it has helped me ease out of an anti-American crowd and go on my way. Most of all, it has given me access to parts of the world I might not have seen otherwise, and that was the case with the visa to Iran. Unfortunately, once I succeeded in getting into Iran, and once I had traveled to the Kurdish area, nationality alone did not insulate me from the suspicion that I was a "fellow traveler" of the Kurds.

Some of the mistrust of foreigners was a residue of U.S. involvement in the 1953 coup that brought the Shah of Iran to power. However, the Kurdish issue had been volatile in Iran since 1919, when a warlord named Simku made nationalist claims and supported a movement for limited Kurdish autonomy. Simku's movement was crushed, and subsequent attempts over the years had met a similar fate. Now it was 1991, but Iran was still fighting Kurdish insurgents, and the insurgents were said to be stepping up activities against government forces, hoping to capitalize on the chaos caused by the huge influx of Kurdish refugees from Iraq. Guerrillas tend to exploit instability, and Iranian officials feared, among other things, that foreign spies disguised as relief workers might slip into the country to support the insurgency.

Guilt by Association

One night as I lay in bed in a Kurdish-owned hotel in Iran's northwest, I had a surprise visit from Iran's secret police. Using the manager's passkey, the *pasdaran* abruptly barged into my room, startling me from a light sleep. They were dressed in leather jackets with baggy pockets—a popular means in many countries for concealing weapons. One of them spoke perfect English. "Why don't you have an *Irish* accent?" he asked with the kind of unhappy smile interrogators seem to manage. I told him I had been born in the United States, just as the Irish passport indicated.

The undercover agents rooted through my camera gear and personal belongings as if it were their own. When they finished their rummaging and opened the door to leave, I caught a glimpse of the manager in the hallway. He seemed to recognize me, probably from the brief pleasantries we'd exchanged the day before. Now he was standing there, helplessly, a Kurd in a police state, a look of embarrassment on his face.

A British doctor was staying in the room next door. He had been working in the refugee camps. I wasn't sure whether he represented an agency or was there independently. I soon heard the passkey turning the tumblers in his lock. I grabbed a water glass off my bureau and flipped it upside down, pressing the mouth to the wall to catch the conversation on the other side. I heard the doctor say, "You can't just *take* my passport like that!" He sounded shocked. I imagined the reaction of the intruders, the cold smiles. As I eavesdropped, I was able to make out the plaintive last words of the doctor, "Don't I at least get a *receipt?*"

The next morning in the lobby, the manager apologized for having surrendered the passkey. He said he had no choice. The British doctor, he added, had been deported.

Urmia

The Kurdistan Democratic Party of Iraq (KDP) had an office in town, which was where I first met Nechirvan Barzani, the twenty-four-year-old nephew of party leader Massoud Barzani and the great nephew of the legendary Mulla Mustafa Barzani, who founded the KDP in 1946. Nechirvan had fled from Iraq in the late 1970s with other Kurdish refugees, and he had learned Farsi, the Persian language, as a youth growing up in exile in Iran. The KDP office was located in a dumpy compound on a dusty street in a working-class neighborhood. What impressed me, however, was part of young Barzani's Kurdish uniform. He had a small revolver in a holster on his belt. It looked tiny and oddly ceremonial. Apparently, the Iranian government permitted him to wear the gun for self-defense, at least within the compound.

I had known the Kurds for only a week, and this was my first lesson: Iran supported the idea of Kurdish revolution—as long as it was in Iraq. Later, I would learn that Syria also supported Kurdish revolution—as long as it was in Turkey.

Iran's support for Iraqi dissidents was Machiavellian, with its own anti-Iraq motivation. Nechirvan's authority to carry the little gun provided a big insight. It was the first symbol of international recognition of the Kurds I had encountered. The Tehran government was fighting its own Kurdish guerrillas, yet it acknowledged the separateness of these Kurds as an ethnic group, *at least in Iraq.* Just for a moment, Iran's political agenda seemed secondary. The modest office took on the feel of an embassy.

I visited the Kurdish refugee camps, met with officials and followed the distribution of the Direct Relief shipments. There were no Americans in sight, but I ran into a Turkish Kurd named Halil Ibrahim and a Swiss journalist named Ruedi Suter. Ibrahim, a refugee living in Basel, Switzerland, was in the process of delivering some fourteen tons of medical supplies to camps along the Iran-Iraq border. Suter had a long history in the region. He had been with Kurdish rebels during the famous uprising of 1975, one of the few journalists at the time to smuggle himself into the mountains of northern Iraq. Unaware of the CIA underpinnings and the U.S-Iranian agenda, he had covered the uprising as a national liberation struggle. During his time with then-obscure Kurds, he had interviewed

Mullah Mustafa Barzani, the legendary guerrilla leader, and had come under fire from warplanes, Saddam's Soviet-made MiGs.

Sneaking into Iraq

Ruedi and I struck up a friendship. When I finished my work for Direct Relief, we set out together to cross the border into Iraq. Kurdish smugglers agreed to guide us over the snow-capped mountains, but the networks of trails on the rugged frontier, the site of the fiercest fighting of the 1980–1988 Iran-Iraq war, were still laced with land mines. The crossing seemed too dangerous.

Instead, we left the Kurdish section of Iran by bus and crossed into the Kurdish section of Turkey. Soon after passing the border, we stopped in a dirt village teeming with refugees who had fled the Iraqi army. We got off the bus and made our way to a teahouse, where I bought a book of Turkish phrases from a local Kurd. Within an hour, we met a Kurdish refugee from Iraq who spoke some Turkish. He was a *peshmerga*, a guerrilla fighter, although at that moment he was unarmed. He was headed home to Iraq and agreed to help us. The first step would be to take a bus for about two hundred miles to get to a trail where he thought it was safe to secretly cross the border.

The Turkish road passed through an area where there had been fighting between PKK rebels, Turkish Kurds, and the Turkish army. Our new guide warned us that the bus would be searched at checkpoints, and that a Kurd sitting next to a foreigner would raise suspicions among the Turkish soldiers. So he taught us a couple of words in Turkish: *şimdi,* which means "now," and *sonra,* which means "later." Now our little smuggling venture had a leader, a common travel goal, and a vocabulary for action based on two time frames: the present and the future. We were passengers in a conspiracy directed by a stranger, who was sitting a few rows away and pretending not to know us. I had been with Kurds in Turkey for less than a day, but already there was an ambience of the underground, of secondary existence that flowed from ethnicity, from life in the shadows.

At times, when the driver wasn't paying attention, our friend would signal by hand, whispering *şimdi* or *sonra,* shaking or nodding his head. For a clandestine operation, the code was crude but effective. Two days later, we were picking our way down a mountain trail into Iraq. Our guide was still joking about our two-word vocabulary, but any sense of triumph we had upon reaching northern Iraq quickly gave way to shock. The abortive uprising by the Kurds, triggered by the liberation of Kuwait weeks earlier, had been savagely crushed, and the landscape around us told a story of destruction and anarchy.

The Kurds had been completely cut off from the world. Everywhere we went, we saw bombed-out buildings, downed power and telephone wires, and the carcasses of dead animals. There was still snow in the mountains, but no one had electricity or heat. Armed *peshmerga* wandered about in no apparent pattern or formation. Some of the roads were blocked by abandoned cars and trucks; many of the vehicles had smashed fenders and bullet holes through the windows. Most of the tires and removable engine parts had been looted. By now, Iraqi troops had pulled back. With the exception of an occasional army helmet, canteen, or military boot, there were few signs of the hated military.

The Kurds were traumatized. We passed them huddled at the side of the road around flickering fires. They seemed dazed, suspended in time, many with a piercing, hollow-eyed gaze that went right through us. The look of horror was mesmerizing, but we kept moving.

No Friends but the Mountains

The Hamilton Road, the highway blasted through the mountains by the British from 1928 to 1932, recently had served as an escape route for tens of thousands of Kurds fleeing to Iran. When we arrived, the road was lined with hundreds of fresh graves, most of them dug for children, the victims of typhoid, dehydration, and dysentery. Some of the panicked refugees had been blown up by Iraqi land mines when they strayed from the pavement in search of a place to relieve themselves.

On one mountainside I saw a father bury his baby daughter, whose body was wrapped in a woven Kurdish blanket. He stood by, tearless, as relatives wielding machetes hacked a grave from the rocky soil. Seen through the lens of my camera, he appeared devoid of expression as he slowly leaned over and placed her tiny body in the shallow hole. Without losing composure, he straightened up again as others covered the child's body with earth. I found myself scanning the frame for clues to his feeling, searching for some familiar grammar of grief.

The faces of these Kurds were cursed by a stoic dignity that ironically or perversely—I don't know which—seemed to contradict the moment. Here, the devastated father stood to attention in traditional dress, looking like a prince at a palace ceremony. However, pictures told only part of the story. I might have been fooled altogether had the mourner not approached me after the burial, patting his heart with the palm of his hand. He embraced me, thanking me in both Kurdish and Arabic for coming to honor his daughter. I was a total stranger. I could feel him trembling.

Another image from the 1991 mass exodus also sticks in my mind—a scene on a dirt road in the Zagros Mountains, near the Iranian frontier. We had caught a ride in a dump truck full of refugees, and we were standing up in the back, bumping along with the others. A teenager with a pistol sat on top of the cab, watching for jackrabbits to appear in the lights of the truck and periodically firing his gun into the night. At the time, there was little access to gasoline in oil-rich northern Iraq, and our vehicle was one of the few on the road. It was cold at that altitude, and the moon was almost full.

Sometime after midnight, the truck came to a narrow passage, where the road was rutted and muddy. Alongside us was a sharp drop-off, a gorge that looked to be hundreds of feet deep. At that point, two trucks full of refugees returning from Iran tried to squeeze by us. After a few minutes of delicate maneuvering by the drivers, we were on our way again, headed downhill. It was then I saw a man on foot climbing the hill from the opposite direction. He was walking in front of a farm tractor and holding up an oil lantern, a human beacon in the darkness. The seat and fenders of the tractor behind him were piled with refugees. Following the tractor was another Kurd, a man carrying a little girl on his back. She was sleeping, exhausted from the long trek. Then came a woman trying to hoist a sleeping boy in the same manner, pausing frequently to catch her breath before continuing the climb. They were big kids, maybe seven or eight years old, too heavy to be carried for long.

The image of lantern and flight seemed to place the wandering Kurds in a feudal context. As we passed the woman, the headlights of the truck played across her face. For a split second I saw the world on her back, raw survival in her eyes, a crazed will to live for her child. Then the truck began to bump and lurch down the hill. The teenager fired his pistol again, and a bizarre feeling of adventure returned.

During the war to liberate Kuwait, the allies had bombed Iraq's sewage treatment and water-sanitation facilities. Dysentery, typhoid, and bronchitis were everywhere: Coughing, spitting adults in filthy clothes sat on the roadsides next to hacking kids wearing the wrong-sized shoes or just pieces of shoes. There wasn't enough for anyone to eat. At almost every turn, we confronted hungry children, barking dogs, and the wretched stench of burning rubbish. Where there was food, flies clung to the remnants on dirty plates and utensils, swarming over emptied cans of donated tuna fish. The Kurds of 1991 were a people of the Dark Ages, courting pestilence, starving in the snow, trying to light lanterns and gather wood for fire, cradling in their arms the dead and the near living.

Yellow victory ribbons were flying in American yards. In Baghdad, the old regime was regrouping. In Kurdistan, however, disease and hunger were mounting. The war had dragged on far too long. I wondered if the Kurds would ever emerge from their darkness.

Sneaking into Turkey

After ten days in northern Iraq, Ruedi and I needed to find a way back to Turkey. By that time, Nechirvan Barzani had returned from Iran and had set up headquarters in an old building near the border. He arranged for three of his *peshmerga* to guide us over the mountain pass and through the minefields, a climb of about five hours. Just before we made it to the Turkish frontier, the *peshmerga* stopped and sat down on a couple of boulders. They took out scraps of paper and proceeded to record serial numbers from the barrels of their AK-47s. They stuffed the scraps of paper in their socks. If we were captured by the Turks and the weapons confiscated, there would be a record. The precaution had the look of standard procedure, and I marveled at their nonchalance.

We threaded our way through the minefields, following in the footsteps of the *peshmerga*. Several hours later, we reached the designated safe house, a farm just over the Turkish border. There we were able to rest, get food and tea, and make arrangements to hire a car. Unbeknown to us, however, our guides had dropped us in an area of insurgent activity by the PKK, the Kurdish separatists in Turkey. As the guides headed home to Iraq, we were quickly detained by a Turkish army patrol. The soldiers angrily informed us that we were under arrest. They started to go through our backpacks, which contained the precious film and footage from Iran and Iraq. If we were jailed, the material would be confiscated. There would be little to show for the trip.

We had one advantage: Our passport stamps showed no sign of our having *left* Turkey, but the soldiers suspected—correctly—that we had crossed illegally into Iraq. As luck would have it, the lieutenant in charge was a Hollywood film buff, and he knew some English. That gave us a chance.

We pretended to be doctors who were searching the border area for sick or injured refugees. I produced an official-looking letter from Direct Relief, pointing to the words "medical supplies." Ruedi said nothing, but he was prepared. Just before we were detained, he had clipped the cover of his Swiss passport to the outer pocket of his jacket. The passport had a large white cross on the cover, and he was hoping that the soldiers would associate the Christian symbol with humanitarian aid from the West. Looking back on the encounter, it may have helped that Turkey is a Muslim country, where the symbol of medical relief is a crescent. Defying logic, my Swiss companion was banking that his *white* cross would suggest the *Red* Cross. I was too scared at the moment to dwell on the absurdity.

We were lucky. A half hour of interrogation gave way to an hour of tea drinking, some English-language practice for the lieutenant, and then a compromise: The officer would radio ahead to his unit command, about thirty miles up the dirt road. They would be waiting for us. The deeply rutted road was made for four-wheel drive, and our passenger car took more than three hours to reach the soldiers. It was well after dark by the time we arrived at the new military checkpoint.

In the meantime, the shift at the roadblock had changed. The terrain was hilly, and the lieutenant we'd left behind, fortunately, could no longer be reached by radio. The new soldiers made us promise to report to army headquarters in the first big town, which lay ahead, but before we left, there was one more thing. A soldier came up to the window of the car and showed us his forearm, which seemed to be infected by boils or a rash. I couldn't be sure, but I knew a "road-block doctor test" when I saw one: They were watching how we answered before letting us pass. My advice was, "hot compresses, tightly bound, for two hours." That sounded good. Ruedi reached into in his backpack and gave the patient two colored capsules of Advil.

A couple of days later, safely on a plane to Europe, I found myself sitting next to a doctor from Dublin. She had been treating Kurdish refugees in the camps and was aware of political sensitivities in Turkey. "Heat would irritate that condition," she advised professionally. Next time, she said, "Try a *cold* compress."

I was on my way home, happy to still have my film and footage of the Kurds. I didn't think there would be a next time.

3

A Second Visit to Kurdistan

I am strongly in favour of using poison gas
against uncivilised tribes.

—WINSTON CHURCHILL

"No Kurdish Towns"

I returned to Iraq and Turkey in the fall of 1991 with a proper visa and a renewed determination to learn about the Kurds and the reasons for American interests in the region.

My lessons began on a Delta flight from Atlanta to Istanbul. Seated ahead of me was a Turkish graduate student, and shortly before landing we struck up a conversation. He had just completed his MBA at the University of Georgia, and he was headed home to test the job market. Wearing jeans, a college sweatshirt, and a pair of "boat mocs," he would have blended into a crowd of students on any American campus. The only noticeable accent in his near-perfect English was the trace of a southern drawl he had picked up in Georgia. Our all-American small talk ranged from the presidency of George H. W. Bush to the Atlanta Braves, who had just lost a game in the World Series. I nearly forgot we were about to land in Turkey.

We were arriving in Istanbul, one of the most famous cities in the world, an ancient place known in history as both Constantinople and Byzantium, but the stranger was from a community in the southeast of the country. "Is it a Kurdish town?" I blurted out, sensing too late that I'd just forfeited my status as a random passenger. Suddenly, I was an outsider, a foreigner poised to enter the homeland. The young man stared hard at me, searching for hints of other undisclosed information.

In a cool and measured tone meant to conclude the discussion, he said simply, "There *are* no Kurdish towns in Turkey."

U.S. Forces Target the Kurds

I spent the night in Istanbul at an airport hotel. There, I met a young corporal, a computer operator for the U.S. Air Force, who was headed home to West Virginia after a year on a Turkish military base. This corporal had a unique perspective on the Kurds: He processed intelligence and provided the data to the notorious TMP, the Turkish Military Police. The TMP received American money and equipment, he revealed, and the targets of a joint United States-Turkish operation were Kurdish separatists, the PKK. "We get names, locations, and other information on the enemy," he said, "and the TMP breaks down the doors of the safe houses where the terrorists are hiding." At the time, the role of the U.S. military in suppressing the Kurdish uprising in Turkey was largely unknown to the American public, so this revelation came as a surprise—if not a potential security lapse.

It was a decade before 9/11, the small window of time just after the Cold War, when proponents of disarmament spoke wishfully of "peace dividends." The expression "war on drugs" was in vogue at the time, but the words "war on terrorism" hadn't entered the lexicon, and this corporal may have been one of the few Americans for whom the term "jihad" had much of a resonance. He was a homesick nineteen-year-old hungry for conversation with a fellow American, even a reporter. We ended up going to dinner, where he told me he once had dreamed of becoming a fighter pilot or an FBI agent. Now, though, he had a career in computer intelligence gathering. His parents were proud of his service in Turkey, but the Middle East was dangerous, and he was happy to be leaving behind the constant need for vigilance and security. He was going home to the peace and safety of America, home to the sweetheart he had married after graduation from high school.

Diyarbakir

The next morning I flew to southeastern Turkey, to the Kurdish city of Diyarbakir, which is located about 150 miles north of the Iraqi border. The only other Americans on the plane were four Christian missionaries, who were going to a refugee center near Diyarbakir. A colleague met them at the airport. We were all headed south, to Iraq, so I caught a ride with them to the bus station. The colleague explained that many of the Kurdish refugees he worked with had walked over the mountains into Turkey after the Iraqi gas attacks back in 1988. Now, those who fled Saddam's army in spring of 1991 had begun to return to Iraq, easing the pressure on Turkey and, in turn, on Kurds in the older camps.

There was enough time for a walk before the bus left for the Iraqi border.

The guidebooks describe Diyarbakir as an ancient trade center for grains, melons, cotton, copper ore, oil, and textiles. The city certainly retained its medieval air. A historic way station on the Silk Road, it was still surrounded by black basalt walls twelve to sixteen feet thick and more than three miles in circumference. Remnants of the remarkable fortifications date to pre-Roman times, but the present walls were mainly built in the fourth century, during the reign of Constantine I. Diyarbakir was later occupied by Persians and Arabs, and then, in the year 1515, it was captured by the Ottoman Turks. After the Great Wall of China, these walls are said to be the best preserved in the world.

The rawness of the Kurdish region contrasted sharply with cosmopolitan Istanbul, the only city in the world that straddles an international seaway (the Bosporus) and has a foot in two continents. Diyarbakir was only eight hundred miles east of Istanbul, but it felt as though the clock had been turned back fifty years.

It was winter in Diyarbakir, and the city was grim and sooty, the air dark with coal smoke and diesel exhaust. Sheep and goats were grazing in open lots between tall apartment buildings within sight of the downtown area. The streets had the look of military occupation: jeeps full of soldiers and army trucks alongside the old buses, horse-drawn carts and tractors pulling farm wagons. An armored personnel carrier with rubber tires passed by, a pair of eyes scanning the traffic visible in a gun slit. Despite the cold weather, vendors were roasting chestnuts and cooking kebabs over curbside fires, and the sidewalks were clogged with pedestrians and merchants holding forth in front of their shops. The sound of honking horns mixed with the blare of police loudspeakers mounted on vans, barking at drivers to keep moving.

On one block, women in bright Kurdish dresses were walking back from the market holding squirming chickens in their hands. It was freezing cold, but groups of Kurdish men in their traditional balloon pants, wrapped at the waist by a long sash, stood outside the storefronts drinking steaming tea from tiny glasses. Overhead, a pair of Turkish-based U.S. warplanes passed to the south, screaming toward Iraq on their daily overflights.

In 1991 there were only about three hundred thousand Kurds living in Diyarbakir, but the Kurdish uprising in Turkey was gathering momentum, and the Turkish army, in an attempt to dry up rural support for the Kurdish guerrillas, was turning large areas of the countryside into free-fire zones. Tens of thousands of displaced persons had begun to flee to the cities. Within six years, the population of Diyarbakir would triple, straining housing and employment resources and crippling the city's social service system.

Following Iraq's invasion of Kuwait, in the months before the start of the first Gulf War, the U.S. Army set up a helicopter base in Diyarbakir. The base was one of several American military installations in Turkey. Diyarbakir also was rumored to be an urban base of support for the PKK, the separatist guerrillas.

Regional Capital

Diyarbakir was—and is—regarded as the unofficial capital of Turkish Kurdistan. The key word, of course, is "unofficial." Until the end of the first Gulf War, the Turkish government pursued a policy of forced assimilation, similar in some respects to U.S. efforts to "mainstream" Native Americans in the late nineteenth and early twentieth centuries, especially in mission schools, where children were forbidden to speak their languages or to practice their native religions.

In Turkey, the government's target was language and ethnic identity, not religion. For the first forty years of the Turkish Republic, the authorities viewed the Kurdish region as a trouble spot of latent, if not actual, resistance, and the area was sealed off by the military until the 1960s to prevent contact with outsiders. Before 1991, Kurdish identity was simply denied, and even the use of the word "Kurd" was proscribed. Despite the fact that the Kurds were the first to populate the area, and despite the fact that they possessed a distinct language that experts believed was centuries old, the Kurds were designated as "Mountain Turks." Officially speaking, they were an assimilated part of Turkish society.

Before our bus left for the Iraq border, the local missionary gave his colleagues a friendly warning. Foreigners who work with Kurds in the area, he said, ought to be aware of government restrictions. Turkey regarded Kurdish separatists as terrorists, and, according to human rights monitors, PKK attacks already had caused many civilian casualties. For the last few years, eleven provinces in southeastern Turkey had been under emergency rule. Special terror laws were in place. People could be detained without charge for thirty days, and in practice were often held much longer. Punishment for crimes was double what it was in other areas of the country. Turkish soldiers, teachers, and oil workers posted to the Kurdish region received bonus pay. The southeast was considered a war zone.

All Kurds were affected. Until February 1991—just a few months earlier—the wearing of traditional Kurdish clothing was prohibited and public use of the Kurdish language itself was banned. Now, Turkey was struggling to deal more openly with its Kurdish minority. Since the Persian Gulf War ended, it was legal to speak Kurdish out in the open, but merchants still were forbidden to advertise in Kurdish on their shopwindows. It was against the law to open a Kurdish school, and broadcasting in Kurdish was banned. It was illegal for parents to give their children Kurdish names.

The previous year, thirty Kurdish representatives with nationalist credentials had been elected to parliament in Ankara. While the electoral victories signaled a political opening, the military was still a more powerful force than the parliament. In Turkish Kurdistan, there still was no freedom of the press or political parties. Pro-Kurdish newspapers, even those published in Turkish, had been shut down by the police. A number of Kurdish journalists had been killed by death squads. Most of the crimes were unsolved, and the Turkish media typically referred to the killers as *faili mechul* (perpetrators unknown).

In the southeast, human rights abuses by the state were frequent and systematic, according to Amnesty International, and ongoing violations continued to compromise Turkey's chances for admission to the European Union. Foreigners, we were warned, should not make the mistake of believing their non-Turkish status gave them immunity from the police. Only the year before, according to the missionary, two German tourists had been detained after a search of their luggage turned up audiocassettes of Kurdish folk music. The Kurds were under the microscope, he cautioned us. Visitors to Turkey who chose to associate with the Kurds would also be scrutinized.

Busting the Sanctions Against Iraq

The trip south to Silopi, the last town before the Iraqi frontier, took five hours. We were crammed inside an old bus that was nearly blue from the smoke of Turkish cigarettes. Looking out the window in the last hour before the border, I began to notice something unusual about the approaching traffic: The northbound drivers had the habit of crossing over into our half of the road and remaining where the pavement was dry and gray colored until the very last moment, when they would scoot back into their own lane, which was wet and dark colored. An English-speaking passenger on the bus, a Kurd who was also headed for the border, told me the secret: Turkish truck drivers had a sanctions-busting deal with Turkish customs to haul diesel over the border from Iraq.

Saddam was selling diesel to the drivers for the equivalent of about four cents a gallon. Back in Turkey, the truckers could resell the diesel for $2 per gallon, and some were clearing $1,000 a run. The round-trip took ten days, most of it spent waiting to load at the refinery near Mosul, Iraq, or waiting to bribe the *peshmerga* of the Kurdistan Democratic Party to cross back into Turkey. The *peshmerga* also took a portion of the diesel load. The oil exports, a direct violation of the United Nations embargo against Iraq, were finalized on the Turkish side by additional "tariffs" paid to customs officials.

It might have been more practical to utilize oil tankers, which are designed to carry fuel, but that would have made the sanctions-busting too obvious. Instead, the entrepreneurial drivers had resorted to freight trucks, canvas-covered loads, dump trucks, flatbeds, and even pickup trucks. Some operators had welded U-shaped tanks under the rear of the vehicles, and others had grafted huge saddle tanks on to the sides of their rigs. Some of the trucks even had gallon drums of oil roped together on deck, their contents sloshing from side to side. After passing hundreds of dripping trucks, I could see why the roadway was soaked and discolored. The trucks had diesel fuel spattered on their fenders, hoods, tires—even the doors and windows. Everything seemed to be leaking.

Free-fire Zone to the Border

I had heard that the public buses in southeast Turkey were frequently stopped by army patrols who forced the passengers to disembark for searching and questioning, but that day I saw no soldiers on the road to Iraq, even at the triangle on the map where Turkey, Iraq, and Syria converge. We did pass about thirty miles of rich farmland north of the Syrian border, an area dotted with Turkish guard towers. According to a man on the bus, the land had become a corridor for PKK smuggling from Syria. He said the PKK had headquarters in Damascus and bases in the Syrian-controlled Bekaa Valley of Lebanon. The Turkish army had planted more than a half million land mines along the border to curtail rebel infiltration. At night, the fertile agricultural strip was a free-fire zone.

The absence of army checkpoints that day may have been due to a cease-fire declaration by the guerrillas, a temporary break in hostilities after recent bombing raids of suspected PKK bases in northern Iraq by Turkish pilots flying U.S.-made jets. Besides, the road between Diyarbakir and the border had seen a lot of foreign travelers in the past year. Thousands of reporters, relief workers, and allied soldiers attached to Operation Provide Comfort, the assistance program for Kurdish refugees, had passed back and forth, presumably sensitizing the powers that be to the presence of visitors in this little-known corridor of insurrection. In 1991, there was no traditional border and no entry requirement for northern Iraq. Unless you wanted a Turkish exit stamp in your passport (in order to reenter Turkey at a different crossing) you could drive right over the frontier to Iraq without stopping. The missionaries wanted the stamp, so we stopped in an oil-soaked parking lot alongside the Turkish immigration building and went inside to hunt up an official. From there we simply drove on across a bridge and into northern Iraq, the wild territory of the Kurds. When the guerrillas at the Kurdistan checkpoint saw the western faces, they smiled and waved us through with their AK-47s.

Lost Statehood

According to an old saying in the Middle East, "the Kurds have no friends but the mountains." Since the time of the Crusades, the Kurds have been used by allies and enemies alike to provide a balance of power in the region. During the Crusades they fought alongside Turkic and Arabic warriors to defeat the Christian armies. In the seventeenth and eighteenth centuries, European merchants paid fees to Kurdish tribes to secure and maintain trade routes to the East. The

Ottoman Empire, which was centered in present-day Turkey, controlled much of the Middle East, and traders were dependent on the Kurds to travel the legendary Silk Road.

During the seven-hundred-year Ottoman Empire, the Kurds were known as ferocious fighters who, because of tribal divisions and clan loyalties, often ended up on opposite sides of the battlefield. After the defeat of the Ottomans in World War I, the victorious Allies sat down and redrew the boundaries of the Middle East. Britain secured a mandate for Iraq and subsequently installed King Faisal Hussein I as its surrogate power. Faisal was not from Iraq (he was a Arasari, born in Mecca Hashemite), but his legitimacy to rule was bolstered by the claim that he was a direct descendant of the Prophet Mohammed, which aided Britain in dealing with the Shiite majority as it tried to cobble together a new and fragmented society of Kurds, Christians, and Shiite and Sunni Arabs.

Following the Great War, the Kurds and other non-Turkish minorities in the Ottoman Empire became a focus of Western attention and concern. President Woodrow Wilson's Fourteen Points urged that such groups be "assured of an absolute unmolested opportunity of autonomous development." The Treaty of Sèvres, signed by the representatives of Sultan Mehmet VI in 1920, was a humiliation for Turkey, but the agreement appeared to guarantee the Kurds a separate homeland. The British at one point favored a Kurdish state as a buffer, primarily because they feared the Turks on their Iraqi border, but that was before Britain grasped the nature and extent of oil deposits in northern Iraq. Most important, it was before the rise of Turkish nationalism, which rejected the Treaty of Sèvres and led to the Treaty of Lausanne in 1923. Instead of granting autonomy, the League of Nations carved Kurdistan into separate pieces. Overnight, the Ottoman Kurds became residents of Iraq, Syria, and Turkey (the Kurds in Iran and the Soviet Union were not part of the empire). British forces, already in Iraq, had defeated the Turks in the Kurdish city of Sulaimaniah in 1918 and had proceeded to occupy the surrounding area. When the Kurds resisted the British, the army tried to co-opt Kurdish leaders by putting a local face on the occupation. In 1919, Sheikh Mahmud Barzinji, the most famous of the leaders, was appointed governor of southern Kurdistan and later took the title "King of Kurdistan." Sheikh Mahmud was the son of Sheikh Said, who in 1909 had opposed the movement of the nationalist Young Turks in Sulaimaniah. In 1920, only a year after his royal appointment, Mahmud mounted his own uprising against British rule.

The rebellion lasted until Mahmud was wounded in combat, which occurred on the road between Kirkuk and Sulaimaniah. Captured by Crown forces, he was sentenced to death but later imprisoned in a British fort in India. In 1922, Britain recalled him from exile to deal with a threat from Turkey, but as soon as he arrived in Sulaimaniah, he allied himself with anti-British, pro-Turkish forces and continued his revolt against British occupation. On December 20, 1922, British forces issued a statement of intent from Baghdad, promising that the Kurds could establish their own government if they wished.

The offer was not accepted, and Mahmud was soon fomenting rebellion again. Beginning in 1924, he fought the British constantly. In 1932, after a coordinated bombing campaign by the Royal Air Force and ground assaults by the British-trained Iraqi army, he was finally subdued. Mahmud was exiled to Iraq's southern desert, a fate that befell many dissidents in subsequent regimes. In 1941, he was allowed to return to his family village, where he spent his remaining years. He died in 1956, two years before the overthrow of the British-installed Iraqi monarchy.

Chemical Weapons

The British were not prepared for the resistance they encountered in Iraq—both from Kurds and Arabs—and the army's response was brutal. The rebellion was crushed with the loss of almost nine thousand lives—and with the Royal Air Force (RAF) playing a key role in defeating the insurgents. Widespread "police bombings," as they were called at the time, caused at least one British officer to quit his post. In 1924, Lionel Charlton, a distinguished air commodore, resigned as staff officer in protest after visiting the victims of a British bombing on an Iraqi hospital. Other officers seemed to enjoy the work, including Arthur Harris, who would later achieve fame directing the bomber offensive against German cities in World War II. Known to his friends as "Bomber" and to his enemies as "Butcher," he first practiced his trade against Kurdish villages in Iraq. Both Kurdish and Arab villages were used as "laboratories" for the development of new weapons. The British Air Ministry experimented with several prototypes, some of them the forerunners of napalm and air-to-ground missiles: phosphorous bombs, war rockets, metal crowsfeet (to maim livestock), man-killing shrapnel, liquid fire, and delayed-action bombs. Many of these weapons were first used in Kurdistan.

While few historians mention the fact, fifty years before Saddam shocked the world by using chemical weapons on the Kurds, Winston Churchill campaigned for the RAF to drop mustard gas on recalcitrant tribesmen in Iraq. The British military used gas against the rebels with "excellent moral effect," although in the end the chemicals were not dropped from airplanes, due to practical difficulties. In 1919, when Churchill was a secretary of state in Britain's War Office, he urged the use of mustard gas against insurgents, saying he could not understand the "squeamishness about the use of gas."

According to British historian Geoff Simons:

Churchill himself was keen to argue that gas, fired from ground-based guns or dropped from aircraft, would cause only "discomfort or illness but not death" to dissident tribespeople; but his optimistic views of the effects of gas were mistaken. Churchill remained unimpressed by such considerations, arguing that the use of gas, a "scientific expedient," should not be prevented "by the prejudices of those who do not think clearly."

Churchill later wrote that it was "absurd" to consider the use of poison gas as an issue of morality, especially in light of the fact that it had been used in World War I "without a word of complaint from the moralists or the church." "To use or not use gas," he claimed, was a "cold-blooded calculation" in which "one really must not be bound within silly conventions of the mind."

Monarchy and Memory

In 1932, the Kingdom of Iraq, with its Arab majority, was admitted to the League of Nations. During the early 1930s, numerous coup attempts were mounted against King Faisal, none of them successful. The British continued to back surrogate powers in Baghdad until the overthrow of the monarchy in 1958. By then, the stage was set for the rise of the Ba'athists, the brutal, nationalistic party of Saddam Hussein.

Kurdish uprisings in the country continued sporadically into the mid-1940s, when the forces of Mullah Mustafa Barzani, the father of Massoud Barzani, the current president of the Kurdistan Regional Government, retreated from Iraq and crossed the border into Iran. Mustafa Barzani spent the late 1940s and much of the 1950s in the USSR. He was invited to return to Iraq after the military coup in 1958, but he failed to reach an accommodation with the new government. In 1961, he relaunched his guerrilla campaign. When Saddam Hussein's Ba'ath Party came to power in 1968, Kurdish insurrection in Iraq, although not continual, had spanned almost fifty years.

In his day, Sheikh Mahmud Barzinji had both friends and enemies in the local population. His supporters saw him as a champion of resistance against British military rule. Some of his detractors were less kind, including Kurdish traders in Sulaimaniah who accused him of operating a patronage system and claimed that he raided caravans between Kurdish cities. Over time and with the rise of nationalist sentiment, however, the Kurds as a whole have come to regard him as a hero. Today, in Sulaimaniah you can see a famous photo of Sheikh Mahmud proudly displayed in shopwindows and in private residences, reminiscent of the images of President John F. Kennedy and Rev. Martin Luther King, Jr. in the United States in the years following their deaths. In the photo, bandoliers are strapped across Mahmud's chest, and a wooden-handled Kurdish dagger is thrust into his waistband. "He never betrayed the cause he fought for," his grandson Mahmoud al-Hafeed told me in 2004. Al-Hafeed, who emigrated from Sulaimaniah to become an architect in Boston, has fond memories of his famous grandfather. "He belongs to the people now," he said.

After the first Gulf War, the Kurdish population in Iraq was estimated at roughly 5,000,000, the majority of whom resided in the north (the figures, based on a 1957 census conducted by the Iraqi regime, were considered inexact). At the same time, nearly 14,000,000 Kurds, almost three times the Kurdish population of Iraq, resided in Turkey. The remainder lived in Iran (about 7,000,000), Syria (1,000,000), and the former Soviet Union (fewer than 200,000). Following the refugee catastrophe in 1991, Iraqi Kurds found themselves in control of about 80 percent of their lands, an area of about fifteen thousand square miles, roughly the size of New Jersey and Massachusetts put together. No such political opening had existed since World War I. Kurds who nursed the dream of independence for generations saw the moment as a turning point in their history.

4

Atrocities

Who can protest an injustice and does
not is an accomplice in the act.

—TALMUD

The wolf repents only in death.

—KURDISH PROVERB

Free and Broken

I crossed the border into northern Iraq and bid the missionaries farewell. By now, Saddam's army had completely retreated. Despite the outward look of a Third World country devastated by war and shortages, Kurdistan was in fact in the throes of a fragile liberation. However, you really had to look for it. There was barely any electricity or cooking or heating fuel. As far as could be seen, the trees and shrubs had been cut down, and many of the hillsides were completely naked from the deforestation. Women and girls continued to hunt for branches, trudging through the fields, bent under their loads. It looked like a born-again wood-burning culture, driven back a century in time.

Bare truck axles, cannibalized engine blocks, and even rusted hulks of army tanks still littered the shoulders of the highways, but with Kurds now free to travel in northern Iraq, vehicles had begun to reappear on the highways. There were plenty of roadblocks, but the checkpoints were controlled—for the first time in Kurdish Iraq—by the *peshmerga*, the fighters who used to be seen only in the mountains. It was a small but important sign of a largely unreported transformation taking place among the Kurds, whose struggle has persisted with little notice for most of the century.

The 1991 exodus of Kurds to Turkey and Iran, one of the largest, most rapid movements of refugees in history, produced large-scale suffering and deprivation for the *awara*, "the people who ran away." At one point the previous spring, an estimated two thousand Kurds were dying every day.

Returning refugees were still dying of diseases traceable to the first Gulf War and to the series of events the war had set into motion. "Our biggest problem is typhoid," said Dr. Wallet Ibrahim Yasin, the director of the Kurdish hospital in the town of Diana. "About one-third of all our beds are filled with typhoid patients, and we can't get enough antibiotics."

Kurdistan was free, at least for the moment, but the Iraqi regime was punishing the Kurds with an economic blockade. Imposed in the fall of 1991, the blockade left the hospital at Diana and the nearby one in Rawanduz without fuel or spare parts to run their generators during electrical outages, Dr. Yasin said. Neither hospital had a working X-ray machine, nor was there oxygen for surgeries. Without gas for automobiles, emergency patients could not be transferred to the bigger hospitals in Erbil.

Dr. Yasin noted that all of Iraq was subject to allied sanctions. "But the Kurds suffer a double embargo," he lamented. In terms of pressuring Saddam, I asked him, were international sanctions working? "Not at all, it has no effect on Saddam Hussein," the doctor said. "He just passes the pain on to us and on to the Shiites in the south—only poor people are hurt."

Oddly, some conflicts disappear from the newspapers, but continue unnoticed and at length to plague people's lives. By the late fall of 1991, most of the refugees had returned from Iran and Turkey. For an estimated forty thousand refugees still hiding in the mountains, however, the Persian Gulf War was not over. Those Kurds were struggling to stay alive under plastic tarps and in tents near the Iranian border, still frightened that Iraqi troops would return. In the border village of Penjuin I met a man named Fagradhin Abdullah, who was tending to his sick mother, and that night I slept in his family's tent. It was covered with snow, but I had the security of a warm sleeping bag. A week earlier, Abdullah told me, a fierce storm had blown through the encampment, and a nearby lean-to had collapsed in the wind. The next morning, the refugees found four children frozen to death in the snow.

At a lower elevation, eighty-five thousand additional refugees, according to United Nations estimates, were crowded into the Saed Sadq camp. Another two hundred thousand had fled north of the thirty-sixth parallel to the so-called Safe Haven, where they were living in abandoned buildings, tents, and makeshift shelters.

"Why picture, picture, picture?" one refugee at Saed Sadq camp demanded as I photographed Kurdish children in plastic sandals walking through the freezing mud. "We want *bread*," she said. I watched her hang the family laundry on a discarded bale of barbed wire, a relic of the war with Iran, which had ravaged the area in the 1980s. "What do you do with all the pictures?" she asked me rhetorically. The question itself seemed to form a picture—an image of Third World countries, where victims sometimes encounter reporters, but not relief workers or food shipments.

Many of the Saed Sadq refugees had come from the oil-rich city of Kirkuk, about eighty miles away. Citing the last official census, which was conducted in 1957, Kurdish leaders said that Kirkuk, a mixed city of Kurds, Turkmen, Christians, and Arabs, had a Kurdish majority. In the last two decades, however, Kirkuk had undergone rapid Arabization, a process accomplished by enticing Arab settlers with housing subsidies, loans, and other government incentives to move to the area. The program, which had been likened to Israeli settlements on the West Bank, already had changed the demographics of Kirkuk. The question in 1991—whether Kirkuk was still a Kurdish city—would still be *the* question in another generation. In 1991, Kirkuk oil represented the same stumbling block to autonomy for the Kurds as it had twenty years earlier, during the Nixon administration. The refugees at Saed Sadq could not go home because Kirkuk was still in the hands of the Iraqi army, and memories of government brutality remained fresh.

Back in 1975, after the CIA and the Shah of Iran first supported, then pulled away from the Kurds, Iraq began systematically depopulating and destroying Kurdish areas. In the mid-1980s, during the Iraq-Iran war—when Iraqi Kurds sided with Iran—the Iraqi regime intensified the campaign, concentrating on "cleaning" a thirty-mile-wide corridor along the Iranian border. It was a way of hitting two birds with one stone.

In all, more than four thousand Kurdish villages were destroyed, and the campaign continued until the invasion of Kuwait in 1990. According to a U.S. Senate staff report, the Iraqi government rounded up tens of thousands of Kurds. The Kurds were placed in resettlement collectives, which were composed of one-story houses made of cinderblock and laid out in large grids. Authorities called the resettlement centers "modern villages." They were not unlike the "model villages" employed as a counterinsurgency tactic by the Guatemalan Army in the 1980s and before that by the U.S. Army with "strategic hamlets" in Vietnam. The major purpose was to cut off civilian support to the guerrillas, the Kurdish *peshmerga*, who, like the Iranians, were fighting the Iraqi government. Iraq's objective, to paraphrase Mao Zedong's famous dictum, was "to get at the fish by draining the sea."

The concrete collectives offered no means of support to shepherds, whose land had been confiscated, or to farmers who had lost their crops and livestock. Now they were dependent on government rations, living in fenced compounds with entry and exit controlled by the military. Males over the age of twelve were separated from their families. Many "disappeared" afterward. One notorious incident occurred in 1983 at a collective called Qushtapa, where more than five thousand Kurdish men and boys, supporters of KDP leader Massoud Barzani, were rounded up by Iraqi soldiers, forced into trucks, and abducted. None of the Kurds was seen again. Saddam Hussein later declared that the abductees had "betrayed the country" by helping Iranian soldiers capture a border town in northern Iraq. "We meted out a stern punishment to them," he said, "and they went to hell."

Government oppression of the Kurds in Iraq did not focus on Kurdish language, clothing, or customs. Unlike Turkey, where the Kurds were forced to hide their ways because all ethnic minorities were classified as "Turks" as a matter of law, Iraqi Kurds had always sung their own songs, spoken their own language, and worn their traditional clothes. In 1932, when Iraq applied for admission to the League of Nations, it issued a declaration guaranteeing protection of minority cultures. The declaration specifically mentioned the Kurdish language. The Iraqi constitution, written in 1958, decreed that the country was a nation of *two* peoples: Arabs and Kurds. At various times, Arab authorities sought to relocate, isolate, and even eliminate Iraqi Kurds, but the goal was submission, not assimilation. That made Iraq different from Turkey, where Kurdish identity itself was a key target. The Kurds of Iraq were not targeted because of their culture. They were singled out because they wanted land and autonomy—because they wanted to be separate.

Anfal Campaign

In February 1992, Middle East Watch and the Boston-based group Physicians for Human Rights released a joint report entitled "Unquiet Graves: The Search for the Disappeared in Iraqi Kurdistan." The report, which detailed a forensic investigation conducted in the Kurdish regions of northern Iraq, concluded, "Iraq [had] committed crimes against humanity in Kurdistan." The report estimated that 180,000 Kurds had disappeared in the 1980s, a period of U.S. aid to the regime, when the Iraqi army was conducting the infamous *Anfal* campaign.

Anfal is an Arabic term taken from a chapter in the Koran in which the followers of Mohammed raided and pillaged lands of nonbelievers; it referred to booty—money, clothes, jewels, and livestock—captured from the infidels. Because it connotes a religious justification, the government's very choice of *Anfal* was sacrilegious to many Kurds. "We are both Muslims, the Arabs and us," my guide, Abdul, told me. "In our mind, Saddam does not respect the holy book."

During the early 1990s, under the protection of a safety zone in northern Iraq, the Kurds began to emerge from a quarter century of secret horror. But *Anfal* was still a household word, and visiting Kurdistan was like taking a tour of the "killing fields" in Cambodia after the reign of the Khmer Rouge. No family had been untouched by the genocide. It was impossible to enter a Kurdish town without someone stepping forward with a story of personal tragedy and an anguished plea for help. In the town of Kalar, a few miles from the front line where Iraqi tanks were poised, dozens of hysterical women surrounded my taxi. When I got out of the car, the women pressed at me with photos of missing family members as they clawed at their faces and wailed in grief.

"We have less than five million people," Abdul said after the encounter. "This is our Holocaust." Indeed, overall losses represented a staggering 5 percent of the Kurdish population. Had the *Anfal* campaign taken place in the United States, by comparison, more than fourteen million Americans would be missing, the presumed victims of government murder.

In February 1992, the United Nations Commission on Human Rights issued a report charging that the rights violations in Iraq were "so grave and are of such a massive nature that since the Second World War few parallels can be found." Among other evidence cited by the United Nations was the testimony of a Sulaimaniah gravedigger who said he had buried up to one thousand Kurds killed by security forces between 1985 and 1989. The report said that thousands of people, not only Kurds, continued to be in danger of execution, torture, and unfair detention. "It is unlikely," the report concluded, that "these violations will come to an end as long as the security forces have the power to decide over the freedom or imprisonment, or even life or death, of any Iraqi citizen."

At the time of the U.N. statement, Saddam Hussein still had another eleven years in power.

Halabja

For eight years, beginning in 1980, Iraq and Iran fought a grinding, brutal war. The Iraqi Kurds, targets of the central government in Baghdad, regarded the conflict with Iran as an opportunity. During the long period of hostilities, Kurdish *peshmerga* units cooperated with the Iranian army by providing sanctuary, supplying intelligence against Iraq, and accompanying Iranian soldiers into battle. In early March of 1988, the Iranian army captured the area surrounding Halabja, the fourth largest city in Iraqi Kurdistan. Saddam's troops still controlled Halabja itself, a city of eighty thousand residents near the Iranian border, and when the Iranians could not dislodge them, Kurdish guerrillas infiltrated Halabja and isolated the Iraqi troops. After several days of fierce, house-to-house combat, all the Iraqi soldiers were dead.

Retaliation was expected, but this time Saddam had a surprise in store for the Kurds. On March 16, 1988, a formation of warplanes from Kirkuk circled low over Halabja, dropping conventional cluster bombs and sending the people scurrying into their fallout shelters. Once the residents were underground, a second formation appeared and ejected new and different capsules. It was gas.

The Iranian army had withdrawn to the outskirts of Halabja where they, like some of their guerrilla allies, availed themselves of face masks. Civilians were unprotected, however, and as the chemical warheads exploded, a yellow cloud arose over Halabja, filling the air with the smell of garlic. Then the poisonous gas, heavier than air by design, began to descend, seeping into the shelters, cutting down the families who tried to run, littering the alleys and streets with corpses large and small. Later, photographers traveling with Iranian soldiers would capture pictures of dead Kurdish mothers and infants locked in wide-eyed embraces. At least five thousand Kurds were dead.

"How many of you Americans remember what happened that day?" a Halabja merchant named Sardar asked me pointedly. He was angry that three years had already passed since the 1988 attack, yet the world continued to ignore his people. "Or do you know about the Kurds only because this man Saddam [later] invaded Kuwait?" he continued with rapid-fire questioning, noting that many of his own relatives had perished in the chemical attacks. "Do you know that this is our Hiroshima—the Kurdish Hiroshima?" he asked. "If America had noticed [then], maybe Saddam would never have invaded Kuwait."

Indeed, the Kurds had no friends. The international community took little notice of the Halabja massacre, and the Kurds were unable to mobilize world opinion for even minimal measures against Iraq. A few U.S. senators proposed trade sanctions against Iraq, but they were blocked by the Reagan-Bush administration. The administration, it later turned out, was underwriting Saddam's war against Iran and, indirectly, his campaign against the Kurds. Unbeknown to the American people, President George H. W. Bush later signed a top-secret directive ordering even closer ties with Baghdad and paving the way for $1 billion in new aid. Late in 1991, disclosures that Bush was at least partly responsible for the Iraqi aggression that spun the world into war and later drove the desperate Kurds to their deaths in the mountains came in the publication of government documents by the *Los Angeles Times*.

The once-classified records indicated that American taxpayers during the 1980s footed the bill for more than $5 billion in loans to Saddam. The Bush administration overrode concerns by U.S. officials that the loans were indirectly financing the Iraqi military and that they would never be repaid. The *Times*'s report also raised the possibility that the White House had taken steps to prevent Congress from finding out about the administration's secret aid to Iraq. Committees in both the House and Senate reacted by announcing hearings to probe these allegations, but by then the war in Kuwait was almost a year old, and the presidential election cycle for 1992 had begun. What a dictator had done with U.S. money in the 1980s—or actions he'd taken against the Kurds or anyone else—seemed like old news. The investigations eventually petered out.

Sulaimaniah, 1991

Sulaimaniah, a city of seven hundred thousand Kurds, is located 210 miles from Baghdad. Since Kurdish uprisings against the British in the 1920s, the city has been known as the center of Kurdish culture and nationalism. Until Saddam came to power, the major Kurdish university was located in Sulaimaniah. Saddam moved it to Erbil, closer to government scrutiny.

The quality of life in Sulaimaniah stood in stark contrast to Zakho, Dohuk, and Kurdish cities near the Turkish border, where food and fuel were available. "Suly," as reporters would later call it, was far to the south, near the isolated Iranian frontier. There was some smuggling from Iran: fruit, eggs, tea, and a few vegetables to fill the void from 1991, when harvests were ruined after farmers became refugees and could not plant their crops. Before the invasion of Kuwait, rice, the staple of the Kurdish diet, cost one dinar per kilo, the equivalent of ten cents for more than two pounds. After 1991, the price of rice rose to seven dinars for the same amount, a painful increase in a country where the average wage was just a few hundred dollars a year.

The problem was isolation. All roads into Kurdistan were blocked at the time by Iraqi troops, and only a limited supply of food was permitted to pass. Saddam's economic stronghold, one of the rare times in history when a central government had embargoed food from its own people, also extended to fuel. It was winter, and the critical shortage was heating fuel. Existing supplies came from stockpiling the previous year, before the roads from the rest of Iraq were sealed by the army. A few gas tankers were allowed into Sulaimaniah, but only a fraction of what was needed. Before the Gulf War, benzene—as gasoline is called—cost a few pennies a gallon. Now the price was fifty cents a gallon, when it could be found.

At one station, near the entrance to the city, where Saddam's portrait had been ripped from a roadside monument, there was a queue of cars more than a mile long. Most of the vehicles were taxis, a central link in Iraqi public transport, and some drivers said they had been in line, sleeping and eating in their parked cars, for the past thirty hours. When I arrived, an angry mob was fighting over a hose to a gas pump that had just gone dry. A couple of *peshmerga* with AK-47s were trying to restore order. "Imagine," one of the fighters told me, "what it feels like to be out of benzene in a country of benzene."

Most of the workers at the large cement factory in Sulaimaniah were laid off, because there were no spare parts to keep the machinery running. The cigarette factory in town had employed two thousand Kurds, but now it was closed. The local tobacco crop had been harvested, and the warehouse was full of dried tobacco, but the factory had run out of cigarette papers and filters. Despite the loss of jobs, the major crisis was medical.

When I visited a Sulaimaniah hospital that year, I saw three wards set aside strictly for land mine victims. There was no fuel to power the hospital generator, so there was no electricity in the entire building. The overflowing wards, filled with Kurds with missing legs, arms, fingers, and eyes, were so dark that

I found it difficult to film. It was impossible to refrigerate blood for transfusions, complicating the already makeshift surgeries, and many patients were being operated on by candlelight.

A hospital spokesman estimated that the Iraqi army had sown twenty million land mines throughout Kurdistan. Many of the mines were planted *after* the war with Iran ended in 1988 to prevent Kurds from returning to their destroyed villages. The high estimate may have been exaggerated, but no visitor in those days could spend even an hour in the countryside without hearing an explosion. Wherever I traveled, people warned me not to stray from the road.

An injured patient named Taymur Muslih told me he lost his hand while rebuilding his home about thirty miles from Sulaimaniah. He blamed the Iraqi Army's *Anfal* campaign. "I saw my children playing with the land bomb [land mine]," he recounted, "and I be afraid [*sic*] and I want safety for them and I jump on it, to take it outside of the house. But it explode in my hand." Muslih said he stayed in his car for "one day and two nights" because there was "no benzene" to transport him to the hospital.

"Almost 100 percent of the hospital beds in Kurdistan are taken up by victims of land mines," said Dr. Azad Jalal, one of the resident surgeons. "All our lands are undermined with bombs, five to six feet on the sides of all the roads," he said, as he inspected a cavernous leg wound of a twelve-year-old boy. The patient had lost most of his left shinbone and two of his fingers in an explosion near Kalar, in the southern part of the governate. The boy's friend, walking ahead, took the full thrust of the blast and was killed. Because of the embargo and the lack of adequate antibiotics, antiseptics, and surgical dressings, Jalal said, "We just cannot cope with a large number of [land mine] patients."

The war with Kuwait was over, and the Kurds had been forgotten once more. There was little interest in land mine victims in a remote area of Iraq. Without international aid, the surgeon said, the greatest danger at the poorly equipped facility was the spread of infection. "So many of the patients, you didn't see them," he said after my tour, "because they died." The Sulaimaniah hospital alone was receiving an average of five amputees per day, he said, with the daily number of mine victims as high as a dozen. "We need a radical solution [in Kurdistan]," Jalal said. "This is no treatment. The job of mine removal is too big for the Kurds," he said. "What is needed is an international corporation with high-tech expertise— like the Texas company that put out the oil-well fires in Kuwait—to clear away the land mines."

"Perhaps," he added, with a touch of bitterness, "some of the executives in Europe" from the companies that sold the land mines to Saddam in the 1980s "might be able to think of a solution."

Hunger Strike

To break free from their isolation, the Kurds needed the media, but in northern Iraq there *were* no media. That point came home to me one day in Sulaimaniah, when two dozen Kurds went on a hunger strike. With no reporters to listen to them, the strikers set up a protest camp at the gates of local headquarters of the U.N. guards. They hoped to persuade the United Nations to enlarge the existing "safe haven" in northern Iraq to include Sulaimaniah, where nearly half of the people of Iraqi Kurdistan live. The goal was not accomplished, but Kurdish response to the hunger strike was overwhelming.

For a period of several weeks, tens of thousands of Kurds poured into the narrow streets around the U.N. complex. Strikers huddled by fires outside the walled building, and supporters showered them with flowers. While U.N. guards with walkie-talkies watched from the roof, crowds pushed and jockeyed for a glimpse of the fasting protesters. Desperate for outside recognition, strike leaders used a public address system for appeals in both Kurdish and English. When the word spread that a Western journalist was on the roof of the U.N. complex, the crowd waved placards and chanted slogans in English. Cries of "Help, Help Kurdistan!" were mixed with shouts of "Down, Down, Saddam!" I pointed my camera at the crowd, filming misspelled signs in English such as PLEASE HELP THE KURDISH PUPELS. The scene became part of a story I was doing at the time for *NBC Nightly News,* but the protesters failed otherwise to get their message to the outside world. As a morale booster, however, the demonstration appeared to have strengthened the city's will to survive in the face of the brutal Iraqi blockade.

Torturing a Schoolteacher

The remnants of the Iraqi security headquarters in Sulaimaniah in late 1991 were a living testament to government horrors in Kurdistan. The sprawling fortified complex of buildings, which included a dreaded prison and torture cells, was attacked spontaneously by mobs of Sulaimaniah residents on March 6, 1991. News of the civilian attack brought the *peshmerga* down from their mountain hideouts, and the headquarters was captured after two and a half days of intense combat. As many as seven hundred secret policemen were killed during and after the fighting, and tales of the bloody uprising have been emblazoned into the history books—the oral history books—of the Kurds. I heard several versions of one revenge story—the knife-wielding mother of a dead prisoner who took her revenge on a captured Iraqi guard.

According to most accounts, about 120 of the 150 prisoners were rescued. "I was in my cell when I heard the Kurdish language shouted from the streets," said former prisoner Jamal Aziz. "They were yelling, 'We are your brothers, and we have come to free you from the Iraqis!' I was afraid the guards would kill us right away, but I wept for joy that my people finally had risen up."

Aziz, a schoolteacher by profession, was a member of a clandestine network in Sulaimaniah that provided food and supplies for the *peshmerga* in the surrounding mountains. A few months before the uprising, Aziz was arrested by the secret police after a colleague broke under Iraqi torture and revealed his name. "He was so ashamed when I was brought to the prison," Aziz said, "that I never again saw his eyes looking into my eyes."

The Iraqis kept extraordinary notes on the Kurds they imprisoned, tortured, and "disappeared." In Sulaimaniah, the *peshmerga* discovered a storehouse of documents: psychological profiles of prisoners, step-by-step records of forced confessions, and videotapes of beatings and executions. However, with the exception of the removal of these captured files, little had been done to the security police headquarters in the months since the liberation. The walls of the Stalinesque gulag were still riddled with bullet holes, and hulks of burned police cars still rusted away in courtyards behind the fallen iron gates. The stench of refuse was everywhere. High above the fortified front entrance hung the watchful symbol of the Iraqi security system: a three-foot piece of green steel in the shape of a human eye.

In one four-by-six-foot concrete cell block, an old message in Kurdish was still scrawled on the wall: "There were two of us in here. The guards tortured my friend. He admitted he was a *peshmerga*. They killed him. They tortured me, too, but I did not admit it. I am still here." In the main interrogation cell I saw steel hooks for stringing up prisoners from their backs and a rotating fan on the ceiling for spinning them in circles. "We were ordered to climb a little set of stairs made of automobile tires," Aziz said, "up to a chair, where we had to stand. Our hands were tied behind us—that is how they attached us to the hooks and to the fan. Then the guards kicked the chair away. You were swinging from above, your arms and shoulders were breaking behind you, and the guards were hitting your legs with sticks." Someone had scribbled crude graffiti on a wall in English: "They hanged men here."

The Iraqi guards also used electrical torture, Aziz said. "They put wires on our tongues, in our ears, and on our private parts." Kurdish women, as well as men, were victims. "I can still hear one woman screaming in the night, 'Oh, God, no, my *breasts*! Oh, God, *no*!' "

"My only chance with the guards was to fake a medical condition," Aziz said. "They had a cleverness to take you near the point of death and then to pull back. You could not give them information if you were dead, so they needed to keep you alive until you broke. When I could hold out no longer, I lied that I had a bad valve in my heart. It may have kept me from telling what I knew. I was screaming in my pain, and I was so close to talking. That man who gave my name was transferred to a Baghdad prison. I am sure he is dead by now."

The largest cell block was a room about twenty by forty feet, which Aziz said had contained fifty prisoners. The iron cell bars, now rusted, were still festooned with tiny swatches of colored prayer cloth. Aziz told me the knotted mementos were offerings to Allah. Mothers of liberated prisoners had tied them on the cells in thanksgiving for the deliverance of their loved ones. Another Kurd, an expatriate visiting for the first time since the early 1960s, was overcome with emotion when he emerged from a self-guided tour of the abandoned prison. "They shouldn't even clean it. Someday this will be a museum, like Dachau or Auschwitz," he told me haltingly. "I hope they don't touch a thing."

5

The Leadership

The mountains isolated the Kurds,
but it kept their culture intact.

—MAN ON A BUS IN TURKEY

2005

By 2005, when Jalal Talabani became president of Iraq and Massoud Barzani was sworn in as president of the Kurdistan Regional Government, news of suicide bombs and other attacks aimed at undermining the new U.S.-supported government dominated the headlines from Iraq. However, the inaugurations of the two Kurdish leaders represented a historic coming of age for the Kurds of Iraq, and both events were charged with political symbolism. Officially, Talabani's term in office was limited to nine months and would expire in December 2005, after the drafting of a new constitution and the holding of a referendum and national elections. Even the temporary appointment of a minority Kurd to the presidency—one of the victims of ethnic cleansing in Iraq—had importance that went far beyond the position's traditionally ceremonial role. For much of their lives, Talabani and Barzani had been rivals and mortal enemies. Now, finally, the leaders and their parties appeared united; in his inaugural speech Barzani thanked "all the *peshmerga* and strugglers of our nation." The twin inaugurations were the climax of a long struggle by the two Kurds and their followers.

1988

There were eight main Kurdish parties in 1988. In November of that year, in the wake of Iraqi gas attacks, with winter approaching and tens of thousands of Kurdish refugees in the mountains of Turkey and Iran, the eight came together for the first time to form a unified umbrella group, the Kurdistan Front. The divergent groups represented a political and religious spectrum from the Islamic Movement in Kurdistan to the Kurdish Community Party. They had lightly armed militias and they had aided one another in battle, but until then they had been independent and uncoordinated, with no centralized command.

Four years later, following the first Gulf War, most of the same parties would participate in international supervised elections in northern Iraq. The most powerful, Talabani's Patriotic Union of Kurdistan (PUK) and Barzani's Kurdish Democratic Party (KDP), would win equal shares of the vote. The election subsequently would be contested, leading to four years of civil war.

1991

Jalal Talabani was fifty-six when I met him in the fall of 1991. Unlike Massoud Barzani, who was younger and more withdrawn, Talabani was talkative and outgoing. Worldly, educated, and politically savvy, he had been trained as a lawyer in Baghdad. In the 1960s and 1970s, he had been a leading minister in the KDP under Massoud's father, Mullah Mustafa Barzani. After the latter's unilateral decision in 1976 to terminate the Kurdish uprising, Talabani branded Barzani's leadership "feudalist, bourgeois rightist, and capitulationist." In 1978, he broke with the KDP to form the Patriotic Union of Kurdistan (PUK).

Talabani spent part of the 1970s living in Damascus, where the fledgling PUK came to maturity. It was the heyday of leftist groups like the Palestine Liberation Organization, and, like many Kurdish leaders during the period, Talabani flirted with socialism. He was not alone. The elder Barzani had come under the influence of Marxism during his fifteen years of refuge in Russia after World War II, but he had rejected the philosophy. Abdullah Ocalan, the leader of the Kurdish rebels in Turkey, believed that Kurdish nation building was tied to Marxism, and he publicly espoused the doctrine until the early 1990s.

Talabani's PUK received Syrian support, as Ocalan's PKK would in the years that followed. The support provided Talabani a back channel for smuggling fighters and weapons through Syria, across the Tigris River, and into northern Iraq. The Syrian route had also been a favorite of the Barzani clan in the 1960s and 1970s; in the 1990s, it would be used to supply PKK rebels in their war against Turkey.

By the late 1970s, Talabani's breakaway PUK was engaging Barzani's traditional rebels in bitter territorial clashes throughout Iraqi Kurdistan. Saddam Hussein, who assumed the Iraqi presidency in 1979, exploited the rivalry between the two leaders, a practice that would persist until the collapse of his regime in 2003. When I met Talabani's followers in 1991, they portrayed their leader as a self-made man who had inherited nothing and who had built the PUK from the ground up. Talabani's critics saw him as a flip-flopper, courting the Americans with tough anti-Arab talk but willing to be photographed in Baghdad by Iraqi television, as he was shortly after the Gulf War, when he greeted Saddam Hussein with a ceremonial kiss.

Talabani had taught himself English, and he spoke the language with greater fluency than Massoud Barzani. (Barzani usually insisted his interviews be conducted in Kurdish.) In 1991, Talabani's headquarters were in the mountains above Sulaimaniah, near the Iranian border. At the time, the PUK enjoyed a reputation for being more sophisticated than the KDP in public relations, including a willingness to court the occasional reporter who wandered into the territory.

In those days vehicles and fuel were scarce in Kurdistan, so I was happy when Talabani dispatched a carload of *peshmerga* to bring me to his headquarters. Two of the men worked in the Sulaimaniah hospital, which may have explained why I was picked up in a shiny new ambulance with Kuwaiti license plates. The ambulance, which had been "liberated" from the Iraqi army, was *double* war booty, as the Iraqis had first looted it from the Kuwaitis. It was a 1990 Chevrolet, fully outfitted with emergency medical equipment for paramedics. Except for a stretcher full of machine guns in back and a bullet hole in the windshield, the ambulance might have fit in nicely on the streets of San Francisco or New York.

I sat in front with the PUK driver. He reeled off the names of countries Talabani had visited and the world leaders he had met. He told me that Talabani had a photocopier, a fax machine, and a satellite telephone in his office—all of which were "firsts" for Kurdistan. I asked him to sum up the differences between the two prominent Kurdish leaders. The driver paused, searching for the right word. Barzani was "tribal," he finally said, whereas Talabani was "more scientific."

When I arrived, Talabani was working at a cluttered desk in his study. A small kerosene stove heated the room, and the PUK leader was bundled up in an overcoat, his throat wrapped in a scarf. The day before, I had watched him on Kurdish television rallying an outdoor audience of thousands in the city of Erbil. It was cold, and he had spoken nonstop for two hours. Now, he had laryngitis.

Talabani's battery-powered radio was broadcasting the news from Ankara, and the PUK chief wanted to talk about "positive political developments" in Turkey. Talabani told me that Turkish Prime Minister Suleyman Demirel was just beginning to recognize "the Kurdish reality." Demirel had just sent a message to Baghdad that Turkish armed forces would not sit by if Saddam's troops tried to drive more refugees across the border. The development contained a glimmer of hope for Talabani, and he had seized on it. The Turks were the Kurds' nemesis in many ways, so the PUK leader really was embracing the old Middle East axiom: The enemy of my enemy is my friend. Other Kurds had expressed it to me in blunter terms: A clash between Turkey and Iraq, although unlikely, could be good for the Kurds. Turkey was a staunch U.S. ally. An attempt by the powerful NATO power to confront the Baghdad regime would bring the forgotten Kurds one step closer to the Americans. Frankly, it was difficult to read Ankara's message to Baghdad as much more than a pro forma warning. Turkey simply did not want a new refugee crisis on its borders. The Iraqi Kurds, however, were desperate for economic and political survival. When it came to good news, they could not be picky.

A few months earlier, Talabani and his rival Barzani had negotiated an autonomy agreement with Baghdad, contingent on the willingness of Saddam Hussein to meet certain demands. It was just after the Gulf War. Saddam, as usual, was playing the Kurdish parties against each other, exploiting their divisions, and the autonomy deal was faltering. Now, though, as far as Talabani was concerned, the sputtering negotiations were finished for good. Barzani and other members of the Kurdistan Front had just announced plans to send another delegation to Baghdad, but Talabani was taking a hard line, underscoring a growing split with Barzani. "Negotiation with a dictatorship is useless," he told me. "We cannot reach any kind of agreement with a dictatorship."

Talabani was angry, seemingly bitter, at the way the Gulf War had ended. "The allies are to blame," he said. "Saudi Arabia, Egypt, and [Mikhail] Gorbachev deceived Mr. Bush. They deceived him and convinced him to stop the war. The United States of America did not know the realities of Iraq. The USA was told to be afraid of Shiites in the south and Kurds in the north, to be afraid there would be chaos in Iraq if Saddam collapsed. They told the USA to fear a fundamentalist movement connected with Iran. For this reason, the Americans preferred to keep Saddam Hussein in power."

Talabani said he wanted the United States "to finish the job, to topple the dictatorship." Publicly, at least, he opposed a CIA assassination attempt against Saddam, an action that he branded "terrorist action and contrary to our goals." He said he preferred that the U.S. support "another uprising of Iraqi people, or inside the Iraqi army, or perhaps both." The Kurdish leader would get his wish, but not for a dozen years. Not until the presidency of George W. Bush.

No Access to Washington

The biggest problem for the Kurds, Talabani acknowledged, was a lack of allies. Most of all, he said, the Kurds needed to position themselves on the *American agenda*. At this point, only months after the 1991 Kurdish uprising had been crushed, a PUK member told me, they could not even land a meeting with "a lower [U.S.] official." Talabani had already visited Washington, D.C., seeking U.S. support for a renewed Kurdish struggle, but according to one of his aides, he came away disappointed, without an opportunity to make his case before Secretary of State James Baker or another high-level member of the Bush administration. His rival, Massoud Barzani, had a similar experience soon after the Gulf War, when he made a goodwill tour of European cities. The itinerary called for him to continue to Washington, but Barzani reportedly canceled those plans after KDP feelers to the State Department indicated only a low-level reception awaited him in the U.S. capital.

Despite the rebuffs, Talabani said that the PUK planned to contact both the Democrats and the Republicans during the upcoming 1992 U.S. presidential race. He hoped that American elections would bring some attention to the "Kurdish cause." The media was powerful, he said, and he believed that the graphic pictures of Kurdish refugees on television the previous year were responsible for White House intervention in northern Iraq and the generous relief effort. "The Kurdish people are grateful to the American people for helping them," he said. "We would be [even] more grateful if the American people would exert pressure on the administration to support the just struggle of Kurdish people for democracy in Iraq."

"We are very vulnerable here," he said almost plaintively as I left.

Barzani Family

While Talabani appeared frequently on television in 1991, it seemed a toss-up whether his rival, Massoud Barzani, even watched the medium. Barzani was a small man with a boyish-looking face who had joined the Kurdish uprising against the Iraqi government in 1961, when he was sixteen. My first impression when I met the KDP leader was that he was a reluctant participant in a family drama not of his own making. One supporter told me, he "would just as soon retire to an estate in the mountains and hunt partridge." But first impressions are often wrong.

Massoud was a member of the most famous clan in modern Kurdish history. His father, Mullah Mustafa, was born in 1903. In 1905, when Mustafa was still a toddler, he and his mother were imprisoned for several months by the Ottomans. His uncle, Sheikh Ahmad, led an uprising against the British, which was put down in 1931 in a brutal bombing campaign by the RAF. The bombings destroyed eighty Kurdish villages and some thirteen hundred homes belonging to the Barzani clan and forced Sheikh Ahmad and Massoud's father to flee to southern Iraq. Mullah Mustafa led his own rebellions against the Baghdad government in the 1940s. In 1946, he and a force of twelve hundred *peshmerga* crossed the border to Iran, where they united with the forces of Qazi Muhammad, a respected judge, Muslim cleric, and the leader of the new Kurdish Republic at Mahabad. Later the same year, Massoud Barzani was born in Mahabad. He was, as he later told me, "a child of revolution."

Mahabad Republic

In 1945, in the little town of Mahabad, Iran, the dream of an independent Kurdistan briefly came to fruition. The chain of events that gave birth to the world's only Kurdish republic began in 1941 with the British-Soviet invasion of Iran that toppled the pro-Nazi regime of Reza Shah Pahlavi. Mahabad, located in the center of a large mountainous area between British and Soviet forces, was populated by Kurdish tribes. In 1943, only twenty-one years after a controversial post–World War I treaty denied the Kurds a promised homeland, a dozen young Kurds in Mahabad founded a secret society called *Komala-i-Zhian-I-Kurd* (Committee of Kurdish Youth). The group, which was strongly nationalist, restricted membership to those of Kurdish descent on both sides of the family. Komala, which had pan-Kurdish aspirations, soon opened chapters in Sulaimaniah and other Iraqi cities, as well as in Turkey.

When World War II ended in 1945, Qazi Muhammad assumed the leadership of Komala. In the same year, he and more than one hundred leading Kurds signed a manifesto urging all Kurds "to take advantage of the liberation of the world from fascism and to share in the promises of the Atlantic Charter." Many of the signers were dressed in *shirwal,* the traditional Kurdish pantaloons, which had been banned under the Shah and were still prohibited in neighboring Turkey. The manifesto spelled out demands for cultural, economic, and legal freedoms denied to the Kurds under the Shah.

The Cold War was beginning. Some of the Kurdish tribes in Iran opposed the new political movement, branded it a Soviet puppet, and threatened to destroy it. As so often is the case in Kurdish history, however, the misfortune of one Kurdish group would benefit another Kurdish group. The occasion was the retreat from Iraq in October 1945 of Massoud's father, Mullah Mustafa Barzani, and his battle-hardened *peshmerga.*

Barzani's forces had scored victories against British-supported government troops in Iraq, but the Baghdad regime had countered by enlisting the aid of rival Kurdish tribes (a similar divide-and-conquer strategy would be pursued against Kurdish rebels in Turkey a half century later with the hiring of Kurdish "village guards"). The coordination of Iraqi soldiers, Kurdish tribesmen, and British backing succeeded in putting down the uprising, and Barzani was forced to retreat. Rebel troops escaped across the frontier, arriving in Iran with a large cache of captured British rifles and machine guns. Barzani immediately allied himself with the forces of Qazi Muhammad, giving the Mahabad experiment the strength it needed to proclaim the new republic. On December 15, 1945, the Kurdish flag of independence was triumphantly raised in the presence of Komala founders, local tribes, Mullah Mustafa Barzani, members of his Kurdistan Democratic Party (KDP), and several Soviet military officers. The Kurdistan People's Government, a ministate of four towns in the mountains, was officially declared. During the Mahabad's brief tenure—slightly less than one year— Archie Roosevelt Jr., a U.S. assistant military attaché in Tehran, visited the republic. One of only four Americans to meet Qazi Muhammad, Roosevelt characterized the new leader as "the symbol of Kurdish nationalists everywhere."

Later, he published his impressions of the Kurdish leader in the *Middle East Journal:*

> A short man of fifty, dressed in an old army overcoat, he had a lightly bearded, slightly ascetic face, slightly yellowish in complexion from a stomach ailment. He neither smoked nor drank and ate very little. His voice was gentle and well modulated, his gestures quiet but effective. Something of an internationalist, he was interested in all the peoples of the world and knew many languages, including Russian, a little English, and Esperanto. His desk was littered with grammars and readers and literary works in foreign tongues. . . . [He] himself thought the Kurds were the descendants of the Medes, and liked to give his own etymology of Mahabad—"abode of the Kurds" . . . Politically at least, Mahabad was the focal point toward which all Kurdish eyes now were turned. . . . Couriers brought communications to him from groups of Kurds not only in Iraq but in Syria and Turkey as well.

Roosevelt went on to say, "[Muhammad's] demands were simple: Kurdish autonomy within the Iranian state." The objectives, not coincidentally, mirrored those of the Iraqi Kurds, Turkish Kurds, and Syrian Kurds, all of whom would challenge the governing structures of their respective countries. Oil production, often a factor in Kurdish political fortunes, played a part in the early collapse of the Mahabad Republic. The Shah's successor was equally opposed to Kurdish nationalism. The new regime offered Moscow oil, a vital commodity in the growing arms race between the superpowers, in partial exchange for a Soviet withdrawal of support for the miniature Kurdish state. The Iranian army, together with Kurdish tribes suspicious of Muhammad's Soviet connections, finally defeated the forces of the fledgling republic. The government moved quickly to reinstitute pogroms against the Kurds, smashing Kurdish printing presses, publicly burning Kurdish books, and banning the teaching of the language.

Shortly before the Soviet forces pulled back to allow the advance of the Iranians into Mahabad, a Russian army car arrived and took Mullah Mustafa Barzani to safety. The Kurdish leader spent the next decade in Moscow, not returning to Iraq until after the overthrow of the British-supported monarchy in 1958.

Qazi Muhammad refused the Soviet offer to escape, telling colleagues that Iranian reprisals against his followers might be less severe if he stayed behind. Soon after the Iranian military arrived in Mahabad, Qazi Muhammad and other Kurdish leaders were executed by hanging. As a warning to the local population, the Iranian army displayed their bodies in the town square for a week.

Museum

Kurdistan felt like a living history museum, disorganized but open to chance discovery. I'd first heard the story of Qazi Muhammad on a visit to a junk store in Sulaimaniah. The shop sold old Kurdish carpets, guns, daggers, photos, and other paraphernalia. On one of the walls was a crumpled image of a man in short hair hanging limp from a rope. It was a photo of the Mahabad execution. The shop owner proceeded to tell me about his affection for Qazi Muhammad. The picture, he said, was not for sale.

Later, in the Iraqi Kurdish city of Erbil, on my way to interview Massoud Barzani, I stayed in a hotel called the Chwar Charra. The name means "Four Candles," a reference to the separate "fires" of Kurdish nationalism that were reunited at Mahabad. It was almost a half century after the collapse of the little Kurdish republic, but the Kurds in Iran, Iraq, Syria, and Turkey still employed the image of four flames to symbolize the dream of one Kurdistan.

General Ali

At the time of my visit to the KDP in 1991, Massoud Barzani made his headquarters in an old hotel in Salahuddin, a former resort town located 180 miles northeast of Baghdad. Salahuddin was named for the most famous Kurd in history, the twelfth-century warrior who saved Jerusalem from the crusaders. But history is written, as the saying goes, by the scribes of the conquerors. In official Iraq, that meant that Salahuddin was an Arab. Saddam Hussein portrayed himself as a direct descendent of the legendary leader, heroically defending Muslim Iraq against the threats of the West in the twentieth century (he also traced himself to the rulers of Babylon, who in reality were Assyrians, the forerunners of today's Iraqi Christians).

Until the Kurdish uprising in March of 1991, the mountain village of Salahuddin represented a temperate getaway from the hot summers in the south—at least for those who could afford it. During the Gulf War bombing of the capital in 1991, wealthy Arabs and Baghdad officials flocked to the gambling casinos of Salahuddin. The last place the allies would look for government big shots, according to conventional wisdom, was a poker palace in Kurdistan.

In its glory days, the Salahuddin was a three-star hotel, and the gold-colored stars were still displayed above the former reception desk. The most striking room in the onetime resort hotel was a huge main lobby with ballroom-high ceilings, six unlit chandeliers, and two motionless fans. On the day of my visit, armed *peshmerga* were lounging in the lobby in overstuffed couches, lazily drinking tea. The couches were soiled and threadbare, with noticeable gouges in their fat, vinyl armrests. Everyone seemed to be smoking—not an uncommon sight among the Kurds at the time—and the ashtrays on the tables overflowed with cigarette butts. It was wintertime, but there was no electricity or heat in the hotel. What light existed came from a window. The air was heavy with smoke and exhaled breath.

There was a lot of chatter in the guerrilla redoubt and a constant coming and going of men with Soviet-made Kalashnikov rifles slung over their shoulders. Messengers with urgent looks arrived periodically carrying folded scraps of paper, which their seated commanders read and initialed before dispatching the couriers on additional errands. Large oil paintings of Mullah Mustafa Barzani, Massoud's father, hung in both the main and secondary lobbies. The paintings were at least ten feet high, and they depicted the legendary mountain fighter with one hand at his belt resting on the trademark *khanger,* the curved ceremonial dagger, and the other hand reaching for a *piala* of Kurdish tea.

At the time I arrived, Massoud Barzani had just returned from Baghdad and was busy informing the KDP officials of his latest efforts to persuade the regime to lift the economic blockade against the Kurds. Accordingly, my interview was set for later in the day. That gave me time to renew acquaintances with the man they called Zahim Ali (General Ali), who was Barzani's top military commander. I had met him the past spring during the *rakeerden,* the mass exodus to the mountains.

Traditionally, the KDP had not employed a military ranking system, and Ali was the only rebel called general. His real name was Omar Osman. The KDP said that the title of Zahim Ali was a special recognition by Mullah Mustafa Barzani because Osman had waged a fierce hit-and-run campaign against Saddam's troops after the 1988 gas attacks drove most other *peshmerga* from the country.

Ali had spent seventeen years in the mountains, and he looked trim and fit. He was of medium build with black hair and a moustache. His head was wrapped in a red-and-white *qafiya*—the Barzani colors—and he wore the latest badge of Kurdish honor: a U.S. Army fatigue jacket. The coveted article of clothing, which the Kurds saw as an emblem of American interest in their desperate cause, had been left behind by U.S. troops after the first Gulf War. He carried a sidearm under the field jacket, holstered over his *pishtwen,* the wide, ruffled cummerbund that Kurdish men use for a belt.

Ali seemed more rested than he had the previous spring, when I had encountered him in the midst of the refugee nightmare. He introduced me to his friend, Qazi Atrushi, another Kurdish commander. Atrushi spoke English and would translate the interview. As it turned out, he had lived in San Diego, California. Although he was on track for U.S. citizenship—he showed me his green card—his allegiance was Kurdish. He was a member of the Kurdish diaspora in North America and Europe who had come home to northern Iraq after the Gulf War.

Both he and Ali were forty-four years old. They had served together as officers in the Iraqi army in the early 1970s, members of a small, elite group of Kurdish students. As part of ongoing negotiations for Kurdish autonomy, the Iraqi government had invited them to enroll in the military school in Baghdad known as "Iraq's West Point." In 1972, the two friends graduated as commissioned officers in the Iraqi army.

Less than two years later, Kurdish autonomy talks broke down with Baghdad. Mullah Mustafa Barzani issued the call for Kurdish officers to shed their uniforms—and careers—and to join the uprising. Some of the Kurds chose to remain with the army, and some were killed trying to desert. Others, like Ali and Atrushi, escaped to Kurdistan, where they integrated inside knowledge of the Iraqi military with the old techniques of guerrilla warfare Barzani had employed off and on against the central government since 1961. These were heady times, Ali said, through translation. "We had the Americans behind us, we were getting trained in Israel, and we had weapons for about one hundred thousand *peshmerga*."

In fact, the CIA was funding the Kurds through the Shah of Iran, although the American public knew nothing about it. As a favor to the Shah, Secretary of State Henry Kissinger secretly had arranged for the CIA to bankroll a Kurdish uprising against Saddam Hussein. According to a 1991 staff report for the U.S. Senate Foreign Relations Committee, it was the Shah's way of settling a border dispute with Iraq and gaining strategic access to the Shatt al Arab seaway between the two nations. In 1975, Kissinger brokered a deal with the Shah and Saddam called the Algiers Accord, which gave the Shah the land and navigation concessions he wanted. In return, the Shah, the Kurds' principal patron, canceled sanctuary for Kurdish rebels in Iran, and the United States immediately cut off the flow of secret arms. Overnight, the Kurds were abandoned.

According to the 1976 findings by the House Select Committee on Intelligence, chaired by New York Congressman Otis Pike, it was shameful manipulation. After encouraging rebel hostilities by infusing the conflict with $16 million in secret aid approved by President Richard Nixon himself, Kissinger personally restrained the insurgents from an all-out offensive on one occasion when such an attack might have been successful. The weapons were Soviet-made and successfully delivered by Israel, but the U.S. never wanted the Kurds to win, according to the once-secret congressional report:

> The President, Dr. Kissinger, and the foreign head of state [the Shah] hoped our clients [Kurds] would not prevail. They preferred instead that the insurgents simply continue a level of hostilities sufficient to sap the resources of our ally's [Israel] neighboring country [Iraq]. This policy was

not imparted to our clients, who were encouraged to continue fighting. Even in the context of covert action, ours was a cynical enterprise.

The Iraqi regime, knowing in advance that aid would be cut off, was able to launch a search-and-destroy campaign against the unsuspecting Kurds only one day after the agreement was signed.

According to the *Pike Committee Report*, had the U.S. not encouraged the Kurdish rebellion,

> . . . the insurgents may have reached an accommodation with the central government, thus gaining at least a measure of autonomy while avoiding further bloodshed. Instead, our clients fought on, sustaining thousands of casualties and 200,000 refugees.

Once again, the Kurds had no friends. The new Ford administration refused to extend humanitarian assistance to the refugees, whose condition had been created by the abrupt termination of military aid. Iran forcibly returned approximately forty thousand Kurds to face the wrath of Iraqi authorities. An untold number were executed or simply never seen again. There were few official tears. Kissinger reportedly told a Pike Committee staff member at the time, "Covert action should not be confused with missionary work."

At this point, the elder Barzani was suffering from cancer. In 1976, the CIA arranged for the rebel leader to be brought to the United States. He was treated at the Mayo Clinic in Minnesota and then transferred to Georgetown Hospital. He died there in 1979, just a few miles from Langley, Virginia, the agency's headquarters. Before his death, Barzani gave one last interview—to the *New York Times* columnist William Safire. With his then twenty-three-year-old son Massoud at his side, the ailing Barzani said, "We do not want to be anybody's pawns. We are an ancient people. We want our autonomy. We want *sarbasti*—freedom. I do not know who will take my place one day. But they cannot crush us."

Barzani had a son who might have taken his father's place, but he was assassinated later by Saddam's secret police. Another son died in Iran of a heart ailment. The leadership fell to Massoud.

It was time for lunch. General Ali extended an invitation to join him and other *peshmerga* leaders in what had been the dining room, where still another mammoth portrait of KDP founder Barzani was displayed. There were a dozen men at a long table. Atrushi did his best to translate the lively banter, which included Ali's teasing of a Kurdish military doctor who had recently defected from the Iraqi army. Ali pretended to apologize to the newcomer because the simple lunch was "below the standards of Baghdad." The physician, a former colonel in Saddam's forces, joined in the laughter. Later, I asked the doctor why he hadn't defected sooner.

"Until now," the doctor replied, "the circumstances were not ready for revolution." His only regret, he said, was that he had put in nineteen years and was slated for promotion to general the coming year. Before the Gulf War, he said, generals made six hundred dinars a month ($60 at the 1991 black market exchange). In the months since the end of the Gulf War, according to the doctor, Saddam had doubled the salary of everyone in the military.

Had the doctor stayed in the system, he now would be earning twelve hundred dinars a month, a fortune by Iraqi standards. Instead, he was here, eating guerrilla food in an unheated dining room. I asked myself, was he a *spy?* Later in the day, I raised the issue with Atrushi, asking him how the KDP protected itself against Iraqi infiltrators. "We don't put ['suspects'] in sensitive positions," he said simply.

The interview with Atrushi and General Ali continued in another room. Atrushi said that during the secret funding in 1975, he had been trained in Israel how to fire missiles. The Kurds had been promised a shipment of surface-to-air missiles. He said the advanced weapons might have forced the Iraqis to recognize the Kurdish autonomy, saving countless lives, but U.S. aid was cut off before the missiles could be delivered. Late in 1975, realizing the revolution had failed, Atrushi walked over the mountains to Iran, beginning his life as a refugee. Later, he immigrated to Canada, where he started Kurdish support groups in Toronto.

In the mid-1980s he moved to the United States. He bought a corner market in San Diego, and remained in California until 1990, when Iraq invaded Kuwait. "I knew instantly what was coming for the Kurds," he said, "and Massoud wanted me to come home."

Despite its weaknesses, the 1970s agreement for Kurdish autonomy from Iraq almost succeeded, according to Atrushi. In fact, Saddam Hussein made a rare state visit to Kurdistan in support of the agreement, and the Iraqi government announced on state television that the Kurds would be autonomous. "We nearly realized the state of Kurdistan in the 1970s—we were that close," he said, holding two fingers together. The fortunes of the Kurds at the time—as so often in modern history—were dependent on oil. "Saddam was much weaker then because there was an oil glut and [foreign] money wasn't flowing into Iraq to buy arms. We were strong then, so he had a reason to settle with us."

"But we were betrayed by the Americans," he added without hesitation. "Don't get me wrong—I like the States, the standard of living and all. But I'll never understand their foreign policy—for so many years the Kurdish people have been used by the United States for the balance of power in the Middle East."

General Ali chose his words more carefully. He had regrets but no bitterness about the 1975 collapse of the revolution and his own decision to remain in Iraq. The government knew he had escaped to the mountains, and it did what it could to pressure him to give up. His clan was offered money and special status—an invitation some Kurdish leaders accepted during the period in exchange for not causing Baghdad trouble. When that failed, the family house was confiscated, and his father was imprisoned and repeatedly tortured.

Ali stayed on the run, launching his raids against Iraqi positions from a series of moveable guerrilla camps along the Turkish border. There was a price on his head, he said, and he survived two assassination attempts. Ali was one of the few members of the Kurdish command with personal knowledge that in the 1970s, the CIA had bankrolled the movement. "It was a secret from our own people back then," he said. "It was also a secret from your people," he added. "That was the part I did not like."

Today (1991), Ali said, the East-West conflict was over, and there was only "one force" (the United States) left in the world. "We could do more to fight Saddam today if we knew the Americans were backing us again militarily." Instead, Ali said, the Kurds were constantly trying to second-guess the United States, worrying that they might be left alone if they mounted an all-out offensive campaign against the superior forces of the Iraqi army. "The key to our struggle is Turkey," he said. "At the least, Washington could pressure its friend Turkey to give the Kurds more rights up there. That would be a signal to Baghdad to deal with our problems politically, not by force."

"That will never happen," Atrushi said, interrupting his own translation of Ali's words. "America is just not committed to the Kurds. After the war, President Bush encouraged us to rise up, but he allowed Saddam to fly his helicopters— which he used to massacre us!" What about Operation Provide Comfort? I asked him. (The generous U.S.-led program provided assistance to refugees in northern Iraq.) "That was realpolitik," Atrushi said bitterly.

According to Atrushi, the Kurds were always looking for "leftovers." Ironically, Saddam's continued hold on power was, in a strange way, *good* for the Kurds. Had there been an army coup in Baghdad, and Saddam replaced by a dictator of lesser notoriety, the outside world might have completely forgotten the Kurds by now.

As he spoke, I recalled some refugees singing the praises of President Bush the year before, when I had visited their tent cities in the mountain snow. Many grateful Kurds had joked to me that the name of Kurdistan ought to be changed to "Bushistan." It brought to mind the expression of earlier Kurdish gratitude reported by Daniel Schorr, the former CBS correspondent and, later, a news analyst for National Public Radio. (In 1976, Schorr was threatened with imprisonment for contempt of Congress for refusing to disclose how he had obtained the secret *Pike Committee Report* on the Kurds.) Mustafa Barzani, like so many of his people, according to a column Schorr wrote, so identified with the United States, he actually wanted to *give* his oil-rich country to America. Barzani was quoted as saying that he "trusted no other major power," and that, if his cause succeeded, he was ready for Kurdistan to become the fifty-first state.

"We have fought enough. Some of our [rebel] recruits are just boys and old men holding guns. We want to negotiate now," General Ali said, referring to the ongoing KDP entreaties to Saddam Hussein. "Our people are in the snow again and the killing must stop."

Ali criticized the "confrontational" tactics of PUK Chief Jalal Talabani and claimed that PUK guerrillas had provoked some of the recent skirmishes with the Iraqi army. He said that the TV stations run by Talabani were whipping up people's emotions, and that the hunger strikes across Kurdistan had been orchestrated by the PUK.

Ali's spirits had been buoyed by Operation Provide Comfort. He said it was the first aid to the Kurds since the CIA delivered supplies in the 1970s. He wanted to make sure I understood he was grateful for American help to the refugees during "the running away" in 1991. What worried him was the Kurds' vulnerability—the same thing that concerned Jalal Talabani. At the time of my visit, in late 1991, there was a skeleton crew of only seven American soldiers in all of northern Iraq. In addition, the U.S. jets enforcing the no-fly zone were based in Turkey, and the Turks were increasingly dissatisfied with the mission to protect Iraqi Kurds, fearing it might undermine Turkey's control of its own Kurds. Ali said Iraqis were beholden to the Turkish parliament, which was scheduled to vote in just a few months to extend or terminate the U.S. mission. "If Saddam attacks again, our forces cannot defend the people in the flatlands and in the cities. We will all be back in the mountains again."

At first, General Ali said he had been suspicious of journalists like myself who arrived to cover the recent refugee disaster. Two of them had official-looking press credentials, but their only interest seemed to be Kurdish troop deployments, rebel weapons, and the condition of old Iraqi air bases. The questions reminded him of the secret CIA involvement during the Nixon administration. I asked him if the prospect of CIA agents passing themselves off as legitimate reporters angered him. "Oh, no!" he exclaimed. "The chance [the agents] might be back here made me very happy!"

Massoud Barzani

The interview with Massoud Barzani took place in the dining room, near one of the portraits of his father. A soft-spoken man, Massoud chose his words carefully with his American visitor. He had wanted the interview to be in Kurdish and had come with a translator, but he agreed, out of courtesy to me, to speak in English.

Barzani played down the differences with Talabani and defended the need for rapprochement with the Iraqi government. The Kurds would never have security, he said, without an agreement for autonomy. The *peshmerga* simply could not defend the people against the superior forces of the Iraqi army.

A few weeks before my visit, Turkish pilots flying U.S.-made jets had bombed northern Iraq, targeting sanctuaries of Turkish Kurds, the PKK rebels. No bases were hit, Barzani said, but the attacks had taken place in the Barzan Valley, the heartland of the Barzani clan, where the RAF had bombed in the 1930s. A dozen Kurdish civilians had been killed in the Turkish bombings. He conceded that the Barzani tribe had a history of both alliance and conflict with the PKK, but he said that the PKK had pledged not to use Iraqi territory for raids into Turkey. The KDP leader insisted the PKK was honoring the agreement. He told me he was angry and saddened by the "foolish" bombing.

Barzani drew his greatest support from the northern territory, where Turkey, Iran, and Iraq meet. (Talabani's stronghold, southeast Kurdistan, comprised a much smaller land base.) When the revolution began in 1961, Massoud dropped out of Baghdad University and came home to the mountains to fight against the government. In the thirty years since then, he had seen his people under constant stress and pressure: gas attacks by the army; thousands of Kurdish villages dynamited; tens of thousands of Kurds killed or disappeared; many more driven into foreign exile or into diseased refugee camps (many of which were off-limits to relief agencies and to the press); Arabization of key Kurdish lands; a "false" autonomy negotiation with Baghdad; and internal feuding—even armed conflict—with other Kurdish tribes.

Like Talabani, he had tried to hold on to the long view, the hope of national liberation, while trying to determine who were the *real* friends of the Kurds. If experience had taught him anything about the Middle East, Barzani said, it was the old "balance of power" squeeze: the Kurds stuck in hostile Iraq between the Turkish and Iranian governments, strong regional powers who view Iraqi Kurdistan as a bad example for separatism in their own countries. It was a classic double bind: adversaries inside and adversaries outside.

Barzani said that the publicity generated by Saddam's oppression of the refugees in 1991 had been a mixed blessing for the Kurds. He told me he appreciated humanitarian aid from the West, but he stressed that the central question for the Kurds was not humanitarian. He said that he did not want his people to duplicate the fate of displaced groups such as the Palestinians, whose successive generations are born into camps and never achieve a homeland. "We are thankful for the blankets and the food, but we do not want the world to remember us as refugees," he said. "Our case is *political.*"

Before the interview, Atrushi had informed me of Barzani's recent meetings with the American army colonel who headed the token U.S. military presence in Zakho, near the Turkish border. The colonel was only a midlevel officer with no role in setting policy, but because Barzani was anxious for any official word of support from Washington, he kept in regular touch with the commander, believing him the appropriate channel for messages to the United States.

I was the only U.S. reporter in the country at the time, and the interview offered Barzani a chance to send out a message. I asked him repeatedly what he expected from the United States, but he was wary and politely deflected my questions. The closest he would come to a direct answer was to say, "The American government *knows* what it should do." It may have been self-serving of me to expect the Kurdish leader to bare his soul, but the Kurds, dependent and skittish from past betrayals, were still a long way from using the media to negotiate with Washington.

After the interview, Atrushi took me aside. "The Kurds are bound by protocol," he said politely, but bluntly. There was no hint of disloyalty, but I could hear the "American" in his voice. "Let's face it," he added, "a lot of people in Iraq still think that an army colonel has more power than a journalist."

The remark was characteristic of the Kurdish timidity of the early 1990s, a time when Barzani and other Kurdish leaders were forced to rely on Turkish diplomatic passports to travel abroad. By 2004, a year after the U.S. invasion that toppled the Iraqi regime, Barzani would display no such reluctance in using the press to send a political message. In that year, when Turkey threatened to protect its stated interests in oil-rich Kirkuk by invading northern Iraq, Barzani summoned the media. He pointedly warned the NATO power to keep its troops at home, lest Kurdish fighters turn northern Iraq into a "Turkish graveyard."

The Iraqi Front

In late 1991, the Kurdish leaders had their backs to the mountains, and Iraqi troops seemed poised for another attack. The front was a line that zigzagged from the bottom of the Sulaimaniah governate, near the Iranian border, all the way north to the Turkish frontier, a distance of more than 250 miles. In some places the two sides were so close they could view each other. Near Kalar, in the south, where the Kurdish guerrillas were dug into earthen bunkers across a long ridge, they could look across a shallow valley and see the faces of the Iraqi Republican Guard.

I was close enough to hear the Iraqi tank motors start and stop, a sound that triggered my adrenaline. In the nearby village of Kifri, the rebels gladly took me on top of Kurdish houses, the ones that had not been destroyed by mortars. After sneaking from roof to roof, I got so close to an Iraqi checkpoint that I could capture the soldiers with a video camera. Occasionally somebody in the distance would trigger a burst of machine-gun fire, and the sound was enough to keep us low on the rooftop. Nevertheless, I got the sense that I was witnessing the early stages of the Kurds taking charge of themselves for the first time since World War I. The Iraqi-Kurdish conflict had reached a stalemate.

In the eight months since the end of the first Gulf War, a line had been crossed; a point of no return had been reached. Despite the let's-wait-for-outside-powers-to-support-us attitude (a syndrome that remained a constant), the 1991 refugee nightmare had triggered a more radical strain in Kurdistan. The legacy of the *rakeerden,* the "running away," had produced a do-or-die mentality among the Kurds. I sensed it at a wedding in Sulaimaniah in the frenetic dancing of the guests, who twisted around, waving colored pieces of cloth in the air. A guerrilla was getting married. "Before, there was no time for this kind of thing," his friend told me as the band played and guests wearing traditional costumes spun around the room. "They were in the mountains before, hiding. Now they take time to marry. There is no more hiding."

By now, almost everyone had had a taste of life on the run as refugees. Nearly everyone was armed, both young and old. In a space of less than a year, Kurdistan had become a guerrilla society. It was still no match for the well-equipped Iraqi troops along the front, but by now, the Kurdish population was so deep into rebellion that resistance cut across all social and tribal lines. There would be no going back, even if what lay ahead was a bloodbath. For the moment at least, the genie was out of the bottle. The Kurds were running their own affairs.

The writer Albert Camus once suggested that the slave starts to be free the day he decides to say no. As far as I could tell, that day had come for the Kurds.

6

Illusory Borders,
Part I

If you cannot break a hand, you must kiss it.

—KURDISH PROVERB

Civil war is a species of misery which introduces
men to strange bedfellows.

—WALTER SCOTT

November 1992

The Gulf War had been over for more than a year, but the television networks still had an appetite—albeit a modest one—for stories about Saddam Hussein and Operation Provide Comfort, the U.S.-led mission to protect the Kurds. I was a freelance producer/cameraman in those days, and my usual way to get into northern Iraq was to fly to Istanbul, then travel eight hundred miles across Turkey to the Iraqi border.

The first part was easy, but flights to and from Turkey's remote southeast, the Kurdish area, often were overbooked with Turkish soldiers en route to the Kurdish uprising. By then, the southeast was occupied by tens of thousands of troops, and everyday life for the Kurds was not unlike that in northern Iraq before 1991, when Saddam's soldiers controlled the Kurdish area. Saddam was still in power in Baghdad, but the Iraqi Kurds now had an autonomous zone. In Turkey, by contrast, Kurdish villages were burning, and refugees were being driven from their homes in a hidden but spreading war. Despite the fact that U.S. taxpayers were underwriting a large part of the war, the story had been largely ignored by the *New York Times* and most of the American media.

The Kurdish uprising in Turkey had intensified since 1991, an unintended consequence of allied protection of Iraqi Kurds. The reason was simple: The Kurdish areas of Iraq abutted the Kurdish areas of Turkey. Before the U.S. Army pulled out of Iraq in the spring of 1991, rebels from the Kurdistan Workers' Party

(PKK) descended into Iraq from the mountains along the Turkish border and captured large quantities of weapons abandoned by the Iraqi military as it retreated south. The Iraqi retreat and U.S. troop pullout left a power vacuum in the region, with plenty of room for the PKK to establish a rear base.

The rebels already had camps in the Syrian-controlled Bekaa Valley in Lebanon, where over the years the PKK had trained thousands of young recruits. Many recruits had grown up poor in Kurdish ghettos in Europe, their passions stirred by reports of Turkish repression. For years, the PKK had smuggled the recruits and black-market weapons across Syria, into northern Iraq, then over the frontier to the Turkish front. It was an established route long before the advent of the PKK. Since the early 1960s the Kurdish rebels from Iraq had used Lebanon and Syria for refuge and resupply in uprisings against Saddam Hussein, including in 1975 when the United States was secretly supporting them. The transit route had also been used in the 1980s and 1990s by the rival Kurdish parties during factional conflicts among themselves.

Saddam Hussein's decision to invade Kuwait and the subsequent creation of the "safety zone" in northern Iraq had been a boon to Kurdish separatists in Turkey. Northern Iraq was becoming the PKK's Ho Chi Minh Trail. The loosely governed enclave offered the guerrillas the kind of supply routes and sanctuary that Laos and Cambodia had provided the Vietcong in the Vietnam War. With the PKK on both sides of the Turkish border, the rebels also had a chance to sell Iraqi Kurds their plans for *regional* revolution. With its dream of a pan-Kurdish state, a presence in two countries offered the PKK political, as well as military, opportunities.

Operation Provide Comfort

When coalition forces withdrew from Iraq in the spring of 1991, they left a token contingent at the MCC (Military Command Center) in the town of Zakho. The MCC housed teams of U.S., French, British, and Turkish officers, all of them part of Operation Provide Comfort. The multinational MCC was linked to Incirlik, the Turkish air base used by coalition aircraft to enforce the no-fly zone, the territory above the thirty-sixth parallel, commonly referred to as Iraqi Kurdistan or northern Iraq. At the time, the Iraqi Kurds' lifeline to the outside world was a single highway from Turkey. With no airport in northern Iraq, the MCC had the responsibility of coordinating vital relief supplies that arrived by road from international humanitarian groups. Increasingly, security in Iraqi Kurdistan was tied to security in Turkish Kurdistan. Under pressure from the United States and Turkey, Iraqi Kurds had agreed to fight the PKK. It wasn't long before PKK guerrillas announced their revenge: They would attack relief trucks inside Turkey bound for northern Iraq.

From a distance, it appeared that the United States, not Turkey, was in charge of Operation Provide Comfort, but my trips to the MCC gradually convinced me otherwise. Turkey was the gateway to northern Iraq, geographically and politically. Despite the international character of the coalition, the Turks knew the neighborhood, in many cases the language, and they commanded the coalition in all but name.

The focus was supposed to be the Iraqi regime. However, U.S. policy now pitted Iraqi Kurds against Turkish Kurds, and before long the MCC was gathering information on PKK rebels to help Turkey suppress its Kurdish rebellion. Each U.S. AWACS, the radar planes that coordinated overflights of Iraq, carried a Turkish intelligence officer on board, and all AWACS data was downloaded through a Turkish tracking center. Soon U.S. fighter pilots were also supplying the Turks with reconnaissance on the Kurdish uprising. A F-15 pilot from the Incirlik Air Base revealed to me in an interview that cameras on his jet had photographed PKK movements. Copies of the data apparently were supplied to Turkish intelligence as part of the MCC agreement.

As the uprising in Turkey spread, Ankara ratcheted up pressure on Iraqi Kurds to attack the bases of Turkish Kurds in northern Iraq. If Iraqi Kurds resisted, badly needed food and medical supplies could be delayed on the Turkish side of the border. Iraqi oil smuggling could also be halted, resulting in a backup of hundreds of trucks at the border, depriving cash-strapped Kurds of valuable bribes exacted from drivers. In addition, Kurdish leaders, landlocked in their remote enclave, lacking diplomatic relations abroad, depended on Turkey for visas to travel to Europe and the United States. They knew that vital trips could be cancelled or delayed if they incurred Ankara's displeasure.

Leveraging Washington

Turkey also had leverage over the United States because the fighter jets that patrolled northern Iraq were based at Incirlik, Turkey. The Turkish parliament periodically hinted it would not renew the privilege of overflights if the United States failed to keep the Iraqi Kurds in line—in this case, if Iraqi Kurds refused to fight PKK Kurds. Since U.S. policy toward the Iraqi regime was containment, not confrontation, the Turkish threat went to the heart of the American mission. Without the ability to use the nearby base at Incirlik, Operation Provide Comfort would be in jeopardy, allied soldiers at the MCC could not be protected from the air, and Saddam's forces might soon be at the throats of Iraqi Kurds.

A Turkish Journalist

On my way to cover Iraqi Kurdistan in the fall of 1992, I stopped in Ankara to interview Ismet Imset, the editor of the English-language *Turkish Daily News*.

Imset was one of the few Turkish journalists who had good sources in the Kurdish community and solid connections to Turkey's powerful military, which saw itself as the guardian of the state constitution and the legacy of Atatürk, the country's legendary founder. That unlikely combination had emboldened him to write what no other Turkish journalist had written: that there might be a legitimate distinction between "terrorism" and "armed resistance" on the part of Turkey's restive Kurds. Few Western journalists in today's post-9/11 climate would try to differentiate these phenomena, especially when the conflict concerned an American ally, but using a newspaper to make such a distinction in the 1990s, during a time of war, was unheard of in Turkey.

A number of Turkish intellectuals, including Yashar Kemal, the country's most famous writer, whose books had been translated into seventy-seven languages, already had been prosecuted for questioning government practices in articles published outside of Turkey. Kemal was put on trial under Article 312, which prohibited the "provoking of hate" between ethnic groups. He was convicted of writing an essay that appeared in the *New York Times* and in the respected German magazine *Der Spiegel,* the first paragraph of which reads:

> One of the greatest tragedies in Turkey's history is happening now. Our Kurdish brothers are being slaughtered, and apart from a couple of hesitant voices, no one is standing up and demanding to know what the government is doing.

In the week I visited Ankara, the Turkish army released figures claiming that two thousand Kurdish rebels had been killed in a recent campaign. Imset told me that the Turkish press routinely published inflated PKK casualty figures for the sake of public opinion. Turkish journalists were still feeling the effects of the 1980 coup, which had muzzled the press. Most reporters went out of their way to support the army, but there were exceptions. A month earlier, Turkey's best-known television anchor had been indicted on criminal charges for airing an interview with a soldier who opposed deployment to the Kurdish region. The police also had arrested a Turkish photographer for publishing a photo of a tank dragging a dead Kurdish rebel around a field on a rope. Imset told me that he had received threats on his life because of his own reports. (In 1995, he was forced to leave Turkey.)

One of the most controversial aspects of Turkey's counterinsurgency program involved the alleged use of napalm by the Turkish army inside the no-fly zone of northern Iraq. On October 20, 1991, Chris Hedges of the *New York Times* reported, "Turkish jets struck several times at what they said were rebel camps inside Iraq last week, dropping canisters of napalm and apparently wounding several civilians, according to allied military officials who monitor the security zone."

On October 14, 1997, ABCNews.com quoted a report from *Jane's Defence Weekly* which stated, "F-16s were dropping napalm on Kurdish villages." On October 31, 1997, Representative John Edward Porter (R-IL) was quoted in a *Washington Times* article saying, "I firmly believe that Turkey feels they can attack civilians in another country with napalm as they are doing right now because we have let them get away with it. We have emboldened them to carry their campaign of terror across borders into other nations." A week later, in a speech delivered in the House, Representative Steny Hoyer (D-MD) charged, "Turkish forces have actively supported the Kurdistan Democratic Party (KDP), which has been engaged in years of bloody fighting with its rival, the Patriotic Union of Kurdistan (PUK)." Hoyer said that widespread reports "indicate[d] Turkey is using napalm and cluster bombs, despite international covenants banning their use." Travel restrictions in the war zone made it impossible for me to confirm the napalm accusations, but Imset, the Turkish journalist, told me he doubted the claims. He said that military commanders indeed had requested napalm, but the Turkish general staff, fearful of alienating the United States, had not approved the use of the chemical. Memories were still fresh of the U.S. arms embargo imposed in 1974 after Turkey's invasion of Cyprus. American weapons were key to controlling the Kurdish uprising, he said, and the generals did not want to risk another suspension.

Imset predicted the war would soon escalate into an even more violent and bloody conflict. One of the reasons was drug trafficking. According to Imset, 80 percent of the heroin smuggled to Europe from Iran and Afghanistan passed through Turkish Kurdistan. Both the army and the guerrillas took part in the narcotics trade, he said, and "no one's hands were clean."

Recently he had published an exclusive interview with PKK leader Abdullah Ocalan, which had been conducted in Lebanon. The encounter led him to believe that Ocalan actually *wanted* Turkey to intervene in northern Iraq, because that would enlarge the conflict and potentially alienate the Iraqi Kurds. He maintained that Ocalan kept ruthless control over the PKK and had ordered the killing of several of his own commanders. He believed Ocalan was prepared "to lose another two thousand fifteen to sixteen year-olds [rebels]" to advance the objectives of the uprising.

According to Imset, both sides in the war were vying for control of the Kurds. The war had trapped the population between "the terror of the PKK and the terror of the state." The only way the state could win was to the divide the Kurds, a policy that he said was known in Turkey as *Kurdu Kurde Kirdimak* (Kurds breaking Kurds). Imset said the strategy had been used against Kurdish tribes since Ottoman times. The tactic was familiar in the nineteenth-century American West, as well. The U.S. Cavalry had used it to divide tribes like the Sioux and Crow, and I had seen a variation of it at Wounded Knee in 1973, in the divisions between traditional and assimilated Indians.

Turkey was adept at playing Turkish and Iraqi Kurds against each other. At the time, Iraqi Kurds were desperate to preserve their revolution against Saddam Hussein, but doing so was only possible on Turkey's terms. For that reason, according to Imset, Iraqi Kurds were under pressure from the United States to meet secretly with Turkish intelligence. Imset claimed that Jalal Talabani, the chief of the Patriotic Union of Kurdistan, had arranged one such meeting the year before in northern Iraq, and that a Turkish general and three other officers had attended—dressed like Kurdish *peshmerga*. If true, the report provided a telling snapshot of local infighting: one group of Kurds using foreign spies against another group of Kurds.

I stayed overnight in Ankara at the Sheraton Hotel. The reception clerk, assuming my presence was connected to the Turkish-Kurdish conflict, pointed to a colorful lapel pin with a miniature F-16 fighter jet on his Sheraton blazer. "I got this from an American who worked for General Dynamics," he said proudly. It was a sign of the times, for the Kurdish uprising and for the arms business it generated. According to news reports that day, Turkish F-16s were conducting bombing raids in northern Iraq. The targets were suspected PKK sites, but witnesses told me later that civilian villages also were hit by the air strikes.

Northern Iraq During U.S. Election Week

A week before the 1992 presidential elections in the U.S., I crossed the border into Iraq. According to news reports in Ankara, twelve thousand Turkish troops were pushing south in the Kurdish enclave. Iraqi Kurds, equipped and funded by the Turks, were pushing north, trying to trap PKK rebels in the Bradost Valley, where the borders of Turkey, Iraq, and Iran all come together. The strategy, known in military circles as "hammer and anvil," would be attempted a decade later in Iraqi Kurdistan by U.S. forces against Ansar al-Islam, the al-Qaeda-linked group. In both cases, that of Turkey and the United States, strategists failed to use the "anvil" component effectively, and many of the militants managed to slip away.

The eyes of the world may have been on the Bush-Clinton campaigns at the time, but the united focus of Turkey, Iran, and the regime of Saddam Hussein was on the Kurds. Turkish jets had just bombed a border village named Demka, reportedly killing fifteen and wounding forty. The bombing took place near the Iranian border, angering Tehran. Iran responded by sending its own fighter jets into Iraqi Kurdistan and threatened a ground incursion, ratcheting up tensions with Turkey. Northern Iraq was a breakaway enclave with a semi-independent status, but for Turks, Iranians, and Iraqis, the area was still an important sphere of influence.

As it turned out, Kurdistan's neighbors could get what they wanted more easily by diplomacy than by confrontation. Before the month was out, Turkey had invited the foreign ministers of Iran and Syria to a meeting in Ankara, where the three powers issued a solidarity statement on "the Kurdish question." True to the history of the twentieth century, one of the few things the quarrelsome neighbors could agree on was the need to limit the power of the Kurds.

When I walked over the Habur bridge into northern Iraq, carrying my backpack from Turkey, one of the first things I saw was streets freshly damaged from the tracks of Turkish tanks. To old-timers in the area, it may have been a familiar sight. While World War I ended in 1918, the League of Nations didn't settle a border dispute between Britain and Turkey at Habur until 1926, eight years later. Even after all this time, however, the "Kurdish question" still transcended the border envisioned by Western planners. What had never been settled was reflected in the broken cement. Turkey had invaded the so-called Kurdish safety zone from one side, and the regime of Saddam Hussein was harassing the Kurds from the other side. Despite the appearance of progress, the Kurds were still fragmented and under siege.

The fighting against the PKK was centered in the Hawkurk region of the Zagros Mountains, in the extreme northwestern corner of Iraq. On my way to the front, I passed scores of local buses carrying Iraqi Kurds recruited to assist the Turkish army. Most of the fighters came from villages, where, according to tradition, the tribal sheik or local leader could round up volunteers simply by putting out the word. He was rewarded by the KDP or PUK or other political parties, enabling him to dispense favors in the village as he saw fit. Turkey was said to be the source of the overall funding. At the front, where I slept for a couple of nights, I saw Iraqi Kurds eating Turkish military rations, and I filmed the arrival of two dump trucks full of Turkish-made tennis shoes. Like everyone else, the Kurds in Iraq and Turkey have product loyalties. Rebels in both countries went to war in the same brand of tennis shoe (Mekap) and of the same color (tan).

The *peshmerga* looked rusty. Northern Iraq had been mostly free of Iraqi troops for almost two years, and few of the Kurdish fighters had recent experience in battle. The ones with access to the Land Cruisers—I counted more than one hundred parked on the mountain roads—seemed more interested in going home to their villages at night to watch the new Kurdish television stations than to huddle under Turkish blankets at the front. Some of those who stayed in the mountains overnight traded mortar fire with PKK forces, but I saw others singing romantic songs around campfires, the light giving away their positions.

Most Iraqi Kurds were divided about fighting the Turkish Kurds. One man said he thought it ironic that the PKK agenda was exactly the same as that of Iraqi Kurdish leaders fifteen years earlier. "Barzani and Talabani want so badly to please the U.S.A.," he added bitterly, "that they will kill their own brothers." Later, at an overcrowded hospital in the town of Diana, a wounded *peshmerga* told me he thought the PKK presence was selfish. There was an epidemic of typhoid and malaria in the area, and he said the hospital had been forced to discharge more than one hundred sick patients to make way for emergency surgeries coming from the battlefield. "They are brothers," the *peshmerga* said angrily, "but they must leave our area."

Northern Iraq was feeling the pressure from Iraqi saboteurs. The Baghdad regime had timed a series of terror attacks to coincide with U.S. elections, and everyone seemed on edge. On my first day in the country, a grenade on a timer blew up in a crowded market in Erbil, the largest city in the north, wounding nineteen people. When I visited some of the injured, I found a darkened hospital, short-staffed, low on medicine, without electricity or running water. When I asked about the shortages, the physician on duty, Dr. Med Dzayi Azzaddin, complained that the Kurdish dam that produced the hospital's electricity had run out of spare parts. The hospital had only fifteen hundred gallons of diesel on hand for a backup generator, and authorities were trying to conserve fuel. In an apparent effort to be polite, he ordered an aide to start the generator and provide a little light for his American visitor. At that time, the cost of diesel in areas controlled by the Iraqi regime was only about two cents a gallon. Being out of oil in this country of oil struck me as an "only in Kurdistan" story. It had the irony of running out of coffee in Colombia or cheese in Wisconsin.

The nearby cities of Mosul and Kirkuk, where large concentrations of Kurds were still under Iraqi control, were some of the richest oil-producing areas in the world, but the Kurds had no share of those resources. What made it worse was that the allied embargo against Iraq caused the Kurds to suffer twice: first from the international sanctions and then from a secondary embargo imposed by Saddam's regime. In other words, the Kurds received only a fraction of the meager food and medicines that Baghdad was permitted to import. According to the Erbil doctor, the United Nations had an agreement in place with Baghdad to allow fuel transports from Mosul, but so far "it was only words."

Hospitals Treating Enemy Kurds

Dr. Azzaddin had worked in Europe for twenty-two years and spoke good English. Like so many other professionals, he had returned to Kurdistan after the 1991 uprising in order "to build the place." After chatting for a while, he revealed that his institution was quietly treating PKK fighters who had been injured in the current fighting in the Bradost Valley. Some thirty wounded Turkish Kurds were in the hospital. That piqued my curiosity. I knew Ankara had demanded that prisoners be turned over to the Turkish army, so that the issue of what to do with wounded PKK was sensitive, but blood is thicker than water and despite the statements of their leaders, Iraqi Kurds had little stomach for fighting the Turkish Kurds. "How can we refuse to treat our brothers?" the doctor asked rhetorically.

Both political parties recognized that publicity about Iraqi Kurds treating the Turkish Kurds would trigger backlash from the Turks, and officials refused to let me interview the prisoners. I did manage to see one rebel in a hospital ward, but the prisoner said PKK "discipline" prevented him from talking to me. He was the first PKK member I'd met by that time, and I'd hoped by talking to him I'd get some idea of what made the rebels tick. In any case, the generator was too loud to talk and the machine's exhaust was being pumped directly into the ward, so I was just as happy to leave. I later heard that most, if not all, the prisoners had been released by the PUK. That made sense, since the KDP, the rival party, had closer relations with Turkey at that particular time.

"My grandfather is Saddam," said another doctor, introducing himself as Dr. Majed Hussein. "I'm only joking," he added quickly. "Hussein is a common surname in Iraq." Dr. Hussein, a cardiologist trained in Britain, was a Shiite Arab, not a Kurd. I wanted to tape-record an interview with him, but he said he was afraid to do so because he still traveled to Baghdad for consultations. If Iraqi agents abroad saw the broadcast and reported him to the secret police in Baghdad, he would be killed. Dr. Hussein said that despite international sanctions, open-heart surgeries and heart-valve repairs were still being performed in Baghdad, "but there is no heart surgery at all available in Kurdistan." That meant that a politically active Kurd with heart trouble had little or no medical options in the country. "There is very little medicine here," he said. "We examine the patients, and we examine them again," he added, smiling. "Then we ask God to help them."

It was the day after the presidential election in the United States. I was curious how Bill Clinton's victory would impact the Kurds, both in Iraq and Turkey. Dr. Hussein didn't have an opinion on Turkey, but he felt that Clinton would continue the Bush policies of disengagement in Iraq. Life for the Kurds, he feared, would get worse. "Saddam is preparing for a victory carnival," he said. "The Kurds were betrayed."

When the West established the safety zone for Kurds in 1991, according to Dr. Hussein, people in northern Iraq were so thankful they called Bush *haji* (holy), comparing him to those who make the sacred pilgrimage to Mecca. Now the *haji* reference had been replaced by *shaitan* (devil), he said. "People here now think the opposite of America. They thought Bush would save their future and their children's future, but he let Saddam kill thousands of Kurds since the [Gulf] war. In the U.S.A. war, every person in Iraq thought, 'This is the *end* of Saddam.' But Saddam stays. Now the one who goes is Bush."

Saddam's Terror Continues

The next day, I was driving through the town of Akra when Kurdish police stopped my car. Only hours earlier a bomb had exploded in a nearby café, killing seven civilians and wounding twenty-one. When I arrived in the rubble of the destroyed cafe, I met Zedan Zekakya Namat, the local police chief, a young man of twenty-three. He was wearing a pearl-handled .38 Special on his hip, and for a moment he looked like a Kurdish cowboy in the middle of a destroyed saloon. Zedan showed me the remains of the cafe's toilet, where he guessed the device had been hidden. He speculated that the powerful explosive was supplied by Iraqi agents who, he said, had been in town offering money to cash-strapped Kurds. I had heard about the bounties. Saddam reportedly had put $10,000 on the head of foreign journalists. An unemployed Kurdish friend, someone known for his gallows humor, had teased me the day before, claiming, "No more than $2,000" would be necessary in my case.

Only hours earlier, the café had been a place for drinking tea and playing dominoes. One of the dead was a twelve-year-old boy who had been sweeping out the building at the time. The boy had been buried almost immediately, in accordance with Muslim tradition, and Zedan took me to his home to meet his family. The young police chief introduced me to the victim's mother. She took my hand, searching my eyes as she told me the deceased was her only son. Then she escorted me to a courtyard where about thirty other woman dressed in black were sitting by themselves on carpets, wailing rhythmically. One of the women offered me a chair. I sat down for a moment, surrounded by chadors and grief. Nearby, in the room set aside for the men, the father clutched a school photo of his dead son. A friend of the victim, who had been helping him sweep out the café, sat on the floor with a leg and an arm bandaged. He looked dazed, murmuring the same words over and over. Someone told me that he had said only one thing since the explosion, "Where is my friend?"

Iraqi Opposition Conference

My next stop was Shaklawa, where a meeting of the newly constituted Iraqi Opposition Conference was underway. This was the first attempt by Iraqi exiles, mostly Sunni and Shiite Arabs, to forge a unified front with the Kurds, who had the largest resistance force in the country. Security was tight on the way into town, and I saw local police checking car trunks and emptying rice bags in search of weapons. Lobbying openly on Iraqi soil for a regime change and discussing how to avoid partitioning the country in a post-Saddam era was a provocation unlikely to escape notice from Baghdad.

The major Kurdish parties were at the conference, as well as a cross section of expatriates, including Ahmed Chalabi, the U.S.-educated Shiite Arab who left Iraq in 1958 after the British-supported monarchy was overthrown. In 2002, in the run-up to the U.S.-led invasion, Chalabi would rise to prominence as a Pentagon favorite, arguing that regime change and postwar stability in Iraq could be swiftly imposed. Later, the intelligence he had supplied the U.S. regarding Iraq's nuclear capability would prove to be false, and, in a separate development, Chalabi would be accused of leaking U.S. secrets to Iran. In 2003, news stories highlighting an outstanding arrest warrant for bank fraud in Jordan would further discredit Chalabi, and he would suffer a temporary fall from grace among U.S. officials. Chalabi, ever the survivor, would remain active behind the scenes in Iraqi politics. Following a good showing in the 2005 elections, he would land the position of Iraq's deputy prime minister, prompting a congratulatory phone call from Condoleeza Rice, President Bush's national security advisor, who had championed his cause before the war. Soon after, Chalabi would become Iraq's acting oil minister, a controversial appointment in light of his previous public statements that Iraq should give preferential treatment to contracts with U.S. and British petroleum companies.

The taxi driver who drove me to Shaklawa told me he had graduated from college in Baghdad with a degree in electrical engineering. His brother had immigrated to Toronto, and he had tried a couple of years earlier to join him. The cabbie said he'd been arrested by the secret police at the telephone office when he tried to make a call to Canada. He had spent a year in prison, during which time Iraqi jailers attached electric cables to his head and tortured him. During an episode of U.S. bombing in the 1991 Gulf War, he managed to sneak back to the Kurdish area. Now he was driving a taxi.

Would Kurds and Arabs cooperate, I asked him, if the regime were overthrown? No, he said, not if the Shiites came to power. "The Shia do not love the Kurds or America," he said. "I don't like Shia." That was 1992, and I remember thinking at the time that such views did not portend well for a unified opposition before—or after—Saddam Hussein.

Cooperating with Turkey

I caught up with Jalal Talabani at the opposition meeting. I asked him why there had been no mention in newspapers controlled by the PUK about Iraqi Kurds joining forces with the Turks against the PKK. In Turkey, the story of the Kurdish infighting was front-page news. I had seen photos in an Ankara newspaper of Iraqi Kurds in solidarity poses with Turkish commandos as they faced the PKK Kurds across the battlefield. There was also the matter of "Kurdish federation," a controversial proposal being floated by some delegates at the Iraqi Opposition Conference. Years later, in 2005, federalism would prove to be a stumbling block when Shiites, Kurds, and Sunni Arabs tried to find common ground in the drafting of a new constitution for Iraq. In 1992 Turkey already regarded "federation" as a code word for Kurdish autonomy and had warned the Kurds to steer clear of it. Did Talabani think the Turkish military incursion had been timed to send Iraqi Kurds another message?

The PUK chief played down the presence of Turkish troops in Iraq, as well as the sensitive issue of Kurds killing Kurds. "It's just a small story," he claimed. "No one is interested." Had Talabani been referring to the international media's lack of interest in the subject, he might have been right. Without a clear Western angle, one that involved a superpower, internecine Kurdish conflict was too obscure to merit much foreign coverage. In Turkey, however, where war casualties were mounting and the public was frustrated by the protracted conflict, news of Iraqi Kurds fighting Turkish Kurds meant the army's "hearts and minds" strategy was working. Whether or not Talabani liked it, the war had become a political hot potato for all the Kurdish leaders. Hundreds of Iraqi Kurds had been killed and wounded from PKK combat or Turkish bombing. Four ministers just had resigned from the local Kurdish parliament to protest Iraqi Kurds aiding Turkey against their "brother Kurds." And many ordinary Kurds were concerned that their fledgling government's survival might cause it to yield to demands that PKK rebels captured in Iraq be turned over to the Turkish army. For the Iraqi Kurds, regardless of their politics, the war with the PKK was the biggest issue of the day.

Another conference delegate, Sami Abdul Rahman, was more forthcoming. Rahman, in those days the leader of a splinter group called the United Party of Kurdistan, told me in a recorded interview, "We hope the allies appreciate everything we have done against the PKK, because we did all we could, we went to the limit." Rahman, who went on to become an official with the KDP and who was killed in a suicide bombing in 2004, said it was "unreasonable and irresponsible" of the PKK to use northern Iraq for a sanctuary. He told me that local Kurds were vulnerable, and he insisted that the rebel presence was an ongoing "catastrophe."

Was it as simple as one Kurdish revolution endangering another? I asked Rahman about the past, when the shoe was on the other foot. Hadn't Turkish Kurds in the 1980s given sanctuary, food, and supplies to Iraqi Kurds escaping from the Iraqi army? "You have to be pragmatic," he said, sidestepping the question. "We don't want a bullet in our backs. You can't fight on two fronts."

Rahman had harsh criticism for Abdullah Ocalan, the PKK leader known to both friends and enemies alike as "Apo" (uncle). He had met Ocalan in Damascus a few years earlier. "Apo is a puppet of the Syrians," he said. "He hasn't put a foot on Kurdish soil since he left Turkey twelve years ago." Rahman said Ocalan had "a huge ego," and he claimed he had counted seven photos of the rebel leader in the PKK safe house he visited in Syria, including "a *mural* in the toilet." Years later, I went to Syria to interview Apo for the CBS program *60 Minutes*. I met the rebel leader in a Damascus hideout. I did see prominent pictures of him displayed on the walls, although none in the bathroom.

I asked Rahman during the interview about Turkey's demand that PKK prisoners be turned over. No, he said, emphatically. When it came to the POW issue, he drew the line. "We have been tortured all our lives," he said. "We would never do that."

Rahman may have been right about the prisoner policy in 1992, but six years later, after Rahman had switched parties to become a leader in the KDP, concerns about Kurdish abuse in Turkish prisons had given way to realpolitik. In 1998, a senior PKK commander named "Fingerless" Sakik—so called for his war injuries—surrendered to the KDP in northern Iraq (his real name was Semdin Sakik). He came from a famous family in Kurdistan, and one of his brothers had been a member of the Turkish parliament (until he was jailed on separatist charges). After Apo Ocalan, Sakik was the best-known leader in the PKK, and his battlefield exploits had been popularized in Kurdish folk songs. His legendary status ended, though, when he defied Apo's authority by breaking a PKK-ordered cease-fire. In that incident, perhaps the most notorious in the entire Kurdish uprising, Sakik's unit massacred thirty-three unarmed Turkish cadets near the city of Bingol. Afterward, Ocalan recalled Sakik to Lebanon, where he embarrassed him in a videotaped session that was widely distributed in Europe and the Middle East. Humiliated, Sakik returned to the front in Turkey, where he tried to defect from the PKK. Making contact with high-level KDP agents, he received what he believed was a safe conduct agreement from his Kurdish brethren to escape through northern Iraq, but shortly after his arrival in KDP territory, Turkish intelligence was given precise information about his location. Army helicopters swooped down on an Iraqi highway, ambushing Sakik's car. He was captured alive and flown north to a Turkish jail. According to news accounts, the police extracted a treasure trove of information from him about the inner workings of the PKK.

For the next six years, little was heard of the legendary commander. Then, in 2004, Turkish officials at the Diyarbakir military prison, where Sakik was serving a life sentence, promoted a showing of fifty works of prison paintings. The unusual and highly publicized exhibit opened at a state-run gallery in downtown Diyarbakir. There, the warden announced that all fifty works of art had been painted by a single inmate: Fingerless Sakik. According to the Turkish daily *Hurriyet*, the warden informed the assembled crowd that the notorious terrorist had been rehabilitated. "We have reclaimed him for society," the warden said, noting that the ex-separatist had personally assured him that henceforth, "he would work for a living, instead of being a parasite on society."

7

Illusory Borders, Part II

Theirs not to reason why,
Theirs but to do and die.

—ALFRED, LORD TENNYSON, 1854

November 1992

The more time I spent with Iraqi Kurds, the more I realized the larger story was being driven by Turkey's relationship with the United States. One day, I went to the KDP office in Zakho to get permission to visit the Iraqi side of the border, an area off-limits to reporters. Turkish F-16s had been bombing border villages, and there were rumors of dead civilians inside Iraq. I had already tried to reach the area, but I had been turned back at KDP checkpoints. When I arrived at the KDP office, I saw a Land Cruiser pull up with Kurdish *peshmerga* and a uniformed man with sandy hair who was wearing sunglasses. Few Kurds wear sunglasses or have light-colored hair. I took the man for a Turkish intelligence officer, and I quickly reversed direction.

The police chief in Zakho, a man named Nizar, told me that he had orders not to let foreign press travel to the front. The Kurds, for the first time in my experience, were practicing news management. When I asked the chief if the order was for his protection or mine, he flashed a cool, knowing smile that reminded me of Captain Louis Renault, the charming but cynical police chief in *Casablanca*. In the end, he did provide me with a letter of introduction written on police stationery, very much like *Casablanca*'s letters of transit. In years of working in conflicted areas, I have found that the more emblems of legitimacy a reporter has—letters, business cards, IDs—the better the chance to escape difficulty. A few days later, on a deserted Iraq road at dusk, Turkish soldiers detained me at gunpoint after I tried to film a military convoy. I was quite happy to have Nizar's letter in my bag of tricks.

Yazidi Kurds

The next day I managed to get to the front, following a chance encounter with a former Iraqi air force officer who had defected from Baghdad during the 1991 uprising. His name was Ahmad Hussein, and he was then a colonel with the PUK, the rival Kurdish party. Until he was wounded in an air raid that week, he had commanded a *peshmerga* unit fighting the PKK on the Turkish-Iraqi border. He was a Yazidi Kurd.

Fortunately for my need to get to the front, I knew a bit about Colonel Hussein's religion and the role the Yazidis played in the region. Kurdish religion is far from monolithic, but the clear majority of Kurds are Sunni Muslims, from the school of Shafi. "Feili Kurds," originally from Iran, are Shiite. Other believers include Alevis, Christians, and Jews. Iraq is home to some 300,000 members of the Yazidi religion, which has about a million members worldwide, and it is in Iraqi Kurdistan that the Yazidi headquarters and most important shrine are located. The burial spot for the Yazidi founder, a twelfth-century Sufi mystic, was only a two-hour drive from my hotel in the border town of Zakho, and his crypt is the site of a major pilgrimage every fall.

Yazidi is a mixture of Islamic, Jewish, Christian, and ancient beliefs like Sufism, Nestorianism, and the Zoroastrian religion of Iran. Yazidis hold that they were created separately from the rest of mankind and are descended from Adam alone, not Adam and Eve. They believe that the world's original tongue was Kurdish, and that God gave that language to them in present-day northern Iraq, which they consider the center of the universe. Many Yazidis have been branded "devil worshippers" by others in the region and persecuted over the centuries by their Sunni neighbors. In the 1970s and 1980s, more than fifty thousand Yazidis left Turkey, Syria, and Iraq and settled in Europe in search of employment and asylum. Many still long to return to Iraqi Kurdistan. The year before my visit to Colonel Hussein, during the annual Yazidi pilgrimage to northern Iraq, I had met a group of Yazidis who had immigrated earlier to Germany.

Colonel Hussein told me he'd recently been wounded in a Turkish air raid. It wasn't a serious injury, but he found it humiliating and he was furious. He said the attack, which had taken place on Halloween near the small border village of Batufa, killed thirteen *peshmerga* and civilians, including three children. At the time, Hussein's men had been serving as "spotters" for the air strikes, a job sometimes performed by Special Forces in the U.S. Army. He said his forces were a full kilometer from the PKK and that they were driving Land Cruisers, which he believed could be identified from the air (the PKK didn't have vehicles). He said eight to ten F-16 jets flew over the area during the course of the attacks, which he said lasted more than an hour. I asked him how he knew the same planes hadn't just circled around. He said he knew from his air force experience that, due to fuel usage, the same jets could not linger in a target area for more than fifteen minutes before returning to base.

When the first Turkish jet rocketed Hussein's position, he assumed it was a mistake, and he immediately radioed the Turkish ground controller, his designated contact. The controller confirmed the message, and Hussein was informed that the pilots in turn had been notified. But ten minutes later, another wave of F-16s flew even closer, bombing his precise position and killing two of his men. Hussein claimed the attack was deliberate—meant to send a message to the PUK, which was known to be less enthusiastic than the KDP about the joint campaign against the PKK.

I don't know what prompted Colonel Hussein to defy the ban that kept journalists from visiting the bombed villages. Maybe it was the same maverick spirit that had triggered his defection from the Iraqi military or the independence of people in society who follow a minority religion. Maybe it was simple bitterness at being wounded and having his men killed by "friendly fire." Whatever the motivation, he assigned six armed *peshmerga* to escort me to the front. The next morning, they picked me up in two official-looking SUVs. The vehicles were not challenged at the checkpoints.

That day, I filmed destroyed houses and large bomb craters in the road in Demka, Kashon, and a place called Soriya. I interviewed several villagers about the terrifying ordeal and photographed a handmade baby cradle near one of the rocketed houses. A villager told me an infant had died in the attack.

Up to that point, my experience had been limited to "primitive" bombardment. I had seen the results of low-tech bombing in rural Central America and in impoverished West Africa. In Nicaragua, I had witnessed rocketing by Sandinista pilots flying Soviet-made helicopters against the U.S.-backed Contras. In El Salvador, I had seen bombing by small government planes in pro-guerrilla civilian areas along the Honduran border. And, in the 1980s, during a pathetic African border war between Mali and Burkina Faso—pathetic because both countries were so impoverished they could barely afford jet fuel—I saw a few mud huts burned when an aging Soviet MiG dropped a single bomb before limping back to base. This was different. The Turks had the latest satellite intelligence and state-of-the-art F-16 Lockheed jets. The damage in the two villages included flattened houses and several large bomb craters in a field.

The high-tech war in Turkey had come to Iraqi Kurdistan.

Back in Zakho I visited the MCC, the allied command center. When I arrived, guards were using mirrors to check under cars for hidden Iraqi bombs. Recently, several devices had been detonated under oil trucks and U.N. vehicles, and everyone was on alert. The coalition had hired Kurdish guards at $5 a day to watch the perimeter of the compound; a British antiterror specialist with experience in Northern Ireland was reviewing security procedures. Inside, I met Col. Robert Wilson, the senior U.S. officer, and his British, French, and Turkish counterparts. I had known Wilson from an earlier visit, and I pumped him for whatever new information he could provide. Wilson said Jalal Talabani was pleading with allied powers to exclude Turkey from the MCC, but that was out of the question. He had heard on the radio that war fever was running high against the Kurds in Turkey. BBC was reporting from Ankara that mourners at a funeral for Turkish soldiers killed in the war with the PKK had taken revenge on two randomly chosen Kurdish pedestrians. The unwitting passersby were spontaneously lynched. Locally, according to Wilson, the Turkish tanks "shook a lot of people up when they came through town," but he downplayed the importance of the overall invasion.

Colonel Wilson invited me to the compound for dinner, a delicious meal of lobster and rice, which had been flown in on a Black Hawk helicopter from Turkey. In two days another Black Hawk was scheduled to arrive with Gen. Richard E. Hawley, the U.S. commander of Operation Provide Comfort based at Incirlik, Turkey. The two choppers would pick up Wilson and the other MCC officers, then fly south for a courtesy visit to Massoud Barzani at KDP headquarters in Salahuddin. There was room on one of the Black Hawks, if I wanted to go.

Detained by Soldiers

The next day, I decided to go after footage of Turkish military, an undertaking I might not otherwise have tried unless other journalists were in the area to follow up if something went wrong. I was the only reporter in northern Iraq at the time, but rubbing elbows with the coalition powers must have emboldened me to act as though the international press was present in numbers. I hired a taxi and filmed several tanks on a road near Zakho. I received a few puzzled looks from soldiers, but no hostility. When I got back to town it was late afternoon. On my way to the KDP dormitory, where visitors like me were permitted to sleep on mattresses on the floor, I spied a Turkish jeep and a "deuce and a half" army truck, but when I tried to film the convoy, the soldiers blocked the road and forced my taxi to stop.

Eight soldiers surrounded the car, motioning for me to get out and to climb aboard a nearby jeep. One of them tried to take my camera, but I managed to keep it out of his reach. I knew if I moved from the taxi, I would be apprehended. One soldier was speaking broken English, telling me I had violated the law and that I now would be brought to the "fort." I figured the "fort" was across the Habur bridge to Turkey, only a ten-minute ride away. If I agreed to go, I'd probably never get back in northern Iraq, my equipment and film would be confiscated, and I'd lose my belongings at the KDP guesthouse. I refused to get out of the taxi.

One of the soldiers started to threaten the driver. He grabbed the man's shoulder and ordered him out of the car, preparing to commandeer the vehicle himself. I glanced at the driver. I could see the fear in his eyes, and I sensed he was about to comply. Another soldier opened the back door and got in behind me, ready to go. Impulsively, I reached over and grabbed the keys from the ignition. "I am an American! I am an American!" I shouted. "This is *Iraq!* You have no authority here." Under the circumstances, of course, a geography lesson was absurd. In war, guns are authority. They were armed, and the moment was theirs.

I kept shouting, reeling off the name of the Turkish colonel I'd met at the lobster dinner, the name of the American general who was due to arrive the next day, and bluffing as convincingly as I could that I was a special guest of the coalition. If this went any further, they'd have an "international incident" on their hands, and so forth.

As if to prove my point, I reached in my pocket and produced the letter from Nizar, the charming but cynical Zakho police chief. It was in Kurdish, and I doubted the soldier could read it. I only hoped the fancy letterhead and Nizar's oversized, stylish signature—a common flourish for Kurdish officials—would work to my advantage.

One of the soldiers, probably a sergeant, asked to see the driver's identity card. Then he grabbed Nizar's letter and motioned one of the other soldiers to the rear of the taxi to confer. The second man wrote down the license plate of the car. The one in charge returned and said something to the Turkish soldier who spoke English, who then told us we could go. My driver was shaken. As we drove away, the cabbie warned me to be careful the next time I tried to cross the bridge to Turkey. He said a report of the incident would probably be given to guards at the border.

Black Hawks

The next day I flew for the first time on a Black Hawk helicopter. The Black Hawk is a troop transport produced by the Sikorsky Aircraft Corporation in Stratford, Connecticut. During the Kurdish insurrection in Turkey, Ankara bought or was given by the United States more than one hundred Black Hawks. The helicopters proved vital in the rapid deployment of Turkish commandos to remote, mountain strongholds of the PKK. Although the war received little notice in the U.S. media, most of the military equipment used against Kurdish rebels in Turkey was of U.S. manufacture, and powerful political forces were often involved behind the scenes in shepherding the necessary transfers through the American political process.

The Spoils of War

Political scientist John Tirman dissected one of these transactions in his book *Spoils of War*. In 1988, according to Tirman, Turkey wanted to buy fifty Sikorsky

Black Hawks to suppress the Kurdish uprising, but congressional critics of Turkey's human rights record voiced objections to the helicopter sale. The Sikorsky contract was worth $460 million, and the deal was being vetted by U.S. Senator Chris Dodd (D-CT), whose district included the Black Hawk manufacturing plant, and whose political campaigns had received contributions from Sikorsky. Dodd, a liberal who was trying at the same time to attach human rights improvements as a condition to U.S. military aid to El Salvador, needed Republican support for the Black Hawk transfer. In the end, Senator Dodd agreed to remove the human rights rider holding up the El Salvador appropriation. In return, key Republicans agreed to support the helicopter sale to Turkey. Ironically, the vote in Congress approving the Black Hawk sale to Turkey came on the same day that a U.S.-trained Salvadoran army unit massacred six Jesuit priests and two workers in San Salvador.

Turks Want to Shoot Us Down?

Traveling by Black Hawk in Iraq in those days felt a bit like riding in an aerial motorcycle. U.S. military practice was to fly at a low altitude so potential enemies on the ground could not see the helicopter until the last minute. For us, that meant flying at 150 mph, hugging the rolling hills at only about one hundred feet—so low I could see the shocked expressions on the faces of Kurdish shepherds when we appeared above them, scattering their flocks of sheep.

The Black Hawk I flew on that day carried two U.S. pilots, Colonel Wilson, the French colonel, and several Kurdish officials. I sat across from General Hawley, the task force commander. Hawley, a plainspoken career officer from Wyoming, informed me before liftoff that our normal route that day had been altered. While Operation Provide Comfort was only a year and a half old, the increased air traffic in the conflicted area was fueling anti-Americanism in Turkey. Newspapers in Istanbul and Ankara had just reported threats by a Turkish general to shoot down U.S. aircraft in border areas where his units were engaging Kurdish rebels. Considering generous U.S. tax support for Turkey and the Turko-American military alliance, which was then more than forty-five years old, I could barely believe it. The notion of a U.S. ally shooting down an American helicopter was stunning.

According to Hawley, the Turkish general claimed that Turkish helicopters rely on ground markings in the form of an H, but T markings, the telltale marks of a landing by U.S. helicopters, had been found in abandoned PKK bases, leaving the Turkish military to conclude that the U.S. was rescuing wounded PKK fighters. "The hell with that," General Hawley said, adding that he considered the PKK an enemy of the United States and that the Turkish claim was a preposterous piece of paranoia. Nonetheless, he was taking it seriously. The Turkish general had warned low-flying aircraft in Iraq to stay at least ten kilometers (6.2 miles) from the Turkish border. "I just told our guys to make it *twenty,*" Hawley said.

Everyone on board the flight wore a helmet, which helped to deaden the near-deafening roar of the helicopter engine. Each helmet had a microphone and a receiver, which enabled us to monitor cockpit radio transmissions. I couldn't decipher all of the shoptalk I was hearing, but at one point Hawley got angry, and it was clear something had just gone wrong. It turned out we had just been "painted," locked on to by a missile-carrying American fighter jet in the area. Apparently, the jet pilot had misread our radar profile and took us for one of Saddam's Russian-made gunships. General Hawley didn't like it. He pushed his microphone to the side and leaned over to Colonel Wilson to give him a piece of his mind.

"Friendly Fire"

I think of the "painting" because I spent a lot of the helicopter trip taking video footage of the door gunners and the other Black Hawk, which was flying near us in formation. When we landed, I took shots of the choppers on the ground, including their tail markings.

Seventeen months later, on April 14, 1994, the same Black Hawk I had ridden in that day in 1992 was hit by friendly fire. It was one of two Black Hawks shot down in Iraqi Kurdistan by U.S. F-15s.

The downing was a tragic incident, illustrative of U.S. pilot error, the influence of the Turkish military, and the political impotence of the Kurds to protest American negligence. A decade later, during the 2003 U.S. invasion of Iraq, there would be another incident of friendly fire from U.S. jets in Kurdistan.

The 1993 mishap took place during a routine mission. The helicopters were en route to meet a Kurdish delegation. U.S. officials had wanted to fly early that morning, but the Turkish army, reportedly, was bombing Kurdish rebels at the time. The Turks had grounded the U.S. mission until late in the morning. It was a dramatic example of Turkish power, which in those days could effectively make northern Iraq a no-fly zone for American as well as Iraqi aircraft.

The shooting occurred about midday. The F-15 pilot later said that he had mistaken the Black Hawks for Russian Mi-24 Hinds, despite the fact that the Soviet-made gunships, according to experts, exhibit a radically different profile on the radar screen. Fifteen Americans and eleven Kurds were aboard the Black Hawks.

All twenty-six passengers were killed.

A year later, after the official investigation, *ABC Primetime Live* devoted a half hour to the incident, and the program included footage I had shot on my earlier trip with General Hawley. The final minutes of the broadcast were the most dramatic, when family members of the dead Americans, who were assembled in the network studio, reacted with grief and anger as ABC played the tape it had acquired of the F-15 cockpit transmissions that day. The screen shows black-and-white video from the automatic camera mounted on the fighter jet. A fireball erupts when the missile hits the first Black Hawk. At the moment of impact, as the helicopter and passengers inside are incinerated, the families and the viewing audience hear the voice of the F-15 pilot. It is the rarely heard language of war and killing, and the friendly fire context makes the moment especially grotesque.

"Stick a fork in him," the pilot says of the fireball below. "He's done."

Smuggling Videos

General Hawley invited me to accompany him to the reception in Salahuddin, the headquarters of the Kurdistan Democratic Party, where a sumptuous lunch had been prepared for the American VIPs. For the KDP, this was a chance to schmooze with Hawley, the ranking U.S. official in Iraq, a living symbol of the superpower that had taken the Kurds under its wing. Because I had arrived with Hawley's entourage, no one questioned my presence at lunch or in the policy exchanges, and I was able to film at will. Part of the meeting was social. Colonel Wilson was winding up his tour of duty with the Kurds, so there were the customary photos, going-away presents, and ceremonial kisses, but there was also business to be addressed.

The Americans were keen to praise the KDP leader, Massoud Barzani, for his cooperation in fighting the PKK rebels. For his part, Barzani asked for U.S. help in expediting relief supplies delayed at the Turkish border. His comments were translated by Hoshyar Zebari, Massoud's uncle and the KDP bureau chief in London at the time. In 2003—a dozen years later—following the U.S. invasion of Iraq, Zebari would be picked as the new Iraq's foreign minister in the governing council set up by the United States and would retain the position after Iraq's first elections in 2005.

With the military and diplomatic mission accomplished, the Black Hawks flew back to Zakho. Everyone in the delegation appeared to be in a good mood. I had been studying General Hawley the whole day, ever since he had revealed the Turkish threat to U.S. aircraft. He seemed friendly to the press, and I began to hope he would let me fly back to Turkey with him. I was reluctant to go by ground, in case the Turkish border guards had been apprised of my run-in with the soldiers. The bridge was the only way out of Iraq, and I was afraid I could be arrested once I crossed into Turkey. During the incident in the taxi, I had kept the camera rolling. At a minimum, I feared that the footage of my brief detention would be confiscated, but it was likely that I'd also lose the rest of my Iraq videos, including what I'd shot in the Black Hawks.

General Hawley was sympathetic. "I'll contact the Turkish general staff in Ankara," he said. "You're an *American*—they ought to give me that courtesy—and you can do the entry paperwork at our base in Diyarbakir." A few hours later, however, the reply came back. "Under no conditions" would General Hawley be allowed to transport me. The general seemed a little irritated. "I'd hate for you to lose your material," he said. "Let me think about this."

The two Black Hawks were flying to Turkey the next morning. I made my own arrangements for a taxi to drive me to the international bridge, where I would have to take my chances. If I made it through customs and immigration, Diyarbakir would be only 150 miles away, less than a three-hour ride in a Turkish cab. That evening, my last in Iraq, one of the helicopter pilots I had met earlier in the day showed up at my room. "General Hawley said you might have a small package for me," he said with a smile. I could hardly believe my luck. The *Pentagon* was going to smuggle my footage into Turkey.

The following day, I was searched by Turkish guards at the border, but permitted to continue. I made my way to Diyarbakir, looking forward to hot water, flush toilets, and lights that stayed on. Late that afternoon at the hotel, I heard a knock at my room. When I opened the door, the pilot was standing there with another man in uniform, a Turkish military officer. I caught my breath for a moment, before realizing the stranger was just a *minder,* someone routinely assigned to U.S. military personnel whenever they went off base. The pilot had a package in his hand. "Hey, there," he said nonchalantly. "You must have left this behind."

BOOK II

War in Turkey

8
Passing Down Revolution

We must try to annihilate all languages in our country except
Turkish. . . . Language . . . may be the firmest barrier—perhaps firmer
than religion—against national unity.

—NAMIK KEMAL (NAMESAKE OF MUSTAFA KEMAL ATATÜRK)

Nationalism . . . is the measles of mankind.

—ALBERT EINSTEIN

End of Empire

In 1981 the White House issued a proclamation commemorating the centennial of the birth of the founder of the Turkish Republic, Mustafa Kemal Atatürk.
The proclamation cited Atatürk as "a great leader in times of war and peace," but
made no mention of the strong American-Turkish military alliance, which by
then was thirty-five years old. Nor did it refer to the Turkish army, which only
one year earlier had overthrown the civilian government, rewritten Turkey's constitution, and proclaimed itself the guardian of Atatürk's legacy.

The 1980 military coup in Turkey hastened a Kurdish revolt that had been
brewing for several years. The Kurdish uprising was launched in 1984, and by
1999, when U.S. intelligence led Turkish commandos to the capture of the rebellion's architect and leader, the movement had mushroomed into a widespread rebellion with a nationalist base. Paradoxically, the fifteen-year conflict, the longest
Kurdish insurrection in Turkish history, was a legacy of the mythlike figure of
Atatürk.

Born Mustafa in 1881, he was given the surname of Atatürk (Father of the
Turks) in 1934 by the Grand National Assembly of Turkey for his pivotal role in
shaping the nation. The name Kemal means "perfection" and was bestowed on
him by his high school math teacher. Atatürk was influenced by his father's insistence on secular education, a harbinger of the sweeping changes the young man
would impose on Turkey in the years to come. Atatürk enlisted in military
school, where he joined a secret society that eventually merged with the Young

Turks, a nationalist movement by military officers seeking reforms from the government of Sultan Abdül Hamit II, whom they deposed in 1908 and exiled in 1909. During World War I, when the Young Turks' government under the nominal rule of Sultan Mehmed V supported the Kaiser, Atatürk was posted to Gallipoli, where his troops helped to repel the British and Australians, denying the Allies a foothold in the Dardanelles. After the war, when a true sultanate under Mehmed VI was restored, and during the Allied occupation, he continued his military exploits in Anatolia as a resistance fighter.

World War I left the Ottoman Empire in shambles. The Ottoman government had conscripted more than three million men, only to see half of them desert. Rampant inflation between 1914 and 1918 topped 2,500 percent, commerce and communications were disrupted, and the population faced widespread food shortages. Between 1915 and 1916, the empire lost an estimated 100,000 citizens to crippling famines in Syria and Lebanon. An estimated 500,000 more died of war, famine, and disease in Syria alone between 1917 and 1918. After the war, Greek and Italian armies landed in Turkey and carved up what was left of the empire. Many Kurds were confident that the empire would be restored, but a few Kurdish intellectuals saw opportunity in the demise of the empire (as some separatist-minded Kurds did after the overthrow of Saddam Hussein many years later). Following World War I, those intellectuals sought European support for a Kurdish state, sending representatives to the Paris Peace Conference in 1919.

In August 1920, Sultan Mehmed VI's impotent government signed the Treaty of Sèvres, effectively ending six centuries of Ottoman imperial rule. The treaty recognized the independence of Syria as a French mandate and both Mesopotamia and Palestine as British mandates. The agreement also called for independence in Armenia and Kurdistan.

Kurds and Turks As Military Allies

In 1919, a year before the Sèvres treaty, the Sultan had dispatched Atatürk to the Anatolia region to suppress Soviet forces and to insure the loyalty of the Sultan's troops. According to the historian Kendal Nezan:

> When [Atatürk] arrived in Kurdish territory, he immediately presented himself as the "saviour of Kurdistan," the champion of a Caliph "imprisoned by the occupation forces" and the defender of "the Muslim lands soiled by the impious Christians." He appealed to "all Muslim elements," meaning Kurds and Turks, and called for "complete unity in the struggle to expel the invaders from the Muslim Fatherland." At the time Mustafa Kemal was careful not to mention the Turkish nation. Instead, he stressed either

the fraternity between Kurds and Turks, or the Ottoman nation in conflict with foreign occupation forces.

Kurdish forces were the first to fight for Turkish independence. As Sunni Muslims, they viewed the conflict as religious, not nationalistic, and Atatürk successfully employed the cry of jihad to rally them against threats by Christian Armenia to annex their territories. In only two months, his officers trained Kurdish troops, organized eastern Kurdish districts, and defeated Georgian and Armenian armies—victories that led to a peace treaty with the USSR. Following other battles in the region, the Kurds were enlisted to help Atatürk's growing army in fighting Greek troops for the liberation of Anatolia. Late in 1919, Atatürk broke with Mehmed VI's beleaguered government in Istanbul and joined forces with former sultan supporters in the national assembly. A protocol by the coalition accepted the principle of Kurdish autonomy with a statement recognizing "the national and social rights of the Kurds."

Even as the Kurds fought against foreign occupation in the belief they would be equals in a new republic, contradictory indicators slowly started to appear. Nationalist authorities acting under military law secretly looked for ways to close down civilian Kurdish societies and to disband cultural groups. Turkey had been feasted upon by the victorious Allies, carved up and humiliated. Now, in a fevered rekindling of national pride, the Young Turks assured their followers there would be no more fragmentation of Turkish lands. The country would be cleansed of foreigners. As Greek refugees were driven out of Anatolia, the rallying cry became "Turkey for the Turks." Those whose first language was Turkish could be trusted as patriots, but nonspeakers—the Kurds in particular—were increasingly suspect, as they could be manipulated by outsiders to help divide and conquer.

In 1920, Turkish nationalists rejected the Treaty of Sèvres, with its implicit promise of a Kurdish homeland. Atatürk later wrote that the goal of the Sèvres treaty had been "to crush the Turkish nation." By mid-1922, Atatürk's army had defeated all outside forces. Together, the Kurds and the Turks had driven out the infidel crusader, but now there was no longer talk of a Muslim republic, where Kurdish aspirations for equality might be attained. If the Kurds believed the unifying ingredient of the new nation was Islam, they were wrong. "The state which we have just created," Atatürk told the national assembly in 1923, "is a Turkish state." The words of the charismatic leader, less than three years after the one-sided Sèvres agreement had been imposed, reflected a new day for the vanquished Ottomans, and Europe, exhausted from a war that began in 1914, was ready to listen. The Allies were unwilling to enforce the remaining provisions of the treaty against a reborn resistance. The Kurdish tribes were disorganized, often focused on establishing fiefdoms that had more to do with narrow self-interest than communal ethnic ties. They had few military forces except those under command of the Turks. There was little they could do.

According to historian David McDowall:

The Kurds had fought for the Ottoman Empire, not for a specifically Turkish state. Despite official statements of recognition of "the national and social rights of the Kurds," it quickly became clear that Atatürk's interest following the defeat of the Christian elements was in the creation of a nation-state along European and authoritarian lines, and it was a specifically Turkish and secular state that he intended. The Kurds of Turkey very quickly lost their special identity and the status they had enjoyed as fellow Muslims.

Sèvres was superseded by the Treaty of Lausanne in 1923, which split Kurdistan among present-day Turkey, Iraq, and Syria (the borders in Kurdish areas of USSR and Iran were already fixed)—without mentioning the Kurds by name. Sèvres, while never ratified, would remain the only international agreement in history to refer to a Kurdish homeland.

The Turkish Republic was proclaimed in the same year, beginning a systematic process of secularization in the country. Atatürk outlawed the sharia, the Islamic courts, closed the religious schools, banned the wearing of the fez, and substituted Latin letters for Arabic script in Turkish, even in editions of the Koran. In 1924, on the day that the caliphate was abolished, Turkish authorities shut down Kurdish schools, banned Kurdish books, and outlawed Kurdish organizations. From that day forward, the Kurds were officially on notice. In the words of Atatürk, the state was "indivisible."

What had bound the Kurds to the Turks was not history or language or culture. It was religious fraternity. Under the Ottoman Empire, the Kurds had retained their identity, while at the same time maintaining a brotherhood with their Muslim coreligionists, the Turks. They saw themselves as Ottoman patriots, not Turkish nationalists. For the Kurds, the abolition of the caliphate was an affront that betrayed the goals of the War of Independence. In rejecting the preeminence of Islam, the new republic had abandoned its soul.

The Treaty of Lausanne did not define the exact border between the new Turkish Republic and the British mandate in Iraq. Turkey had a historical claim to the vilayet of Mosul in Iraq, because of its substantial Turkmen population, but the treaty left the status of Mosul up for negotiation with Britain. The early 1920s were marked by intermittent Kurdish uprisings against British forces in Iraq. In 1922, Atatürk sent a small military force to the Mosul area to seek alliances with Iraqi Kurdish tribes who were agitated by the Allied breakup of their territories.

The British, who had used the Greeks to divide Turkey after World War I, now tried to employ the Kurds in the same way. In the fall of 1922, they recalled the Kurdish leader Sheikh Mahmud Barzinji from India, where they had exiled him, in the hopes of crushing a series of nationalist uprisings in Iraq. Instead of aligning himself with British forces, Sheikh Mahmud continued his rebellion against the Crown, allying himself with pro-Turkish forces. His uprisings against British control in northern Iraq persisted into the early 1930s.

Meanwhile, British engineers were becoming aware of the vast deposits of oil at Mosul and Kirkuk. Finally in 1926, after threats of war and a great deal of agitation between the two countries, Turkey and Britain accepted a proposal from the League of Nations fixing a permanent border. Despite the efforts of the Turks, Mosul and its large population of Kurds would remain a part of Iraq. Henceforth, Kurds to the north of the new frontier would be part of the Turkish Republic.

The past did not die easily. For the Turks, the Mosul claim remained an emotional issue, even into the twenty-first century. Every national budget passed by the Turkish parliament, beginning in 1926, has included a token payment into a fund for the "Vilayet of Mosul."

Kurdish Muslims Rebel Against Secularism

Meanwhile in the 1920s, dissatisfied Kurds in Turkey rebelled against the abolition of sharia religious courts and the growing repression of Kurdish culture. Turkish nationalists, who had just overcome the threat from outside the country, viewed the Kurds as fifth columnists and counterrevolutionists. Hundreds of villages suspected of rebel sympathies were burned to the ground, and thousands of Kurds deported to western districts. Independence tribunals handed down death warrants for Kurdish teachers, writers, and organizers. The so-called Sheikh Said Rebellion, the most famous of Kurdish resistance movements in Turkey in the 1920s, was short-lived. On September 4, 1925, Sheikh Said and more than fifty of his followers were hanged in central Diyarbakir.

The radical changes in Kurdistan were made easier by Atatürk's position as head of the Grand National Assembly and his establishment of a one-party regime in Turkey. During the 1930s, the military consolidated control of Kurdish areas and stepped up efforts at compulsory assimilation. The assembly quickly passed the Settlement Law, which designated Kurdistan as an area closed for civilian settlement. Any area where the native language was not Turkish was to be evacuated and its residents distributed to Turkish-speaking districts.

The Law of Maintenance of Order gave the government the power to suppress any form of perceived opposition. Thousands of Kurdish villages were given Turkish names, and the word *Kurdistan* was removed from history books and publications. The objective was no less than to erase the Kurdish identity. In

1936, Gen. Abdullah Alpdogan, the military governor of Dersim—which the Turks had renamed Tunceli—announced that Kurdish people did not exist as a race. He said they were actually Turkish natives who lived in the mountains. He designated them "Mountain Turks," which became official nomenclature in the country until after the first Gulf War in 1991. "Turkey was practicing crude social engineering," according to historian McDowall, "which had currency [at the time] not only in Nazi Germany but among many European intellectuals."

The Kurdish "Guernica"

The fiercest Kurdish resistance to these changes took place at Dersim. By 1936, the town was completely surrounded by the Turkish army. In July 1937, Seyt Riza, a seventy-five-year-old Kurdish cleric and cultural leader, contacted Sir Anthony Eden, the British Foreign Secretary. Riza made an abortive plea for international intervention, complaining of forced assimilation, the banning of Kurdish language and newspapers, and forced deportations. Later, in a plaintive letter to the head of Turkish Ministry, he wrote, "Three million Kurds live in their country and ask only to live in peace and freedom, while keeping their race, language, traditions, culture, and civilization." Riza asked the minister "to let the Kurdish people benefit from the high moral influence of [your] government and to bring an end to this cruel injustice."

By then, a war between 1,500 Kurdish guerrillas and 50,000 Turkish soldiers was already in progress. The uprising, which lasted more than a year, was crushed with the help of warplanes, poison gas, and heavy artillery. Thousands of Kurdish homes were burned, villages permanently depopulated, and civilians massacred. Hundreds of Kurds hiding in caves or barns were burned to death by the army. There were reports of Kurds' collective suicides—tragic escapes from the pillaging soldiers. Foreign military observers were prevented from witnessing the actions of the government, but one Turkish army document listed almost 8,000 Dersim residents killed in the last months of 1938 alone. More than one million Kurds were displaced in the conflict. Estimates of the number of Kurds killed in Dersim between 1937 and 1938 run as high as 20,000.

Rallying Cry

Despite the savage razing of Dersim, the area was considered such a hot spot of Kurdish resistance that it remained under military occupation until the 1950s. For the Kurds, Dersim would become synonymous with heroic resistance, however doomed. In some quarters today, the name still evokes a sentiment akin to "Remember the Alamo!" Several Kurdish guerrillas I met in Turkey in the 1990s listed Dersim as one of the reasons they had gone to the mountains. More than one recited accounts of the execution of Seyt Riza, the leader of the Dersim resistance.

The elderly Riza, his two sons, and several compatriots were hanged together in 1937. By one account, Riza gave an impassioned speech from the scaffold in Kurdish in which he called out, "Down with the oppressors!" and, "Kurdish youth will get revenge!" By another account, he defiantly grabbed the noose from the executioner and hanged himself, depriving the state of its final attempt at control.

By the time of the Dersim campaign, Mustafa Kemal Atatürk's health was in decline. In November 1938, he died of cirrhosis. He was fifty-seven. Atatürk had served as president of the republic for fifteen years. Under his guidance, Turkey had taken radical steps to modernize and to secularize, becoming the first nation to limit the role of Islam politically and socially. Atatürk's new republic had borrowed culturally from Europe, giving women the right to vote, uprooting Turkish commercial law, and copying the foreign policy of countries like Britain and France. His passing was noted by world leaders from Churchill to Gandhi.

The single-party system Atatürk established in Turkey continued until after World War II. In 1946, with rising Cold War fears of Soviet influence in the Middle East, the United States initiated military aid to Ankara. Henceforth, Turkey would be considered an important bulwark against communism. By the early 1960s, U.S. nuclear weapons would be stationed in Turkey.

In a quid pro quo for Soviet retreat in Cuba during the 1961 missile crisis, the Kennedy administration ordered the dismantling of Turkish-based intercontinental missiles, which were aimed at Moscow.

In 1974, after the Turkish invasion of Cyprus, U.S. military aid to Turkey was temporarily suspended.

When the generals overthrew the democratically elected government in Turkey in 1980, the United States stood apart from the strong criticism of the coup voiced by its European allies. In the same year, and in direct response to the Islamic revolution in neighboring Iran, Washington and Ankara signed the Defense and Economic Cooperation Agreement (DECA). Under the agreement, the United States received the right to use military bases in Turkey, which bordered both Iran and the USSR, in exchange for promises to modernize the Turkish armed forces.

Consequences for the Kurds

Today, there are hundreds of statues of Mustafa Kemal Atatürk throughout Turkey. His portrait appears in shops and private homes, and his quotations are chiseled on public buildings. For the millions of Kurds in the country, however, the legacy of Atatürk also includes a collective memory of terror and cultural repression.

By the end of the 1980s, the Berlin Wall had fallen and the Cold War was over. Germany had begun to recede in strategic importance. The fastest spreading religion in the world, from Morocco to Malaysia, was now Islam. Turkey, secularized by seventy years of "Kemalism," would become the center of a new NATO military strategy. Thus, it was not surprising, when the Kurds rose up again in the 1980s, that the Turkish generals would turn to America for weapons.

9

Turkey, 1993

Turkey would never have more than one time zone
—it would indicate division, weakness.

—KURDISH SHOP OWNER

Colonel Young

War tends to make everything crazy, even between allies.

When I returned to northern Iraq to interview American officials in 1993, I could see that the Kurdish uprising in Turkey was straining the U.S.-Turkish alliance in Iraq. On prior occasions, reporters had met alone with U.S. Army representatives in the reception room of the Military Command Center (MCC) in Zakho. No longer. Now Turkish officers insisted on being present for media interviews. The U.S. commander for the Kurdish "safety zone" in Iraq, Colonel Bob Young, was reluctant to speak to me in the reception area. He didn't want his counterpart, the Turkish colonel, to hear us.

As it happened, the allies had scheduled a farewell outing the next day for soldiers finishing their duty rotation, and Young invited me to ride along in the caravan. The only other person in the colonel's Humvee that day was the machine gunner on top, a Kurdish bodyguard paid $5 a day for his services. We were headed for Saddam's summer palace at Sirsenk, about an hour's drive away, and we could talk freely in the Humvee.

Two years earlier, when the Iraqis had retreated from the north, this palace of circular staircases, ornate banquet rooms, and artificial waterfalls had been abandoned. Now a small, multinational force in armored Humvees was parked in one of the sculpted gardens. The soldiers unloaded hamburger patties, packages of Hormel hot dogs, and charcoal for a portable grill. Everyone was in a party mood. As Kurdish machine gunners guarded the barbecue, wine corks popped, and the voice of Jimmy Buffet and his "lost shaker of salt" rose from someone's boom box.

Inside the palace, a group of Kurdish squatters had built a wood fire in one of the rooms and were baking Kurdish flat bread. They looked on curiously as an

American soldier with a battery-operated saw cut tablets of Italian marble from a wall. The tablets would be inscribed as souvenirs and given to departing soldiers as mementos of their deployment to Iraq. It was 1993, there were fewer than a dozen U.S. troops in Iraq—at least officially—and a tour of duty in the country was tinged with a sense of adventure. A decade later, the number of American troops would be 150,000, and soldiers finishing their tours would take home quite different memories.

On the ride back, Colonel Young decided to air some dirty laundry. He was winding up a tour of duty in northern Iraq that had begun while George H. W. Bush was still in office, and soon he'd be heading home to the States. I wasn't sure why Young wanted to talk. Maybe he was disillusioned about the mission or maybe it was because we were both Americans. In any case, he began by declaring that the coalition was appeasing the Iraqis.

Two years after the victory in Kuwait, Young maintained, the U.S. was being outmaneuvered on the Kurdish issue. "Clinton doesn't have the same emotional attachment to the Kurds," he said. Under the Bush administration, U.S. warplanes often flew over Iraq at two to three hundred feet to, as Colonel Young said, "show Saddam who's in charge here." The Clinton administration, he claimed, was eager to avoid confrontation with Iraq; now, no overflights were being conducted below five thousand feet. In the last two months Iraqi agents had blown up fourteen relief trucks. That week, the Iraqi army had killed a dozen farmers on a raid into Kurdistan. According to Young, the previous mechanism for raising such grievances with the Iraqis had been dissolved. The Iraqi officers who used to meet regularly with Colonel Young and his staff were no longer willing to do so. Lately, when Young and his staff showed up for meetings, he said, "they put a gun to our heads." The Kurds no longer had America as an interlocutor. The Kurdish safety zone was no longer safe.

Worst of all, Young claimed, American power within the coalition itself had been eroded. Turkey had usurped U.S. authority in northern Iraq. "I have to watch what I do and say," Young said, complaining that his Turkish counterpart regularly filed reports to Ankara accusing Americans of favoring the Kurds. Colonel Young had studied Middle East history at West Point. In his opinion, the Turkish fears were unfounded, but they were jeopardizing U.S. use of Turkish bases. "There will *never* be a Kurdish state in the region," he maintained forcefully. Nevertheless, the growing Kurdish question was damaging the prestige of the U.S. Army. "Never in my entire military career have I had to kowtow to a *foreign* uniform," he said. "Now I've got a Turkish minder."

Neither Colonel Young nor I could have guessed that a decade later, after a surprise intervention to topple Saddam Hussein, the Turks would block U.S. troops from using their soil, depriving the allies of their northern front and unwittingly empowering the Kurds, their longtime nemesis. The Iraq war would ignite anti-Americanism in Turkey, altering the power ratio between Turks and Kurds in the region. The developments, not anticipated by war planners, would be a product of the law of unintended consequences.

Newroz, 1993

I crossed back into Turkey for *Newroz,* the Kurdish New Year. The Kurds celebrate *Newroz* every March 21, the first day of spring, but this year Turkey had taken measures to restrict the festivities. The government knew that PKK guerrillas were planning to use the holiday to advance their separatist agenda. The previous year, the events had turned violent. In Çizre and other towns, the police had fired into crowds, killing more than a dozen protesters and fatally wounding a Turkish photographer. This year, many local mayors had issued decrees banning public gatherings. The Kurdish mayor of Sirnak, in the center of the war zone, had been removed from office after he questioned the need to prohibit a demonstration in his town. This year, in the days leading up to *Newroz,* there had been "preventative arrests" of Kurdish politicians, labor leaders, and journalists.

According to Turkish newspapers, about three hundred thousand security forces already were in the Kurdish region, including the dreaded Special Teams, the plainclothes police given free rein to deal with security threats. The Kurdish region, eleven provinces in southeast Turkey, had been under emergency law for several years. By statute, the punishment for crimes was twice that of the rest of the country. Violation of Article 8, the catchall law that targeted any expression against "the indivisible unity of the Turkish state," was punishable by two to five years in prison. The police could arrest and hold suspects for thirty days without a charge—as opposed to four days in other parts of Turkey. The *Super Vale,* Diyarbakir's "emergency governor," announced he would impose a curfew, if necessary, to keep the peace. The *Newroz* march in the city could proceed, but no banners or shouting of Kurdish slogans would be tolerated. If any demonstrator produced a red, yellow, and green flag—the colors of the PKK—the police were free to shoot.

Advocates of Kurdish independence claimed that the *Newroz* tradition was thousands of years old. Given the force of the Kurdish uprising, now in its tenth year, the holiday embodied a powerful symbol of defiance. Every Kurdish child knew the legend of Dehak, the notorious tyrant who terrorized the Middle East in the sixth century B.C. According to the fable, Dehak abused his subjects, imprisoning, torturing, and killing many of them. Each night, two Kurdish children were snatched from their parents and ritually slain. Dehak fed their brains to his giant serpents. One day, a Kurdish blacksmith named Kawa was able to get close to the tyrant by bringing a gift of sheep brains, which the snakes devoured. When Dehak wasn't paying attention, Kawa rose up and slew him with a special knife he had forged for the occasion. Great joy greeted the news of the tyrant's death, and bonfires were lit in celebration from the tops of the mountains. It was the first day of spring. It was a new day. The people had been freed.

. Now it was a day before *Newroz*, and all the shops in Diyarbakir were boarded up for the holiday. According to the government press office, about seventy accredited journalists were in town to cover the expected confrontation. With the exception of me, the reporters were Turkish or European. I had spotted bonfires in the nearby hills, and I wondered how the army was responding. I decided to check out the area with two Dutch journalists—a photographer and a gutsy radio reporter named Jessica Lutz, a fluent speaker of Turkish and a frequent visitor to the Kurdish region.

The first Kurdish village we visited was almost totally without government services, a forgotten mudhole where the children had such bad teeth they looked like yellow stubs. The kids and their mothers peered at the foreigners from doorways, bolting liked scared rabbits as we approached. The reason soon became clear. Turkish troops had occupied the hamlet and soldiers were going door to door, rounding up all males over the age of fourteen and herding them into the village square to warn them not to celebrate *Newroz*. We stopped to talk to an old man who had been passed over in the sweep. He said that a day earlier the imam, the local religious leader, had been threatened about traveling to a nearby village to celebrate. According to the old man, a soldier warned the imam ominously, "If you leave home, you will never return." A few years earlier, the man told us, twenty-four hundred people had resided in his village. Some of the young men and women had gone to the mountains to join the guerrillas, but most of the families had chosen to abandon their homes, fleeing to Diyarbakir to avoid the conflict. Now, with fighting almost every night, only five hundred people remained, and the village was almost deserted. The name of the place in Kurdish was Ingaci. The government had renamed it Kirmasiirt, which means "unbreakable back" in Turkish. Ironically, the village's back was all but broken.

As soon as the soldiers realized we were taking pictures, they tried to confiscate the film. It did not matter that we had our special press credentials for the "emergency area." Fortunately, the commander found Jessica's language ability charming, and that got us tea, as well as a chance to argue that Turkey should not censor the international press. Given the fact that we were uninvited guests who had interrupted a military mission, arguing about a right to take photos in public places seemed useless. The commander claimed that our photos "would allow PKK terrorists to identify the soldiers"—even if the pictures were published in California. In the end, however, he let us leave without confiscating the film, asking only that we appreciate the need for special policies in a time of war. "There is no censorship in Turkey," he said, "but you are not permitted to take photos of security forces."

Fewer than one thousand people showed up for the *Newroz* march in Diyarbakir. Most Kurds, it appeared, had chosen to celebrate the holiday safely by staying home. We saw police at the demonstration with automatic rifles chasing protesters and we heard a few gunshots. Afterward, in another part of the city, we photographed about two hundred Kurds dancing to Kurdish drums around a pile of burning tires. I saw one dancer, a portly woman in her thirties, excitedly pull a cloth from under her blouse. It was red, yellow, and green. She put it away after only a few moments. The police didn't show themselves, but I heard that about a hundred Kurds were arrested in the city during the day. In a *Newroz* demonstration in the city of Adana, home of the U.S. consulate, four Kurds were shot to death by the police. Two were killed in other Kurdish towns.

Furtive Photo in a Café

Wherever I went in those days, it felt as if a thousand eyes were fixed on my every move, and twice that number if I carried a camera in plain view. There was no way I could blend in. I was outside the society.

In the town of Çizre my film was confiscated on the street after a passerby volunteered to authorities that I had taken a photo of an army patrol. I was saved from a similar fate another day by the intercession of an English-speaking army recruit who had worked as a bartender in a tourist hotel on Turkey's Mediterranean coast before he was drafted.

There seemed to be spies and counterspies everywhere, some paid, but others acting out of fear or a desire to settle personal scores. Turkish police cars all had signs with a telephone number for confidential informants (IMDAT 155). In the town of Siirt, my cab driver told me people were using the number to settle personal grudges. "The bond between Kurds," he lamented, "has broken down because of the war." There was no way to trust a person anymore, he added, paraphrasing a local proverb, "until you have eaten a kilo of salt with him."

One day in a Kurdish restaurant, I caught sight of a Turkish reporter from an Istanbul paper. He was at another table, and he seemed to be sneaking glances at me as I ate. The place was a dive, with stained tablecloths, old plastic flowers, and buzzing flies. Half the ceiling bulbs were burnt out, but there was enough light to see the guy snap my photo surreptitiously and quickly leave. It was a creepy feeling, like someone slapping a target on my back.

The waiter was friendly. He thought the guy was annoyed that a visiting American, a guest in the country, was sticking his nose into the Kurdish question instead of minding his own business. He had overheard the reporter say to a colleague, "This is not *Clinton's* town!" I didn't know whether the photo was meant to intimidate me or if the man hoped to trade a copy to the military for press favors.

Illegal Colors

A grocer in Diyarbakir told me he was well aware it was illegal to advertise his products in Kurdish, but he was baffled when he got into trouble for the *color* of Turkish words he used on the window of his shop. The police made him remove the color green from the name of the grocery, but allowed him to keep reds and yellows. An officer told him that use of the three colors in the same space was prohibited, because the combination suggested the "terrorist flag" (PKK). There was a similar paranoia about traffic signals. The security chief in the city of Batman replaced the green traffic lights with blue bulbs. Under the new system, drivers were supposed to know that a blue light meant "go." Fortunately for street safety, the chief quickly became a laughingstock in the local papers, and the backlash forced him to come up with a different story. When he said he merely had ordered "the wrong color bulbs," someone pointed out that the bulbs themselves were white. What gave the traffic lights color were the blue *lenses* the mayor had ordered.

One day I stopped in a village for a cup of tea with some old men. The name of the place was Uzumlu, but the Kurds told me they called it Paris. Visits like this often ended prematurely when police chased away would-be conversationalists. After that, I was usually put in a police car and "invited" to the station house for tea. That day, however, we were undisturbed. One resident pointed to TV antennae on the roof of a big building. He was angry that local Kurds were not allowed to watch the private channels, the ones available to the Turkish public. He said the security forces had recently rotated the village's TV receptor away from Paris, so the Kurds could get broadcasts only from the state-run channels. The townspeople were told that the private TV channels had "bad information" about the war.

Some of what I found in the war zone was a matter of outright denial.

A Turkish general told a radio reporter I knew that he'd come to a scheduled meeting "directly from the war." Later in the interview, he got mad when the reporter asked a question about the war. "What *war*?" he snapped. "There's no war."

In one town a policeman got angry after observing me take a photo of Kurdish cotton pickers who were crammed in the back of a truck idling at the curb. He demanded to know the "real reason" I had taken the shot. Because it was a good photo, I answered simply. "I don't believe that," he said. "We know that you *planned* this." Maybe he also thought that I'd *planned* for him to show up at precisely that moment, but I didn't have the nerve to ask.

Near the town of Silvan, the army was burning the fields on either side of the highway with the goal of eliminating potential hiding spots of the enemy. The date was August 16, the day after the anniversary of the Kurds' 1984 uprising. According to a Kurdish teenager I met, the guerrillas had kidnapped eleven soldiers on this stretch of road the night before. Civilians were caught in the middle. The PKK had ordered the shops to close in Silvan in observance of the rebel holiday. Only ten had closed. The next day pro-government forces burnt all ten to the ground. They were still smoldering when another reporter and I arrived in town. An oversized message on a nearby hillside caught our attention. We had seen it before in the Kurdish region. Painted in the grass in huge letters were the words, HAPPY IS HE WHO CAN CALL HIMSELF A TURK.

Minibus on a Low Road

I liked to travel by minibus because it offered me chance encounters with ordinary Kurds and the opportunity to confirm the validity of government claims.

After officials told reporters that the ban on Kurdish music had been lifted, for example, I watched police at a checkpoint confiscate Kurdish cassettes from my bus driver. The incident was repeated at other checkpoints. Bus travel, however, was often problematic. One day, for example, I wanted to go to the town of Sirnak to investigate reports that army bulldozers had destroyed houses of families whose teenagers had joined the guerrillas. A soldier at a roadblock took me off the bus, but he let the other passengers continue. He admitted the road was open to civilians, but he claimed I was an "official" and that the denial was for my protection. He gave me a handout with a photo of corpses lined up on the shoulder of a road. The handout said, "This Is Real Face of the Terrorists."

In two weeks of traveling I'd already counted about sixty ID checks. So many fingers had paged through my passport, I was almost afraid the pages would dissolve. I'd been detained four times for my "protection," but so far not arrested. (I decided to call anything over two hours in custody an arrest.) Because of the soldier's behavior at the Sirnak checkpoint, I surmised that the damage reports from the town ahead were probably true, and I tried even harder to talk my way through. But when the soldier said, "*Yasak!*" I knew it was hopeless. The word means "forbidden." When the Turkish army says that, you just forget it. It's "*Yasak!*"

Batman and Paranoia

The largest city in the Kurdish southeast, after Diyarbakir, was Batman. The official population of Batman was 157,000, but the mayor told me that just in the last year, war refugees had swollen the population to 225,000. Batman was the stronghold of Hezbollah, the homegrown Sunni extremist movement (not to be confused with the Lebanon Shia group). The Turkish military reportedly was arming the local Hezbollah for jihad against the PKK, a government solution that turned out to be successful only in the short term. Following the Iraq war in 2003, Hezbollah would be implicated in the bombings of the British consulate, a British bank, and Jewish synagogues in Istanbul.

On any given day in 1993, a suspected PKK sympathizer was likely to be shot in broad daylight in Batman. The following day, in retaliation, Hezbollah Kurds would be sprayed with machine gun fire, sometimes as they prayed in a local mosque. Each side referred to its dead as *shahid,* the universal term in the Middle East for *martyr.* Once again, it was Kurd killing Kurd, terror versus terror.

A clerk in the hotel told me that the price tag for a daylight murder was $6,000 U.S. Killings after dark could be arranged for $3,000, sometimes less. Both sides favored the use of a signature shot to the neck. The guerrillas often left political messages. For example, an accused collaborator with the state might be found hanging from an overhead electric wire with Turkish *lira* stuffed in his mouth. According to a cop I talked to in the bus station, there were never any witnesses, not even when killings took place in crowded cafés. "No one sees anything," he said, throwing up his hands in despair. Each killing was a case of *faili mechul* (perpetrator unknown). I asked the officer what law enforcement was doing about the problem. "How could *I* possibly tell who does these things?" he replied, a bit defensively. "I'm not a fortune-teller."

According to a PKK flyer I found, "A deaf and dumb society was being created. The Turkish state is putting our brain to sleep. Creating an obedient human being." Another officer I met seemed to agree, as he sought to delineate the difference between police work in the United States and police work in Turkey. In America, he said, police don't ordinarily show up until a crime takes place. In Turkey, he said, police are always visible on the street—that is, until something happens.

Both the rebels and Hezbollah used violence to impose their agendas of prohibition on the Batman populace. Islamic fundamentalists already had banned wedding receptions and gambling. The week before, the owner of a video arcade in Batman had been shot to death and his son badly wounded. They had been warned by Hezbollah: Gambling was *yasak.* Forbidden. The PKK banned alcohol: Drinking was *yasak.* So much, I thought, for rebel concerns about a deaf and dumb society. The hotel clerk, who knew a local bootlegger and was able to buy beer—albeit at an inflated price—told me he had to be careful. He directed me to the last bar in town that was still open (the others had been shot up or blown up). The patrons I met there seemed to know that their days of public drinking were numbered, but they acted with ambivalence, and their sense of hopelessness seemed like a snapshot of civilian life in Turkish Kurdistan at the time.

"I'm married, but I have no job and I drink our money away," said one, morosely. "It's not the Kurdish way." He said the ban was hard for him. He both feared and liked the PKK, but he and his friends at the bar had been brought up in a tightly ordered society, where breaking the rules was met by terror—from one side or another. It was as if they were waiting for direction from a force outside themselves. "Maybe afterward [after prohibition was completely established]," another patron said, "the state—or someone else—will tell us what to do."

If a prize were to be given to a radical group in Batman for generating the most paranoia among its members and for spreading fear among the rest of the population, it would have gone to Hezbollah. Local rumors said the radical sect was about to outlaw Marlboro cigarettes. There were thousands of giant Marlboro Men all over Turkey at the time—red-and-white murals on sides of eight-story concrete-slab apartments—and I had a feeling Philip Morris was not going to be pleased. Marlboro was far and away the most popular cigarette in the country—real American cigarettes, at only about forty cents a pack. The company had just built a Marlboro tobacco plant in western Turkey and was pursuing a vigorous publicity campaign in the country and throughout the Third World. Now, however, Philip Morris had run into an unexpected opponent, and its product was about to be banned. Hezbollah claimed the issue was prohibition. According to rumors, Marlboros were "washed in wine."

Dead Journalists, Terrorism, Self-Defense

In a 1992 report on Turkey, Human Rights Watch said eleven journalists had been murdered during the year, the majority apparently by death squads. All but one were killed in Kurdistan. If the numbers were correct, the total was the highest in the world for the period, including even the far better publicized conflicts in Bosnia and Croatia. It was still almost a decade before the events of 9/11 and the rise of "the war on terror," but the United States had already characterized the Kurdish uprising in Turkey, unlike the one in nearby Iraq, as "terrorism." As the world's only superpower, the United States could pick and choose which Kurdish war was legitimate.

In the town of Bitlis, I met the parents of a twenty-year-old man who had been murdered three months earlier. The young man had been a journalist for the pro-Kurdish newspaper *Gündem*, and his father was still active in Kurdish politics. After the victim's kidnapping, his parents received a phone call telling them their son would be killed unless he quit the paper and his father withdrew from Kurdish politics. The mother and father told me they beseeched the local army commander, but the appeal was to no avail. Then they received another call that said, "Your thoughts the other day were nice, but you did not live up to the conditions we agreed upon. We have finished the work on your son." It was then, his mother said, that she thought she recognized the voice as that of the commander. When they received the body, there were signs of electric torture. She told me that his eyes were "bulging out of his head" and that his underwear was bloody. The father raised four fingers to represent his four children. Then he bent one down, signifying the deceased. He said that the day before, three Kurdish activists had been killed in Batman and a fourth in Diyarbakir. "The police claim the ones responsible are *faili mechul*," he said, "but we know the truth. The killer is the state."

In Diyarbakir, I met a *Gündem* reporter named Hassan, who told me he carried a gun "for self-defense." He lifted his shirt to display what he said was a bullet wound in his back, the product of an attempt on his life. Hassan said that the journalists who'd been killed included newspaper vendors. Recently, two Kurdish boys hawking *Gündem* papers on the street had been shot and killed. The spate of child murders in Turkish Kurdistan had not been covered in the U.S. media, but the choice of so-called soft targets in Turkey in the 1990s foreshadowed a larger use of the terror tactic in nearby Iraq a decade later. Lured to Iraq during the American occupation by the promise of jobs, impoverished workers from Nepal, the Philippines, and other Third World countries would be kidnapped and killed for political advantage, along with hundreds of randomly targeted Iraqis. By then, the world's tolerance for violence had increased, or so it appeared. Eventually, even the killing of innocents—for example, the mass slaughter in 2004 of children in Beslan, Russia—would lose some of its ability to shock.

Tracer Bullets at the Hotel

At a roadblock near my hotel, the Kadioglu in Çizre, a Turkish policeman threatened the Kurdish taxi driver with arrest for failure to update his taxi license. I was sitting in the back of the car, unobserved through the dark tinted windows. After a minute or two, the cop agreed to accept a fifty thousand *lira* note in place of the license. That was about $5—maybe half the fare the cabbie expected from me—and we were allowed to pass.

The power had gone out at the hotel, but the lobby was lit by candles. As I passed the reception desk, I noticed a framed photo on the wall. It was a picture of hotel clerks posing with a group of journalists. One of them was the Turkish photographer killed there, directly in front of the hotel, during *Newroz* the previous spring. It was dark now, and I was happy to be off the streets. My penlight guided me up three flights of carpet-ripped stairs and into the room. Thirty minutes later, I heard the gunfire. I crawled onto the balcony above the neon marquee that advertised the hotel as *turistik*. Yellow tracer bullets were lighting up the street below.

I heard a knock on the door. It was the reception clerk, Halil (not his real name), the friendly one who knew some English. He held out six beers. The beer had come from a bootlegger's storeroom, and the cans were covered with dust. For Halil, the cost of the drinks represented more than a day's wages. Plus, getting them had taken a bit of nerve because alcohol was banned in Çizre, both by the PKK and by Hezbollah, whom one Çizre resident referred to as "the guys with the beards." Halil wanted to talk.

We crawled out on the balcony. *Boom!* The sound of a mortar echoed across the town. Below us, two Panzers, armored personnel carriers made in Germany, scooted into the plaza in tandem, passing the Renault dealer and spitting automatic fire from their gun ports. For a moment, they looked like windup toys chasing each other. To our right, a heavy machine gun thundered from the army base on the hill. Parallel to the balcony, a floor below, tracer fire flew by again in an arc. Whoever it was, they weren't firing *at* us, but freshly patched holes in the concrete wall of my balcony kept that possibility in the forefront of my mind.

It was hard to tell who was shooting. Oftentimes, Halil said, it was both the Kurds and the army. But sometimes, he told me, it was just "suppressing fire" from the police, from one side of town, and the army from the other. The next morning, we would see the shops shot up, and I'd film a distraught woman at the local hospital trying to get a wounded youth loaded into a truck so he wouldn't get arrested as she said, "for being shot."

"Why did God create Hell?" Halil asked jokingly, "as long as there's a Çizre?"

The beer was warm, but it tasted good. By now, the sky over the north side of Çizre was illuminated by military flares exploding and parachuting to the city. It reminded me of nights at Wounded Knee, when the occupied village was bathed in the yellow phosphorescence of FBI flares. Tonight, with the exception of one haggard milk cow wandering in the deserted square below, no living thing was crazy enough to be on the streets of Çizre. The cow strolled leisurely across the intersection, seemingly oblivious to the gunfire, stopping at a pile of garbage for a bite to eat.

Halil used my phone to call the reception desk, lying that he was in his own room, resting. He was scared the police or his new boss might discover he was meeting with a journalist. Kurds in Çizre knew better than that, but he had something important to tell me.

He began with an old Kurdish proverb: A man who becomes rich, late in life, either brings home an extra wife or he kills someone. Then Halil told me the story of his former boss, the hotel owner, who had been killed the month before.

As a border town in the aftermath of the Gulf War, Çizre had experienced a huge influx of Kurdish refugees from Iraq. In those days back in 1991, the hotel was sold out every night, and the restaurant and bar were always jammed with journalists and aid workers. Within months, the old man was rich, but he couldn't handle the sudden wealth, and he started drinking and fighting. That got him into trouble with the local authorities, and finally, after a drunken killing, he was arrested. The charge was dropped, however, when he paid a large "fine" to the Turkish police. Soon after, drunk again, he tried to win a woman away from another businessman, a pharmacist in town. They fought, and he shot the man to death. This time, the hidden authority in town, the PKK, decided to put the hotel owner on trial. "It all started downstairs," Halil said, "they just kidnapped him, took him away." Sixty Kurdish merchants in Çizre were polled by the PKK. Should the man live or die? Thirteen gave him "thumbs up." Let him live. The other forty-seven voted thumbs down. The PKK executed him.

"Don't tell anyone I told you this," Halil whispered.

A searchlight from one of the cruising Panzers swept the balcony and moved on. My companion opened another beer, and his attention turned to the less obvious costs of the Kurdish uprising. Halil liked his job, not the least for the chance it offered to meet female reporters who visited the hotel. In the culture of Çizre, there was no opportunity to approach a woman in public, certainly not for sex. Not even for small talk. You know what I mean, Halil said, the way that kind of thing happens in other places. The war had stopped all that. The PKK rebels had put an end to romance. They claimed the only real love was the love of freedom. They said that Kurds should love the revolution.

Now there was nothing to do. Everyone was scared. Or bored. They were all trapped. He longed for Çizre to be exciting, the way it used to be. "Before the uprising, the evenings were exciting," he said nostalgically. "There were lots of people then, and they were walking in the streets."

10

Turkey, 1995, Ground Level

Fear a stupid enemy.

—TURKISH PROVERB

Eviction

When I met Ali, he was drinking tea and playing cards in Midyat, one of the many Kurdish towns overflowing with refugees from the war in the countryside. Ali and his wife and nine kids had fled Shehtir, a farming village known for its sweet cherries. Long ago, the Turks had changed the name of the place to Kocasirt, which is how it appeared on the map. However, like others who had lived there, Ali still called it Shehtir.

Having agreed to guide me to the village, Ali drove gingerly down a hill toward his old home, carefully scanning the rock-studded road for signs of recent digging. He said the army often mined the access to vacated villages. The week before, on the road to another abandoned settlement, a man and a woman were badly injured when a land mine exploded under their donkey. "I have seen President Clinton on television," he told me matter-of-factly. "If he knew about these bad things, I don't think he would permit them to happen."

Ali was talking about the Turkish security forces. In the summer of 1994, sixteen army tanks had rolled through his village searching for Kurdish guerrillas. Some had rubber wheels, like the kind the Germans sold to Turkey; the others were armored-track vehicles, like the M48 and M60 tanks made in the United States. Even though no rebels were found, the soldiers returned a few months later. They delivered an ultimatum to the people: Become village guards or abandon your homes.

The seventy-year-old *muhtar*, the village elder, was against the idea from the start. He insisted the villagers had never fed or otherwise assisted the rebels. The people wanted to grow their crops, and they made no response to the offer of arms. It was the wrong choice. A few nights later, the *muhtar* was dragged from his home and shot. The townspeople still refused to become village guards, so they gathered up their furniture and household belongings and moved away.

Whatever Kocasirt had been before, it was now a collection of deserted, burned, and dynamited houses. It was a ghost town, with a cemetery. It was there we encountered an old woman who had returned to the village by foot. She was wailing softly and sprinkling red cherries on a grave to feed the spirit of her dead brother. My guide recognized her as the sister of the village elder who had been murdered. The old woman had no idea who had killed her brother. "They came at night with guns and they wore masks," she said tearfully. A few minutes after they took him away, she and the others in the house heard shots down the road. When it got light, they went outside and found his body. Reaching for a weed in the overgrown graveyard, the woman made a sweeping motion with one hand. "They just plucked him like a flower," she said.

Cities

Çizre had been "cleaned," the Turkish policeman told me proudly. In one sense he was right: The largely Kurdish town of twenty-five thousand, located about fifty miles north of the Iraqi border, was firmly under the control of the Turkish security forces.

When I visited in 1993, Çizre had been a hotbed of resistance incited by the PKK. That memory was still fresh as I rented my old room at the ratty Kadioglu. The patched bullet holes in the balcony walls were still visible. The intermittently lit sign outside my window reminded me again that the hotel was *turistik*. I recalled watching the exchange of tracer fire after dark from the balcony overlooking that sign, and it was hard to forget the surreal streams of yellow lighting up Çizre's main intersection below. Nowadays, however, pedestrians walked on the street below, and the town was beginning to return to normal.

Çizre, in fact, was "clean," but behind the scenes, the town was seething with war refugees from isolated, outlying Kurdish villages. Privately, the mood, gathered from conversations away from the watchful eye of the police, seemed to alternate between war-weary depression and outright rage.

There was a similar sense of desperation among the displaced people in the large Kurdish cities of Hakkari, Batman, and Mardin. The population in Diyarbakir, the largest of any of the Kurdish cities, was now more than six hundred thousand, twice what it had been just four years ago. Families were doubled up with extra relatives and friends in concrete box–style apartment buildings throughout the city. In every part of Kurdistan, the refugees were triggering a crisis in social services, housing, and employment.

In Diyarbakir a carpet salesman, a Turk I had met on an earlier trip, told me that jobs were particularly scarce. Rug sales in his own shop had dropped from three hundred a year to only fifty, all because tourists were afraid to visit the region. I inquired about a beautiful carpet on display, one I had seen before. He said he had gotten it a while ago from a Kurdish weaver in Siirt, a province renowned for its handmade rugs, but it was no longer safe to visit the area. The weavers' villages had all been burned.

The Pattern

In a three-day trip behind army lines in the province of Siirt, along the Tigris River, the so-called birthplace of ancient civilization, I witnessed scores of refugees on the run. At one point I saw entire families fleeing a village recently burned by the Turkish army. They were fording the Tigris River, guiding a long line of donkeys laden with refrigerators and other goods. When I finally reached their village, it was in ruins, but a handful of residents, including the local mayor, were still trying to scavenge their belongings. The mayor told me an army commander had arrived prior to the burning, accompanied by government-armed village guards who warned the residents in Kurdish. The commander gave the residents twenty-four hours to get out of town. Some had quickly dug holes in the fields to bury valuables; others just gathered up what they could carry and abandoned the rest.

I walked through the rubble, taking pictures as I went. The destruction was fresh, only a day or two old, and some of it was still smoldering. Then I heard an army helicopter overhead. It was American-made—a Sikorsky Black Hawk—the type the Turkish army used for troop transport. Luckily, the chopper was high in the air, en route to a different mission. I finished my work and moved on.

Much later, I found my way to another district, to a place the map referred to as Alimlikoy but which the Kurds call Bilalya. A month earlier, the army commander from the nearby city of Mardin had informed local residents that they would have to go on the payroll of the state as village guards. The villagers were reluctant to become guards, because that would put them in the middle of the war with the PKK rebels. They were shepherds who had to spend long, isolated hours in the mountains with their flocks. If they accepted weapons from the government, they might become targets for the guerrillas. The Turkish officer gave them two weeks to think about it. When no answer was forthcoming, he arrested the *muhtar*. The shepherd who walked me into Alimlikoy—overland, around the blockaded road—told me the *muhtar* had been kept in jail for several days. He had been beaten, the shepherd said, "but not badly."

On the very day the *muhtar* was released, shortly before my arrival in mid-June, the villagers hired trucks from Mardin to haul away their household goods and as much of the ripening harvest of lentils and barley as they could carry. I arrived in time to see some of the harvests outside Mardin. The grain was piled by the side of the road, where the village Kurds were pouring salvaged crops into plastic bags to be sold at the market. Within sight of the new refugees was another giant hillside sign that said, HAPPY IS HE WHO CAN CALL HIMSELF A TURK.

It was boiling hot the afternoon I climbed down the steep hill to Alimlikoy. The shepherd asked me not to take a picture of his face, but he led me to his home. The house had been ransacked, apparently by the soldiers when they blockaded the road. The TV set in his living room had been smashed. "They think even this [television] is too much of a luxury for us," he said bitterly.

Why didn't you just agree to become a guard? I asked the shepherd. He replied that the people in the village didn't like guns and had no use for the state's money. "Why would we?" he asked. "We have our fields and our animals. We have an income. Besides," he said with some emphasis, "why should we try to do a job that not even the *state* can accomplish?"

Punishment

Near the town of Silopi I visited a half-empty village. The few remaining residents told me how they had been terrorized by shelling from nearby tanks. The school had two large holes in the walls, and a picture of Atatürk still hung, albeit slightly askew, over the blackboard. Kurdish students, giddy from the excitement of a stranger's visit, laughed and posed for pictures, incongruously, in the classroom where debris from the shelling covered their desks.

There were holes in several houses from the shelling, which villagers said came on the heels of a firefight between the army and guerrillas a few miles away. No one had been injured in the attack, which happened at night, but several animals had been killed and most residents were terrified enough to vacate their homes after the incident. The villagers said they had never helped the guerrillas, but there was no way to prove their innocence—and there was no way to prevent the retribution that followed. As one man put it, "We have been punished."

Safe Haven

Across the border in northern Iraq, the town of Atrush was part of the Kurdish "safe haven," the sector in which the U.S.-led allies protected Iraqi Kurds from Saddam Hussein's army. The area also had become a refuge for Turkish Kurds. Just outside Atrush were two camps crammed with an estimated twenty thousand Kurds who had fled the army's scorched-earth campaign in Turkey. After dark, I watched these refugees sit down in a grassy, open pasture, surrounded by mountains. There, two generator-powered television sets brought them MED

TV, daily broadcasts in Kurdish by satellite from Belgium, where expatriates had a production studio. It was the PKK's most potent weapon of propaganda to date.

Like all Kurdish-language broadcasting, MED TV was banned in Turkey, where the police prevented clandestine viewing by frequently confiscating the compact satellite dishes from Kurdish homes. However, this was a corner of northern Iraq, and there was no way to restrain the flow of such information. The broadcasts were a high-tech mix of Kurdish music, propaganda, and war news.

Here in a remote valley just south of the Turkish border, signals from two thousand miles away illuminated the night. Children sat in the weeds in front of television sets, their attention glued to the broadcast of Kurdish music. Singing about resistance, one TV musician turned to the camera and held up two fingers in the familiar victory sign. Scores of excited kids joined in, raising victory signs of their own, mouthing the lyrics back to the performer in harmony, as if this were a live concert.

At that moment it suddenly dawned on me: Forget all the talk about Kurdish feudalism and Kurdish tribalism. That's all over now. The new reality for once-isolated Kurds is Marshall McLuhan's "global village": a place where television communicates a problem (repression) as well as the solution (insurrection). Then, like a climactic scene inserted by a distant producer, the Kurdish kids raised fingers in another salute of victory. The instant audience participation rounded out the picture: electronic propaganda in a pasture, a linked Kurdish diaspora, and a hint of the ongoing struggle that lay ahead.

Postscript at the Kadioglu Hotel in Çizre

By 9:00 A.M., there usually were two cops in the lobby, ready to shadow me for the day. I was friendly with the reception clerk, and one evening when we were talking, he confided that he was supposed to use a different colored pen to record the names of journalists, based on his judgment of the security threat that each presented. He was doing the best he could, but it was an inexact science, and he was frustrated.

The clerk told me he was getting tired—tired of the war and tired of all the unpaid tasks he was forced to perform. Cooperative with the police, like a lot of accommodating Kurds, he struck me as more alienated than ever before. True, the guerrillas had been driven to the tops of the mountains, their logistical bases interrupted by the widespread destruction of villages, but it looked as if the government was losing a battle for the hearts and minds of ordinary Kurds.

The clerk complained that he had to inform the police of the slightest movements by reporters, "When you get up, when you go out, and when you return.

It's incredible," he confided. "We have to make telephone calls to *three* different places each time: the Army, MIT [military intelligence], and the regular police. Why can't we just call one place and let them handle the rest?" I asked him, in jest, if he was proposing a clearinghouse for the surveillance of the press. "What can we do?" he said with a shrug and a bit of a grin.

11

The Business of Killing

The spike in arms spending is a bonanza for the nation's armaments contractors, almost all of which report surging profits and soaring stocks.

—*LOS ANGELES TIMES*, OCTOBER 1, 2004

A Mass Grave, Another Culture

For a reporter, one of the biggest hurdles in covering conflict is the need to stand outside the action. Language and racial barriers increase the challenge of getting "inside" a foreign culture to make the story resonate with readers, listeners, or viewers back home. Until 1973, when I covered the Indian occupation at Wounded Knee, South Dakota, I had never seen anyone shot to death. Then I met Frank Clearwater, a forty-seven-year-old Cherokee from North Carolina. Clearwater and his wife wanted so badly to be part of the confrontation that they'd hitchhiked all the way from their home on the East Coast. By the time they arrived, the famous village was surrounded by hundreds of FBI agents and U.S. Marshals, and federal negotiators had vowed publicly to "starve out" the Indians. After a long hike through the reservation backcountry, the Clearwaters managed to penetrate the government cordon. I bumped into them outside the trading post. It was cold that night, and I told them there were extra blankets inside.

After I found the bedding, Clearwater lit up a "ready-made" cigarette, offering to share it with me and several Indians who were standing around. A store-bought cigarette was special, and we passed it around in a circle, like a form of communion, until a long, red ash could be seen in the dark. Then the newcomers walked up the hill to the little pine church to look for a place to sleep.

The next morning, just after dawn, a small plane rented by Wounded Knee sympathizers flew over the FBI bunkers and parachuted bundles of food into the besieged compound. The dramatic airdrop ignited a hellacious firefight between the Feds and the Indians, rousting Frank Clearwater from the floor of the church. As he sat up in his blanket roll, a bullet ripped through a wall and blew off the back of his head. By the time I got there, Indians were

crouched at the windows with their rifles. There were bullet holes in the
wooden wall, and blond-colored splinters lay on the floor. Clearwater was already dead. A blanket I'd given him had been used to roll him onto a
makeshift stretcher. This was the man I'd shared a cigarette with a few hours
earlier. Now his face was frozen, his lips contorted, and the blanket was covered with blood and tissue. I couldn't help thinking, *Weren't we just talking
about the cold?*

The next to die was a Lakota Sioux named Buddy Lamont, a Vietnam vet-
eran just home from the war. He was hit when he popped out of a foxhole with
his rifle about fifty yards from the trailer where I'd slept the night before. He
was killed by a long-range shot, probably by a sniper with a scope.

Buddy was popular on the reservation, and his mother worked as a cook
for the Bureau of Indian Affairs (BIA). The local connections earned the Lamont family the right to inter him at the Wounded Knee cemetery, next to
the victims of the 1890 massacre. Before the burial, the casket was opened,
and the mourners filed by to pay their respects. At the gravesite, his mother
talked about her great aunt, who was killed at Wounded Knee in 1890, and
how Buddy had gone overseas "to fight communism." When he got home,
she said, his fight was with the BIA. The casket was full of gifts for the trip to
the spirit world: food, chewing gum, and a package of Lucky Strike cigarettes.
Someone had placed a package of razor blades and a can of Gillette shaving
cream on the chest of his corpse. Relatives snapped photos with their Insta-
matics.

Buddy's grief-stricken sister was in the cortege. As I raised my camera to
take a picture of Buddy, she stopped me and asked sarcastically, "How much
money will you make on *this* trip?"

"What do you mean?" I stammered defensively.

"Getting pictures of my dead brother," she said. "I know you reporters. This
is just a *job* for you."

Suddenly, I was a *waiciscu,* a non-Indian, "a taker of the fat" in the Lakota language. The remark at the mass grave, a piece of ground heavy with race and history, impaled me. I put the camera down. As the amateur lenses clicked away, I
would remember this day—without film.

I looked at the mass grave in front of me and thought of the 1890 massacre. In
my mind's eye, I saw the archival image from *Life* magazine, the old picture of
the Seventh Cavalry dumping bodies into the rectangular pit. I thought of all the
skeletons—some three hundred—in the ground nearby. They were eighty-three
years dead. I thought about the soldiers getting their medals, how war distorts
the truth, and history fights to correct it. I thought about killing and the clash of
civilizations. I thought about the role of journalism.

Objectivity and Accountability

At its simplest, reporting is remembering what you saw on the other side of the mountain and faithfully recounting it for people who couldn't make the trip. If I was going to keep doing this work, I had to find a way not to flinch when I got too close. If the truth wasn't available from official sources, I needed to find a low road to travel on, a way to witness events up close, a way to make a foreign story local. I had to learn to get the picture and *not* put the camera down.

Later on, during the 1980s and 1990s, when I'd come home from war and destruction in Central America or the Middle East, people rarely asked about U.S. foreign policy or the role they had as citizens in creating it. Instead, people often would say, with a kind sigh, "Aren't you happy that you live *here*?" Where I lived, of course, was Santa Barbara, a charming seaside resort town in southern California, but I knew they were referring in general to life in America. At some point, the disturbing significance of the question came into focus: ugly, dangerous places in the world were unconnected from the beautiful, safe ones. The distinction bothered me. In effect, they seemed to be saying: Go ahead, have your foreign holidays in hell. Go ahead, bring back your dirty pictures for clean places. But don't forget to shut the door behind you.

Then one day, a couple of years after I'd run into the Kurdish story, I discovered that sunny California enjoyed a direct connection to the war in Turkey. The connection was the weapons business. Kurdistan, like the legacy of American Indian history, was closer than I had realized.

Tax Incentives for Arms Merchants

In the summer of 1995, the County of Santa Barbara Board of Supervisors passed a proposal for the creation of a "foreign trade zone" at the Santa Barbara Airport. The zone was designed to exempt local companies like Delco Systems—ones with government or overseas defense contracts—from paying federal import duties on components and raw materials bought outside the United States. When I looked into it, I found that thousands of county residents worked in the arms industry, producing products sold in the United States and throughout the world. In the local economy, I learned, the weapons business surpassed the oil industry and rivaled tourism. Santa Barbara–made arms helped make southern California the weapons-producing capital of the world. In the 1980s the United States sold more than $134 billion in weapons and military services to more than 160 nations and political movements. American sales increased further during the 1990s. By 1993, the United States controlled nearly 73 percent of the weapons trade to the Third World. The U.S. Arms Control Export Act was intended to prevent American weapons from reaching anti-democratic regimes. In reality, however, strong lobbying by the arms industry ensured a weak oversight of arms exports. According to industry analysts, U.S. weapons were in use in thirty-nine of the world's forty-eight conflicts—*often on opposite sides of the same conflict.* The majority of American arms exports—an estimated 85 percent—went to nondemocratic regimes. Beyond the ethical issues of supporting dictators like Saddam Hussein—as the United States and other countries had done in the 1980s—the glut of weapons sales also posed a danger to American forces. The arming of jihadists in Afghanistan in the 1970s, of Ba'athists in Iraq in the 1980s, and of strongmen in Panama and Somalia had resulted—to use CIA parlance—in "blowback," endangering U.S. citizens and U.S. allies.

By the 1990s, the Cold War was over, but the arms industry still had plenty of customers abroad. In 1994, the armament division of Delco Systems, for example, sold at least $260 million worth of weapons manufactured in Santa Barbara County. In a telephone interview, Delco president Mike Johnston confirmed the figure and conceded that the majority of the sales were made to "foreign customers."

Weapons were big business. Since the collapse of the Berlin Wall in 1989, overseas arms sales for U.S. companies had rung up an eye-opening $82.4 billion. World sales by all other arms makers, by comparison, totaled only $66.8 billion. Since 1986, the United States' share of international weapons manufacturing had skyrocketed from just 13 percent to more than 70 percent. Uncle Sam, in short, had cornered the arms market. My most surprising discovery, however, was the frequent link between taxpayer assistance and corporate military profits. The war between Turkey and the Kurds offered an example of how arms sales and military aid bolstered each other, and how weapons production was enmeshed in the U.S. economy as a whole. From the mid-1980s to the mid-1990s, American companies sold Turkey $9.4 billion in weapons, making Turkey the fifth-largest U.S. buyer (following Saudi Arabia, Japan, Taiwan, and Egypt). The reason, according to William D. Hartung, an analyst at the World Policy Institute and the author of *And Weapons for All,* was the Turkish-Kurdish conflict. It was, he said, "far and away the biggest use of weapons and most aggressive use anywhere in the world." During the same ten years, the American taxpayers gave Turkey a whopping $5 billion in military assistance, part of which went directly to U.S. companies for the purchase of fighter bombers, tanks, missiles, M-16 rifles, and other equipment. There was no doubt about it: The arms business was tax-supported.

Good Kurds, Bad Kurds

Despite the apparent indifference of the U.S. media to the role of American arms in suppressing the Kurdish uprising in Turkey, human rights monitors in the 1990s did their best to report on violations of human rights by the U.S.-equipped Turkish army. In 1996, Stephen Rickard, the director of the Washington office of Amnesty International, told me what Amnesty knew about the abduction of Kurdish villagers in the war zone. "The Turkish military has adopted as a matter of policy the depopulating [of] whole villages," Rickard said in an interview. "Many, many people have simply disappeared. They have been seen taken away by the Turkish forces and then just never seen again."

By the mid-1990s, with the support of U.S. and NATO weaponry, Turkey had leveled, burned, or forcibly evacuated approximately two thousand Kurdish villages. That was roughly one-half the number of Kurdish settlements in Iraq destroyed in Saddam Hussein's infamous *Anfal* campaign during the 1980s, when the defense industry in the West armed Iraq and turned a blind eye to wide-scale human rights violations. In both cases, the public was led to believe that tax-supported weapons sales benefited American jobs and expanded the U.S. economy.

The author Hartung argued that the relative lack of outrage for atrocities in Turkey was "completely based on politics and public relations." In a 1997 interview, Hartung explained how U.S. foreign policy differentiated between what he called "good Kurds" and "bad Kurds." The Kurds oppressed by Saddam Hussein, he said, "are by definition 'good Kurds,' because they help make propaganda against Saddam Hussein. The Kurds who are being slaughtered by our allies in Turkey need to be ignored because it sends a bad message about Turkey."

Anyone who wanted a primer on the use of U.S. military equipment in the 1990s needed only to visit one of the camps in northern Iraq for refugees fleeing the U.S.-equipped Turkish army. One scene in particular stands out in my memory, a visit I made to the Atrush camp in 1996. The camp, located just south of the Turkish border, seemed like an incubator for Kurdish revolution. Young children whose only English vocabulary consisted of the words "Cobra" and "Black Hawk" described through a translator how their villages were hit by Turkish rockets, and how U.S.-made equipment was integral to attacks that caused them to flee. I filmed an old man who told me his eyesight was too bad to distinguish between the Cobra, the gunship built in Texas, and the Black Hawk, the troop carrier manufactured in Connecticut. He said he depended on his ears to warn him that the Cobra was coming. Making guttural sounds, he mimicked the sound of the feared gunship, noting that the frightening noise alerted the villagers to run for their lives:

There are two kinds of helicopters, but because my eyesight is not very good, I cannot recognize them. So whenever I would hear a helicopter coming over our village, I would ask my grandchildren. They would look up in the sky and tell me, "Oh, Grandfather, don't worry, this is just a Sikorsky, you know, the transport helicopter. That cannot harm you, that won't do anything." And sometimes when I would hear one they would tell me,

"Oh, Grandfather, run, run, we have to hide! This is the Cobra coming."
Any child in our village from five to ten years old, they all know which helicopter is which one.

On the day of my visit, residents staged demonstrations against Turkey and in
support of the PKK. Carrying rebel flags and shouting slogans, about fifteen hundred refugees walked to and from Atrush. Among them were hundreds of boys and
girls ages seven to thirteen who marched in practiced formation, coming to a disciplined halt on the command of an adult monitor. It looked like a grammar school
for future guerrillas; most of the children were not even alive when the conflict
started back in 1984. Now they were part of a war that was widening by the day.

In 1996, the year I met the old man in Atrush, the U.S. State Department acknowledged that American arms had been used by the Turkish government in domestic military operations "during which human rights abuses have occurred." In
a report ordered by Congress, the Clinton administration admitted that the
abuses included the use of U.S. helicopters, armored personnel carriers, and F-16
fighter bombers in the destruction of entire Kurdish villages in southeastern
Turkey.

When asked what the difference was between what Saddam did to the Kurds
and what Turkey had done, a State Department spokesman in the Clinton administration was disarmingly candid. According to Assistant U.S. Secretary of
State John Kornblum, "If you're *in the village,* there's no difference whatsoever."

State Department Findings

The State Department report conceded that the Turkish policy had forced up
to two million Kurds from their homes. Some of the villages had been evacuated
and burned, bombed, or shelled by government forces to deprive the PKK of a
"logistical base of operations," according to the report, while others were targeted because their inhabitants refused to join the "village guards," a counterinsurgency strategy that required civilian Kurds to fight Kurdish separatists.
Turkey's village guard system had parallels to Iraq's "modern villages," which
Saddam Hussein had designed in the 1980s to control the Kurds of Iraq. More
than a century earlier, the U.S. Army had forced Native Americans on to guarded
reservations, following a 1923 Supreme Court decision that said that Indians
could not hold title to lands in the United States (the case ruled that the Indians'
"right of occupancy" was subordinate to the United States' "right of discovery," a
decision that led to the controversial strategy of "Indian removal").

The State Department report on Turkey repeated past U.S. criticisms that Turkish forces carried out or at least tolerated "extrajudicial killings" and widespread
torture. The department acknowledged that because U.S. helicopters, fighter

bombers, and personnel carriers were the mainstays of the Turkish military, it could be "assumed that they would be used to transport any security forces perpetrating such acts."

Criticism from humanitarian groups was swift. Human Rights Watch charged that the State Department had issued only "half conclusions" in its report, so as to avoid offending the Turkish government. The New York–based watchdog group, which in the past had also criticized the PKK rebels for rights violations, said that the U.S.-supplied Turkish army was "responsible for the majority of forced evacuation and destruction of villages, usually as punishment for refusal to join the village guard system." A statement issued by London-based Amnesty International declared, "This is not the first time the United States has been sullied by its association with thugs and murderers."

"Sadly," Amnesty's Stephen Rickard told me in a subsequent interview, "I would have to describe the administration's policy on Turkey as a 'yes, *but*' human rights policy. Which is to say, 'Yes, it's tragic what is going on in Turkey, *but* it's a member of NATO. Yes, it's tragic what is going on in Turkey, *but* Turkey [is] so important to the situation in Iraq and Saddam Hussein.' The United States has a sliding scale of values and a sliding scale of human life."

Meeting the Need for Arms

During the Clinton presidency, at the height of the Kurdish uprising in Turkey, Sikorsky Aircraft, the U.S. corporation that manufactures the Black Hawk troop transports, built an assembly plant near Ankara for the Turkish military. Today, the United States has intelligence-gathering posts in Turkey, including a radar installation in the largely Kurdish city of Mardin. The Mardin facility was built by GM Hughes of El Segundo, California, the parent company of Delco Systems in Santa Barbara. The radar site was said to be capable of "seeing" deep into Iraq, Iran, and South Central Asia. In the 1980s, Saddam Hussein had been an important customer of the Hughes Corporation.

There was one way that U.S. arms reached the battlefield in Kurdistan without Congressional oversight. In 1992 and 1993 the Pentagon quietly facilitated a mammoth shipment of heavy weapons slated for reduction after the Cold War under a 1990 treaty on conventional forces in Europe. According to the United Nations Arms Registry, the U.S. government turned over 1,509 tanks, 54 fighter planes, and 28 attack helicopters to Turkey. Instead of scrapping the weapons, they were simply given away. There was no public debate about the transfer and no Congressional oversight. There was little question about the purpose of the unprecedented arms shipment. As the authoritative *Jane's Defence Weekly* revealed in a 1993 report, "a high proportion of defense equipment supplied to Turkey [was] being used in operations against the PKK."

Throughout the 1990s, Amnesty International lobbied the Clinton administration to curtail arms sales to Turkey. With minor exceptions, however, the administration refused to condition exports on certifiable improvements in human
rights. Mark Grossman, a spokesman for the State Department, told me, "Turkey
has a right to defend itself against terrorism, and we look carefully at all weapons
sales." Nevertheless, according to Grossman, "If the Turks would like to buy
them, that's up to them."

Santa Barbara Connection

In the 1990's Delco Systems in Santa Barbara, which was owned by the GM
Hughes Electronics Corporation, made mortar systems and tank turrets. Delco
literature called the Delco/Royal Ordinance 120mm Armored Mortar System
"the most mobile, survivable system available today." A Delco LAV-25 turret, advertised as "combat-proven, mature, versatile, and reliable," had production
commitments at its Santa Barbara plant through 1996 for U.S. and foreign customers, including Kuwait and Saudi Arabia. While most Santa Barbara residents
knew little or nothing of the Kurdish uprising, Delco regarded the conflict in
Turkey as a potential business opening. Company president Mike Johnston told
me that Delco's armament division was "looking at marketing opportunities in
Turkey."

GM Hughes had a long, but largely unknown, connection to Kurdish repression. In the 1980s, during Saddam Hussein's genocidal campaign against the
Kurds, GM Hughes sold sixty transport helicopters to the Iraqi regime. In the
1990s, during the height of the Kurdish uprising in Turkey, Hughes sold thirty
transport helicopters to the government in Ankara. In addition, Hughes sold
Turkey its Advanced Medium-Range Air-to-Air Missile, which the company's
report described as "the international air-to-air weapon of choice."

Santa Barbara Research (SBR), the industry leader in the manufacture of
infrared equipment, made devices for weapons systems and sold them to clients
throughout the world, including Turkey. SBR, a wholly owned subsidiary of Hughes
Aircraft, manufactured the target detectors used in the popular Sidewinder missiles. SBR, which subsequently changed its name to Santa Barbara Remote Sensing,
also sold night-vision equipment to Lockheed for use on its F-16 fighters, a staple
in Turkey's counterinsurgency campaign against Kurdish rebels.

The Lockheed Corporation, one of the largest multinational arms makers, had
about six hundred employees working on military aerospace in Santa Barbara
County, in a joint program with Martin Marietta Materials, Inc. at Vandenberg
Air Force Base. A separate Lockheed division produced the F-16 fighter jet,
which the company sold to fifteen foreign countries, including Turkey. In the
early 1990s, Lockheed built a joint U.S.-Turkish assembly plant for F-16s near

Ankara. By 1995, 152 Lockheed F-16s had been made in Turkey, and another eighty were slated to be built. By then, human rights groups documented a number of civilian fatalities, including the deaths of children, after aerial attacks on Kurdish villages by the Lockheed fighter bombers. In 1992, I personally witnessed the effects of Lockheed bombers on settlements in northern Iraq, where civilian Kurds, including infants, had been killed by aerial bombardment.

Raytheon, a founding member of the American League for Exports and Security Assistance (ALESA), a powerful arms lobby in Washington, made radar-jamming devices in Santa Barbara. The devices were used on F-16s, the fighter jets that conducted the raids on the Kurdish hamlets in northern Iraq. Several other Santa Barbara firms were engaged in the so-called defense business. Toyon Research conducted top-secret research for major military systems; General Research, a recipient of hefty Star Wars contracts in the 1980s, was involved in a variety of arms production deals. Other local companies with military contracts were Mission Research Co., Renco, and Channel Industries.

The proposal for a "foreign trade zone" in Santa Barbara was designed to provide a tax break to companies that imported raw materials from abroad. According to Tim Mahoney, the director of the Santa Barbara Industrial Association in 1995, more than half of the thirty-four corporations in the association had contracts with the U.S. government or with foreign countries, many of them for weapons components. One of the companies was Delco Systems, which imported heavy metals from Canada for tank turrets and sold them to Saudi Arabia and other countries. Turkey had expressed interest in buying turrets from the Santa Barbara plant for use in suppressing the Kurdish uprising. Santa Barbara taxpayers may not have been aware of ethnic strife in Turkey, but arms contracts like this gave them a direct role in subsidizing the conflict.

12

60 Minutes

It's only called fanaticism when you lose.
—PKK GUERRILLA

Pitching a Story

In the spring of 1995, I wrote to *60 Minutes* at CBS proposing a piece on the rising number of rights violations against the Kurds in Turkey and the increasing number of U.S. arms shipments to the Turkish army. At that point, the Kurdish uprising hadn't been on U.S. television, and one of the senior producers invited me to lunch to discuss my proposal for a story. He told me he was interested, but he may have been too busy with other projects to follow up. I never heard from him again.

A few months later, I contacted Jon Wells, an associate producer for Ed Bradley, one of the *60 Minutes* anchors. A former reporter for the *Boston Herald*, Wells had a reputation for hard news. Turkey had caught his attention the year before when *60 Minutes* broadcast a segment on the Paris Air Show, the premier aircraft and technology bazaar that takes place every spring. The big American arms companies Lockheed, Boeing, and Bell Textron were unveiling their newest product lines, and buyers for the Turkish government, he told me, were on a "shopping spree."

Wells did a little research and found out that United States' loan guarantees were behind a plan to build a new Lockheed plant for F-16 fighter jets in Turkey. The number of F-16s needed for the war against Kurdish rebels was increasing rapidly. Wells quickly realized that the American taxpayers were subsidizing Lockheed and helping to underwrite Turkish costs for the ethnic conflict. He was curious as to what the United States was getting in return, so he interviewed an industry representative. The spokesman told Wells that the new U.S.-financed plant near Ankara would "provide American jobs." Wells asked the obvious question: How many jobs?

"One," the representative answered sheepishly.

It was clear to Wells that Turkey's war with the Kurds had a U.S. angle. He was interested, so he brought the idea to John Hamlin, one of Bradley's senior producers. Hamlin, a former ESPN sports producer, had little experience with hard news, but he had been looking for a story with controversy, something that would grab attention. Would it be possible, Hamlin asked me, to land an interview with the notorious leader of the Kurdistan Workers' Party (PKK)?

Hunting the PKK

The rebel boss was Abdullah "Apo" Ocalan. To many Kurds, he was a legend, a leader with godlike status. To the U.S. State Department, he was a terrorist who made war against Turkey, a key NATO ally. Ocalan had never been interviewed on American television. This could be a CBS exclusive. If I could put *60 Minutes* in the same room with the PKK chieftain—and if the producers could convince Ed Bradley to go to the Middle East—Hamlin told me *60 Minutes* would do the story.

The PKK is a clandestine organization in Europe and the Middle East that operated—and still operates—in the shadows. In 1993, I had met what I suspected were rebel operatives in Belgium. The occasion was a large hunger strike staged to bring attention to the war in Turkey, especially to the destruction of Kurdish villages. Neither issue was getting much attention in the press. I was en route from Belgium to Turkish Kurdistan at the time. I already had interviewed Turkish government officials, and now I wanted to interview PKK leaders.

One of the Kurds I met in Belgium went by the name of Ali Saipan. A Turkish Kurd who was rumored to be on the PKK central committee in Europe, Saipan had thick glasses, which gave him more of a European look than a Kurdish one. Few Kurdish men wear eyeglasses, either because they don't need them or can't afford them or because the practice is perceived as a sign of weakness.

Saipan was a cocky guy with a sense of self-importance, which apparently made him feel he could lecture strangers on Kurdish history and world morality at first meeting. Saipan lacked the quiet assurance of the battle-humbled PKK fighters I would later meet in the field, but he tried to impress me by drawing attention to the 9 mm automatic pistol concealed in his jacket. He also had a single-minded agenda, which he hoped to achieve by trading on my need for access to the PKK. He showed me a satellite telephone that he had in a small bag under the table. He wanted me to deliver the phone in Turkey to a "doctor who was helping the Kurds." It wouldn't take up much room in my luggage, he said, and as an American entering Turkey, I would not be scrutinized at customs. After I delivered the phone to the "doctor," he promised, I could visit the rebels. No American journalist had met the PKK, so my interview would be a first. That would be good for the Kurds and good for my career.

I knew the war in the remote mountains of southeastern Turkey depended on such communication devices. It wasn't hard to guess where the satellite phone was really going. The Kurds faced a high-tech army that had jet and helicopter gunships, the latest satellite surveillance, and computerized tanks with thermal sensors to detect the smallest movement by rebels on the ground. I had seen sophisticated Motorola two-way radios in the hands of Turkish officers and village guards. The communication systems were networked, and the PKK was incurring high casualties.

Rebel recruiting had been stepped up in expatriate communities on the Continent, particularly in Germany. Volunteers were being smuggled into Lebanon, trained, and then shepherded through Syria to northern Iraq for more training at rearguard bases, before moving up to the front in Turkey. Money was needed for the war, and Kurdish shop owners in Germany, France, Holland, and other countries were making monthly contributions. The PKK called it "tithing"; critics said that some of it was extortion. In any case, the guerrillas were taking a beating, and the pressure was on. Coordinating logistics between Europe and Turkey was vital, and the guerrillas were desperate for satellite phones.

The meeting went sour when I refused to transport the phone. Saipan wasn't interested in hearing a high-sounding discourse on the values of objective journalism, and there wasn't much I could do to explain my position. Kurds were dying. Talk was cheap. It was a refrain I would hear in the coming years after the events of 9/11, when the shock of the unique and unprecedented attack prompted some foreign correspondents to choose advocacy over accuracy in their reporting. As far as the PKK was concerned, I was "with them or against them."

Despite my refusal to deliver the telephone, Saipan pretended to assist me with my sought-after interviews, but his displeasure was evident. In any event, I set out for Turkey, where I waited several days in a designated hotel to be contacted by the rebels. When no one came, I suspected I had burned my bridges.

Now it was 1995. In the interim, my Kurdish contacts had improved and, from what I could tell, the PKK had become more media savvy. For whatever reason, after only six weeks, I managed to get tentative approval from PKK operatives for CBS to interview Ocalan. Now the big question was where and how the film crew could safely meet the hunted rebel leader. The answer depended on Syrian politics and the guerrillas' need for security.

Syria and the Kurds

It was an open secret that Ocalan was living in Damascus under the quiet protection of President Hafez al-Assad. Kurds had been in Syria for centuries, and, with a population of more than one million, they were the largest ethnic minority in the country. But their current numbers comprised less than 10 percent of the population, and many Syrian Kurds had been Arabized over time. Following World War I and the breakup of the Ottoman Empire, ethnic tensions arose between Kurds and Arabs. In the 1920s and 1930s, French colonists recruited Kurds as a foil to Arab nationalists and gave them a special military unit and other privileges. The practice was similar to the British preference for the Sunni elite in Iraq. In 1946, French troops departed from Syria, but resentment against the Kurds, a legacy of colonial favoritism, continued long afterward.

In 1949, after military officers carried out several government coups in Damascus, it was discovered that some of the coup organizers had Kurdish roots. The discovery intensified friction with the Arab majority. In the late 1950s, during the rise of nationalism and a growing antiforeigner sentiment in Syrian society, memory of the Kurdish role in the coup contributed to a move to purge Kurdish officers from the Syrian army.

In September 1961, the Kurdish Democratic Party launched an uprising in neighboring Iraq. The rebellion caused repercussions in Syria when the KDP tried to open a Damascus branch aimed at securing Kurdish rights in Syria. Unfortunately for the Kurds, the effort coincided with the rising popularity of President Gamal Abdel Nasser in Egypt and a wave of "pan-Arabism" sweeping the Middle East.

Syrian Arabs feared that the Kurdish uprising in Iraq could spread to Syria. In 1962, the government conducted a census that left out tens of thousands of Kurds, stripping them and their descendents of citizenship and the right to own property or to hold government jobs. In the mid-1960s, oppression of the Kurds increased dramatically when the hypernationalist Ba'ath party came to power. Soon the Kurds were required to carry red-colored cards identifying them as foreigners. After the coup that brought Assad to power in 1970, the persecution of the Kurds gradually began to ease. When the Kurds rebelled in neighboring Turkey in the 1980s, Syria allowed thousands of refugees—Turkish Kurds—to resettle in Syria. The Kurds, however, were still noncitizens, subject to discrimination.

Assad's calculated support for Kurdish rights in Turkey was popular in Syria, despite the fact that by now almost two hundred thousand Syrian Kurds lacked citizenship—and might otherwise be clamoring for attention. Assad counted on the support of Turkish Kurds because, among other reasons, Syria still had a territorial dispute with Turkey over Hatay, the predominantly Arab territory on the Mediterranean that Turkey had annexed in 1939.

The current bone of contention—and a key reason that the PKK leadership was allowed to make its headquarters in Damascus—was a raging water dispute between Syria and Turkey. In some areas of the parched Middle East, water was becoming as valuable as oil. In the early to mid-1990s, Turkey made public a controversial plan to flood several ancient Kurdish villages. It was part of an effort to divert the Tigris and Euphrates Rivers for hydroelectric power upstream from the Syrian border.

The massive irrigation project in Turkish Kurdistan, which was known as GAP, involved the construction of twenty-two dams and nineteen hydroelectric plants. It was one of the largest such undertakings in world history. The Turkish government said that when GAP was completed, it would provide irrigation for 1.7 million hectares of land, corresponding to one-fifth of irrigable land in Turkey and accounting for 22 percent of the country's new hydropower. GAP promised to make Turkey a major supplier of water in the region, and government officials soon announced plans to sell tankers of water to other countries, citing Israel, which had provided military assistance in quelling Turkey's Kurdish uprising. (In 2004, Turkey agreed to sell fifty million cubic meters of water a year to Israel, for twenty years.) Proponents used hyperbole to describe the vast network of dams, calling the mammoth project the Eighth Wonder of the World. Downstream in Syria, however, where the giant dams would soon curtail traditional access to the waters of the Tigris and the Euphrates, there was already a water shortage. The Damascus government was using the Kurdish uprising as leverage with the Turks.

While President Assad was playing the PKK card, he was careful to retain plausible deniability. The rebel training bases, after all, were located in Lebanon, a county that was, at least technically speaking, beyond his control. That meant that a meeting between CBS and Ocalan on Syrian soil was out of the question. It would embarrass Assad with Washington, and it would compromise the water negotiations. The Syrian *mukhabarat,* the secret police who monitored Ocalan's movements, would never permit it.

Accordingly, the PKK told me the television interview would have to take place in Lebanon, in the Syrian-controlled Bekaa Valley, an hour's drive from Damascus. The civil war was over in Lebanon, but the Bekaa still had a deserved reputation as a lawless territory. The valley was a training ground for Hezbollah, Hamas, and a number of armed groups—including the PKK. At the time, Lebanon was on the U.S. list of countries Americans were forbidden to visit. As working journalists, the CBS crew would not be subject to the ban, but the Bekaa Valley would be more dangerous to visit than Beirut or Damascus. The CIA and Israel's Mossad were said to be tracking Ocalan. There had already been an attempt on Ocalan's life at a PKK training camp in Lebanon, and a bomb at a wedding in the Kurdish region of northern Syria had narrowly missed him. If word of our trip leaked out and we were followed, the PKK could deal with us as it saw fit and then disappear across the border to Syria. If the guerrillas were going to permit a group of American strangers to see their leader, the meeting would take place at a safe house of their choice, on PKK turf somewhere in the Bekaa Valley.

Story Approval

Once a story is approved at *60 Minutes,* production funds begin to flow. As soon as that happened, I was hired as program consultant, and Jon Wells began buying airline tickets and lining up hotels in Beirut, Cairo, Istanbul, and in southeast Turkey. The wheels had begun to turn, but doubts remained in everyone's mind that we could pull off the unprecedented rendezvous.

On one side, I had to keep convincing *60 Minutes* I could deliver Ocalan—but without sharing confidential sources and contacts that might enable the network to independently assess the risks of the plan while it progressed. On the other side, I needed to assure the PKK that we were journalists, not spies, but security concerns made it impossible to talk to the rebels over the telephone. In the end, I had to rely on messages hand-carried to Damascus by a Parisian who had business in Syria. The system was cumbersome, but it proved workable.

I tapped additional contacts in Frankfurt and Brussels. Germany is a control center for the PKK, which draws support and money from the more than four hundred thousand Kurds who fled Turkey, beginning in the 1960s—some for economic reasons, but the majority in recent years because of the war between the Turks and the Kurds. The contacts promised that if I flew into Beirut, someone from the organization would be there. No one in Europe, however, would give me the name of the person or persons I was to meet.

As a rule of thumb at *60 Minutes,* someone other than the senior producer develops the ideas for stories and does the lion's share of the research. The producer supervises overall aspects of a particular story, tries to keep the weekly segment under budget, and handles internal politics with Don Hewitt, the executive producer and *60 Minutes* founder. However, the journalistic scoop and supporting research on many shows often belongs to someone behind the scenes, a person with the humble title of associate producer. In this case, that was Jon Wells.

Ed Bradley

When the research is finished and the interviews arranged, the correspondent is given a working script that he or she customizes until it feels right. In this case, the correspondent was Ed Bradley.

60 Minutes employs a two-camera setup for interviews, so reaction shots of both the subject and an on-air reporter can be captured in real time. CBS had hired a Greek camera operator, but he encountered a visa problem at the last minute and he couldn't get into Lebanon. We had one camera operator already, an Australian, who would film Ocalan. I ended up operating the camera that filmed Bradley. Like scores of other journalists, Bradley had gone to Iraqi Kurdistan after the Gulf War, but that was 1991 in Iraq, where the underlying story for American viewers was U.S. policy toward Saddam following the liberation of Kuwait. It was clear from talking to Bradley, however, that he hadn't followed the Kurdish story since that time and that he knew nothing about the destruction of Kurdish villages in Turkey. In that matter, he was not alone.

In 1995, at the point *60 Minutes* agreed to the program on American weapons and the Kurdish uprising, no American news outlet even had a bureau in Turkey. Despite the fact that the U.S.-equipped Turkish army had been battling Kurdish rebels for more than a decade, only scant references to the conflict had appeared in the U.S. media. The *New York Times,* which prides itself on being "the paper of record," decided not to base a correspondent in Turkey until 1996. By then, the Turkish army was winning the war, and almost three thousand Kurdish villages had been wiped out. The majority of the estimated 37,000 to die in the fifteen-year conflict (1984–1999)—most of them Kurds—were already dead. The *New York Times* correspondent, who spoke neither Turkish nor Kurdish, settled in Istanbul. He paid little attention to the conflict, with the exception of one attempt to see destroyed villages, an effort that led to an overnight detention at an army garrison. He later bragged to foreign reporters, including me, that Turkey's most senior general had personally apologized for detaining him, ignoring the fact that efforts at damage control were directed at his powerful newspaper, not himself. In any case, the reporter apparently learned his lesson and, as far as I know, he did not seek to re-visit villages in the war zone.

In view of the paucity of news coverage, Bradley might be forgiven for his lack of information. As it turned out, most of what he knew of U.S.-Turkish relations and the Kurdish uprising came from position papers the *60 Minutes* producers had given him in preparation for the upcoming program. Despite the arm-twisting by both producers, the story simply wasn't turning him on. The night before I was to leave Paris for Beirut, two months after the story had been approved, the scheduled program was almost canceled. Jon Wells called me in my hotel room to say that Bradley was having second thoughts about leaving the United States. Wells copied me on the e-mail that Bradley had sent him. It seemed that Ed had gone to dinner with someone in Washington who warned him the PKK was a terrorist group, and that reporting on the rebels could endanger him or compromise his reputation. Apparently, Bradley now believed that the venture was unwise or unsafe, but he was framing his new reservation in journalistic terms. Wells said Bradley was questioning whether *60 Minutes* viewers would be interested in a piece on the PKK: A story on the guerrillas, he argued, could be a flop.

Bradley wanted to call everything off, but Wells and Hamlin convinced him to fly at least as far as Paris, where he had friends to visit, and then to reassess. By then, I would be in Lebanon, where I would do a preinterview with the guerrillas and, if possible, with Ocalan. That would buy time, and let me provide Bradley with an update. It would raise his confidence as well as that of the guerrillas. If the trip looked safe, if things went well for me, Ed and the film crew could follow.

Beirut and the Bekaa Valley

My translator and I landed in Beirut at midnight. As far as I could tell, I was the only American in the airport. Outside the terminal, about five hundred people crowded the reception area, almost everyone speaking Arabic. I heard someone behind me mispronounce my name—something like "Maqurban?" I wheeled around to see two short men with moustaches wearing dark, baggy sport coats, the kind that make it easy to conceal weapons. One of them reached for my bag. The other motioned toward an old Mercedes-Benz at the curb.

I am not sure where I slept that night, but it was somewhere in the Bekaa Valley. It crossed my mind that the PKK had kidnapped dozens of foreigners in Turkey a couple of years earlier. I tried to keep track of the roads, in case the guerrillas took me hostage and I had to make a run for it, but the driver did a lot of circling and doubling back, and after awhile I got confused. We ended up at a safe house in a small town. I was given a tiny room with a bed. When I awoke the next morning, the men who met the plane were gone, and another crew was in the house watching me, making cell phone calls in Kurdish, and occasionally providing me with food. From my window I could see a grape arbor and I could hear the voices of passersby speaking Arabic.

Sneaking into Syria

On the second day a portly man, who was carrying a .38 pistol in a holster under a new leather jacket, showed up. He spoke a little English, informing me that he was a Kurdish merchant from Damascus and that his Turkish-born parents had resettled in Syria in the 1960s. "There has been a change of plans. You're going to meet Apo in Syria," he said. "Leave your luggage here."

A small Ford SUV with a driver waiting behind the wheel was parked outside the house. The merchant got in the passenger side. I grabbed one still camera and climbed in back. As we approached the Syrian border, the man told me to hide the camera on the floor of the car. A uniformed guard at the checkpoint waved us to one side. I had been instructed in advance to stare straight ahead, and at that moment I was quite content to do so. The portly man gave the border guard an official-looking paper to read. After that, he went inside the small security post.

After two minutes or so we were on our way. In less than a half hour, I was looking out the window at thousands of white houses and buildings on a hillside. I was in Damascus, Syria. *Here I am*, I thought, *an American in a terrorist country. Without an entry visa.*

Abdullah Ocalan

Apo's first comment came as an amusing surprise. "I am gratified," he said, "that your government has sent you to meet me." I stared at him in wonder.

Here was the son of a Kurdish farmer from a small village near Urfa, a Turkish city just north of the Syrian border. He had three sisters and two brothers (his younger brother, Osman, would become a PKK commander). Like many Kurdish children, he learned Turkish in school, and it was still his primary language. At an early age he quarreled with his father and left home. In the 1970s, he studied political science at the University of Ankara. He founded a Maoist political group on campus, and, as he told me, began to discover the uniqueness of his own roots as a Kurd. This was in the day when many students had guns, and when political conflicts sometimes were settled abruptly. Scores of killings occurred between right-wing groups like the Gray Wolves and Marxist revolutionary groups like Dev Sol. In 1978, Apo and a dozen associates founded the Kurdistan Workers' Party (PKK).

In 1979, Apo went underground and escaped from the country. In 1980, the Turkish army overthrew the elected government, imposed martial law, and began mass purges of activists, including the urban Kurds. Unlike other left-leaning groups, however, the Kurds had a *land base*. Apo's cadres moved to the countryside, where the PKK began training for organized armed resistance. On July 18, 1984, a small force of Kurds with rifles and grenades ambushed a police station in the town of Semdinli, near the Turkish border with Iran and Iraq. Eighteen policemen were killed. The PKK had launched its revolution.

Apo appeared to be in his midforties, a man of medium height with a barrel chest and a thick moustache. He was bright and personable and quite full of himself. He'd long been estranged from his wife, who, he claimed in a rambling discourse, was a pawn of the Turkish government. Her father had known Atatürk personally, he said, and she was really a "Kemalist" herself. She had used her sexuality inside the PKK, he told me, in the same way Cleopatra had used her own to control Egypt. "I have a Caesar complex," he boasted. "I fell in love with a spy."

Apo quoted Einstein, Mohammed, and Jesus Christ. He also quizzed me about the movie *Forrest Gump*, which was popular at the time. Although he hadn't seen the film, he had heard a lot about the lead character. In Apo's view, Forrest was a little guy who beat the odds. "That is the way I am," he said. That is how Apo got a new nickname. From that time forward, whenever the translator and I needed a code word on the telephone to refer to Ocalan, we called him Forrest Gump.

Apo had no experience in the West. His understanding of the role of the press in society had been formed in Turkey, where the news was subject to military influence, if not control. The only other countries he had visited were Lebanon, Syria, and Bulgaria, places where media freedom was also restricted. In his eyes, it was unlikely that a journalist would be in the Bekaa Valley without the permission of his government.

It followed, then, that this visit had the imprimatur of Washington. Thus, it represented, at least in his mind, the long-awaited "back channel" to the besieged Kurds.

To me, of course, that was absurd.

I wanted to tell him that if American authorities knew his whereabouts at that moment and had an opportunity to kill or capture him, my presence would offer him no protection. Instead, I emphasized that in America the press and the government were separate institutions. Apo listened politely, but I doubted my comments made much of an impression. My job was to convince him that *60 Minutes* was not a CIA front, and that an interview with CBS was worth the risk to him and the PKK. When I told him that the program would be watched by millions of Americans, few of whom had ever heard of the PKK, he acted surprised, betraying an isolation from global media awareness I had not expected. When I said that the Kurdish uprising in Turkey had never been on the front page of *any* American newspaper, and only rarely had an article about it appeared elsewhere in U.S. news, he appeared to be genuinely shocked. "Everyone knew about the *Vietnam War*," he said, visibly puzzled. "How could Americans *not* know about the war in Turkey?"

"It hasn't been on television," I replied.

"It's a 'Go'"

I sent a message to Jon Wells: Ocalan would do the interview.

Wells and Hamlin rounded up the video crew and headed for Beirut. We met in a luxury hotel on the top of a mountain overlooking the Mediterranean Sea. It was high above the city in an isolated spot recommended by the Lebanese bodyguards CBS had hired to protect us. It turned out they were ex-militia types who had worked for one of the warlords in the wake of Lebanon's civil war. They knew the Beirut nightclub scene, boasting that they could get "cocaine and hookers," and they shadowed us around the hotel like comic book heavies.

Ed Bradley insisted the bodyguards be present for the Ocalan interview for our protection. They would be "our guys," he said, in case of trouble. The PKK nixed the idea, making Bradley even more unhappy about doing the story. Wells and Hamlin thought they could convince Bradley to come to Beirut, but were afraid he'd balk at going on to our next scheduled stop, southeastern Turkey. The trip would add a long day of flying and a night in both Cairo and Istanbul. Turkish Kurdistan was in conflict, and Bradley felt that *60 Minutes* could obtain stock footage without our physically going there. He didn't think the trip was necessary, but the producers and I argued that viewers of the show needed to see the correspondent in the context of a destroyed Kurdish village. We had written the "stand-up" for Bradley to deliver. He needed to *be* in Turkey to deliver it.

After Bradley arrived in Beirut, the bodyguards were dispatched to locate some Cuban cigars for him. They found him a $220 box of Habanas. The next day, John Hamlin sent the gunmen to take Bradley shopping in Beirut for antiques for his Manhattan apartment—"to keep him happy." It was a matter of good psychology. "If Ed is happy," the producer said, "things will go better for the story."

PKK security wanted half of the crew to sleep at the Bekaa safe house the night before the interview, in order to set up the equipment in advance. I guessed the guerrillas also wanted to get a look at the strangers who would be so close to their boss. I stayed in a nearby hotel, where Hamlin and I rehearsed the questions with Bradley. A PKK car picked us up in the morning. We did the usual circling and doubling back before we met Apo at the safe house. The place was full of armed men with machine guns, including one guy with a ceremonial, gold-plated AK-47.

The CBS crew posed for souvenir snapshots with the militants, and the interview itself went like clockwork.

Then Apo sent somebody for takeout food. There were eight of us for lunch, including Bradley and myself, and a half dozen armed fighters. The table was piled high with dolmas, kebabs, fish, and large pieces of beef and lamb. Bradley was directed to sit on one side of Apo, and I was placed on the other. A PKK photographer with a point-and-shoot camera circled the table, taking multiple photographs of the special guests.

Apo filled his plate with gusto and started eating. Bradley quietly picked at his food. At one point the PKK chieftain grabbed two large bones of lamb meat, which were dripping with juice. He used his hands to rip apart the bones, snapping them with an audible *pop,* and beamed. Then with a flourish Apo took the largest bone between his fingers, leaned across the table, and plopped it down on Ed's plate.

Just like that.

I glanced over at Ed. He was sitting there, speechless, in his tan safari jacket, a gold earring in his left ear, staring at the hand-delivered meat on his plate, his eyes opened wide. It may be an honor in the Middle East for a man to feed you from his own hand, but from the look on Bradley's face at the moment, I wasn't sure he saw it that way. There was a pause. Apo kept smiling. Ed managed to say "thank you." Then he looked down, his attention refocusing on the new food item.

Highwaymen

Apo and his security detail were the first to leave. The portly man quickly led everyone to the cars for the trip across the border to Damascus.

We loaded the TV equipment into a pickup truck and two cars and then set out for the ninety-minute drive to our Beirut hotel. The drivers wanted to avoid the Syrian military checkpoints, so we split up to lessen attention. I was in the backseat of the old Mercedes, and the same driver who met me at the airport was at the wheel. He motioned for us to fasten our seat belts. The Syrians had recently opened a campaign to promote road safety. There was no reason to break the law.

The CBS soundman was next to me. John Hamlin was in the front passenger seat. The two video cameras and the other equipment, a total value of about $150,000, were safely in the trunk. Best of all, we had our prize, the exclusive interview we had come all this way to get—"the gold," as a Hollywood friend likes to call raw film or tapes after a successful shoot. "We did it!" Hamlin said, clearly relieved.

"Next, can you get me Pol Pot?" he asked me. I couldn't tell whether he was joking.

En route to Beirut, in a crowded market town, the unexpected happened. We were crawling through traffic on a narrow two-lane street when a Volkswagen Beetle tried to pass us on the right. The driver needed part of the sidewalk to squeeze by—and he almost made it. At the last minute his left rear bumper hooked on the right front bumper of our big Mercedes. The little car slammed on the brakes in front of us and stopped, blocking the road. Two athletic-looking Arab men quickly got out. They were more than six feet tall and both were wearing tennis shoes and stylish black running suits with white stripes running down the pant legs. They wore dark glasses.

There was no damage to the Mercedes, but the little VW bumper was twisted like a pretzel. The strangers peered inside the Mercedes, noticing the foreigners. One of them began berating the driver, calling him names in Arabic, pointing to the site of the collision, and demanding money.

We were in the notorious Bekaa Valley, a no-man's-land only partially under control of the Syrians. There would be no recourse to insurance companies or the courts; such niceties didn't exist in the territory. Our Kurdish driver was calm, despite the fact that in all likelihood he was an illegal immigrant in Lebanon. The man had grown up in a conflicted area of Turkey, speaking both Turkish and Kurdish, but here he would always be an outsider, a citizen of neither Lebanon nor Syria. Like Kurds in the diaspora around the world, there was no law he could point to, no piece of paper to guarantee this right or that right. Still, like any good urban guerrilla under the circumstances, he spoke Arabic, the local language of commerce and power. Plus, as we soon would see, he had the moxie of an underground man, someone who knew enough not to overreact when challenged.

It was simple: We were being ripped off. Held up by bandits in running suits. This was just like the scam in the States—someone slams on the brakes, triggers an accident, and tries to collect on the spot. Unlike in the States, however, time wasn't on our side. If this thing were to snowball, we could lose the car, the cameras—and, worst of all, the interview tapes.

The driver slowly maneuvered the big Mercedes to the side of the street. For a moment I thought he might just drive off. That was a potential solution, although maybe not the wisest. One of the "sportsmen" was escorting us, his right hand hanging on the open door of the car, the verbal tirade unremitting.

A part of me was fascinated. This was the first thing in the Bekaa that hadn't gone smoothly. The accident—or whatever this was—wasn't in the PKK's carefully planned script. I tried to guess how our driver was going to get himself—and us—out of the soup. Like a movie viewer with special knowledge, I had seen the bulge in the pocket of his baggy suit coat. At least one of the characters in this drama was armed. The disciplined PKK man seemed more than a match for the two sportsmen in running outfits. In the worst-case scenario—if the episode turned into punks against guerrillas—surely the punks would lose.

Our driver appeared calm, letting on nothing. Only moments earlier the risks to his boss, Abdullah Ocalan, had seemed to be over. The Americans hadn't turned out to be spies, after all. No GPS transmitter had led the CIA to the safe house. Apo seemed pleased at the prospect of landing on television in America, the country that was bankrolling the war against the Kurds. The CBS interview could be a political home run. Now the mission was to get these passengers safely to the hotel. However, if the tapes in the trunk with his leader's words were lost, or if the special guests in the Mercedes were harmed, the driver would pay for it. When a guerrilla army has its back to the wall, there is no room for accidents. The policy on mistakes is zero tolerance. In war, "sorry" doesn't cut it.

As soon as the car was off to the side, the Arab escort quickly thrust his hand to the dashboard. Before the Kurd could stop him, he had snatched the keys from the ignition and disappeared.

"Na-bosh?" I asked the driver in my simple Kurdish. "Bad?"

The driver sat for a moment, saying nothing. Then he opened the door and got out, melting into the small crowd that had begun to gather. The three Americans were alone in the parked car. "This doesn't look so good," the soundman said softly.

The car windows, except for the driver's, were rolled up. Presently, the lead sportsman returned to our car. The crowd of rubberneckers seemed to know him. I guessed we'd had the misfortune of landing in his hometown. I watched him slide along the passenger side of our vehicle, coming up behind the front door.

Then I saw the pistol.

It was probably only a .32 or a .38, far smaller than the automatic I guessed our driver was carrying—but it was a gun—and the PKK man was nowhere in sight.

The gunman tapped the barrel of the pistol on Hamlin's window. Was this a stickup? I felt for the wad of bills I had stashed in my sock. My mind began to race.

This was John's first trip to the Middle East. Now he had a gun at his window. The intruder tried to open Hamlin's door. It was locked. John pretended to ignore him. The man shouted something in Arabic through the closed glass. John kept his back to him for a moment before spinning around in panic to respond. His words sounded annoyed and bewildered. Under less serious circumstances, they might have struck me as comical.

Hamlin turned and gestured at the window, trying to dismiss the Arab with a wave of his hand.

"No *hablo!*" he yelled, coming down hard on the silent *h*.

"No *hah blow!*"

A totally irrational thought entered my mind.

Shoot him, I said to myself, quickly suppressing the thought.

Get it over with.

Here we were trying to escape from the Bekaa Valley with our exclusive PKK videos, and we had some yahoo on board experimenting with his two words of Spanish. This was Lebanon, however, not "an ethnic encounter" with someone trying to wash our windshield on Tenth Avenue in Manhattan.

At that moment our driver returned, sliding into the seat behind the wheel. He turned to Hamlin and asked for money. John quickly thrust a handful of $100 bills at him. The driver got out of the car. We watched him walk across the street with the Arab, who by then had stuck his pistol back into the waistband of his running pants.

Less than five minutes later, the driver was back. He had the keys in his hand. As we drove away, the driver leaned over to John and returned all but $40 of the money. I caught his expression in the mirror. He wasn't gloating, not a trace. Maybe it was the culture, but the Kurd was stone-faced. He acknowledged me, but he seemed too professional to smile.

I quickly took stock of what had happened. There had been a collision in the Bekaa Valley. Our immigrant driver had negotiated a happy resolution. The entire transaction had been conducted in U.S. currency, with change provided. After all the threats and excitement, the whole deal had been settled for a lousy forty bucks.

The PKK man had kept his cool.

The Americans were going home.

The Kurds would be on *60 Minutes*.

13

PKK Visit, 1996

Tea, tobacco and a Kalashnikov: That is a guerrilla.

—DASHIN, PKK GUERRILLA

I have passed with a nod of the head
Or polite meaningless words,
Or have lingered awhile and said
Polite meaningless words.

—W. B. YEATS

Rank and File

It was another year of Kurds killing Kurds. The Iraqi Kurdish factions were deep in civil war; several thousand fighters were dead or wounded on both sides. The Kurdish Democratic Party (KDP) still monopolized revenues from oil smuggling to Turkey, and the Patriotic Union of Kurdistan (PUK) still controlled Erbil, the largest city in the breakaway Kurdish enclave. U.S. efforts to broker a peace between the parties had failed miserably. The previous year, Iraqi intelligence had blown the cover of a CIA team based in northern Iraq, exposing another plot to overthrow Saddam Hussein. U.S. credibility among the Kurds was at an all-time low. More divided and hopeless than ever before, the Kurdish parties now appealed to rival powers in Baghdad and Tehran.

Massoud Barzani's KDP secretly procured artillery and other weapons from Saddam Hussein. Jalal Talabani's party, the PUK, did the same from Iran. The Iraq-Iran war, stalemated in the 1980s, now continued by proxy through the Kurds.

The conflict climaxed on August 31, 1996, when Iraqi tanks, invited by the KDP, crossed into Kurdistan and recaptured the city of Erbil. The bold Iraqi offensive sent chills across the north. The Military Command Center in Zakho, where I had eaten my lobster dinner with American officers, was abandoned in the middle of the night as coalition officials and CIA agents hastily fled across the border to Turkey.

Less lucky were the Kurds suspected of working for U.S. intelligence. Hundreds were captured by Iraqi troops in Erbil and quickly executed. Within weeks, almost five thousand Iraqi Kurds and their families escaped to Turkey. Relief agencies eventually relocated the new refugees to Fargo, North Dakota, and Nashville, Tennessee.

In Turkey, the PKK-led uprising was now twelve years old. Turkish soldiers and Kurdish rebels were killing one another in greater numbers, but the Turkish army was finally getting the upper hand. More than three thousand settlements had already been burned, and Kurdish families were fleeing to the cities by the tens of thousands. Kurdish rebels continued to target pro-government Kurdish village guards and their families. The civilian population was caught in the middle, and human rights groups condemned both the guerrillas and state forces. Representative John Porter (R-IL), one of the few members of the U.S. Congress to express concern, told me the conflict between the guerrillas and the Turkish state pitted "terror against terror."

There seemed to be no end in sight. The war in Turkey, still largely ignored by the U.S. media, had spilled into Iraq, and the region seemed to be spinning out of control. The breakaway Kurdish enclave in northern Iraq, struggling to rebuild thousands of villages destroyed by the Baghdad regime, had already been partitioned by two Kurdish armies. The additional presence of PKK rebels from Turkey threatened to tip the balance in the civil war.

At first, the PKK allied itself with the PUK. That gave the Kurdistan Workers' Party (PKK) fighters sanctuary in Iraq from the Turkish army, and it gave the PUK support against its own nemesis, the KDP Kurds. That meant Iraqi Kurds (PUK) and Turkish Kurds (PKK) were now killing Iraqi Kurds (KDP). In turn, Iraqi Kurds (KDP), allied with the Turkish army, were killing Turkish Kurds (PKK) and Iraqi Kurds (PUK). The border, a constant battlefield of soldiers and guerrillas and Kurdish factions, seemed increasingly arbitrary as an international boundary. Kurdish nationalism had never been bloodier, its adherents never more divided. On both military and political fronts, the Kurds were self-destructing.

In the spring of 1996, I went to a nondescript office on the second floor of a strip mall in Orange County, California. It was the Syrian consulate, and I was there to obtain a visa. Few Americans visited Syria in those days. The assistant chargé d'affaires, a friendly Syrian woman in her midfifties, was eager to describe ancient ruins and other tourist sites in her country, but I was there because I needed to use Syria as a stepping-stone; from there, I was planning to sneak into Iraq and Turkey.

By then, I was familiar with southeast Turkey and with both the Turkish army and the Kurdish population. I had met the leadership of the PKK in Lebanon, but not the rank-and-file rebels at the front. Only a few European journalists had visited the guerrilla camps in the Turkish mountains; no American reporter had done so. The foot soldiers of the twelve-year-old Kurdish uprising were still a mystery to me, and I was determined to see them for myself. With contacts still fresh from the *60 Minutes* trip to the Bekaa Valley, I made arrangements with PKK intermediaries, booked a ticket, and flew to Damascus.

When I landed in the Syrian capital it was midnight; the airport terminal was nearly deserted. I approached the customs table, worried about the professional-looking camera equipment in my bags, but officials only glanced at my tourist visa and waved me through politely without inspection. I proceeded directly to the parking lot, where two men in bulky sport coats, PKK operatives, were waiting by an old Mercedes. Once again, one of the strangers mumbled something that resembled my name. He opened the car door, and I got into the backseat. I was driven to a local safe house, one of many that I would see in the weeks to come. It was the start of a tour of the PKK infrastructure, a chance to see first-hand what made the notorious rebels tick.

The guerrillas lived in a rambling two-story stucco house in Damascus on a street lined with orange and loquat trees. It was a quiet neighborhood of upper-middle-class Syrian families, not at all the seedy address I had imagined would be occupied by a group designated by the U.S. State Department as one of the foremost terrorist organizations in the world. The entryway, full of shoes parked in tidy, disciplined rows, opened into a large living room with a high ceiling, gilded chandeliers, and flowered wallpaper. A white overstuffed couch faced four matching armchairs. On the wall at one end of the couch was a smiling picture of Syrian President Assad. At the other end, in perfect symmetry, was a smiling picture of Abdullah Ocalan.

Down the hall was a bathroom with a matching peach-colored toilet, tub, sink, and bidet. A folded towel and fresh bar of soap greeted each visitor. What an odd introduction, I thought to myself, to the organization responsible for the longest-running Kurdish rebellion in Turkish history.

The dress for PKK men was a study in monochrome: baggy, gray shirts with button-down collars and large, double-breasted pockets. The women wore large, baggy shirts buttoned at the top, tails outside the pants, and simple vests. Most of the women fixed their long, dark hair in a single braid down their backs. Everyone looked scrubbed and ready.

The attention to the Kurdish cause was total and consuming: endless revolving traffic of people coming into and going out of the house or sitting poised on the edges of their chairs. The house was a place of constant motion, nervous energy, and almost obsessive order. Guerrillas answered phones, fingered the TV remote, sliced vegetables, did the dishes, cleaned the terrazzo floors, straightened the woven carpets, and vied to jump up to answer the doorbell. Each rebel carried at least two pens, and everybody seemed to have a specific assignment. Some sat in twos on the couch or the overstuffed chairs, drinking Kurdish tea from steaming glasses, exchanging information in hushed tones, methodically jotting down plans or tasks in their pocket-sized notebooks. Everyone and everything existed for the revolution. There was no time to waste.

The bookcase held photo albums of fighters and refugees, PKK pamphlets, dictionaries in various languages, Amnesty International reports, and political novels like B. Traven's *Rebellion of the Hanged*. Each shelf had stickers in Kurdish neatly labeling the contents. One of the books was Sun Tzu's *The Art of War,* the ancient military treatise. A guerrilla told me the book was about "two wars": the war against the outside enemy, the easy one, and "the war inside ourselves," the hard one.

There were two TV sets and two VCRs in the living room. One of the television sets was tuned to a Turkish satellite station for news of the war, the other to MED TV, the pro-PKK channel based in Belgium. On the wall above was a large clock with a portrait of Dogan, the Kurdish prisoner who burned himself to death in a Turkish jail on *Newroz* day, 1982. The image, an icon to the PKK movement, was reminiscent of the famous photo of the Buddhist monk who immolated himself in Saigon in 1963.

On my first night in the house, MED TV broadcast a spaghetti western about the struggle of American Indians. The subject was a rebel favorite, not surprisingly, and the movie had been dubbed into Kurdish. In the film, the Indians— played by Italian actors wearing wigs—put up a heroic resistance, but in the end, as might be expected, they are massacred by the U.S. Cavalry.

One of the rebels, a young woman whose nom de guerre was Newroz (New Year), told me that she was constantly tired. In Turkey, she had been on the move at night; during the day, she'd napped only for short stretches. Her legs had become accustomed to the ups and downs of the mountains. In Syria, where the land was flat, she managed to sleep four to five hours a night, and she said she felt disoriented.

According to Newroz, the PKK required cadres to "break down time into units smaller than seconds." The relentless attention to time filled every day with multiple activities, a rigor designed to "save your life." Like all the guerrillas, she had a wristwatch, and she consulted it frequently. The face of the watch displayed a photo of Apo. Like the image of the martyr on the clock, the watch kept one question in constant focus: "What time is it now for the revolution?"

The guerrillas referred to each other as *heval,* which means "someone who is heading the same way," in this case, in the direction of Kurdish liberation. Newroz said that every aspect of the rebels' existence depended on discipline, beginning with their equipment.

In the field, she said, she carried one magazine of thirty rounds in her AK-47, four loaded magazines on her vest, and 150 rounds in a backpack, plus sleeping and eating gear, plus "personal luggage" like clothing and photos. In addition, Newroz kept three grenades on her belt. Before each battle the rebels danced and sang Kurdish songs. If they survived the battle, they danced and sang again. "The side that makes the *plans*," she maintained, "is stronger."

Unlike the Turkish army, the guerrillas did not have high-tech weapons, and survival depended on rigorous conservation of limited resources. Except for emergency encounters, militants were forbidden to fire their weapons on automatic. After firefights, they had to account for each bullet used. To prevent capture and torture, they were taught to save the last bullet or grenade for themselves.

Newroz said that fighting Turkish soldiers was different from fighting the Kurdish *peshmerga* in Iraq. The Turks had vastly superior forces and would send one unit directly at the PKK while other units encircled the rebels to trap them from behind. In addition, she said, the Turkish army treated male and female rebels equally as the enemy. In contrast, the KDP fighters, she claimed, made "primitive" attacks from a single direction, sometimes yelling things like "Barzani is great!"

She dismissed the KDP tactics as "feudal," a common PKK term of contempt for Iraqi Kurds. She claimed the KDP members were "burdened by wives, children, and gardens," that they fought by day and went home by night. "People who have nothing to lose cannot make war," she said, because they have "no ideology" to sustain them. "They are fighting for their *villages*, not for Kurdistan."

According to Newroz, the KDP believed that Kurdish women "should be in the kitchen and not on the battlefield." For this reason, they sometimes tried to "catch"—to capture alive—a female PKK member without shooting at her. Newroz snickered when she said the word "catch," as if to underscore her claim that the *peshmerga* were backward people.

Upon overhearing Newroz's remarks, a male PKK fighter took issue with her view of the KDP. "Actually, they fight well, one-on-one," he said. "They don't have the military planning of the Turks, and they are unpredictable, but they have experience as hunters in the mountains and they come on like wild animals."

The conversation moved to other subjects, beginning with the use of tobacco. The PKK discouraged smoking, but it was not forbidden. "After ten years in the mountains," Newroz told me, a smoker "doesn't have the lungs for running." She said the guerrillas had few material possessions, that they didn't drink, and they were not allowed to have sex. I didn't see anything to dispute that claim, at least not among the rank and file. (The practice among the leadership, away from the mountains, was rumored to be otherwise.) "Our clothes, even our personalities belong to the PKK," she said. "We marry the party."

In the words of another rebel, the guerrillas were like an octopus: many arms "with one brain." The brain, of course, belonged to Abdullah Ocalan, the founder and chief of the Kurdistan Workers' Party. Whether from blind loyalty to the dream of a Kurdish homeland or total indoctrination, the secret movement had survived.

Waiting to Sneak Across the Border

A lot of journalism is waiting for an appointment or contact or lead, or for someone to return a phone call. At this point, I was waiting for a crop of PKK recruits and supplies to arrive from training camps in Lebanon. Together, I was told, we would be smuggled across to Iraq and on to the Turkish border. It wouldn't be safe to go for another week, one of the commanders said, "until the moon was dark."

I was impatient to understand what drove so many young people to sacrifice their lives in this uprising, but I tried to keep in mind that my primary goal wasn't getting footage of "bang-bang" between the rebels and the Turkish army—although that might guarantee my story got on TV.

After a couple of days without leaving the house, I had a good case of cabin fever, so the guerrillas suggested we take a tour of the capital. Damascus is considered one of the cornerstones of world civilization, with roots in Roman, Jewish, Christian, and Islamic history. The story of St. Paul's conversion on the road to Damascus plays a key part in the early development of Christianity, and the city was once the headquarters for the Umayyads, the Muslim empire that controlled the Middle East. Damascus was first settled as early as 6,000 B.C., making it the longest continuously inhabited city in the world. There were plenty of tourist sites, but our first stop was the tomb of Salahuddin (Saladin). The tomb, which is adjacent to the Umayyed Mosque, a masterpiece of Islamic architecture erected about A.D. 700, is a major attraction in the Arab world. Oddly, the famous burial crypt offers no clue to the ethnicity of the deceased. As a result, many visitors may not realize that Salahuddin, the legendary warrior, was a Kurd, not an Arab.

My escort that day was a twenty-two-year-old PKK woman, the daughter of Turkish Kurds who had immigrated to New Zealand in the 1970s. Her older brothers were members of the PKK, and she had been steeped in the Kurdish movement since childhood. As I left the building, I looked back, catching her in an unguarded moment. She was running her fingers over an old, embroidered cloth that was draped over the tomb, examining the weave of the fabric. It appeared she was meditating.

In fact, she was getting ready to remove one of the gold threads surreptitiously. With a single stealthy twist of the wrist, she snapped it off, quickly exiting the burial crypt with her prize. When she realized I'd seen her, she smiled and looked away with a hint of righteousness, as if to say: Look here, I am a partner in this history, not a tourist. This souvenir *belongs* to me.

Five hours north of Damascus lay Aleppo, a city of two million in Syria near the Turkish border. Aleppo had a large Kurdish population, many of them refugees from Turkey. The PKK had recruited heavily in the area, and the militants were eager to show me the depth of their following.

Most of the Kurds were poor, living in dingy eight-story, Soviet-style tenements without an elevator. On one of several visits, I met about a dozen old men. We sat on flowered couches around a table and a vase or two of wilting roses. Everyone was smoking, and the clean lace tablecloth, apparently set out in expectation of my visit, competed for attention with several overflowing ashtrays. The walls displayed photos of Apo posing with guerrillas, the sons and daughters of local families who left their homes in Syria and crossed the nearby border to fight the Turkish army. The corners of the photos were curled and the color had shifted from years of exposure to the light. Later I would learn that many of the young people smiling in the pictures with their leader were already dead.

The host in each apartment filled and refilled my tea glass, insisting on extra spoonfuls of sugar; the others nodded and whispered their approval in Kurdish. I was the first American the men had met, and at times they would lean forward to get a better look at the stranger.

One man spoke English. "Are you *really* an American?" he asked.

I was taken aback by the innocence of the question. Could the presence of a real, live American be a sign that Kurdish luck was changing? Would the foreigner sitting in the home of Syrian Kurds make a difference after he left, when he returned to the faraway places where things were decided? The sense of isolation and helplessness seemed palpable.

I showed him my passport.

"Please tell your people about the Kurds," he said.

Fresh tea was offered. Most of the men were content to stare respectfully, but one wanted to speak. He leaned forward, fingering a worn cigarette case: "Kuwait has only four hundred thousand people, yet they are a nation, with *ministries and passports*. We have thirty million Kurds, but we have nothing. No country. *Nothing.*"

The tenement dwellers reminded me of the old Indian traditionalists I'd first met on the South Dakota reservation in the winter of 1973. They lived in log shacks with mud plastered between the logs to keep out the wind. They, too, were the keepers of the flame.

In one particular place, the Indians were gathered around a woodstove talking Lakota and rolling tobacco by the light of an oil lamp, and their shadows flickered across the wall. An icebox dominated one corner, and mattresses covered the loose boards on the floor. A bag of Wonder bread lay on one mattress, and kids in pajamas were eating jelly sandwiches.

Out back, behind the shack, there was a little junkyard where carcasses of "Indian cars," as they call them on the "Rez," had been put to rest. After supper, the old men went there to build a fire, to cook the rocks for their sacred sweat lodge.

At first, it seemed like an incongruous place to pray. The men seemed like diehards as they stood outside in the snow in their droopy skin with only towels around them, quoting the famous Lakota warrior Crazy Horse. "One does not sell the land upon which the people walk." They were passing around a pipe, pretending it wasn't winter. Making believe this was still Indian country, not the United States of America.

Were these people feeding a dream? Or was it a fantasy—even fanaticism—a goal line stand against extinction of a race?

I could see that they drew their power from those who came before them. I asked them what they thought of AIM, the American Indian Movement, the militant group founded in the Minneapolis ghetto in 1968. At the time, AIM was only five years old, but already it had instigated the armed takeover of Wounded Knee and caused a number of other civil disturbances. One grizzled old guy looked at me, unimpressed. He replied in Lakota-accented English, "I was AIM in 1920."

For some Indians—and for some Kurds in northern Syria—a different sense of time existed: The past, indeed, was prologue.

Syrian Kurdistan

The network of PKK supporters in Syria made me feel I had entered a protective bubble: People fed me and my guides, families offered their beds, cars with drivers showed up to take us places. For the believers, it was all part of nation building. Everything was provided, everything understood, and nobody asked for a receipt. In one Kurdish village I sat on the floor in a circle of Kurds, eating flat bread, chicken, and rice from communal pots. One of the group, a man in his late sixties, was something of a local hero. He told me he had fought against the governments of Iraq, Iran, and Turkey, at different times in the 1970s and 1980s. Everyone called him "the oldest guerrilla." He said his twenty-year-old son had tried to follow his example, but had been captured in Turkey two years earlier and had died in police custody. His body had showed signs of torture. "Kurdistan is one," the man declared a little loudly—possibly for the benefit of my escorts. "Kurdistan is the key to Mesopotamia—the question of the Kurds must be solved or there will be no peace in the Middle East."

OK, I said, so you have crossed borders of three countries to fight for your people, but here in Syria the Kurds are not even allowed to have their own schools. Why not fight *here*?

He was reluctant to tell me, adding, a little more quietly, that no one wanted trouble with the government. Someone else said, "The circumstances are different. We have no mountains in Syria. We cannot fight here. We must think of our international interests."

At that point, Dashin, one of my escorts, jumped into the conversation. Dashin had lost two of his three brothers in the war, and the PKK was keeping him and his other sibling, a sister, away from the front lines. The uprising was in Turkey, he said, because that was the country where the Kurds were treated the worst.

"The Kurds are fifth-class citizens in Turkey," he explained, "fourth class in Iraq and third class in Iran." In Syria, he said, the Kurds are second-class citizens. "If we are stopped by the police," he said, suddenly concerned about my ability to be discreet, "please don't say anything about the Kurds."

We spent one night in the house of a Kurdish olive farmer near Syria's border with Turkey, close enough that we could see the gun towers and minefields on the Turkish side. Like other PKK supporters I'd met, the farmer had photos of Apo and PKK fighters on the walls of his home. I knew by now that Apo did not command from the field, so I assumed the photos had been taken in the relative safety of the training camps in Lebanon.

The next morning we sat in a sunlit orchard alongside the farmhouse, eating olives and talking about "tithing" to the revolution. Everyone was still in slippers, and the air smelled of jasmine. The farmer told me and my rebel escorts that olives had been harvested on the land for at least a thousand years. He said that he contributed several barrels of olive oil to the PKK every month. The men smoked and drank tea and talked politics, as was their custom. Nearby, the women swept and washed the stone path.

In the city of Afrin, a well-to-do Kurdish restaurant owner treated me to lunch. With his flashy print shirt and his thin moustache, he might have passed for a local movie star. I was surprised to learn he had sent all three of his sons across the border to Turkey to fight for the PKK. Before joining the guerrillas, he said, they had been careful to complete their military service in the Syrian army. "I am ready to give their lives in the war against the Turks," he said. "When we get news of another *shahid* [martyr], there is rejoicing in the town, because that proves they [the rebels] are fighting." While I couldn't be sure, I thought the man was boasting. From everything I knew, the PKK was losing the war, and a disproportionate share of the rebel canon fodder was coming from Syria. "Within a couple of hours of the news [of a death]," he said unconvincingly, "another eight to ten volunteers leave for the border."

He asked me why the United States supported Turkey. I told him it was because of Turkey's strategic location near the former USSR and because it borders the trouble spots of Iraq and Iran. Look at the map, he said. "If America agreed to make a deal with the Kurds, you could have your jets on our land." I was sure that the Kurds figured in U.S. strategy, but I did not think American plans included the PKK. "Whose group could we make the deal with?" I asked. "With Apo? Or Barzani? Or Talabani? Aren't the Kurds too divided to make deals?"

The owner nodded his head politely. I ordered a bottle of Syrian beer, asking him to join me. He declined politely. "I will drink many beers," he said, "when there is a Kurdistan."

By now I had been waiting in Syria for seven days. Each night, the moon was waning. I kept trying to imagine what lay ahead. The guerrillas kept making calls from pay phones to Damascus to report on their "charge" and to get more direction about what to do with me. Things were beginning to drag. Maybe all the logistics—arranging cars, guns, routes, bribes, fake documents—just took extra time. I hoped I wasn't undergoing a test, being observed over a period of time before being allowed to see the "family jewels," the PKK troops. I wasn't a prisoner, but my time wasn't my own. No one could—or would—tell me what was going on.

My next escorted activity was a trip to Palmyra, the desert oasis on the old Silk Road. Palmyra is famous for a group of well-preserved Greco-Roman ruins dating to the reign of Zenobia, the powerful queen who drove the Roman armies from Syria in the third century A.D. On the day of my visit to the famous ruins, however, the only power in evidence was the *mukhabarat,* the secret police, whose many jobs include monitoring foreigners at Syrian tourist sites. Up until the point the plainclothes agents came within earshot, my PKK escorts had expressed little interest in the famous archaeology. When the police approached, Dashin abruptly started gesturing toward the crumbling columns of the amphitheater, holding forth in spotty English as if he were my tour guide rather than an official "sitter" of journalists. I was aware of the fact that he had false identity papers, so I played along. "If the mind of the human is strong," he said, pointing to an ancient arch and colonnade while he drew on his PKK ideology, "the victory will stay for a long time for the people to see." Later, over dinner in the Damascus safe house, I recounted the Palmyra story and Dashin's sudden, police-inspired interest in antiquities. The other guerrillas laughed uproariously, one of them to the point of tears.

The next day my guide was Sirwan, a valued PKK asset. Sirwan had lived in Damascus for twenty years and could pass for a native, well-educated Syrian. He was a quiet, self-effacing guy in his midforties who had a university degree in chemistry and had taught at a Turkish secondary school. He longed to return to Turkish Kurdistan, but PKK membership made that impossible. Syria was too crowded, and he especially disliked the traffic in Damascus. "The Arab people," he said disdainfully, "know only the camel." The statement surprised me, although I wasn't sure why at first. Later on, I realized that I was so used to Kurds being at the bottom of the Middle East pecking order that I had never heard a Kurdish person express superiority over another ethnic group.

Before joining the PKK, Sirwan had owned a small factory in Damascus, where he employed five workers. He told me he had earned the equivalent of $60,000 U.S. a year, a princely sum in Syria, and that he had purchased a nice home for his wife and three children. He had given up everything for the party, however, and now he saw his family only one or two days each month.

Sirwan was a true believer in Ocalanism, the ideology of the PKK chief that Western critics dismissed as Marxist-Leninist. He didn't brag about it, but I found he'd articulate his beliefs if I dug a little. He called the founder's philosophy a blend of Islam, Christianity, and socialism: "a special mixture for the Kurds." He said that history had taught the Kurds they were losers for so long that they had come to accept failure as a racial characteristic. Because they weren't allowed to express themselves, the Kurds had come to believe they were *incapable* of doing so. The power of Apo's philosophy, Sirwan said, lay in its ability to transform their negative self-image.

The thought was similar to what another rebel, a German Kurdish woman, told me a few days earlier. Her chosen nom de guerre was Tohildun, which means both "revenge" and "transformation" in Kurdish. The current uprising, she said, was "the Kurds' last chance." If they failed, there would be a major massacre by Turkey to make them afraid to try ever again. Tohildun told me that PKK cadres were taught to rid themselves of "internal flaws." She said that before the Kurds were forcibly converted to Islam, in the seventh century, they believed in Zoroastrianism. One of the teachings of Zoroaster called for followers to give away what they had to others. "The Kurdish prayer," she said sarcastically, amounted to "Oh, God, let others get theirs first, so please make me *last*." She said the fact explained why many local Kurds allowed their offspring to join the Syrian army (the government had done a major call-up the month before, after Israeli bombing in Lebanon). "But Israel is not our fight," she said.

According to Tohildun, Iraqi Kurdish leaders like Barzani and Talabani had been unable to identify characteristics common to all Kurds, so their movements had failed to unite the different Kurdish factions. Ocalan taught his disciples that throughout history the Kurds had fought other peoples' battles, that they had always given away their services and their lands. In Turkey, the Kurds helped Atatürk drive out foreign aggressors, naïvely believing that a free Kurdistan would be their reward. Apo said that such generosity was a character flaw of the Kurds. The current uprising, Tohildun said, was the time for Kurds to *take* what belonged to them. "The only real obstacles are inside [our] heads—our first battle is to achieve 'Kurdistan of the mind.'"

Sirwan, my guide, agreed. "Because of Islamic domination," he said, "Kurds always had a small brain." The trick was to free the mind from control by religion and the state. Both, he argued, preach human limitation: "What you are *not* capable of, what you *cannot* do." Sirwan said he was Muslim in name only, and he expressed disdain for Islamic believers. "One hour they are praying in the mosque," he claimed, "and the next hour they'd slit your throat for money in the name of Allah."

In Sirwan's opinion, Turkish Kurdistan already was free. "The physical liberation," he predicted confidently, would follow "within five years." Considering Turkey's military superiority, though, I questioned the prediction. "What about all the soldiers and the high-tech weapons?" I asked. "Before his downfall," Sirwan replied, without missing a beat, "the Shah of Iran had all those weapons, too."

Sirwan took me to the immigration center to get my visa extended. The visit provided a firsthand insight into Syria's support for the PKK. After getting visa photos on a street corner—snapped by a photographer with an ancient-looking wooden box camera—I followed Sirwan into a government building, where he made the equivalent of a $2 gift to a uniformed man behind a marble counter. That allowed us to jump a queue of waiting Arabs, and we were ushered directly into the office of the director of immigration.

The office looked like a storage closet, with a ratty, overstuffed chair stacked on one of the two desks in the room. A balding army general sat behind the other desk, surrounded by several men who were standing. They were smoking and talking Arabic all at once, as if they were old friends. The general wore a tan dress uniform with large, detachable epaulets, similar to those worn by President Assad in a photo on the wall. He held his cigarette with his left thumb and forefinger, ash upward, as he rose to shake my hand.

I had never met a Syrian general. I looked around the hot and cramped office. Six plants were wilting away from lack of water or the dense cigarette smoke—or both. A window-mounted air conditioner rattled away, making little headway with the smoke or the temperature. A sign on the wall read NO SMOKING in Arabic. A hotel keepsake on the general's desk read AMERICAN EXPRESS CARDS WELCOME in English.

There was a constant parade of supplicants coming into the room for immigration favors. At one point, I counted fourteen people standing at the desk, passports in hand. The general had a calm and friendly manner, patiently initialing papers as they were placed before him, ordering an assistant to bring us cups of Turkish coffee—which in Syria is called Arabic coffee. The general took my passport and old visa, the one I'd gotten in the California strip mall, and gave it to a policeman, who immediately left the room. The next day was a Muslim holiday, and the office would be closed, he said pleasantly, but we could get what we wanted if we waited a few minutes.

The general ordered another round of coffee, and then he said to Sirwan, "So how are things going over there?" Sirwan told me later that "over there" meant the war against the Turks. In truth, things were not going very well for the Kurds, but Sirwan answered, "Fine," and the general moved on to other pleasantries. We drank our small coffees, and the policeman returned. The general initialed my new visa, stapled it into the U.S. passport, and handed it back to me. The extension gave me another thirty days, twice the time of the original visa. He rose from his seat, shook hands with me, and said "good-bye" in English.

Now I had enough time on my Syrian visa for the trip "over there." The guerrillas transferred me to another safe house, this one in a Damascus ghetto, a Kurdish neighborhood of dusty, unpaved streets, where shop owners openly displayed photos of Apo in their windows. Dashin, my escort to the Palmyra ruins, bid me good-bye. "Say hello to the mountains," he said, laughing. When I entered the house, an adolescent boy wearing a Chicago Bulls sweatshirt was watching cartoons in Arabic. A young Kurdish woman greeted me in English. She had a Swedish accent and I figured her for a new recruit from Europe, but she clammed up when I tried to get her name.

My new escort was Ahmad, a high school English teacher. He was not a member of the PKK, but the guerrillas had given him the job of getting me to Qamishli, the border town on the Tigris River, five hundred miles to the north. Ahmad had a virulent dislike for Turkish, informing me that the Turkish vocabulary was derived from a mixture of Persian, Arabic, English, and Kurdish. He claimed it was not a "real language." He was also acutely sensitive about his ethnicity. "Why are all the nations of the world against the Kurds?" he asked. My question to him was, Why wouldn't the PKK fight in *Syria* instead of Turkey, since Syria didn't permit Kurdish schools and the government imprisoned dissident Kurds. "We have no mountains, so we cannot fight here," he replied.

"Incidentally," he said, "is Kevin your real name or your *unreal* name?"

Ahmad warned me not to wear sunglasses on the bus so I wouldn't attract police questioning. I went along with the advice, although—as a 6'3" American—I didn't consider the glasses my distinguishing characteristic. After a ten-hour ride across the Syrian desert, we arrived in Qamishli, a Kurdish city with horse-drawn carts and 1950s cars like Kaisers and Studebakers. The next safe house belonged to a wealthy, middle-aged flax merchant named Fars. He lived within sight of the Turkish border, and he was given to relaxing on his balcony, smoking a water pipe, and watching the Turkish sentries with binoculars. Fars had photos of himself and Apo on the walls of his spacious home, as well as about twenty snapshots of Apo posing individually with young graduates of the PKK training camp in Lebanon. All of them had been killed in Turkey.

"They were *shahids*," Fars said. He also had a sculpture of Apo, which no doubt would have pleased the rebel leader. The piece depicted Apo balancing the planet Earth in one hand and a reunited Kurdistan in the other.

I had been in Syria twelve days. Supplies were beginning to show up at Fars's house. When no one was looking, I peeked into one of the boxes. It was full of syringes and bandages. The moon was almost dark now, and the war was getting closer. I stayed one night in Qamishli. The next morning, a plainclothes guerrilla commander picked me up in a late-model Mercedes-Benz. We headed east along the Tigris River into the heart of Kurdistan, following what he called a "PKK road": through dusty villages and farmland dotted with Syrian oil derricks, past horses pulling rubber-tired wagons and tipsy hay rakes, past a yellow 1950 DeSoto taxi with eight passengers and a bulging roof rack, past smoking Soviet-era military trucks, past shepherds beating their flocks out of our way, past Kurdish women picking cotton and wearing flowered dresses like folklore dolls, and past the PKK lookouts disguised as peasants who signaled us that the coast was clear. When we passed a vegetable stand, the driver made a U-turn and stopped. "Are you hungry?" he asked. Yes, I said, noting that tomatoes were my favorite fruit and offering the opinion that the tastiest ones in the world were grown in the Middle East. It was a gratuitous comment between strangers on the eve of a risk-filled adventure, and he responded in kind. "When there is a free Kurdistan, you will be our U.S. importer," he said with a smile. "We'll give you an exclusive franchise for California—you can call your vegetable stand '*Kevin's Kurdish Tomatoes.*'"

The last stop was a farmyard surrounded by mud walls. Inside the walls I found one hundred guerrillas, most of them recruits, sitting cross-legged on the rocky ground, lacing up their new PKK-provided sneakers and wiping grease off an unearthed cache of grenades, AK-47s, and sniper scopes. The owner of the farm was distributing plastic bags and duct tape for the young rebels to waterproof their bedrolls and backpacks. A PKK commander handed out red plastic canteens, hard candies, and tins of Moroccan sardines soaked in what looked like Pennzoil. As a final going-away treat, he passed around paper cups of ice cream. Somehow, it all had the look of a familiar ritual.

I bagged my camera, film, and lenses and put on a dark T-shirt for the twenty-five-mile overnight hike. The guerrilla next to me, a stringy man in his thirties, took out his harmonica and played a few bars of "Oh, Susanna." He smiled and introduced himself as a medical doctor. He showed me a bag of new surgical instruments he'd bought in Damascus. He said he was walking back to Mount Ararat, the highest point in Turkey, where the PKK had a large camp. The mountain is the legendary resting place of Noah's Ark, and I knew from a news story that the rebels had recently kidnapped a group of Christian missionaries who'd been searching for the fabled ruins. Mount Ararat was about eight hundred miles away. He said he hoped to make the camp in two months.

"No problem, I've done it before," he said. "I am walk man."

"Sony Walkman?" I asked him.

"No," he said, laughing, "*Kurdish* Walk Man."

By all appearances, morale was high among the rebels, but in truth, they were badly outmatched by Turkish troops and superior technology, especially the U.S.-supplied helicopter gunships. At this point in the war, casualty estimates indicated that for every Turkish soldier killed, five guerrillas lost their lives. PKK recruiting, whether in Turkey, Syria, or the Kurdish ghettos of Europe, could not keep up with the demand.

At dusk, the recruited warriors assembled their gear and listened silently to a pep talk from the commander. Some were just teenagers; a few were small-framed girls who seemed to be drowning under the weight of the fifty-pound packs and the five magazines of bullets on their gun belts. Then a group of local Kurds formed a send-off line and showered the recruits with hugs and kisses. Some of the would-be fighters were just sixteen, my daughter's age. If the scene hadn't been so serious, it might have reminded me of booster parents at a kid's soccer game.

The final bit of business before departure was a photo session, a ritual of remembering the living. Point-and-shoot cameras were passed around, and the young rebels took snapshots of one another. One of them told me the PKK provided the film "to take pictures of friends that may not be here tomorrow." I had to wonder how many in the group would end up in the photo gallery in Fars's house.

The PKK assigned a twenty-one-year-old named Hocki as my translator and guide so I wouldn't get lost in the dark. An hour later, near the shacks of the Syrian border guards, we were snaking our way through the tall grass in an oil field, a long, disciplined line threading the spit of land where Syria, Iraq, and Turkey come together. Hocki was a Turk, not a Kurd, who had taken up the cause of the PKK as a high school student in Germany. He was going to war for the first time and relished the prospect of fighting the Turkish soldiers. He had picked up English from watching movies like *Terminator,* and he was eager to quote lines like "*Hasta la vista,* baby!" for me as we made our way down the trail.

It occurred to me that Hocki might get his wish that night, courtesy of a Turkish or Iraqi patrol. We were close enough to see the lights of a Turkish village on our left, and we knew Saddam's Republican Guard was somewhere on our right. Fortunately, it didn't happen, and, while I was glad my gung-ho escort knew some English, I didn't want to rely on his judgment in a firefight, especially in a dark place that neither of us knew. Sometime around midnight, I moved up the column and fell into line behind the Walk Man.

It was daybreak when we reached the Tigris. My T-shirt was soaked in sweat, the muscles in my legs on fire from the all-night march. Lookouts were posted on the river, while the rest of us opened food or rested in the high weeds along the bank. I ate some sardines, hoping that would lighten my backpack, while I fielded pointed questions from the doctor about my independence as a journalist ("Is your pencil *free*?") and why the 1988 chemical attack on the Kurds wasn't broadcast on American television until the invasion of Kuwait in 1991 ("Propaganda?"). Then I fell asleep. When I awoke, the guerrillas were inflating rubber rafts in preparation for crossing the river after dark. I joked with the doc that I needed light for pictures, so I'd be happier if we crossed the river before the sun went down. "No, we are happy when it is night," he said. "The guerrilla is *not happy* with light. After the freedom, we will be happy with light."

When we finally rowed to the other side of the Tigris, we found high-sided gravel trucks waiting to take us to a PKK staging area near the Iraq-Turkey border. The hired truck drivers were Iraqi Kurds, and I noted that they were wearing the red-and-white scarf of the Barzani clan. That might have made them sworn enemies of the PKK, but the chance for a paying job had overridden party allegiance.

After a rough ninety-minute ride standing in the crowded trucks, we arrived at the base camp, slept for a couple of hours in our bedrolls, and then began climbing a mountain along the Zab River. About noon, we arrived at the "mother camp," where some three hundred fighters formed a single reception line, kissing and hugging the tired recruits.

I spent the next three weeks in the main camp and in various subcamps along a hundred-mile stretch of the Turkish border. The main camp was nestled in a deep gorge between two mountains, which made low-flying Turkish aircraft vulnerable to rebel fire from both sides of the narrow pass. The walls of the canyon were honeycombed with caves, which were stocked with weapons and food supplies bought from Iraqi Kurds and brought in by pack mule. There were no aerial attacks on the camp during my visit, but PKK members usually stayed close to the cave openings so they could take refuge inside quickly. The guerrillas had called a unilateral cease-fire the week before, hoping to better their position by negotiation. But U.S.-made Cobra gunships sometimes hovered near the camp at high altitude, and I saw Lockheed F-16s bombing suspected rebel positions in other locations.

When they weren't fighting, the guerillas traded a variety of jobs among themselves: cooking, caring for the wounded, guarding the Turkish POWs, herding the pack animals, repairing the cable car they'd built over the river, fixing walkie-talkies, running the satellite TV system with news from the MED TV station in Belgium (during my visit, I watched a Clinton press conference with Kurdish narration), gardening, typing messages on an old Royal typewriter, and gathering wild plants for food. A large oven, constructed from mud and operated by rebel bakers, supplied the camp with wispy-thin flat bread, a Kurdish staple. The nearby Zab River provided occasional fish—obtained by pole, gun, and, sometimes, by grenade. There was even someone assigned to organize the volleyball games, which took place in the late afternoons.

"The guerrilla life is a big university," said one fighter.

After only a few days outdoors and nights sleeping on the ground, my clothes were filthy, but the rebels who washed their uniforms in the stream, carried sewing kits, and exhibited almost a manic discipline, always managed to stay clean. I thought to myself: If a Kurdish state could be built on the basis of willpower alone, this might be it. "Once the Palestinian problem is solved," a guerrilla named Radar told me confidently, "we are next in line."

The guerrillas had two rules. The first was to keep moving, and the second was to stay hidden. The lifespan of a typical fighter, according to everyone I talked to, was about thirty months. They slept with their sneakers on, the tops of their socks taped to keep out the insects, ready to move at the first indication of danger. Spring and summer were the guerrillas' favorite seasons, because leaves and foliage camouflaged their movements. A few fighters claimed they liked inclement weather, because it offset the strength of the Turkish technology, "and the enemy doesn't expect you." According to one PKK member, the rebel advantage was motivation. "If you are not strong with ideology," he claimed, "you don't have the willpower to stay outdoors in the rain."

The rebels used old smuggler trails that crossed in and out of Turkey. There were dozens of these paths, and they had been used for generations by Kurdish fighters against both Saddam and the Turkish government. "The best trail," an older rebel told me, "is the one you know."

A five-hour hike from the camp brought me to the PKK "school," an outdoor space camouflaged by trees and branches that had been carefully laid over a couple of large boulders. A larger-than-life-sized painting of Ocalan attested to the movement's fascination with the Damascus-based leader.

By 1996, the time of my visit, the rebels were preaching a pan-Kurdish nationalism, emphasizing pre–World War I borders for the Kurds and drilling into the cadres the belief that the Kurds had a right to the oil, gold, water, and other resources in their territory. For the most part, they had given up the Marxist rhetoric they had favored in the 1980s and early 1990s, but the rebels clearly saw Turkey, their U.S.-equipped enemy, as a proxy for American interests in the region, and the word "imperialist" punctuated their lectures. In addition, they still utilized the Maoist tactic of self-criticism. Each session of the school included presentations in which individual rebels analyzed the strengths and weaknesses of given actions (i.e., being lax with radio codes or making a fire that could be seen from the air at night). One rebel, a woman, stressed the power of ideas. "Everyone is a teacher," she said, "and everyone is a student." Then she added something that I would think about years later, when the world seemed to be inching toward a clash of civilizations. "The side with the *strongest ideology* wins."

I remember musing at the time: Is that really the case? Years later, during the Abu Ghraib torture scandal in Iraq, I recalled her point of view as a new question surfaced. Did ideals like democracy and human rights—the centerpiece of America's "ideology"—still have the power to win? Or would victory go to the side with the most weapons, be they cruise missiles or suicide jalopies?

The most common language in the camp was Kurdish, despite the fact that most of the fighters in the camp knew Turkish better than they did Kurdish. The majority had grown up in Turkey, where the teaching of Kurdish was illegal. The same prohibition existed in Syria, so usually, Syrian Kurds were better versed in Arabic. For the rebels, Kurdish offered a practical alternative to Turkish and Arabic, and the language was a strong political bridge to European-born Kurds.

My translator during the visit was a fighter named Delil, a twenty-two-year-old man born in Turkey to a Turkish father and Kurdish mother. His family had immigrated to Germany when he was a child. He still remembered life in Turkey, unlike his younger brother, who was born in Germany. His brother, Delil said, loved soccer and had "a taste for money." Besides German and English, Delil spoke Turkish and the Kurdish he'd learned in the mountains. "My mother forgot her Kurdish," he said, somewhat wistfully. "My father had plans for me, but I decided to come here."

The commander of the camp was a Turkish Kurd named Fuat, a small, sunburned man with white hair and lots of wrinkles. He was forty-five years old, but looked more like sixty. Fuat was one of the twelve-member steering committee of the PKK and, with Apo, one of the original founders of the movement. I interviewed him in the shade of a tree, both of us occasionally scooping water from the nearby stream as two bodyguards stood at attention by his tent.

I couldn't help noticing the word CAMEL emblazoned in large letters on the side of the tent. An ad for the R. J. Reynolds Tobacco Company in a war zone struck me as a bit bizarre, to say the least. It conjured up images of Camel hats, lighters, gym bags, and other premiums people won by sending in thousands of cigarette coupons. Fuat didn't smoke, and I never found out how he got the tent.

Unlike most guerrillas, Fuat didn't grow up in Turkey's southeast. He was reared in Istanbul, where his father was a dockworker. "Until I was nineteen," he told me, "I thought I was a *Turk*." His radicalization began at the University of Ankara in the 1970s, where he met Apo and joined a group of students and began to discuss the 1938 uprising at Dersim and other debacles in Kurdish history. When he went home and quizzed his parents, he discovered that they were born in Dersim. They had been removed from the area along with his grandparents after the rebellion was crushed.

"For the Kurds in Turkey, 1938 was the final resistance point," he said. "They were like *The Last of the Mohicans*," he said, referring to the American movie. "After the Dersim massacre, our families were afraid to say 'we are Kurds.' It was Apo who told me I was a Kurd."

In 1978 the PKK was created, Fuat said, and the founders began to collect their first weapons.

Motivation

I was given freedom in the camps to interview anyone I wanted, although my translator presumably reported my questions and interactions. I found that most of the PKK members were former villagers or farm kids who had never spoken with a reporter, and, unlike party officials, they tended to tell their stories in a straightforward, unvarnished way, without a political or ideological spin. A few came from families with roots in earlier uprisings, like the PKK woman whose grandparents died in the Dersim massacre in 1938. A few had been in jail for political activity; a few spoke of torture.

Most, however, had been radicalized by small, personal experiences connected with the military occupation. A teenager said Turkish soldiers had taken his parents off a bus and searched them; another remembered being slapped by a teacher in school for speaking Kurdish. That reminded me of Black Elk, the American Indian medicine man who'd told me in my early days of reporting about his experience as a child in a mission school in South Dakota. When he spoke Lakota, Black Elk said, his teacher washed out his mouth with Ivory Snow soap. Kurdish, like Lakota, was considered *dirty*.

A seventeen-year-old fighter, Ferhat Tepe, was only thirteen when his brother, a pro-PKK journalist, was tortured and killed. He related the story as he squatted next to me, drinking tea, fingering an AK-47, and smiling, his still-good teeth a sign that he was new to the mountains.

The PKK women went into battle with the men, but they had separate units for training. Many told me that their reduced status in Kurdish society—a place where women sometimes were subjected to "virginity tests" before marriage, and where so-called honor killings of women suspected of premarital sex took place—played an important role in their decision to join the guerrillas. "In the history of Kurdistan, the Kurdish people were always at the bottom," Commander

Fuat said, "and at the bottom of the Kurdish people were the Kurdish women." The PKK promised equality and had spread the word in villages that political and sexual freedoms were connected. The party taught that if women didn't *pay* for their freedom, they would never obtain it. "If we get our freedom with our own hands in this war," said a battle-hardened female commander in her thirties, "no one can take it away."

Sexual equality, however, referred to the promise of equal treatment in the ranks, plus emancipation in a postrevolutionary Kurdistan. It did not include a right to have sex in the mountains, a practice prohibited for both sexes. "Apo told us that love affairs are bad for the war," one woman told me, "because one of the parties usually convinces the other to leave the mountains." It struck me as ironic that rebel women had escaped patriarchal Kurdish society only to have the male-dominated PKK leadership make such decisions for them.

War Games

During my time in the mountains I learned never to take a bath in a stream without having a lookout nearby, how to use a swatch of rice sack as a scouring pad for washing clothes, how to shave using a bullet (stick the blade in the groove near the primer cap and use the projectile as a handle), how most wild plants can be eaten, and how toothaches and diarrhea eventually go away, even on long marches.

Some problems, however, like the lack of electricity for charging camcorder batteries, were daunting. One day, after filming live-ammunition training drills, my camera batteries died. I set off with escorts to climb an eight-thousand-foot mountain, where the PKK had a generator powering a radio that connected battle stations along the border. By the time I reached the site, the guerrillas were low on gas, so I couldn't power my battery charger.

Just then, a pair of Turkish F-16s appeared overhead. The radio operators dove into a bunker and prepared the Doshka, a Russian-made machine gun they'd hauled up the mountain in parts by mule and reassembled on a big tripod. It was a heavy machine gun, .50 caliber, but puny by comparison to the powerful jet fighter that was rocketing the base of the mountain a mile away. I hunkered down in the bunker with my dead camera. I was happy that we weren't the targets of the F-16, but sorry that rare images of a forgotten war would not have a chance to be on American television.

During my three weeks in the mountains, I walked about 120 miles, a figure I based on a log of my hours and estimated speed. On several mornings I was awakened by artillery booms or the sound of gunfire in the distance. I saw Turkish soldiers, but only through binoculars. The longest march, a seven-day hike along the border and into southern Turkey, gave me a greater sense of the Kurds who were fighting the war. Besides Delil, my translator, my escorts were two rebels from Syria and two from Turkey.

Sozdar, a small, athletic-looking woman with a pixie haircut, took her nom de guerre from a fallen comrade. She spoke Arabic and Kurdish and told me her parents threw a big party for her when they found out she was going to the mountains. "They took four rolls of film," she said proudly. Habet, a Turkish Kurd, had a bullet scar on his leg, and he wore a photo of Apo on his belt. He wrote poetry in a notebook and told me that the film *Midnight Express* didn't show enough "real truth" about torture in Turkey. Like most of the rebels, he was an atheist but, like the PKK leadership, he professed respect for Mohammed, Jesus, and Buddha "as teachers."

Dilsad was a little guy from Turkey whose job it was to carry the teapot, six glasses for tea, and enough flat bread for a week. He rolled cigarettes by hand. In the time of war, he said, "no one worries about cancer." His friend was Cesur, another Syrian Kurd, who sang and played his transistor radio and was always looking for green figs or wild grape leaves. I told Cesur I'd played a little basketball in high school. He wanted to know about Michael Jordan and the NBA.

Cesur had entered the war in 1992 after his father, an olive farmer "who spends too much time in the mosque," reluctantly gave him a "ticket" (i.e., blessing) to go to the war. When Cesur arrived in the mountains, his father sent him a message imploring him to come home or at least to visit, and promising "to sew [him] a new uniform"—the way Kurdish fathers fashion suits and dresses by hand for children who are getting married. One day, after being absent from home for more than two years (and during which time he'd worn the same clothes), Cesur received a package from a PKK messenger. It was the new uniform, and in one of the pockets Cesur found an audiotape with his father's voice. In the recording, his father said he'd finally reconciled himself to the Kurdish war. At the end of the tape, he exhorted his son "not to be shot in the back while running away in battle."

Terrorism

The PKK committed widespread abuses during the fifteen-year uprising (1984–1999), primarily against rural Kurds perceived of collaborating with the government. The height of the rights violations was reached during 1991 and 1992 in a PKK campaign targeting "village guards"—Kurds on the state payroll—and their families. Reports of those abuses quickly turned into a public relations disaster for the PKK. In subsequent years, the violations decreased, but they did not disappear.

During the 1990s, the State Department repeatedly accused the PKK of terrorism, but the department refrained from accusing Turkey of acts of terror, even as it admitted that the U.S.-equipped Turkish army had committed human rights violations against civilians. Amnesty International and Human Rights Watch accused both the PKK and the Turkish army of widespread abuse, including torture, and both groups tried to publicize death-squad killings, even when there was no clear evidence which side had committed the crimes. Credible allegations by both Amnesty and Human Rights Watch were rejected routinely by both Turkish officials and Kurdish guerrillas. During a *60 Minutes* interview in 1995, Onur Öymen, Turkey's deputy foreign minister, declared that all such practices were "prohibited in Turkey and punishable—severely punishable—by law." He said, "We cannot accept such allegations, and we consider it is a pity that a friendly country [the U.S.] can write such reports without proven facts."

The PKK used a similar circular logic. Apo often threatened to bring the conflict to cities such as Ankara and Istanbul. The tactic would have resulted in civilian casualties, and with isolated exceptions, the threat never really materialized. When I interviewed Apo in Damascus, before setting off for the mountains, I asked him why he had not brought the war to the cities. He replied that the Kurds had the right to do so because the government had attacked their region, but that the PKK had not done so for fear of negative publicity. He also contradicted Amnesty's figures on PKK abuses. "The Turks have nearly destroyed all of the Kurdish villages," he said. "They have committed thousands of unsolved murders. And they say we have killed a few civilians. Can those two things really be equated?" Unlike the U.S. media, the European press regularly covered the Kurdish-Turkish war, and assessments on the Continent differed sharply from those in Washington. Hugo Paemen, the European Union ambassador to the United States, told me that arms sales to Turkey should be restricted, because "every day we hear about violations of human rights."

When I asked Paemen whether the military held the real power in Turkey and the civilian government was just a "façade," he replied, "Up to a certain point, yes, it is clear." But John Shattuck, the assistant secretary of state for democracy, human rights, and labor during the Clinton administration, disputed the view. Shattuck, a one-time professor at Harvard and a former member of the advisory board at Amnesty International, told me in an interview that Turkey was "the one democracy in the area." Shattuck defended U.S. arms deliveries to Turkey, adding, "I don't think the United States is responsible for Turkey's internal policies."

When I talked to U.S. officials, they usually stressed that Turkey was making "progress" in human rights, although Turkey would not permit State Department rights monitors free access to the southeast—usually "for their protection"—and data gathered by the U.S. embassy in Ankara was rarely based on eyewitness accounts by staffers. Embassy personnel were not permitted to travel to the Kurdish area—unless escorted by Turkish officials. The restrictions made independent assessment of army abuses difficult, and the reliance on Turkish versions of events sometimes made State Department figures unreliable. In one case of apparent disinformation, the government blamed the massacre of ten villagers in a minibus near Guclukonak, Turkey, on the PKK, but William Shultz, the executive director of Amnesty International-U.S.A., told me, "The government claimed that that was a PKK bombing, [but] an independent review of that case seemed to indicate it might well have been the government itself."

Kurds versus Kurds and PKK Terror

I never went into battle with the PKK and never witnessed abuses firsthand, but in 1995, a year before my tour with the rebels, I investigated an incident in Gorumlu, Turkey, near an army base, where village guards and members of their families had been killed. I went there with Jessica Lutz, the Dutch radio reporter. We interviewed eyewitnesses to the PKK attack, which had taken the lives of several civilians, including children, and came away with the opinion that the PKK was at fault.

We both had visited the village in 1993, when Gorumlu exhibited support for the rebels and was the scene of almost daily firefights with the army. Nevertheless, in 1995 the men in Gorumlu had decided to go on the government payroll and joined the village guards. Here, the guards were especially valuable because they knew the PKK trails: They had served as scouts for soldiers during the March invasion of Iraq.

The state gave the villagers weapons, bullets, American-made two-way radios, and a salary of $250 a month, far more than they could make as farmers. Kurdistan was the poorest, most backward region in Turkey, and there was widespread unemployment. By 1995, eighty thousand Kurds had signed on as village guards in the region, saving their villages from destruction by the army. With their help, the army had driven the guerrillas deep into the mountains, and clashes in places such as Gorumlu had been less frequent.

However, the changeover was not without cost in Gorumlu.

The PKK, many of whose local members had been recruited from Gorumlu, viewed the guards and their families as Turkish collaborators and argued that both were legitimate military targets. Soon after the invasion began, a coordinated attack was launched against the garrison and the village, resulting in civilian deaths.

During the battle, the Turkish commander told us he had intercepted a radio transmission that he said came from a PKK superior urging his fighters to "hit the little mice as well as the big mice." According to the officer and several villagers, four children were killed, and three adults were injured when the PKK threw a grenade through a window of one of the houses. At the time the PKK denied responsibility for the attack, blaming instead the *kontra gerilla* death squads, which they claimed were linked to the Turkish security forces.

The PKK commander of the Gorumlu region, whose name was Cemal, happened to be in the Zab camp during my visit in 1996, and I asked him about the incident. At first he said that the Turks had lured the PKK into the attack and then had "taken protection behind civilian houses"—a familiar excuse, regardless of the perpetrator, when civilians die in war. When I told him that my own investigation suggested more than collateral damage, Cemal maintained the attack was "a mistake" and that the rebel unit later had been "disciplined." He claimed that the practice of killing Kurdish village guards had been discontinued altogether in 1995, "unless the guards were involved in attacks with Turkish soldiers."

Going Home

It was June 1996. I had been away a month, and I wanted to go home. My son was graduating from elementary school, and I'd promised him I'd be there for the ceremony. Commander Fuat didn't find the reason compelling and asked me to wait "until the moon was dark." Still, he relented when I insisted, and after several days of coded radio transmissions, the arrangements were made, and a number of rebels came by to wish me a safe trip.

In all, it would take fifteen guerrillas to smuggle me back into Syria. Eight were assigned to take me across the Tigris River and halfway to the Syrian border. At a prearranged spot and time, they would hand me over to a new unit of guerrillas, who would be walking toward us from Syria. One of the responsibilities of the new unit was to scout the Syrian border guards. "Is it true the guards look the other way and let you pass?" I asked one of my escorts when we were underway. It was midnight. The moon had risen late, and I could see his face. "It is only a *little true*," he said. He took off his backpack and showed me a bullet hole in the flap, which he had sewn up with coarse thread. A month earlier, near the border, someone had fired at him.

At the midway rendezvous, the two units met to rest, chat, and smoke. I took off my shoes to check for blisters. One of the Syrian-based guerrillas noticed the deteriorated condition of my socks. There would be fresh socks waiting for everyone at the safe house, he promised, After all the walking I'd done in the mountains, my old socks, he said, were *shahid*s.

We were in a gulley, in the narrow spit of land between Saddam's Republican Guard and Turkish forces, and we could see the lights from the Turkish village of Silopi. Suddenly tracer bullets from the Iraqi side appeared overhead, seemingly random, and abruptly stopping after a short burst. "They are just letting us know they're there," said another guerrilla.

About 4:00 A.M. we found ourselves lying in the dirt in the oil fields near the border, watching the shacks of the Syrian border guards, hoping they were asleep. We could see gas fires on top of an oil rig in the distance, behind the police post. The man alongside me, a clean-cut Kurd in his early thirties with good teeth, told me his name was Qahram. He said he had finished thirteen years of schooling "to become an English teacher," but he had changed his mind. Now he was leading a double life in Syria, part-time in the classroom and part-time as a Kurdish rebel. He picked up a handful of soil from our hiding place. He let it run through his fingers.

"This mine," Qahram said. "All Kurdistan mine."

14

Well-Founded Fear of Persecution

In 1991, when I got home after the first Gulf War, few people knew much about the Kurds. A humorous, but not atypical, response at the time came from a Santa Barbara woman who asked me in a video interview, "K-U-R-D? Is that a radio station?"

"Kurds?" a man asked. "Kurds are Arabs—from Arabia somewhere, right?" Another woman laughed as she responded, "Is it a musical group—or just some language?"

Kani Xulam

Soon after my return, the League of Women Voters asked me to present a slide show at the public library in Santa Barbara. The event drew only about thirty people. When the presentation was over, two young men, Kani and David, approached the rostrum. They were brothers, and both were students at the University of California. Except for their clothing—a casual California look—they resembled the people in the slide show. It turned out that they were *Turkish* Kurds, members of the only Kurdish family in Santa Barbara, where they had settled after fleeing poverty and ethnic warfare in their homeland.

A few weeks later, Kani and David invited me to their home for tea. They lived on a busy downtown street in a weathered duplex. At their request, I removed my shoes at the front door, surprised as I stepped into a room full of used washers and dryers. David ushered me past the old appliances to a living quarters located in back, where I joined the brothers cross-legged on a floor that was strewn with sleeping bags and American paperback novels.

The brothers, as I soon discovered, made their living repairing and selling old appliances. Kani, a history major in college with only vague plans for what he would do after graduation, had stumbled on the idea after a previous tenant moved out of the apartment, leaving behind a Frigidaire. The refrigerator was scratched and dented, so the landlord allowed Kani to keep it. Kani cleaned up the old unit and advertised it in the local paper. When the ad got eight responses, Kani and David realized there was an untapped market in town for used appliances. With a typical immigrant can-do spirit, they took out a display ad in the yellow pages of the telephone book. They cheerfully called their new enterprise the Yes Brothers.

Within a year, the fledgling business had transformed itself into a Maytag appliance franchise, but Kani soon moved to Washington, D.C., leaving the Santa Barbara business to David. In Washington, Kani, increasingly affected by the Kurdish uprising in his homeland, founded an organization called the American Kurdish Information Network (AKIN), with the stated mission of providing news on the plight of the Kurds. This nonprofit group was the first of its kind in the United States.

By the time I met Kani and David, I had already traveled to Turkey and seen some of the war between the Turks and the Kurds with my own eyes. Later, when I needed a refrigerator, I ended up buying one from the family appliance shop. The fact that a Kurdish family lived in my hometown made events eight thousand miles away seem closer than they were. By then, Kani had embarked on a high-profile public life. Many of the estimated twenty thousand Kurdish immigrants in the U.S.—most of them from Iraq, not Turkey—soon knew his name, and hundreds had begun to support the work of AKIN with $5 and $10 contributions. Kani was pleading the Kurdish cause at libraries and universities, lobbying members of Congress on Capitol Hill, picketing the Turkish embassy in Washington, and making appearances on CNN and other news outlets.

In 1993, Leyla Zana, a controversial advocate of the Kurds in Turkey and the first Kurdish woman to win election to the Turkish parliament, traveled to the United States and spoke to a Congressional committee about human rights abuses in Turkey. Two years earlier, during her swearing-in ceremony in the Turkish parliament, she nearly had triggered a riot when she spoke the Kurdish language to the assembled legislators, and the session had to be adjourned until order was restored. Shortly before her trip to the United States, I interviewed her in a Diyarbakir restaurant, and I found myself surprised by the sense of calmness she projected in the midst of the otherwise chaotic news events.

Kani met Zana during the Washington visit and served as her translator. Zana, a mother of six, returned to Turkey, where in 1994 she was stripped of her immunity as a parliamentarian, tried for treason, and sentenced to fifteen years in a Turkish prison. Among other charges, the indictment alleged that her speech on

Capitol Hill had falsely accused Turkey of human rights abuses. While in prison, Zana was awarded the Sakharov Peace Prize (her incarceration prevented acceptance of the award in person until after her release in 2004). She later was nominated for the Nobel Peace Prize.

With Zana's visit and subsequent imprisonment, American Kurds had a new cause to champion, and Kani was leading that fight from AKIN's Connecticut Avenue office in Washington, D.C. Over the next couple of years a string of successes rolled in. He acquired more than 150 signatures from members of Congress in support of efforts to hold Turkey accountable for its human rights abuses against the Kurds, and he lobbied with some success against U.S. arms shipments to Turkey. In 1995, Kani mounted a thirty-six-day hunger strike on the steps of the Capitol for Zana. President Clinton's ambassador to the United Nations, Bill Richardson, visited him and his fellow strikers, giving the Zana case a small amount of publicity in Washington newspapers. Kani also used his staff of volunteers to create a Web site for AKIN. Within a few months, the Web site was registering hundreds of hits per day. It appeared Kani might put the little-known struggle of Turkish Kurds on the map.

Then he was arrested.

On Friday, April 12, 1996, a group of twelve federal agents raided the offices of the American Kurdish Information Network, confiscated AKIN's computers, files, and petty cash, and placed Kani in handcuffs. The official charge: the use of a false name in application for a U.S. passport. Kani's brother David was arrested in California on the same charge and rearrested later for obtaining (but repaying) a California student loan under a false name. The rest of Kani and David's family had fled the growing turmoil in Turkish Kurdistan and entered the country legally, but the two brothers had applied for American passports under fictitious names. There was more to the story of the Yes Brothers than I had realized.

Over the next six weeks, U.S. Marshals shuttled Kani from Washington to California via county jails and state and federal prisons in Pennsylvania, Oklahoma, Oregon, Arizona, and Nevada. Once he arrived in Los Angeles, Kani was held on $250,000 bail. The charges carried the potential penalty of deportation, and so Kani began the long fight to achieve political asylum rather than return to an uncertain fate in Turkey. It was still years before the events of 9/11, and the disparity between the offense and the bail figure struck me as disproportionate. Still, Kani and David *had* used illegal methods to obtain U.S. passports. I needed to do more investigation.

At the time of Kani's arrest, Turkey publicly branded him a terrorist, charging that he was in cahoots with the PKK in Turkey. Kani's American supporters maintained the Turkish government had brought his case to the attention of the U.S. Justice Department to stop his lobbying efforts on Capitol Hill. When I began to investigate, I discovered that one prominent advocate, Ralph Fertig, a U.S. administrative judge in Los Angeles, had put up his residence as a surety to release both brothers from jail. Kani was "crimping the Turkish government's style," according to Judge Fertig. "Once they found out through an intelligence network that Kani had come to the United States without proper papers," Fertig claimed, "they informed the Justice Department."

I decided to file a Freedom of Information Act request.

Two years later, I received copies of internal Immigration and Naturalization Service documents that made me suspect that international politics had intervened in the legal case. Both the INS hearing officer and her superior had concluded that Kani had a "well-founded fear of persecution" in Turkey, and they had recommended him for political asylum soon after his arrest. Then I filmed an interview with a representative of the California Department of Education, who acknowledged that federal authorities had encouraged the state prosecution in David's student loan case. The released documents revealed that despite the finding that Kani had met the test for sanctuary in the United States, higher-ups in INS headquarters in Washington had overruled the asylum recommendation, labeling his case "high-profile, politically sensitive."

By contrast, the U.S. District Court in Los Angeles treated Kani's arrest as a garden-variety case. The federal judge found Kani guilty on the passport charge, dismissing the $250,000 bail and sentencing him to just four hundred hours of community service—in his own office, the American Kurdish Information Network.

Political Asylum in Limbo

Kani still faced the challenge of political asylum, and the Justice Department continued to agitate for his deportation. Thanks to his efforts in Washington, however, Kani had acquired some influential friends. Several prominent members of Congress, including Representative John Porter (R-IL), flew to Los Angeles to testify in the INS court trial in support of his application for political asylum. The outpouring of vocal interest assuaged my concerns that the brothers had misled me, and I continued to follow the case. On December 4, 2000, the INS judge concluded that Kani had met the test for political asylum, and that deportation would jeopardize his safety. According to the court, Kani had "a well-founded fear of persecution" in Turkey. The ruling against the Justice Department was rare, if not precedent setting, for its commentary on human rights abuses by a NATO ally.

Nonetheless, the Justice Department appealed the finding to the INS Appeals Court. A final INS ruling from was not expected until 2007, eleven years after Kani's original arrest, but in all likelihood the INS verdict would not be the end of the matter. Whatever the outcome, the case still could be appealed to the Ninth Circuit Court of Appeals.

The family of Kani and David reacted differently to American life. Adam, the oldest brother and the first in the family to immigrate, had come to the U.S. on a high school scholarship in 1977. Since then, he had graduated from college, received a master's degree, and earned a pilot's license (the first American Kurd with his own airplane). Adam and his brother David were enjoying a successful practice in commercial realty in Southern California. While Kani awaited the results of his legal proceedings, he continued to work on behalf of the Kurds at the AKIN offices in Washington, while he pursued a Ph.D. in international service at American University. The youngest brother, Ned, who with his sister, Mila, had inherited the Maytag franchise, sold the business to pursue real estate in Santa Barbara. In 1998 Kani's mother became a U.S. citizen, but she ultimately left Santa Barbara and returned to Turkey, as did Kani's other brother, Abdul, who took his Maytag repair training and opened an appliance dealership in Diyarbakir. Mila, Kani's younger sister, became a U.S. citizen, but she did not adjust to American society. She returned to Turkey and, in 2004, she married a Kurd and started a family in Diyarbakir. In 2005, Ned married a Kurdish woman in Diyarbakir. The couple announced plans to settle in Santa Barbara.

BOOK III

War in Iraq

15

2002: Northern Iraq

It was a storm that had been gathering for years. Just because
it burst, you cannot blame the thunderbolt.

—ANONYMOUS (FRENCH REVOLUTION)

February 2002

It was my first visit to Iraqi Kurdistan in almost four years. Across the region, the political fortunes of the Kurds had changed. Three years earlier, Turkey had deployed troops on the Syrian border and threatened to invade. Once again, the issue was that Syria was fomenting Kurdish unrest in Turkey. The threat of invasion was real, and Syrian authorities responded rapidly by expelling Abdullah Ocalan and his guerrilla cadres from the country. The Kurdistan Workers' Party (PKK) leader subsequently sought refuge in Russia, Italy, the Netherlands, and elsewhere. Eventually, Ocalan was captured in Africa, following a brief sanctuary in the Greek embassy in Nairobi.

U.S. intelligence tracked Ocalan's desperate cloak-and-dagger odyssey across three continents and, reportedly, supplied the information that set up his capture by Turkish commandos in the Kenyan capital. As Kurdish demonstrations shook a dozen European capitals—some Kurdish protesters set themselves on fire, and three were shot to death trying to force their way into the Israeli embassy in Berlin—Ocalan was handcuffed and flown to Turkey. He was incarcerated on an island near Istanbul, the only inmate in a specially constructed prison. Charged with capital offenses, he was later convicted and sentenced to death. The sentence subsequently was changed to life imprisonment, in part to keep Turkey's application alive for admission to the European Union (the EU bans capital punishment). After his arrest, Ocalan issued a cease-fire declaration from his prison cell and ordered all PKK fighters to leave the country. It appeared that the fifteen-year rebellion, the longest Kurdish uprising in Turkish history, was over.

In Iraq, the prospects for the Kurds could not have better or more starkly different from those of their cousins in Turkey. Revenue from the United Nation's Oil for Food program had revitalized the local economy, and the political situation was largely stable. A cease-fire between the Patriotic Union of Kurdistan (PUK) and the rival Kurdistan Democratic Party (KDP) was holding, encouraged by the prospect of a U.S.-led war. For the Kurds of Iraq, the lean, troubled 1990s were history. They had been free of Saddam's control for eleven years. Now they were playing their cards right, and they were prospering. The last thing on anyone's mind was a political assassination.

The Populist Kurd with the British Manner

Barham Salih, a Kurd, was the prime minister of the eastern territory, the part of northern Iraq controlled by the PUK from January 2001 to June 2004. Back in high school, Salih had been known as a whiz kid. He'd scored in the top one percent of all Kurdish, Arab, and Christian students in his class, and some of the other Kurds were envious. One day, according to Mohammed Hussein, a former classmate, a few of the students grabbed Salih on the playground and threatened to give him a beating. Hussein told me the story in 2002—by then, he'd become the deputy security chief of Sulaimaniah—and the recollection caused him to laugh. Barham was a nice guy, he said, but his high grades were putting too much pressure on the rest of the students. "We liked him," Hussein said. "We just needed a break from all the homework."

Salih started secondary school in 1975, the same year the Kurdish insurrection in Iraq was crushed and two hundred thousand refugees were forced to flee the country. By 1978, the year he graduated, Saddam Hussein's Ba'ath Party had been in control for a decade. After consolidating control over the country, the regime began to concentrate on military research, civil construction, and oil exploration. Development was becoming a national priority, and the Ba'athists had given engineering, in particular, an official mandate. Soon, a strategic decision was made to underwrite scholarships for promising Iraqi students to study abroad. Salih, a bookish eighteen-year-old from the Kurdish city of Sulaimaniah, was offered a full ride to a British university. The arrangement required him to return to Iraq after completing his education abroad.

The Sunni elite controlled Iraq in 1978, as it would for the next quarter century. The Kurds were looked upon as uneducated mountain people, hillbillies with subversive tendencies. It was a unique honor for a Kurd to receive such a scholarship. Unbeknownst to the Iraqi teachers who sung his praises in the classroom, however, Salih's interests went beyond getting high marks. Like many in his generation, he had seen his parents and their friends mistreated by the central authorities. He hated the Iraqi regime, and he harbored separatist ideas for the Kurds. America had withdrawn its support for Kurdish independence in 1975, but the dream was still alive. By night, Salih and other high schoolers were secretly printing handbills denouncing the lack of Kurdish rights under the dictatorship.

A few weeks before Salih was to leave to study in the United Kingdom, the police captured one of the group and forced him to confess. Salih and several other youths were arrested later and sent to a jail in Kirkuk. As luck would have it, Salih's father was a respected judge who knew the ins and outs of the criminal justice system. His father had been temporarily exiled to an Arab-speaking area of southern Iraq in the early 1970s, a common experience for educated Kurds whose loyalties were suspect.

The elder Salih knew the jails were torture centers, and he felt he had to act quickly. It might only be a matter of time before the torturers got to his son. The judge used all his connections to get a bribe to the warden at the prison. After only eighteen days of confinement, Salih was released. His parents bought him a fake passport on the black market and gave him what savings they could. With the counterfeit passport in his hand—and his heart in his throat—he slipped by police at the Baghdad airport and boarded an airplane. The Kurdish teenager, embarking on his first flight, was going to London.

Within a few years, Barham would earn a Ph.D. in engineering from the University of Cardiff in Wales. He would be fluent in English, and he'd speak it with a cultured British accent. By then he'd also be an outspoken dissident, organizing protests in the exile community and condemning his scholarship benefactor, the Ba'athists, in public forums.

Barham Salih became a U.K. citizen and now had a real passport. With British citizenship and an advanced degree, he might have landed a lucrative engineering job almost anywhere in the United Kingdom. Nonetheless, Salih decided to continue his political work. Iraqi spies in Britain, however, had been monitoring Salih's political activities and reported back to Baghdad. Once again, his parents were banished to southern Iraq. In the late 1980s he took a job in the London office of the PUK, where he eventually became the party's representative and spokesman. He was comfortable in London society, grateful for his education, and he remained quick to defend his adopted country, despite the conflicts of history. Many years later, during an interview, I would ask him about the British occupation of Iraq and Churchill's reported use of gas against the Kurds. By then it was the eve of the Anglo-American attack on Baghdad. He demurred to answer; this was not the time for a swipe at British foreign policy or to criticize an icon like Churchill.

After the first Gulf War, when the Kurdish factions started killing each other and the economy in northern Iraq broke into shambles, PUK chief Jalal Talabani tapped Salih for the party's most important foreign position, PUK representative in Washington, D.C. Salih was educated and personable, with the manner of a British diplomat. Most important, he understood Anglo-American thinking.

For the Kurds, the selection represented a break with the past. Salih's experience was limited to having been a student, an organizer, and a party official. He had never been a *peshmerga,* a Kurdish guerrilla whose leadership stripes had been earned in the mountains under fire. The Gulf War had put the Kurds of Iraq on the map, and Talabani recognized that the new battleground was international relations. If the Kurds were going to compete, they needed people like Salih— Kurds who were comfortable at embassy functions, at corporate cocktail parties, and, notably, under the lights at *Nightline* and *Meet the Press.*

The twentieth century was almost over. Leaders of the Kurdish parties in northern Iraq knew their people had been isolated long enough. It was time to come down from the mountains. Thus began the 1990s, a decade of small diplomatic steps for the Kurds in Washington, a time, as one put it, of "learning the Americans."

By the mid-1990s, the Kurds of Iraq represented only 15 percent of the estimated 25 to 30 million Kurds in the region. The majority of the world's Kurds— some 14 million—lived in Turkey, but the United States–Turkish military alliance had obscured the struggle of Turkish Kurds. About 7 million Kurds lived in Iran, but Tehran had no diplomatic ties with the U.S., and America had shown no interest in supporting Kurdish resistance in Iran. There were a million Kurds in Syria, but they were largely unknown to the outside world. That left the 3.5 million Kurds of northern Iraq (and an estimated 1.5 million in the rest of Iraq). They had fought for decades against the central government. Soon, with the election of George W. Bush and a changing American foreign policy toward Iraq, their old struggle would be validated. Politically, it would be the equivalent of waking up one day and winning the lottery. A minority in greater Kurdistan, the Kurds of Iraq would find a new sense of empowerment in Washington.

Salih's star rose quickly in Washington. In 2001, the PUK recalled him to become the prime minister of the Kurdistan Regional Government in Sulaimaniah. By that time, he owned a house in a Washington suburb in Maryland, and his wife worked for the U.S. Department of Agriculture. Like the rest of the kids on the block, the Salih children spoke American slang and liked to hang out at the mall. Whatever the future held for the Kurds in Iraq, Salih would need to visit Washington frequently. Salih decided his family would stay on temporarily in the United States, while he returned to his hometown of Sulaimaniah. A cease-fire with the Kurdistan Democratic Party had been in place since 1996, but the rival Kurdish parties had yet to unify their positions, and each had its own prime minister. Nechirvan Barzani, the nephew of Massoud Barzani and the young Kurd I had met in Iran in 1991, was the new prime minister for the KDP.

Salih took up residence in the well-appointed family home where he had grown up as a child. His mother, who had been active after the Gulf War in lobbying for the rights of Kurdish women, moved to a nearby house to continue her work. Sleeping quarters for Salih's retinue of bodyguards were set up across the street.

2002: "Welcome to Kurdistan"

It had been nearly impossible for journalists to enter Iraq from Turkey since 1995, when Ankara restricted news access to PKK sanctuaries in northern Iraq. Access to Iraqi Kurdistan from Iran was time-consuming and often problematic, but it was relatively easy to cross the border from Syria. In the case of my trip, the Kurds in Damascus applied to the Syrian police for transit permission. In February 2002, after a wait of two months, the *mukhabarat* approved my application.

I hired a taxi in Damascus and rode five hundred miles through the desert, arriving at dawn at the Tigris River, the border between Syria and Iraq. A small wooden shack stood by the river, a makeshift office for the *mukhabarat*. An hour later, a plainclothes policeman found my name, handwritten in Arabic, in his dog-eared ledger.

Despite its appearance, this was an international frontier, but I was going to the land of the Kurds, a *noncountry*. There would be no visa or exit stamp in my passport, no paper trail to alienate the Iraqi regime in Baghdad. Transit would consist of just a wink and a nod, nothing at all to indicate I had left the country. The passage would be low profile, almost undercover. I crossed the Tigris in a leaky plywood boat. A sign on the other side greeted me in English: WELCOME TO KURDISTAN. I looked back across the river. Officially speaking, I was still in Syria.

I had no way of knowing, but a little more than a year remained until the U.S. invasion in Iraq. At this point there was still a rivalry between the KDP and the PUK and no unified Kurdish military command for Pentagon planners to count on. The KDP controlled the western two-thirds of the breakaway enclave, giving it access to the Turkish and Syrian borders. The PUK controlled the eastern portion along the border with Iran. I was headed for the PUK city of Sulaimaniah, but when I stepped out of the boat in northern Iraq, I was still in KDP territory. That meant I needed a KDP fighter to escort my taxi to the last KDP checkpoint, a ninety-minute drive to the east. After that, there was a demilitarized zone of several miles, a beautiful but haunting stretch of land, where, following the 1996 cease-fire in the bitter civil war, Kurdish artists had painted roadside boulders with doves and other emblems of peace. A mile later, we stopped at the first PUK checkpoint.

The road surfaces in the region were just as cracked and potholed as they had been in 1991 after the Gulf War, when I had first visited the Kurds. There still weren't any gas stations. The only place to fuel up were narrow shoulders off the highway, where Kurdish kids sold the benzene from plastic jugs. No banks or post offices or movie theaters were open yet. At the same time, I was struck by the number of new hotels, Internet cafés, and luxury cars. Since my last visit, in 1998, in many ways, Kurdish society and economy seemed transformed. Two American-looking supermarkets had opened in the last year, lessening Kurdish isolation from the West, and others would open soon. While there weren't any tourists yet, picture postcards were on sale in the markets. Everywhere I went, people were jabbering away on cell phones and shopping in stores. The changes were astonishing.

U.N. Resolution 986

Most of the population was still poor, but the malnutrition I'd seen in the early 1990s was no longer evident. "The problem now," a Kurdish doctor told me, is "unemployment, not hunger." He said that college graduates were vying for jobs as truck drivers with foreign relief agencies, because the pay was stable, and the currency was in U.S. dollars, not *dinars*. Nevertheless, even with the widespread lack of jobs, most people in 2002 now had enough to eat. Under the Oil for Food program implemented in 1996 (U.N. Resolution 986), Iraq had been permitted to sell oil to buy food and medicine and to invest in water and energy projects. The Kurds were getting 13 percent of the oil revenues. Every Kurdish family was now guaranteed a monthly allotment of goods such as flour, cooking oil, sugar, soap, and tea.

However, the aid process was slow and cumbersome, with rumors of widespread corruption. Any delegate on the U.N.'s fifteen-member Security Council could block an import to Iraq on the grounds of potential "dual use," arguing that the Baghdad regime might convert the product to military use. The definition covered a lot of material needed for reconstruction. According to Kurdish leaders, 90 percent of the goods then on hold—about $5 billion—had been blocked by the United States. The remaining 10 percent was being held up by Britain.

The program had other deficiencies. Instead of supporting local farmers, Saddam was forcing the United Nations to buy agricultural products for Iraqis on the international market. Local farmers in Kurdistan were caught with rotting stores of their own barley and wheat and had nowhere to sell them. Meanwhile, they were receiving grain subsidies marked "Thailand," which did nothing to increase their income. "They sell our good oil," one farmer told me, "and we get expired rice in return."

Worse yet, the Iraqi regime was suspected of channeling payoffs to U.N. officials who administered Resolution 986. Among other things, Baghdad had held up visa approval for technicians hired for development projects, and official foot dragging often spelled failure for critical programs. I saw an example of that shortcoming at a Kurdish hospital in the city of Dohuk, where an air-conditioning system intended for the operating room languished in packing crates, unassembled. The manufacturer's warranty required installation by company technicians, but the installers could not get Iraqi permission to cross the border from Jordan. After two years, the Baghdad government still had not processed their visa applications.

Oil for Food was a welfare juggernaut, but it was necessary, and many Kurds addressed the program with self-deprecating humor. One of several jokes I heard went something like this: A Kurd brought a jug of oil with him when he went to a restaurant for dinner. When it came time to pay the bill, he put the jug on the table and said to the waiter, "This is oil for food." Another Kurd, a man who owned a neighborhood liquor store, gave me another view. An alcoholic who had quit drinking five years earlier, he spoke of the period before the advent of Resolution 986, when life was hard for the Kurds. In those days, he said, his customers drank "for sadness." Things were different now, he said with a wink. "Now people drink for pleasure."

The Difference a Decade Makes

Despite Iraqi meddling, corruption, and the convoluted bureaucracy of humanitarian relief, U.N. Resolution 986 had set up a safety net in Kurdistan. What a contrast life seemed to be now, compared with the early and mid-1990s, when the Iraqi Kurds, largely ignored by the West, were barely scraping by. In those days, there were few jobs, people were hungry and desperate, and beggars would approach foreigners in restaurants for food or handouts. In some villages, foolhardy residents tried to convert land mines to use as depth charges for fishing, often with disastrous results. Economic crime was rampant, especially auto theft. Chop shops to dispose of car parts sprang up all over Kurdistan. As feuds, domestic abuse, alcoholism, and violent crime increased, armed guards protected the haves from the have-nots.

In 1993, a month after my visit to Kurdistan, my loyal driver, a gentle, easygoing man named Azad, was murdered on the open highway. On a subsequent trip, I visited family members in the KDP town of Salahuddin and gave them photos I'd taken of him. Azad's wife told me the little she knew: His taxicab had been forced off the road; when the body was found, his money was gone.

Now it was 2002. For more than a decade, the Kurds had largely been forgotten by the world. The public's memory of the Kurds—an image of refugees living in tents, washing dishes in mountain streams—was still frozen in 1991.

However, the Kurds had changed, and the differences could not have been greater. When I returned in 2002 to Salahuddin to visit Massoud Barzani, the office of the KDP leader was no longer in the dilapidated ex-casino where I interviewed him ten years earlier. Now he and a large staff were housed in a palacelike headquarters called *Sari Rush* (Black Head), five miles outside of town. A few days after renewing acquaintances with Massoud, I ran into Shirko Abid, a former KDP *peshmerga*. Shirko's father had fought with Massoud's father, KDP founder Mullah Mustafa Barzani, and he'd been a part of the short-lived Mahabad Republic in Iran in 1946. After the collapse of the Kurdish republic, Shirko's father returned to Iraq, where, Shirko said, Iraqi agents later killed him with a poisoned glass of orange juice, but that was *then,* Shirko said. "This is a new time."

Shirko had immigrated to England after the abortive Barzani uprising in 1975. In the years since, he had amassed a fortune in an electronics business in London. Now the ex-guerrilla was back in Kurdistan with a contract to provide all the KDP offices with a state-of-the-art computer system. He told me the prospect of war against the Iraqi regime was opening up widespread investment opportunities, and he boasted, "Kurdistan would become a 'Hong Kong' investment center or the 'Switzerland of the Middle East' for tourists."

It was clear that the dark years of the 1990s were finally over. The Kurds now had their own ministries of health, agriculture, and redevelopment, as well as other earmarks of a fully functioning government. They were in the midst of a golden era, economically and politically.

New Freedoms

The PUK leaders saw signs of even more progress ahead. Inviting me to lunch soon after my arrival, Barham Salih seemed effusive. Kurdistan, he maintained, would soon be "a beacon of democracy" in the region, especially to neighboring countries, where freedom for other Kurds was so restricted. Already, dozens of periodicals were available in northern Iraq, including the official Ba'ath party newspaper from Baghdad.

One of the Kurdish dailies was exercising its freedom, he said with a mixture of pride and dismay, by attacking him in editorials. Nineteen Kurdish television stations were broadcasting in northern Iraq. Some of the broadcasts, beamed to Europe and North America, were in English. The Kurds, he said, had a fully functioning legal system, which could boast the only female judge in the Islamic world. There were signs of progress on every front. Ever the optimist, Salih predicted that Kurdistan would soon have gun control laws, seat belt rules, and even traffic tickets for bad drivers.

Plan for Iraq War Begins in 2001

Most important, Uncle Sam, the old suitor, was calling again, and, according to news reports, the Kurds were answering the call. In fact, from what I could gather from the Kurdish prime minister, plans to remove Saddam Hussein from power were *already* in motion by the fall of 2001. Salih revealed that only three months earlier—in November 2001—he had been invited to the Pentagon to meet with Donald Rumsfeld, the secretary of defense. Salih was visibly excited when he recounted the meeting, telling me he'd been "very impressed" with Rumsfeld. This time, he said, "the United States is serious" about regime change. When I tried to pump him for details, however, he clammed up. The Kurds, it occurred to me, were now in the confidence of the United States.

The Kurds weren't members of the United Nations, and they had no representation on Embassy Row. Their offices in Washington were still as small and cramped as they had been in the 1990s, when I'd seen them waiting, hat in hand, for low-level meetings on Capitol Hill. However, the Kurds were the only dissident group in Iraq with an army on the ground, and now they were getting access to the highest levels of the Pentagon—not the usual channel for marginalized groups seeking diplomacy. Political authority to negotiate, normally the province of the State Department, had been usurped by Defense, a department that usually *implemented* policy. Salih's meeting, coming just weeks after the attack on the World Trade Center and at a time when the Pentagon had its hands full with the war in Afghanistan, seemed more than a coincidence.

The private talks with the secretary of defense, the highest official in U.S. history to receive the Kurds, had not been reported in the press. Salih's revelation of the special audience came in February 2002. At that point, the U.S. invasion of Iraq was still thirteen months away, and no one was discussing war—at least not publicly. Salih's disclosure suggested that the Kurds were being recruited for a purpose. Why else, I remember thinking, would the largely neglected group suddenly be in demand in Washington? I felt as if I had just gotten a look at the government's cards. "I think the war will be here by September [2002]," Salih said confidently.

Preserving Kurdish Gains

Salih told me the Kurds were still afraid of antagonizing Saddam Hussein. At that point, the issue involved an anti-regime radio transmitter, which the CIA wanted the Kurds to set up in their territory. That would be a flagrant provocation to Saddam, Salih indicated, and reprisals were likely. The Kurds had no way to stand on their own unless the United States guaranteed their survival, preferably with a written pledge. He hoped the United States would afford Kurdistan the same protection as Kuwait. The Iraqi regime needed to know that Uncle Sam would shield the Kurds. Nevertheless, despite the likelihood of war, the Americans had made no such promises to the Kurds. Therefore, the transmitter was a no-go. "Besides," Salih said wryly, "we already *have* our own radio stations in Kurdistan."

Then there was the matter of Turkey. A guarantee of U.S. protection also might allay Kurdish fears of Turkish "preemption" in northern Iraq. The Kurds were worried the Turks would move troops into northern Iraq before the arrival of U.S. forces. Some Kurds referred to possible deployment as "pulling a Cyprus," a reference to Turkey's 1974 invasion of the Greek-controlled island. The Cyprus invasion was condemned by both the United States and the United Nations in 1974, but Turkey had justified it on the grounds of an emergency, a temporary need to rescue Turkish Cypriots. The Turkish occupation in Cyprus was still in place, almost thirty years later. Lately, the Turkish press had been running stories about the Turkmen minority needing similar protection from the Kurds in northern Iraq. Salih was headed to Ankara for meetings designed, he said, to "raise the comfort level" of the Turks. The prospect of war, he said, had Ankara nervous about a secret U.S. agenda in the region. Turkey was paranoid. "It's so bad," Salih told me, "that now they're asking us what *we* know [about American plans]. Our stock with Turkey is going up," he said with a smile, "because we have access in Washington."

The biggest fear of the Kurds was whether the United States would include them as full partners in the war effort. Iraqi Kurdistan wasn't Afghanistan under the Taliban, where people were desperate for change. Yet the Kurds were being asked to risk everything. Would the war effort be a one-way street, with the superpower controlling every aspect of the alliance? What if the invasion didn't go as planned, I asked the prime minister, and the Kurds ended up with *less* power than before? Did the Kurds have any options other than war? With the eyes of the world on Saddam, why couldn't the Iraqi threat be *contained*? Why risk the golden era of the Kurds by provoking a madman? Paraphrasing a local proverb, I asked, "Isn't the devil you know better than the one you don't?"

Salih emphatically disagreed.

The only way for the Kurds to preserve the gains they had made over the last decade, he argued, was to remove the lingering threat of the Baghdad regime. The task would be less difficult than the critics realized, and he sought to draw distinctions between challenges the United States faced in Iraq and in Afghanistan. In both countries there were ground forces to aid the Americans. Admittedly, the Iraqi army was stronger than the Taliban, but it was far weaker than it had been in the first Gulf War. More important, the Kurds controlled more land than the Afghan Northern Alliance and could provide a large and secure gateway for U.S. troops, presumably via Turkey. Once Saddam was gone, the Iraqis would welcome the Americans as liberators.

A new and better world lay ahead, and the Kurds were eager to do their part.

Assassination

It was April 2, 2002, late in the afternoon. *Newsweek* magazine had just published an article about the Iraqi Kurds—with the politically loaded word *Kurdistan* in the headline. Barham Salih, a careful observer of the U.S. media, took note of the prominent placement. "The 'K' word is finally out there in the U.S.," he joked to an American visitor. "We are making progress."

Parked in front of Salih's house that day were three Toyota Land Cruisers, and Karzan Mahmoud was seated in the one he'd used a few weeks earlier to ferry me around northern Iraq. Normally, this would have been his day off, but he was filling in for someone who'd called in sick. It was drizzling, and Karzan and the other bodyguards had taken refuge inside their vehicles. They had just escorted Salih to a memorial service for a Kurdish poet, a nationalist who'd died of a heart attack, and now they were waiting for Salih to check his messages at home before whisking him to the Palace Hotel for an important meeting. Ryan Crocker, the head of the Iraq desk in the State Department, was in town to continue U.S. efforts to patch up the old feud between the PUK and the KDP.

Just then, a fourth Land Cruiser pulled up in front of Salih's two-story home and Dr. Khasrow Gool, the PUK intelligence director in Sulaimaniah, got out with three bodyguards. The security men were dressed in camouflaged green uniforms and they carried the standard AK-47s. Karzan's team did not recognize the men, but Gool was an old friend of the prime minister and everyone knew him. The two Kurdish leaders had gone to high school together, years before Khasrow became a detective in Baghdad and, eventually, a double agent for the Kurds inside the Iraqi *mukhabarat*. His cover had been blown in 1991, just before the first Gulf War, and he'd been arrested. After the war, the Iraqis freed him in a prisoner exchange with the Kurds.

It was a rare experience for a representative of the U.S. government to visit Kurdistan, and Gool was anxious to accompany Salih to meet the Washington envoy. Now, Salih's bodyguards assumed their boss would invite his old friend for a customary *chi* before leaving to see the American, and Karzan figured the delay would give him enough time to run down to the corner store for a cold drink. As he emerged from his SUV and began walking, he saw what looked like a normal taxicab approaching from the opposite direction. It was a 1983 or 1984 VW Passat and was painted the orange and white colors used by Iraqi taxis. When Karzan was about thirty feet away, the car came to a stop in the middle of the street. Karzan noticed that the three Kurds in the car were wearing camouflage uniforms. Thinking they needed directions, Karzan moved toward the curb and called out, asking them what they wanted. The next thing he saw was the passenger door open, and then the muzzle flash from a machine gun.

Salih was on his way out of the house and had just reached the vestibule when his assistant called him back for a phone call from a Kurdish woman, a writer in Germany. He was in a hurry, but he had been playing international phone tag with the writer for a couple of days, and he decided to go back to take the call. That was when the shooting started.

Amange, Salih's nineteen-year-old cousin, was in the kitchen at the time. Amange—the name means "goal" or "target' " in English—had joined the security detail only a few weeks before, after proudly informing his family he had scored 85 percent on the PUK bodyguard test. He grabbed his rifle and opened the door of the vestibule, stepping onto the front steps and directly into a hail of bullets. The assassins cut him down before he could fire a shot. (A month earlier, I'd met Amange in a local teahouse, a popular place known for its baklava. I'd been drinking tea and eating the sweet Kurdish dessert that day when I'd seen him by the window. He was standing in a shaft of sunlight, laughing and talking on his new cell phone, and I'd taken his photo. At a memorial service held after his death, I would give his mother a copy of the picture.)

Karzan's abrupt exit from the Land Cruiser had startled the attackers, apparently forcing them to trigger the attack prematurely, before they were directly in front of Salih's house. Karzan thought of the 9 mm machine gun he'd left in the pocket of the driver's door, but it was too late. As he raised his arms to cover his face, he felt the hot flash of bullets tear into his leg, hands, sides, elbow, and wrists. Two rounds passed through his arm, creasing his head. As he dove for safety under his car, shots rang out from behind, hitting him in the back and side. The other bodyguards—his own men—were confused by the fact that Dr. Gool's men and the assassins were both dressed in camouflage uniforms, and everyone seemed to be firing wildly. In all, Karzan was hit twenty-three times. Still conscious, he heard one attacker yell to his comrade, "Shoot him again! He's still alive—shoot him again!"

When he heard the gunfire, Nijat was across the street from Salih's house in the security building, taking a break. Nijat was an especially alert bodyguard, a fact I'd discovered the month before when Salih assigned him to a detail to protect me on a trip to Ansar-infiltrated territory near Halabja. On that day we'd stopped for lunch at a hole-in-the-wall kebab joint. It was late afternoon and everyone was hungry. The other bodyguards and I hurried indoors, where we wolfed down plates of lamb and rice, but Nijat remained outside by the sidewalk grill, scanning the crowd that had gathered to peek at the foreign visitor. He also monitored the cook, to make sure he didn't try to poison me. I didn't discover the part about the cook until later, when we were in the car and headed back to my hotel. Nijat started scolding one of the other bodyguards in Kurdish, and I persuaded my translator to tell me what he was saying. It turned out he was admonishing the other guard for giving in to his hunger and not remaining *outside* the restaurant. Rushing to eat was not "according to training" for bodyguards. With a foreign guest present, he said sternly, the lapse of discipline was a serious breach of security.

When the attackers started shooting, Nijat grabbed his gun and raced up the stairs to the roof of the dormitory. He and another guard poured fire onto the

Baghdad, 1983: Secretary of Defense Donald Rumsfeld represented the Reagan-Bush administration in efforts to restore diplomatic relations with the regime of Saddam Hussein. Iraq later used converted U.S. helicopters to gas the Kurds. *(Video capture courtesy of Getty Images)*

In 1988, approximately five thousand Kurds were killed by chemical bombs in the town of Halabja. In 2003, the administration of President George W. Bush listed the massacre as one of the justifications for going to war with Saddam Hussein. *(Courtesy of IRNA/AFP/Getty Images)*

Operation Provide Comfort, April 1991: A Turkish soldier watches the arrival of U.S. aid in Turkey. The Kurds later returned to their homes in Iraq where, under Allied protection from 1991–2003, they built a prosperous, semiautonomous zone.

A Kurdish refugee camp near Urmia, Iran, March 1991: One and a half million Kurds fled to Iran and Turkey following a failed uprising in northern Iraq. Today, many Kurds in Iran would like to duplicate the success of Kurds in neighboring Iraq.

Kevin McKiernan (left) interviews Massoud Barzani, current president of the Kurdistan Regional Government, in 1991. Barzani told the author, "We do not want the world to remember us as refugees. Our case is *political*."

Turkey, March 1991: A Kurdish father prepares to bury an infant in the mountains after fleeing the Iraqi army. Tens of thousands of Kurdish refugees died in their rush to escape Iraqi troops.

Kurdish rebels (PKK) in southern Turkey, 1996. After the capture of their leader in 1999, the PKK called a unilateral ceasefire with Turkish troops. In 2004, the guerrillas resumed attacks, claiming promised reforms in Turkey had not been carried out.

Sirnak, Turkey, 1994: Kurdish refugees, their donkeys laden with refrigerators and other household goods, flee after their village was burned by Turkish troops. Approximately three thousand villages were destroyed in the Kurdish uprising in Turkey.

Diyarbakir, Turkey, March 21, 1994: Protesters demonstrate for independence during celebrations for *Newroz*, the Kurdish New Year.

Soriya, Iraq, 1992: Kurdish villagers after an attack by Turkish F-16 fighter jets. Turkish officials said cross-border raids into Iraq targeted PKK rebel bases, but Iraq's Kurdish leaders said civilians also suffered casualties.

Syria, 1995: Abdullah "Apo" Ocalan at a PKK rebel safe house in Syria. In 1999, Turkish commandos captured Ocalan in Africa, reportedly with U.S. assistance. He is serving a life sentence in a prison on an island near Istanbul, Turkey.

Iraqi-Turkish border, 1992: Iraqi Kurdish fighters point to the positions of PKK rebels. During the 1990s, Iraqi Kurds fought Turkish Kurds and also fought among themselves. U.S. officials helped Iraqi Kurds settle many of their differences.

Diyarbakir, 1995: A Kurdish woman passes a U.S.-made M60 tank. During the course of the Kurdish uprising (1984–1999), the United States was Turkey's primary supplier of weapons. Human rights groups sought to limit U.S. arms exports.

Barham Salih (left), Iraq's current minister of reconstruction, in a photo taken in 2002. A month later, an al-Qaeda-linked group tried to assassinate Salih. Attackers killed five bodyguards, and the author's former driver was badly wounded.

Halabja valley, Iraq, 2002: McKiernan (center) with his driver, Karzan Mahmoud (third from left), and body-guards. Mahmoud was wounded by twenty-three bullets in the assassination attempt. The author helped to arrange medical care in the United States.

Qais Ibrahim Khadar, a member of Ansar al-Islam, tried to kill Kurdish official Barham Salih. He told the author, "If I got out of jail tomorrow, I'd try to kill him again." Qais claimed al-Qaeda was a state of mind. "You cannot kill it," he boasted.

An Ansar al-Islam commander in a 2003 photo. Known as the "Bombmaker" because he rigged cars for suicide bombers, he was also suspected in the double bombings that killed a hundred Kurds in 2004. He was captured later that year.

Yazidi religious ceremony in northern Iraq, 2002: The Yazidis, who claim three hundred thousand followers worldwide, believe that the world's original tongue was Kurdish. They regard Iraqi Kurdistan as "the center of the universe."

An Ansar al-Islam camp in northern Iraq. The United States pinpointed insurgents in 2002, but held off bombing their camps until the attack on Saddam Hussein in 2003. Some militants escaped to Iran and later merged with the insurgency in Iraq.

Shinerwe Mountain, Iraq, 2002: Kurdish *peshmerga* ("those who face death") man a bunker on the frontlines in the war with Ansar al-Islam. Iraqi Kurds tried to convince the United States to bomb Ansar camps several months before the U.S.-led invasion.

The Kurds, the largest minority group in Syria, have been emboldened by Kurdish advances in Iraq. Since the fall of the Iraqi regime, Kurdish demonstrators in Syria have repeatedly clashed with Syrian authorities.

A member of the Kurdish *peshmerga* in northern Iraq. Iraqi Kurds have special units of women fighters, as do PKK guerrillas, the Kurdish separatists in Turkey. So far, only Turkish Kurds have allowed women to go into combat.

Kirkuk, Iraq, April 10, 2005: Kurdish fighters destroy a poster with Saddam Hussein's image during the liberation of the city.

Wagea Barzani, Kurdish army commander: Barzani suffered permanent head injuries in a "friendly fire" attack on his caravan by U.S. fighter jets in 2003. Eighteen Kurds were killed in the incident and forty-five injured.

Kirkuk, Iraq, April 10, 2003: A Kurd raises banner with the words "Thank you Mr. Bosh [sic]." Kirkuk is home to Kurds, Arabs, Turkmen, and Christians. Today, the oil-rich city is considered a tinderbox of ethnic tension.

A sign at the border of northern Iraq. Iraq's neighbors—Turkey, Iran, and Syria—fear that Kurdish autonomy in Iraq will agitate their own restive populations. Already, visitors to the Kurdish region have their passports stamped "Iraqi Kurdistan."

Baghdad, 2005: Jalal Talabani (left), the first Kurdish president of Iraq, with Karzan Mahmoud in the Green Zone. Mahmoud was the author's driver before being wounded in a terrorist attack. He is currently working at the Iraqi Embassy in Canada. *(Photo courtesy of Karzan Mahmoud)*

Baghdad protests, April 2003: Before the war, two-thirds of the American public backed the U.S.-led invasion. By the fall 2005, an AP poll said that 59 percent of Americans believed "The United States made a mistake in sending troops to Iraq."

fake taxi below, emptying the banana clips from their AK-47s in a matter of seconds, reloading until the gun barrels burned their hands. A bodyguard named Serbest—which means "free" in Kurdish—later told me that he saw one of the assassins peel off a heavy coat. Underneath was a green camouflage uniform, just like the ones worn by Dr. Gool's guards. Amid the panic and chaos of the firefight it was hard to tell Kurdish friend from Kurdish foe.

Salih's other driver, the man parked across from Karzan's car, dove to the floor of his own SUV just as bullets blew out the windshield. Karzan saw one of the attackers pull the pin on a grenade and lob it under the driver's seat. Karzan waited for the explosion, but he heard nothing. The grenade was a dud.

From where he lay, Karzan could tell that the license of the attacker's car was red, indicating it was from Erbil. He tried to memorize the plate number, but blood from his scalp wounds had trickled into his eyes, making it difficult for him to read. It was raining steadily now, and he was lying on the pavement underneath the back of the Land Cruiser. He thought of what was directly overhead—the cans of gas, weapons, and ammunition he'd loaded earlier that day—and it occurred to him that the car might explode. His attention turned to the droplets of water bouncing off the concrete near his face. He felt cold and wet and he was getting dizzy. Suddenly, bolts of lightning lit up the street. A peal of thunder followed, mixing with the crackle of the gunfire. Karzan closed his eyes, trying to distinguish between the sounds. He was puzzled why anyone would want to shoot him. When he opened his eyes again, everything was quiet. He could see several of his friends lying on the street. They seemed to be sleeping, and he wondered why.

This had always been a quiet, residential street, without checkpoints, providing ready access to Salih's house from either end of the block. Now the façade of the prime minister's stucco home was pockmarked by dozens of bullets, the upscale Kurdish neighborhood was littered with shell casings, and the air smelled of cordite. Salih's assistant, Azad Sabir, arrived a few minutes later, and was devastated by what he saw. Five bodyguards, all friends, lay dead. Four more were wounded, three of them seriously. The bodies of two of the assailants, both men wearing the long beards favored by the extremists, lay sprawled near their bullet-riddled taxicab. The third man, the leader of the hit squad, Qais Ibrahim Khadar, had escaped, but only after wounding Karzan and killing at least two of his friends. The ferocious gun battle had lasted ten minutes, a remarkable time for any firefight, much less an urban battle in a contained setting. In all, Khadar had fired some 140 bullets, a feat that required him to reload several times in the heat of combat. Barely injured—he had suffered only a flesh wound to the leg—the brazen killer had vanished.

He would be captured later, and I would meet him.

16

Stranger in My Cab

A coincidence is worth a thousand appointments.

—ARAB PROVERB

A day before the attack on the prime minister, I found myself stuck at the airport in my hometown of Santa Barbara. I was en route to Washington, D.C., to give a talk on Iraq. My plane had mechanical problems, and I was waiting to be rerouted.

In more innocent times, before the attacks of 9/11, a travel agent I know, a transplanted New Yorker who had left the Big Apple in the 1980s, liked to refer to Santa Barbara as the "Little Avocado." He bragged that his adopted city had "the world's cutest little airport": a tiny terminal with a red tile roof, palm trees around the outdoor gates, and a set of runways perched on the bluffs of the Pacific Ocean.

After 9/11, the agent's description of the little airport might have been updated to include the presence of National Guardsmen with M-16 rifles.

I passed the time at the airport that day talking with the soldiers. The conversations, like a lot of things in the United States after 9/11, reflected the strains of our common, transformed reality. Earlier that week, on an Amtrak train, the conductor had confided to me that he dealt with feelings of helplessness by holding a second job, making videos on "psychological ops" for the Army Reserve. "You know," he said hopefully, ". . . to *influence* things." And then there was the municipal worker I saw in the front seat of his parking enforcement van, staring straight ahead. The city vehicle had a photo of Osama bin Laden on the door with a bull's-eye superimposed on it. Under the photo were the words WANTED DEAD OR ALIVE. I guessed he was not the kind of guy you could talk out of a ticket.

My friend Abdul, a Kurdish lawyer, believed that the world entered a "new time zone" on September 11, 2001. In the future when people look back, he predicted, they would talk in terms of before 9/11 and after 9/11. The divide, he predicted, would be as significant as B.C. and A.D.

The guardsmen were patrolling in front of the United counter with their automatic rifles. One soldier told me he was a single father, a self-employed earner on his other, regular job. He said the guard work paid only the equivalent of minimum wage. He had been checking travelers at the airport for five months, but he "hadn't found anything yet." The worst problem was boredom, and it was getting on his nerves. "I don't expect Osama to come through the line in Santa Barbara," he said. "So I pick out certain passengers and play mental games about which one is the terrorist."

Journalists are trained to be suspicious but not paranoid. Were I paranoid, I might have been spooked by an encounter that took place much later that day, after a new routing landed me in Baltimore. By then, it was almost midnight. I was outside the terminal waiting to get a cab to Washington, and I had finally made my way to the head of a long taxi queue. The taxi dispatcher estimated the fare to Washington would be $50. The man in line behind me stepped forward. He was a middle-aged guy with sandy hair, wearing a crumpled suit and a trench coat. He said he was in a hurry and politely asked if he could share my car. He jumped in the back with his rolling suitcase, and we fell easily into conversation. It was the last night of the NCAA basketball finals, and the Maryland-Indiana championship game was on the radio. The driver was a Russian immigrant who lived in Baltimore. He was rooting for Maryland, the home team. The passengers were pulling for Indiana.

We hadn't gone far before the stranger revealed the reason for his trip: He had come to Washington to meet Tom Ridge, the director of Homeland Security. He owned a bioterrorism countermeasure company, a start-up venture launched after the events of 9/11, and he was scheduled to meet Ridge at the White House at 8:30 the following morning. The objective was to choose several cities to conduct readiness demonstrations in the case of another terrorist attack. I settled back to listen.

My new seatmate announced that he was an ex-CIA agent who had specialized in bioterror in the agency's Directorate of Operations. The disclosure, not something strangers mention so casually, startled me. The man told me he had a Ph.D. in both chemistry and East Asian studies, and he said that he had taught Cantonese at the University of Maryland. That stuck with me, because my daughter is fluent in Mandarin Chinese. It was uncommon, she had told me once, to find Westerners who were fluent in Cantonese.

The man said that the big fear in government circles today was biological, not chemical terrorism. He said that America was the "new battlefront" and that he and his colleagues expected suicide bombers to attack the country in the near future. All that was necessary to wreak havoc was for a smallpox-infected terrorist to get on an airplane. Passengers breathing the air inside the plane, he said, would not realize they had been infected for three days, when the symptoms would appear. By then, they would have transmitted the disease to three million people. "It's exponential, logarithmic," he said.

The taxi was passing some kind of installation, which I couldn't see because it was dark. "This is Fort Meade," the man said, volunteering that this was the site where the army had developed viruses in the 1980s. Some of the viruses, he added, had been shipped to Iraq. The conversation turned back to smallpox. I asked the stranger about government tests on people who'd contracted the disease and about whether I was still protected by the inoculation I'd gotten as a child.

That is when he offered that the government of Saddam Hussein had used Kurdish prisoners for smallpox experiments. Iraqi scientists learned from the tests that old inoculations prevent death, but not disfigurement. The control group of inoculated Kurds, the stranger said, had survived the infection with scars. "People our age may be OK," he said. "It's our kids—unprotected—who will die." At the time, I knew that a war was coming and that I would be returning to Iraq. Not surprisingly, I found the smallpox information mesmerizing.

The man spoke knowledgeably about the components of the so-called Halabja cocktail used in Iraq. It was thought to be a mixture of sarin, VX, and mustard gas, which verified what a doctor I'd met in Halabja only a month before had told me. Unlike the doctor, however, the stranger claimed that *Iran*, not Iraq, was responsible for the notorious Halabja attack. I knew that both countries had used chemical weapons in the 1980s, and I knew that on the date of the Halabja attack both Iranian and Iraqi forces had vied for control of the city, which is located near the border of the two countries.

What gave me pause was the fact that I also knew—long before the conversation in the taxi—about the CIA claims of Iranian culpability. Contrary to the views of most experts in the world, the agency had concluded *the government of Saddam Hussein was not responsible for the Halabja attack*. The bloated condition of the dead Kurds' bodies, according to the CIA report, indicated they had been killed with a blood agent—a cyanide-based gas—which Iran was known to have possessed. The report claimed that Saddam's troops had mustard gas—but not blood agents—in their arsenal.

If the man in the car *wasn't* a CIA agent, he sure was talking like one. "By chance, have you read the latest *New Yorker*?" I asked him. The magazine had just published a long, controversial story claiming that Saddam Hussein still had an arsenal of weapons of mass destruction (WMD) and purporting to link his regime to al-Qaeda. The story was set in Iraqi Kurdistan and opened with a dramatic account from Halabja, the most exhaustive focus on the 1988 attack to appear in U.S. mass media in more than a decade. The recent story had reignited the dispute about who actually had gassed the Kurds. Conservative columnist

Jude Wanniski, a former editor at the *Wall Street Journal,* had just attacked the *New Yorker* writer in an open letter to presidential advisor Karl Rove. Wanniski, the advisor to President Ronald Reagan who coined the phrase "supply-side economics," warned President Bush not to be deceived by the Halabja account. Wanniski claimed that the *New Yorker* author, whom he said was an Israeli citizen and a former soldier in the Israeli Defense Forces, was motivated by an interest in advancing the war against Iraq. The letter had little apparent effect on the president. A few days later, I heard the *New Yorker* writer on the radio expressing satisfaction that the president was citing his piece as evidence of Iraqi atrocities.

The man in the taxi said he had read "every word" of the *New Yorker* article. He dismissed the piece as "part naïveté, part disinformation." I didn't give an opinion or counter his arguments, as I wanted him to keep talking. He asked me only one question during the long ride: "What brings you to Washington?" For a second, I wondered if the well-informed passenger was aware of my scheduled talk on Iraq, but I dismissed the impulse as paranoia by responding, "A conference on the Middle East." I assumed he took my response to mean something about Israel and Palestine. And that was it.

Twice during the cab trip, he replied to my questions by saying, "The answer to that is probably classified." The first time was when we were still in Maryland, not far from Fort Detrick. I knew that during the Cold War anthrax had been brewed by the gallon and successfully weaponized at Fort Detrick. I asked whether the anthrax recently found in the letters to government officials had come from inside the U.S. "The new thinking," he finally said, "is that it was foreign-made."

We were almost to Washington. The man in the taxi made a cell phone call to someone he called "sweetie." He said he'd landed at Baltimore and was sharing a cab to D.C., "with a friend."

Despite his belief that Saddam had not gassed the Kurds, the stranger had no reservations about a war with Iraq. He said that U.S. intelligence had firm evidence of at least seven chemical weapons sites in Iraq. He thought the United States would attack Iraq by the end of 2002, about eight months away. The trick, he said, would be to destroy all those sites in the first few minutes of bombing, before the regime could retaliate with WMD. I was planning to be in Iraqi Kurdistan by that date. This wasn't the first time I'd focused on those initial minutes as Saddam's window of opportunity for chemical or biological reprisal. The Kurds would be at risk, and I would be with them.

The stranger said the next issue of *Vanity Fair* magazine would have information on the target sites and would be on newsstands in a few days. I didn't ask him how he knew.

We arrived in Washington and stopped at the Mayflower Renaissance Hotel. The taxi meter read $49, exactly. The man got out and handed me $26 in cash. He told the driver he didn't need a receipt—odd, I thought, as businessmen often get receipts—and he was gone.

The next day I telephoned a friend in Washington, someone who had worked for a U.S. senator and was knowledgeable about Saddam's use of WMD in the 1980s. I asked him why the CIA would blame *Iran* for the gas attack at Halabja. My friend said he thought that any plans to attack Iraq could embarrass the CIA for the close connections the agency had with the Iraqi dictator during the 1980s. "It is possible," he said, "that Saddam was secretly supplying the CIA with bioterror results, like the human guinea pig experiments on the Kurds."

Later that week, *Vanity Fair* appeared on the newsstands. The stranger in the cab was right—at least about the magazine. Inside the May 2002 issue was an article entitled "Saddam's Deadly Arsenal."

17

Fall 2002: Six Months Before the War

Anything more than the truth would
have seemed too weak.

—ROBERT FROST

Reserving a Seat

In the fall of 2002, ABC News asked me to go to northern Iraq to set up a base for the network. Threats of a U.S. attack were taking shape, and the news outlets were making plans. It was just a week after the White House announcement that U.S. agents had intercepted large quantities of aluminum tubes bound for Iraq. Vice President Dick Cheney said the seized tubes were "irrefutable evidence" that Saddam Hussein was building atomic weapons. In a live television address to the American people, President George W. Bush spoke about the attacks of September 11 and made a powerful argument for the need to confront Iraq. "We cannot wait," he said, "for the final proof—the smoking gun—that could come in the form of a mushroom cloud."

Four years before, in 1998, U.N. inspectors reported they had destroyed most of Iraq's WMD capability. According to the administration, however, the WMD program had been reconstituted, and America was now in imminent danger. The president said Saddam Hussein had already "gassed his own people," directly invoking the fourteen-year-old Kurdish tragedy at Halabja as a casus belli and claiming that new inspections could not contain the growing risk of WMD in Iraq.

Secretary of Defense Donald Rumsfeld was also speaking out, and I listened carefully for clues that could impact my personal welfare on the coming assignment. Rumsfeld's claims about Iraq were supported by a menacing logic. "The absence of *evidence*" of weapons of mass destruction, the secretary assured a group of reporters "was not evidence of *absence*." The rhetoric reinforced my belief that a decision had already been made. As far as I could tell, there was a war coming. If I went to Iraqi Kurdistan, I'd be in it.

Donald Rumsfeld

Donald Rumsfeld seemed an unlikely champion for the Kurds or for other victims of the Iraqi regime. The secretary of defense did have a key role in Kurdish history, but it was a dark one, certainly not what the Bush administration wanted to highlight when it spoke of Saddam's atrocities. In the 1980s, Rumsfeld had been instrumental in promoting the U.S.-Iraqi reconciliation and reestablishing military support for the Iraqi dictatorship. The result was a catastrophe for Kurds and Iraqis alike, abetting some of the very abuse now being used as a justification for war.

In 1980, following the collapse of the Algiers Accord, whereby Iraq and Iran had agreed to settle their border disputes, the two countries launched what would become an eight-year war. By 1983 the conflict was in full and bitter bloom. To much of the world at the time, Iraq was a pariah state and Saddam Hussein was the "Butcher of Baghdad." The U.S., however, quietly favored Iraq, and the Reagan administration had a secret plan to rehabilitate Saddam. The plan had its roots in the overthrow of Mohammed Reza Pahlavi, the Shah of Iran, by Shiite fundamentalists in 1979, just four years earlier. The pro-Western monarch, installed by the CIA in a controversial coup in 1953, had been a supplier of oil and a major buyer of American arms for the past twenty-five years. The Shiite coup replaced the shah with the world's first Islamic state, quickly provoking the student-led seizure of the American embassy in Tehran and the taking of fifty-two U.S. hostages. That humiliating episode lasted 444 days, setting the stage for U.S.-Iran antipathy that would reverberate into the twenty-first century.

The Reagan White House and Saddam Hussein saw eye to eye on the issue of Islamic fundamentalism, and both seemed determined to rid the Middle East of the growing phenomenon. The year before, the administration had removed Iraq from the list of state sponsors of terrorism, despite Baghdad's harboring of Abu Nidal, the notorious terrorist implicated in the Black September massacre at the 1972 Munich Olympics, as well as later attacks at El Al airline counters in Rome and Vienna. The removal opened the way for a resumption of American-Iraqi oil trade, which had been frozen since Iraq nationalized U.S. oil interests in 1972. Significantly, it also lifted the ban against the buying of U.S. weapons. Rehabilitating Iraq and arming it against the ayatollahs offered the United States a chance to even the score with Iran.

In December 1983, the Reagan-Bush administration dispatched an American diplomat to Baghdad to negotiate, among other things, an oil pipeline for the Bechtel Corporation. The envoy was none other than Donald Rumsfeld. He had been White House chief of staff, as well as secretary of defense, in the administration of President Gerald Ford during the height of the U.S.-Soviet arms race in the 1970s.

When Rumsfeld arrived to negotiate with Saddam Hussein, he had something to trade for the Bechtel pipeline. Rumsfeld carried a handwritten letter from President Reagan himself—an offer to the Iraqi dictator to restore full U.S. diplomatic relations (ties had been severed in 1967 because of the Arab-Israeli war).

Rumsfeld and Saddam discussed a variety of issues of mutual interest, including a shared enmity toward Iran and Syria and the U.S. efforts to find alternative routes to transport Iraq's oil. U.S. facilities in the Persian Gulf had been shut down by Iran, and Iran's ally, Syria, had cut off a pipeline that transported Iraqi oil through its territory.

By this time, Iraq's use of nerve gas was well known, but according to declassified notes of the meeting, Rumsfeld did not broach the subject with the Iraqi dictator. After the talks, Rumsfeld spoke to the media about the value of mending fences with the notorious strongman. A new U.S.-Iraqi relationship, he claimed in a *New York Times* interview, could be useful in solving the problems of the Middle East.

Three months later, the fighting between Iraq and Iran had intensified, and Washington was alarmed that Tehran might prevail. Once again, Rumsfeld was dispatched to Baghdad. From news reports at the time, Rumsfeld would have known that the dictatorship was actively engaged in the use of weapons of mass destruction on or near the borders of the country he was visiting. A United Press International story dated March 24, 1984, chronicled both the war and Rumsfeld's visit in the same dispatch. According to the UPI report, a team of U.N. experts had concluded, "Mustard gas laced with a nerve agent has been used on Iranian soldiers in the forty-three-month Persian Gulf War between Iran and Iraq. . . . Meanwhile, in the Iraqi capital of Baghdad, U.S. presidential envoy Donald Rumsfeld held talks with [Iraqi] Foreign Minister [Tariq] Aziz."

It was not until 2002 that widespread reports confirmed Iraq had gassed Iranian troops in 1984—after their positions were pinpointed by U.S. military intelligence. The gas attacks took place at the precise time when Rumsfeld was negotiating with the Iraqi government, a time the former (and future) secretary of defense might have alerted the world to Iraq's chemical threat. Nonetheless, according to a *New York Times* story datelined Baghdad, March 29, 1984, "American diplomats pronounce themselves satisfied with relations between Iraq and the United States and suggest that normal diplomatic ties have been restored in all but name."

Later that year, when full relations were officially restored, Rumsfeld's negotiations with Saddam Hussein began to bear fruit. By then, the CIA and other U.S. intelligence agencies were inviting Iraqi generals to classified briefings. U.S. taxpayers were providing hundreds of millions of dollars in loan guarantees to Iraq. The war against Iran had begun to tilt in Baghdad's favor.

U.S. weapons companies such as Hughes, Boeing, and Sikorsky had a new customer, and Saddam had a long shopping list. Washington quickly approved sales of UH-1H "Huey" helicopters and Hughes MD-500 Defender helicopters. The transfers were slated for civilian use, but no one in the Reagan administration objected when the helicopters were converted quickly to gunships for the war with Tehran. Later, the regime of Saddam Hussein fitted some of his U.S.-made helicopters with nozzles and used them to spray cocktails of mustard gas, sarin, and VX gas on Kurdish villages.

Overtures to Iraq by the Reagan-Bush administration soon laid the groundwork for U.S. biological shipments. In 1985, the Commerce Department granted an export license to the Centers for Disease Control and Prevention in Atlanta to export West Nile virus samples to Iraqi researchers. A Virginia lab, the American Type Culture Collection, became an important supplier to Iraq of anthrax and other germ samples, later using the Department of Commerce approval to defend the shipments. U.S. samples of botulism, developed at a top-secret military germ warfare lab in Maryland, were also sent to scientists in Baghdad. According to Jonathan Tucker, a former U.N. weapons inspector, "At that time, the U.S. government was tilting toward Iraq, was trying to improve relations with Iraq, and the tendency was not to scrutinize these requests."

By this time, Iraq had developed a voracious appetite for mustard gas. German suppliers, using the cover of dual-use exports, could barely keep up with the demand. At the height of the Iran-Iraq war in the mid-1980s, the CIA was supplying Baghdad with steady intelligence on Iranian troop deployments. In the so-called tanker war, the two nations were attacking each other's oil shipments in the Persian Gulf. By 1987, U.S. jets were aiding Iraq by destroying Iranian oil platforms and firing on Iranian naval vessels in the gulf, a policy that culminated in 1988 when an American destroyer shot down an Iranian civilian airliner. In the same year, Iran agreed to accept a U.N.-brokered cease-fire. The war ended in a stalemate, for both sides, but U.S. aid in ending the conflict enabled Saddam to return his full attention to the bothersome Kurdish insurrection.

Bechtel did not get its pipeline from Saddam, but the negotiating efforts of Donald Rumsfeld opened the door for the corporate giant to secure other investments in Iraq. In July 1988, only four months after the Kurds were gassed at Halabja, Bechtel signed a contract with Iraq to build a petrochemical plant near Baghdad. The Bechtel design involved the popular dual-use technology, enabling the Iraqis to employ the chemical ethylene oxide to produce mustard gas. Financing for the plant was guaranteed through a program of the U.S. Department of Agriculture.

When Iraq defaulted in 1990, repayment of the loans reverted to the United States. Of the $5 billion in economic aid provided to Iraq over an eight-year period, $2 billion in defaulted loans were still outstanding. It was a cruel and bitter irony. Six years after Rumsfeld's boast that a restored relationship with the Iraqi dictator would be useful, a bill for gassing the Kurds and committing other atrocities had landed in the lap of the American taxpayers.

September 2002

Given the record of aggressive U.S. support for Iraq in the 1980s, the sudden concern for Kurdish victims in 2002 seemed a bit like crying crocodile tears. However, there was little time to review past atrocities or to apportion responsibility for Saddam's crimes. War correspondents usually focus on the *what's,* not the *why's,* of war. My job would be to report from Iraqi Kurdistan, not Washington. Saddam Hussein had been accused of stockpiling WMD. A news hurricane was brewing, and I had my assignment. Politics could be left to the commentators. I was headed to the front lines. The clock was running, and my mind was racing.

ABC News was already anticipating the possible use of WMD in the impending war, and the network wanted me to stop in England for special training. The London bureau, which coordinates news coverage from Europe, Africa, and the Middle East, had set up a course for staffers who might suffer exposure. The hazards seminar for journalists was being offered by an outfit called Bruhn NewTech. According to Bruhn NewTech's four-color brochure, the company conducted training for "nuclear, biological, and chemical (NBC) events both on the battlefield and in the civil emergency response environment."

I had covered northern Iraq on a dozen trips since the early 1990s. I knew the region pretty well. I was used to doing my own risk assessments, but these dangers were different, and the offer of a free disaster course was welcome. I knew precious little about biohazards and nerve agents. Saddam had already dropped chemicals on the Kurds. I could hardly afford to be in denial about where I was heading. Still, I had questions about the ABC offer. When it came to end-of-the-world scenarios, I suspected that my company would put its own interests first. Iraq was a catastrophe in the making, and I was en route. I asked myself: Were the network bean counters in New York sitting in their Central Park West suites calmly figuring the odds of my survival?

I hoped I was more than a dot of ink on an actuarial table, but my fears had been fueled by a negative experience with a previous employer. A few months earlier, in May 2002, a PBS producer in Washington, D.C., had pressured me to sign a liability waiver before leaving for northern Iraq. By then, some observers already believed a U.S. attack was a done deal, and television companies were making contingency plans to produce shows about WMD. The company that hired me, Safe World Productions, a subsidiary of Turner Productions, was planning a two-part series called *Avoiding Armageddon.*

Producers at Safe World Productions said the series was intended to expose the growing hazard of biochemicals in the world. That seemed like a worthwhile objective, but only a week after I'd agreed to be part of the production in Iraq, Safe World lawyers sought to protect the company from liability for injuries I might incur on the job. Safe World needed authentic footage of Kurdish gas survivors to promote the program, but the company wanted to insulate itself from any financial risk entailed by my travel to a war zone. On the eve of my departure, Safe World insisted I sign a statement saying that travel to Iraq "was not a condition of my employment." Travel to Iraq was the *only* way I could participate in the production. The waiver meant that if I were hurt or killed, my dependents would have no claim. It was clear that Safe World executives were as desperate to get the job done in Iraq as they were to avoid responsibility for my doing it. Everyone knew it was dangerous, and the liability release struck me as absurd and hypocritical. In the end I managed to accept the assignment and to make the trip without signing the release, but the experience made me cautious.

I wondered if the ABC executives knew something I didn't. Could agreeing to attend the disaster training serve as a waiver in a future worker's compensation case? Did course attendance mean that I had been warned about the dangers that lay ahead in Iraq—but chose to go anyway? If I were injured, would the ABC lawyers fight claims from my family with the argument I had "assumed the risk," the legal doctrine that railroad companies back in the nineteenth century had used as a shield against lawsuits for negligence?

Time to Go

I spread out my batteries, cables, chargers, lights, videotapes, digital flash cards, tripod, laptop, and other gear on the Kurdish carpet in my Santa Barbara home. I tested the cameras and the lenses, proceeding through my usual inventory of equipment. Most of the supplies I needed for work would not be available where I was going. I couldn't afford to forget anything. Kurdistan did have the Internet—access became available in 1999—but it was impossible to order products or services online. There was no mail service, UPS, or FedEx. Forget checks—there was no such thing as a bank or financial institution. American Express cards could be left at home; northern Iraq was a cash-only economy.

Despite its tragic past, some visitors saw Kurdistan as a kind of charming kingdom, a welcome bubble of isolation in a busy, over-connected age, but for a television journalist with periodic needs for spare parts, there might as well have been a sign on the banks of the Tigris River that said YOU ARE LEAVING THE REST OF THE WORLD.

I sorted out my trip pharmacy: water purification tablets, bandages, tourniquet, burn medicine, antibiotics, and malaria pills. This time, I added bottles of Rad Block, potassium iodide. The tablets were supposed to block thyroid cancers caused by radiation exposure. They had become widely available in the aftermath of the Chernobyl disaster. I had seen them on the Internet, on a sobering Web site called www.NukePills.com.

If I were exposed to nuclear contamination, I'd probably be a goner, but I grabbed the Rad Block anyway. Then I called Mike Brabeck, the friend from high school who was now a doctor in Boston, to see if he could get me some doses of atropine, the antidote for exposure to nerve gas. U.S. soldiers assigned to the Middle East were being supplied with atropine injectors, but Brabeck told me that access to the drug was beyond the reach of civilian physicians. Then I contacted my cousin Billy, an officer in the U.S. Army. Billy wasn't optimistic, either, but he said he'd try to help.

I had been following the Kurds for years, and it would be difficult for me to opt out of this assignment. The Iraq war was the story of a lifetime—for them and for me. I called my insurance agent and mailed in a check for extra accident and dismemberment coverage. Afterward, I fretted silently about the fine print in the policy: Would a gas attack qualify as an *accident?*

Little about the trip looked routine, so I'd put getting the extra coverage at the top of my checklist. That placed it ahead of items like needing yellow fever shots, buying a canvas belt with a secret money slot, and getting another tourist visa to get me through Syria for the river crossing to Iraq.

It was slowly starting to dawn on me: *Hey, I could die on this assignment.*

Covering conflict wasn't a new experience, but this was the first where the use of chemical and biological weapons was possible, if not likely. ABC was providing a bulletproof vest, but in light of the unique dangers that seemed to lie ahead, the notion of body armor struck me as irrelevant, if not farcical.

I couldn't shake the fear that this time I was pushing my luck.

As a journalist, I had seen a fair amount of violence, beginning in the 1970s as a radio reporter for NPR's *All Things Considered,* when I went to the Pine Ridge Indian Reservation in South Dakota. Since then, I had covered the Sandinista-Contra war in Nicaragua, civil wars in El Salvador and Guatemala, the Zapatista rebellion in Mexico, as well as conflicts in the Philippines, the West Bank, and Iraq. I had been under fire in Central America, and I had traveled in war zones with government soldiers in Africa. I had covered the Irish Republican Army (IRA) on active service in Northern Ireland, PKK guerrillas in Turkey, and Hamas cells in Israel. However, those conflicts were "low intensity." The assignments usually lasted a matter of weeks, limiting any long-term exposure to physical risk.

Death by Gas

In many countries, my U.S. citizenship had served as a kind of protective shield, but in northern Iraq, where I was headed, Americans could well be targets, even before the war. I suspected that once U.S. bombing began, Saddam Hussein would strike back. The Iraqi regime, once cornered, undoubtedly would use any weapon it had, even WMD. Most countries would do the same as a last resort. That was the whole point of having such weapons.

The media were citing Israel and Kuwait as the likely targets for an Iraqi retaliation. That didn't make sense to me. Northern Iraq was closer and easier. The regime did not need advanced missiles to reach Kurdish targets in the north; Kurdish cities were only miles from launch sites in Iraq. Chemical and biological shells could be loaded into artillery canons. "Old" technology would do the trick. Plus, unlike other potential targets, the Kurds had a history: They had been gassed already. Saddam already had threatened that if he were about to be killed, he would "leave a country without people."

In terms of risk assessment, gas was in a class all by itself. It wasn't like the challenge of a roadblock, which a clever journalist might dodge by knowing the terrain or by having good connections. It wasn't a case of matching wits with gunmen at checkpoints, hiding incriminating film footage in your sock or in the bottom of a backpack under dirty laundry, your heart beating fast while they did their searches.

Gas could outsmart "reporter tricks." It was heavier than air. You couldn't see it. You couldn't hide behind a concrete wall, escape beneath the ground, or hunker down in a foxhole on the battlefield. You couldn't duck. I found that out in a gully during the 1973 Wounded Knee siege, when federal forces fired CS gas—a noxious compound with little or no residual damage—into the village.

This was irregular war, which stood normal thinking on its head. If the Iraqis dropped gas on Kurdistan again, the only chance for survival might depend on getting to higher ground. I tried to remember that as friends and well-wishers, concerned I was leaving for another war zone, cautioned me to keep my head *down*.

To Iraq

I arrived at the Santa Barbara airport on September 28, 2002. National Guardsmen carrying M-16s searched my things, confiscating a two-inch Phillips screwdriver from my camera bag. With that, I was on my way to Iraq.

After landing in London, I took the train to Salisbury, a medieval-looking town near Stonehenge, the famous circle of standing stones. From there, I caught a cab to Winterbourne, the nearby British air force base. The RAF had provided a classroom for a media course on NBC hazards: nuclear-bio-chemical—as well as an airtight chamber for gas-mask testing.

The other journalists—all eighteen of them—worked for BBC, which recently had mandated the hazards training for all staffers traveling to the Middle East. The course was hosted by Dave Butler, an ex-British commando who said he had fought the IRA in Northern Ireland. Since the events of 9/11, according to Butler, his company had had more business than it could handle.

The training was a mixture of note taking, trying on protective gear, a fair amount of nervous laughter, and, finally, a trip to the "gas chamber" for exposure to tear gas. For two days, we sat at crowded tables in a prefab trailer as Butler strolled back and forth with his large-pocketed military pants tucked into combat boots, regaling us with war stories. His specialty was gallows humor. ("Be careful with your gas mask—death can be fatal.") On the second day, he made a PowerPoint presentation on viruses and toxins, with "practical tips" such as how to get *radiation dust* off our television cameras.

In light of where I was going, I figured I could use all the help I could get, but the variety—and intensity—of information was overwhelming:

- With the prevailing winds in Iraq—northwest to southeast—you are vulnerable to sarin gas for 19 miles, nuclear radiation for 26 miles, and a biological attack for 60 miles.
- You have a 98 percent chance of survival if anthrax only gets on your skin (but only a two percent chance in your lungs).
- If you get a blister agent in your throat, you will choke.
- There are eight different strains of smallpox to worry about.
- Bug sprays such as Raid contain nerve gas; under large doses of nerve gas, a goat will die in 37 seconds.
- Nuclear blasts cause blindness at night from a distance of 200 miles.
- The hairy parts of your body are the best traps for biological agents. Clean them out.

Then we went outside to get measured for boots, masks, and protective suits. As part of the cost of the course, the company provided a rucksack to tote the gear, with bright yellow stitching on the front flap that said SURVIVOR.

We tried operating our cameras with the bulky rubber gloves.

Butler told us how to change canisters on the face mask during an attack, so the nerve gas didn't get in. ("Watch for dented seams—they can be fatal!") Butler had a bouncy, can-do spirit that seemed just short of a Monty Python skit, an attitude that almost made me forget the reason I was there. He repeatedly warned the group not to get discouraged about the dangerous assignments that lay ahead. News people in today's world, he said cheerfully, face "a plethora of hazards."

We took lunch at the base, outdoors on the grass, nibbling on finger sandwiches and making small talk over the roar of RAF fighter jets that were practicing nearby for deployment to Iraq. It all seemed like a mixture of fun and doom, a nuts-and-bolts school trip for grown-ups anticipating an apocalypse.

Then we climbed into our hooded hazard suits. The instructors escorted us into the airtight chamber, doused the lights, and dropped pellets of pepper spray on the cement floor. Someone yelled, "Gas! Gas!" I fumbled for a moment, tangling the straps to my mask before I could pull them over my head, inadvertently sucking in pepper spray. In small doses the gas is harmless, costing only a few tears. When we went outside, my eyes were still tingling.

Before we climbed out of our suits, Butler wanted group photos in front of the gas chamber. Smiling for the camera only tended to remind me of the "plethora of hazards" that seemed to await me in Iraqi Kurdistan, but Butler was exceedingly cheery. I was confident if something bad befell me, he would find a place for my picture in one of his PowerPoint presentations.

I was on my way to see the Kurds, who had been gassed before and who might well be gassed again. I had not expected a philosophy course, but it occurred to me that no one in this bizarre, albeit necessary, course had spoken a word about *context*, about the madness of the post-9/11 world all of us had landed in so suddenly. Maybe it was our conditioning. Journalists seem to adjust to escalating crisis like the proverbial frogs in a hot tub of water. If the temperature is turned up only a degree per hour, we don't think to get out. Not until the water boils.

If anyone had a larger perspective, it was Ian, the friendly, overweight ex-commando who gave me a lift back to my hotel the first night. It was a thirty-minute drive, and he felt like talking. Ian had joined Bruhn NewTech five years before, after a stress-related discharge from British army intelligence in Northern Ireland. "The only way we beat terrorism there," he said, "was to address the root causes—jobs, housing, poverty, and especially humiliation. We knew who all the terrorists were. But no matter how many we killed, we couldn't beat them militarily. There were always new ones to take their place."

Ian said he had lost seven friends in the IRA conflict, and he was a backer of strong military response. "But diplomacy also has to play a big part," he added. "What America didn't understand from 9/11 is that the country was being targeted for its policies."

The following afternoon, ABC sent a VIP car to meet me at the gate of the military base. It's one of those network touches—a bit of "pastry" before the big mission—designed to make you feel like a big shot, even if you're not. I climbed into the seat and settled back. We were off to the ABC office in London for a final meeting before my plane left for Syria.

ABC, like the other networks, is a subsidiary of a large, multinational corporation. Time Warner owns CBS, General Electric owns NBC, and Walt Disney owns ABC. I checked in at ABC, which has offices in the huge Disney complex in London. Before going upstairs to the news bureau, I was given a security badge at the reception desk. It was a numbered, laminated pass. Riding up in the elevator, memories of the many trips to Kurdistan flooded my mind. Now, they were mingled with Dave Butler's descriptions of nuclear and biochemical apocalypse.

I looked at the cartoon logo on the Disney security pass and thought of the news assignment ahead. Suddenly, I was struck by an absurd thought and it made me smile. I was going to Iraq for Mickey Mouse.

18
Suly: October 2002

Consider keeping potassium iodide in your emergency kit, learn what
the appropriate doses are for each of your family members.

—U.S. DEPARTMENT OF HOMELAND SECURITY

War Fever

It was still six months before the U.S. invasion, but the winds of war were already blowing. U.S. bombers were striking Iraqi missile installations and radar sites almost daily. From some vantage points in Kurdistan, it was possible to spot the U.S. jets and to hear the explosions. The U.N. mandate to protect the Kurds in northern Iraq gave allied pilots the right of self-defense if fired upon, but the scope and intensity of the bombing suggested that Iraqi targets were being softened up for war. So far, no U.S. planes had been hit, but the persistent antiaircraft fire raised the prospect that an unexpected downing could kick-start the war. "Maybe the Iraqis will get *lucky*," one of my editors mused on the phone, "and we won't have to wait anymore."

The U.S. invasion of Iraq seemed inevitable, and a psychological campaign was already under way, with U.S. planes dropping Arabic leaflets warning Iraqi soldiers not to fight. The question was whether Saddam would allow his military to be crippled, day by day, in advance of the major U.S. attack. Or whether, knowing his cause was lost, the Iraqi dictator would launch a preemptory strike with WMD—perhaps on a "soft" target like Kurdistan.

The Kurds were banking that they would not be targets of convenience, a parting shot from a dying regime. In the absence of that horrifying prospect, it was hard to argue that the impending war would be bad for them. By an accident of timing, the interests of the Bush administration and the Kurds had converged. Distrust for U.S. intentions was now a thing of the past, and the Kurds seemed to be bathing in their new fortune. With regular visits from the "relatives"—as they affectionately referred to CIA agents—Iraqi Kurds hoped they'd soon become honorary members of the American family. "The U.S.A. is good," my friend

Barham declared one day, genuinely and without apology. "The Americans will help us because [they] believe in human rights."

The atmosphere of anticipation in some quarters approached giddiness. Kurdish military commanders hoped the conflict would transform their arsenals from small arms to state-of-the-art weaponry. Wagea Barzani, brother of KDP leader Massoud Barzani and a top commander for the KDP, told me he had his eye on acquiring advanced American M1 Abrams tanks for the Kurds. The military commander of the PUK, Mustafa Qader, who said he had been visited by CIA agents, told me he hoped to receive surface-to-air missiles.

With everything going so well, the worst imaginable development, as the Kurdish leadership saw it, would be a palace coup in Baghdad. If Iraqi military officers overthrew Saddam, it would be more difficult for the U.S. to justify the anticipated invasion. To those who had studied U.S. affairs, there was also the fear that a surprise domestic issue in the States could postpone or even derail the war train. Barham had lived in Washington long enough to know that American foreign policy was fickle, and he was afraid the push to topple Saddam could fall victim to an unrelated scandal. "I'd like it [the operation] to begin *now*," he told me six months before the war, "before there's another Enron or Watergate."

Golden Era for Kurds

The mood among rank-and-file Kurds was less certain than that of the leaders. A prime reason for ambivalence about the war was a fear of damaging the surging economy. By the fall of 2002, Kurdish shops were full of Swiss chocolate, German sausages, Dutch beer, and other imported goods. While access to the Internet was prohibited in the rest of Iraq, dozens of Internet cafés were open and thriving in Kurdistan. Video and DVD rental stores abounded. Pizza parlors were decorated with Domino's posters, which their owners had obtained during visits to the United States and Canada. The shops were selling Kurdish pizza (chicken and olives), and business was booming. The Kurds even had their own oil refinery. They still depended on Iraqi and Iranian oil for the bulk of their needs, but the refinery, the only one in the country not under the control of the regime, symbolized a growing independence.

With basic food staples—but not meat—provided by U.N. Resolution 986, a growing sector of the Kurdish population now had disposable income. Several supermarkets with American-style pushcarts and electronic registers for price scanning had opened. On a visit to one of the new markets, I was surprised to see a cosmetics counter, where teenage Kurdish girls were experimenting with lipstick and mascara.

Despite the fact that Kurds drank tea almost exclusively, many stores now sold instant coffee—usually a Nescafe patent-busting brand known as Nice Café [sic]. Cheap appliances called Sqny [sic] and Bhilips [sic]—Chinese knockoffs of brand names like Sony and Philips—were also available. In the last year, cellular telephone usage had exploded. So far, the technology did not allow calls between mobile and nonmobile phones, and the phone systems between the areas controlled by rival Kurdish factions still were not compatible. Nonetheless, cell phones were in such demand that the overtaxed phone company in Sulaimaniah would not issue any more customer lines—except to journalists or those with political connections.

Parts of Kurdistan had begun to resemble other twenty-first-century societies—for good and for bad. The loud and often rude chatter from cell phones in public places seemed to be everywhere. I even heard a couple of Kurds complaining about the racket. If having both noise *and* noise critics counted as a sign of progress, the Kurds were well on their way.

Despite great economic growth, Kurdistan was still a cash economy, with no central banking system in Kurdistan. Journalists all handled the situation differently. One reporter I knew hid his money in his backpack, but he also had a secret compartment in his belt. "If anything happens to me," he confided, "there's $2,000 in my belt."

I didn't know where I'd be when the war broke out, but I didn't want to be stranded without enough dollars if I couldn't get back to my hotel. For that reason, I seldom left any money in my room when I wasn't there.

In countries where theft and street crime were concerns, I've sometimes taped money behind hotel mirrors or under bureau drawers. But I had brought a large amount of cash to Iraq—enough to make a difference if I needed to smuggle myself out of the country—and I carried all of it with me. That meant that when I was walking back to the hotel late at night I'd often have $10,000 to $15,000 wedged in my pockets. I never was mugged or even had a close call, which is probably a testament to stability and social control in prewar Kurdistan.

Population Shift

While some Kurds believed that another uprising was the only way to consolidate the gains they had made in the previous decade, others thought that international pressure had boxed in Saddam, and they were wary of the risk of endangering the self-government they already enjoyed. "Saddam's in a cage," one man told me. "Let's leave him there, or we could lose everything."

There were those who favored regime change only on a risk-free basis—as I discovered one day when I was invited to address an adult English class at a local school. I asked the students how many supported a U.S. invasion. A majority of hands went up. Then I asked how many would support the war if they knew their own city might be involved. Only a few hands went up this time, suggesting how much had changed since the uprising of 1991, when the Kurds were under Iraqi rule and desperate to be free.

After eleven years of autonomous rule, Kurdish demographics had shifted. Many Kurds had no personal experience with the Iraqi government. In fact, the majority either had not been born by the time of the 1991 uprising or they were too young to remember any authority but the Kurds. Few high school and elementary students regarded Arabic as a foreign language worth learning and few could speak or write it any longer. The Kurds now had almost a dozen television stations of their own, including satellite channels that broadcast in Kurdish to Europe and North America. When younger viewers came across Arabic language on television, usually from the official Baghdad stations, most kept channel surfing.

While some leaders were saying privately that they'd love the United States to build air bases in Kurdistan and even to take over the oil fields of Kirkuk and Mosul, not all agreed. "The oil has been a curse on the Kurds," my friend Azad Sabir, a PUK official, told me one day. We were sitting in "MaDonal's"[*sic*] at the time under a counterfeit set of McDonald's Golden Arches. Kurdish cooks were carving Happy Meals from a crackling spit of lamb, and Azad was talking about his family. Iraqis had jailed his mother. One of his brothers had been killed by an Iraqi tank in the 1991 uprising; another brother had fled to Sweden. "If it weren't for oil," he said, "We might have had our own country fifty years ago."

His words recalled those of KDP founder Mullah Mustafa Barzani in the 1970s. Before his revolution was betrayed by the White House, Barzani had offered to *give* Iraqi Kurdistan to America as "the fifty-first state." Now the Kurds were riding to war again on America's coattails, and the outcome was anyone's guess.

When the Kurds made the alliance with Washington, they became a silent, nonvoting partner, who could hope for—but not demand—protection from America. In that sense, their predicament differed from their neighbors. Under the terms of the 1991 surrender, the Iraqi regime was permitted to retain missiles with a range of less than hundred miles, a limitation aimed at protecting Israel, Kuwait, and parts of Turkey. Those countries had the additional safeguard of Patriot antimissile systems, as well as sophisticated civil defense plans that guaranteed gas masks for most of the population. The United States had publicly pledged to defend all three nations, but the Kurds, Saddam's closest target, had no safety net.

The risk to Kurds wasn't limited to missiles equipped with chemical warheads. When it came to reaching the Kurds, old-fashioned, gas-tipped artillery shells would do.

No Gas Masks

As the threat of war grew larger, health professionals across the Kurdish enclave became increasingly worried.

In Dohuk, the northern governate located on the Turkish border and controlled by the KDP, the director of public health was Dr. Abdullah Saeed, a surgeon. Dr. Saeed told me the impending war could produce two million internal refugees and might leave a large portion of the population without food or potable water. He said that if Saddam used WMD, aid workers would be unable to reach victims, which could produce mass panic. "It would be a health catastrophe."

Saeed had already organized twenty-five emergency medical teams to cope with the expected emergency, but none of the teams had first-aid kits or gas masks for ambulance drivers (under current U.N. sanctions, gas masks were prohibited to prevent their appropriation by Iraqi soldiers). He said the health department had no atropine or antitoxins for nerve gas. Saeed had raised the need with American officials when they had scouted the area back in January 2002. He said the officials had promised that the civilian population would get the same protection as Kuwait and Israel, where everyone had masks, but nothing had been delivered yet. His emergency teams were advising people to put wet rags over their faces and go to high ground in the event of a chemical attack.

In view of U.S. certainty that Saddam possessed WMD and was poised to use them, Dr. Saeed was "shocked" that Kurds had not been provided for and that so little planning had gone into the consequences of the war. Given the risks, I asked him, should the war proceed?

"We have to get rid of him," he said, meaning Saddam Hussein.

What if ten thousand Kurds die? I asked.

"We still have to do it," he said.

What if fifty thousand die?

"No, that is too many," he said.

Okay, what about twenty-five thousand?

Dr. Saeed paused to ponder my hypothetical. "Maybe it is needed."

No Atropine

It was clear by now that I was heading into war with an unprotected population, with risks unevenly distributed. The day after I interviewed Dr. Saeed, I sent another e-mail to my cousin Billy on a U.S. Army base, pestering him again for atropine, the antidote to nerve gas. I was looking for the military-type auto injectors, the kind soldiers can jab though a pant leg in a matter of seconds. Getting antitoxins seemed like an issue of survival, and my connections gave me a potential advantage over most of the Kurds. I didn't want to draw attention to my efforts but I couldn't help feeling like someone on a leaky boat quietly snagging a life preserver.

19

A Sheikh in a Suit

Revenge is a wild kind of justice.
—FRANCIS BACON

Shalaw Askeri

I first met Shalaw Askeri, a mid-level official with the Patriotic Union of Kurdistan, in May 2002 in the tiny village of Goktapa, where—as he related graphically—many of his relatives had been gassed in a 1988 air raid. Goktapa is less well known than Halabja, the site of the chemical attack sometimes cited by the Bush administration as one of the justifications for regime change in Iraq. Almost five thousand Kurds died at Halabja, but Goktapa was one of more than two hundred hamlets in the late 1980s where horrific cocktails of tabun, mustard, and VX nerve gas had also been used. An estimated 400 Kurds died at Goktapa, Askeri said, of whom 45 were relatives, mostly his first cousins and their families.

As I spoke to Askeri, I gradually began to realize that he was more than just a survivor of the widespread repression in Iraq. His story was larger, and it embodied important aspects of modern Kurdish history: the long-standing tragedy of internecine conflict among the Kurds; the diaspora of the Kurds abroad; and the nervous hopes for a stable freedom in a post-Saddam era.

I met Askeri again in October 2002, and we went for dinner at a fancy restaurant in Sulaimaniah. By then, he'd been promoted to the position of PUK minister of agriculture, and it was clear that he was a rising star in party politics.

Askeri, a young-looking politician of forty-two with an athletic build, had an easy smile, jet-black hair and, like most Kurdish men, a full moustache. He had a reputation as an equestrian, and he kept several horses in a stable at Goktapa, but when he met his constituents in the city, he wore a European tailored suit and tie. His English was nearly perfect, and he was a popular figure in ministry circles. With a bit of a swashbuckling manner, he bore some resemblance to a young Errol Flynn in one of those old movies that PBS stations run late at night.

What distinguished him from most Kurds, however, was the fact that he was a tribal sheikh. Like his father and his grandfathers before him, he was the traditional chieftain of a large clan. "If I were in trouble," he said matter of factly, "I could call on a thousand men, and they would come to my side."

In his position with the PUK government, Askeri officially commanded 160 Kurdish *peshmerga*. That number didn't include twenty-four private bodyguards, including three fighters in the restaurant who were drinking *chi*. The men were seated nearby in camouflage dress with AK-47 automatic rifles slung over their shoulders. Other *peshmerga* were outside in the alley, watching the parked Land Cruiser. Askeri told me his bodyguards earned $110 a month, almost double the salary of the rest of the workforce.

Askeri was born in the city of Kirkuk, an ethnically mixed city of almost one million located about one hundred miles west of Sulaimaniah and still occupied by Iraqi forces. With its vast petroleum deposits, the Kirkuk region remained an important reason Iraq was the world's second-richest oil-producing area after Saudi Arabia. The oil accounted for Baghdad's long-running attempt to alter the ethnic ratio in Kirkuk. The regime's Arabization program, accelerated after Saddam took over as president in 1979, provided housing allowances and other incentives for Arab settlements in Kirkuk.

The Kurds claimed that, until World War I, Kirkuk had been the unofficial capital of Iraqi Kurdistan for centuries under the Ottoman Empire. The history-making autonomy talks between the Kurds and Iraqis, nearly realized in the 1970s, had collapsed over the Kurds' insistence that they control the Kirkuk oil fields. For the last eighty years, the resistance of the Kirkukis to domination had made the city, in Askeri's words, "the heart and soul of Kurdistan."

Askeri didn't say so, but Kirkuk also had quite a sizeable population of Turkmen, the third largest population group in Iraq (after Arabs and Kurds). They received political support from Turkey, and they strongly disputed Kurdish claims to represent the bulk of Kirkuk's population.

In 1912 Britain converted from coal to an oil-fired imperial navy, and in the 1920s British Petroleum began building the first pipelines across northern Iraq. Around that time Askeri's grandfather was arrested by the British Army and taken to a garrison in Kirkuk. The army, according to Askeri, had underestimated the power of a Kurdish sheikh. Loyal tribesmen—twenty thousand of them—marched on the British garrison, prompting his release. In 1930, Askeri's great uncles, who were also sheikhs, joined a fierce uprising against the British, the one led by the legendary Sheikh Mahmud Barzinji. Sheikh Mahmud's uncle, Askeri said, was his *great* uncle, and both men were killed by a RAF bomb in the same battle against Crown forces in the early 1930s.

We were eating lamb kebab and drinking *arak*. Askeri was treating me to a bit of the famous Kurdish hospitality and weaving accounts of Iraq under British occupation forces with Kurdish history and stories of his family.

Ali Askeri

Shalaw's father, Ali Askeri, first made his name as a student organizer against the Ba'ath party in Kirkuk in the 1960s. He had a reputation for a common touch and had a large populist following. In the 1970s, he went underground and became a wanted man after engaging in daring raids on Iraqi targets in and around Kirkuk. Long before I'd met Shalaw, I'd been aware of the elder Askeri's place in the pantheon of Kurdish heroes. He was a legend, especially to the PUK, and for many Kurds he inspired the kind of personal loyalty reportedly attributed to supporters of Emiliano Zapata during the Mexican Revolution.

In 1975, the U.S. secretary of state, Henry Kissinger, brokered a secret deal between Baghdad and Tehran, the Algiers Accord, which led to the sudden collapse of the Kurdish uprising. No longer sponsored by the United States, the Kurdistan Democratic Party (KDP) ordered rebels to lay down their arms. Ali Askeri and hundreds of dissident fighters refused and, instead, joined the PUK, the breakaway faction. Civil war followed, with Turkish and Iranian forces supporting the KDP to suppress the upstart PUK. In 1978, with infighting crippling a unified resistance to the Iraqi regime, Ali's forces went to Turkey to procure arms to rekindle the Kurdish revolution. Inside the border, they came under withering attack from Iranian, Turkish, and Iraqi jets.

Turkish ground forces and KDP *peshmerga*—Ali's former comrades in arms—surrounded the renegade PUK fighters and began to destroy them. What happened next remains an especially bitter moment in Kurdish history. It was winter, the snow was deep in the mountains, and Ali Askeri was sick—too sick, it turned out, to elude the trap the KDP Kurds had set with the promise of a weapons cache. The KDP captured Ali and two other PUK leaders not far from the Iraqi border.

It had been three years since the collapse of the Kurdish revolution, the last time Askeri had been an ally and confidante of Mullah Mustafa Barzani, the legendary founder of the KDP. So close had the two been in 1975, his son Shalaw told me, that Barzani had entrusted Ali with personally spiriting the Barzani family across the border to Iran to escape advancing Iraqi troops. Since then, however, Ali had defied General Barzani's order to cease and desist. Now the political parties were locked in bitter warfare, Kurd killing Kurd.

Barzani's revolution was over. Now, the aging leader followed developments in the internal blood feud from a Georgetown hospital in Washington, D.C., where he lay dying from cancer. When he received the news of Askeri's capture, he quickly issued a death sentence for his former compatriot. KDP *peshmerga* executed all three PUK rebels with a shoulder-fired RPG, the large, rocket-propelled grenade launcher primarily designed to attack tanks. According to Shalaw (and several other Kurds I'd already interviewed), the KDP commander on the scene sarcastically remarked that he had chosen "a big weapon for a big man."

Guns and Refugees

When he heard the news of his father's death, Shalaw Askeri was an eighteen-year-old refugee in Syria, a high school student and a basketball player. The following year, he crossed the Tigris River to Iraq and made his way up the mountains where, in the familiar Kurdish coming-of-age ritual, he picked up his first gun. Now he was a PUK rebel.

That might have been the end of the story, but in 1985, six years later, something happened that would change his life again, a twist of fate for a young man who was now twenty-five and a battle-hardened guerrilla in his own right. It was an accident of a temporary cease-fire between the PUK and Saddam's forces, one that allowed Shalaw to leave the country for medical help—a hearing disorder caused by a battlefield explosion—and to go to Czechoslovakia. While he was undergoing treatment in Prague, the Kurdish civil war erupted again in northern Iraq, stranding him abroad with no way to return.

The Kurds in Europe had an active underground railroad. Askeri's colleagues managed to bribe an official at the Prague airport, enabling Askeri to fly to Sweden to visit his older brother. Shalaw settled in Stockholm, learned Swedish and English, married a Kurdish immigrant, and started a family. He educated himself and, with the organizing skills he'd learned from his father, landed a job as a social advocate and translator in a Kurdish refugee camp. With time out for basketball pick-up games, political debates about the Kurds in Stockholm cafés, and a new hobby—visiting Swedish health saunas—Shalaw had traveled a long way from the mountains.

Then came 1991. When the West attacked Saddam after the invasion of Kuwait, the far-flung Kurdish diaspora held its collective breath in anticipation that all of Iraq might be freed. In the end, the United States allowed Saddam to remain in power. Instead, President George H. W. Bush exhorted the Iraqis to rise up against the dictator and to accomplish the regime change themselves. The Kurds were the first to fight, capturing Kirkuk overnight, but the lightly armed rebels had misread the White House.

There would be no help from the United States.

As Shalaw sat glued to radio and TV reports in Stockholm in early 1991, his PUK guerrilla colleagues in Kirkuk were cornered in a last stand. By the terms of the Iraqi surrender, U.S. General Norman Schwarzkopf had given Saddam back his Russian-made helicopters. Within days, the powerful gunships, with their fierce electronic cannons, had crushed the uprising. The Iraqi army quickly retook Kirkuk and the rest of Iraqi Kurdistan, driving almost two million Kurds into the mountains of Iran and Turkey.

Return to Iraq

Now it was 2002, and we were in a restaurant, drinking steaming tea from glass *pialas*. Askeri was smoking a British cigarette and fingering a set of prayer beads. I told him that I'd been with refugees in the mountains in 1991, when he had made his decision to abandon his new life in Sweden and rush back to Kurdistan. He told me that after the allies reacted to TV reports on the slaughter of the Kurds and declared northern Iraq a no-fly zone, he'd walked over the snowy mountains from Turkey and into his homeland. In his absence, thousands of villages had been razed, and dozens of mass graves now dotted the countryside.

Upon his return in 1991, Askeri said, he was reluctant to ask about the whereabouts of his old friends. Kirkuk, freed for only a week in the short-lived rebellion, was lost again, outside the safety zone, sucked back under Saddam's control. During the brief liberation of the city, seven hundred of his contemporaries had been killed, many by summary execution. Together with the panicked exodus to Iran and Turkey, the overall spring uprising had taken the lives of tens of thousands of Kurds.

Revenge

As I listened to Shalaw Askeri, I wondered what the coming war would do to change Kurdish history and how, as U.S. allies and potential victors, they would deal with the phenomenon of victory. Much of the history of the Kurds had been marked by loss: the loss of land and power, the loss of self-rule, and the loss of life, especially of family and friends. Loss was a routine occurrence in Kurdish culture, a common commodity. And the outlet for release—the traditional salve passed down through the generations—was revenge.

I recalled visiting Sulaimaniah in the fall of 1991, just six months after the brutal suppression in Kirkuk, and meeting with Kurt Schork, a young correspondent for Reuters. Schork had just witnessed the surrender of a group of demoralized Iraqi troops to a large force of Kurdish *peshmerga* in Sulaimaniah. The *peshmerga* were bitter about the deaths of comrades in Kirkuk, and an argument with one of the prisoners spontaneously triggered a spate of revenge killings. Dozens of unarmed Iraqis were executed on the spot by their Kurdish captors. Schork told me that when he heard the first shots, he'd just "waltzed" into the room where the captives were held and proceeded to photograph the executions. Midway through the killing frenzy, Schork realized his photos might be confiscated, and that he might be in personal danger. He fled north with the pictures to the territory of the rival KDP, where he stayed for a while, keeping a low profile.

Looking back, he told me, he thought he had benefited from the then-isolation of the Kurds. It was fortunate for him, he observed, that the PUK *peshmerga* had limited experience with the international press at that point and didn't immediately appreciate the potential for damage to the party's image. He credited his escape with the photos to their lack of media savvy—and to his own naïveté, but the incident, he said, "kind of took the sparkle out of Kurdistan." (Schork, who was known for his bravery in covering wars in Bosnia and Africa, was killed in 1999, in a rebel ambush in Sierra Leone.)

More than a decade after the PUK prisoner massacre, the subject was still touchy with PUK officials, even ones like Shalaw Askeri, who had nothing to do with the notorious incident. "In war," my dinner host said tersely, "terrible things happen."

For Askeri, freshly arrived from Europe in 1991, the days of fighting were not over. By 1994, he was caught up in the renewed civil war between the PUK and the KDP. Late one night, his SUV was ambushed near Sulaimaniah on the same road, coincidentally, where British forces had wounded Sheikh Mahmud Barzinji in 1919. The attackers were KDP *peshmerga,* members of the same party that had executed his father. The assailants fired machine guns from both sides of the highway, riddling Askeri's vehicle with dozens of bullets and wounding all six PUK men inside. Miraculously, no one was killed.

Askeri told me he was hit in the leg and the right arm. The driver, who was also shot, managed to pull over, and Askeri was able to exit the SUV and to fire his AK-47 with his left hand, balancing the weapon on the roof of the car. The attackers escaped into the night.

Second-Guessing the Americans

As we finished our dinner, I asked Askeri what he'd learned from all his adventures. He recalled playing basketball as a young man in Syria and joked that his gunshot injuries had cut short a promising career in the NBA. On a serious note, he said his experience had taught him to cast a cold eye on the possibility of more U.N. inspections in Iraq. A war in Iraq was a sure thing, he predicted, and the timing would have nothing to do with resolutions in the U.S. Congress or U.N. inspections, he said. The issue was American power.

Askeri predicted that the U.S. would delay the attack for several months, until early 2003 in order to strategically position its forces. The postponement would be due to the weather, he opined, because American soldiers would be too hot in their protective gear to schedule a war before winter. The Pentagon preferred the cooler air, he speculated, because it would slow down dispersal of the expected gas clouds from the Iraqi positions. Saddam, once cornered, would use chemical weapons as a final act of defiance.

He maintained there were two scenarios for U.N. inspections, but they both led to the same outcome. Either the U.N. inspectors would find weapons of mass destruction or they would not. Finding WMD would prove that Saddam had lied, which would be grounds for attack. If, however, the inspectors found nothing, the United States would claim that Iraq was hiding the weapons, which would also trigger the attack. In either case, he said approvingly, war was inevitable.

No Reprisals

During the eleven years that northern Iraq was free of control from Baghdad, the PUK and KDP factions had quarreled with each other over everything from politics to oil revenues. More than two thousand *peshmerga* were dead in internal fighting—often tit-for-tat attacks—including a number of Askeri's friends. In 1997, the rival Kurds had signed a Washington-brokered cease-fire and, for the past three years, the State Department and the Pentagon had been working to bring the parties closer together.

For Shalaw Askeri, planning for what came *after* the U.S. attack was equally important. "The Americans need to help us prevent revenge killings," he said. With all the war talk following years of suffering under Saddam, ordinary Iraqi people were "sharpening their knives," he said, itching for the chance to settle old scores against "every Iraqi policeman on the corner and all the members of his family." Before the first bomb falls, he warned, the Americans needed to spell out a postwar plan for the Ba'athists. There must be an announcement, he warned, of a general amnesty for all but "the really bad guys."

Askeri told me that he and other Kurdish leaders wanted the kind of truth and reconciliation commission set up here that worked so well in South Africa after apartheid. "We have to give people their justice, but we need to do it through the law." As for what happened to his father, Askeri seemed to have come to terms with whatever demons he once had. "We did bad things to them [the KDP], *too*," he said. "They hated us. We hated them. We both hated the Iraqis. But someday the Kurds must come out from this revenge. We must leave it, or we will never go forward."

20
Ansar al-Islam

The magician should be careful not to be
overtaken by his magic.
—KURDISH PROVERB

Biarra

Ansar al-Islam is an Islamic fundamentalist terrorist group operating in Sulaimaniah province. When I first saw their guerrillas, they were deep in the valley, at least a mile below, and they looked like specks in my binoculars. It was early October 2002, I was with PUK fighters, and we were crouching behind sandbags in a bunker on Shinerwe Mountain.

We were looking down toward the village of Biarra, which sits right on the Iranian frontier. At the time, Ansar was headquartered in Biarra, but the growing insurgency controlled dozens of small villages along the border. Among the Islamic militants, according to Kurdish intelligence, was Abu Musab al-Zarqawi, the Jordanian who would rise to infamy as the most wanted terrorist in postwar Iraq.

PUK officials maintained from the outset that Ansar had links to al-Qaeda, and that Iran was providing weapons and other supplies to destabilize the Kurdish enclave in northern Iraq. By the time I first saw their positions, the militants were stepping up raids and mortar attacks. They had already killed more than one hundred Kurdish government fighters, and they seemed to be getting stronger and bolder. The mountain was a lonely outpost, and the *peshmerga* squatting with me in the bunker were on the defensive.

The Biarra region is about one hundred square miles, a Switzerland-like pocket of snowcapped mountains, rushing streams, and waterfalls. The area is several thousand feet above sea level, and it is known for its delicious pomegranates, walnuts, and peaches. Before the arrival of Ansar in 2000, Biarra had been a retreat for Arabs and Kurds trying to escape the boiling hot Iraqi summers. It is one of the prettiest spots in Iraqi Kurdistan, but is accessible only by rutted dirt roads and numerous switchbacks that snake down the mountains.

The approach was vulnerable to snipers, and the road was known to conceal land mines.

By the fall of 2002, Ansar had assembled a force of about seven hundred guerrillas. A few of the fighters were foreign, like Zarqawi—so-called Afghani Arabs, because of their experience with the Taliban—but 90 percent or more were Kurds. They shared a motivation similar to that of al-Qaeda, with whom they sometimes traded expertise or personnel. In all likelihood, some were equally approving of monstrous acts such as the World Trade Center attack, but despite news accounts at the time suggesting a common command and control center with al-Qaeda, the guerrillas were predominantly Kurds. They drew their primary inspiration from mosques in Kurdistan; most had never been out of the country.

When U.S. jets bombed Biarra in March 2003, some reports misleadingly described Ansar as a foreign group "fighting the Kurds." In fact, Ansar was a homegrown terror organization, a radical offshoot of a legal Kurdish group, the Islamic Movement in Kurdistan (IMK). Ansar had evolved from two extremist strains of the IMK, Hamas and Tawid (belief in the unity of God), which had come together in September of 2001 to form a new group called Jund al-Islam (Soldiers of Islam). Soon after, perhaps in an attempt to soften the terror image and broaden its recruiting base, Jund remorphed into Ansar al-Islam, the "*Supporters* of Islam."

Tawid's deeds included the assassination of Franso Hariri, the governor of Erbil, the largest city in northern Iraq. Hariri was a close family friend of both the Barzani clan and the KDP, the Kurdish faction that controlled the western part of Kurdistan. Hariri was an Assyrian Christian whose native language was ancient Aramaic, reportedly the language of Jesus Christ. He was fluent in Kurdish and he was enormously popular in Erbil. Tawid claimed he was an agent of Israel and marked him for death.

According to KDP spokesman Fawzi Hariri, the late governor's son, the PUK itself had made an earlier attempt—during the KDP/PUK civil war in the 1990s—to kill the elder Hariri. Fawzi had immigrated to London in the 1980s. At the time of his father's death in 2001, the younger Hariri was pursuing a career at British Airways, but following the Tawid assassination, he returned to Kurdistan to work for the KDP in media relations. He told me that KDP suspicion at the time of the murder had fallen on the rival PUK, but PUK chief Jalal Talabani immediately notified Massoud Barzani that extremist Tawid members were to blame—and then delivered the men responsible to KDP control "with uncharacteristic speed."

After Hariri's assassination, KDP intelligence set out to eradicate Tawid, which at that time was an urban group centered in Erbil, a city of almost a million people. More than a dozen militants were killed before the group fled to PUK territory, to Qandhil Mountain, the highest mountain in Iraqi Kurdistan.

Qandhil Mountain is located on the Iranian border, about one hundred miles north of Biarra. If a favorite guerrilla sanctuary were to be chosen, Qandhil Mountain—with its snowy peaks, deep canyons, and networks of honeycombed caves—would be high on the list. During the 1970s and 1980s, when the Kurds were fighting the Baghdad regime, Talabani's PUK guerrillas had relied on Qandhil's rugged terrain to escape the Soviet-made MiGs flown by Iraqi pilots. At other times, Iranian Kurds used the mountain to stage guerrilla raids against the regime in Tehran. PKK separatists still use the area today to hide from the F-16 fighter jets flown by Turkish pilots. For Tawid, a group that spurned the "infidel" life of most Kurds and the increasingly pro-U.S. Kurdish leaders, the isolated retreat of Qandhil Mountain seemed like a good choice.

Before long, the militants decided to relocate to the Halabja Valley, where Islamic fundamentalism—the peaceful variety—had flourished since the 1980s. Surprisingly, the PUK not only turned a blind eye, but also seemed to encourage the move. The party provided drivers and vehicles to transport militants and weapons to Biarra, where the nearby border offered easy escape to Iran. On the surface, the PUK assistance seemed designed to curry favor with conservative Muslims in Kurdistan, but the PUK also was indebted to the Islamic government of Iran, and some officials in Tehran reportedly were friendly to the militants.

The Islamic militants' strong-arm evangelicalism in the valley soon pitted them against local farmers, shop owners, and small-time smugglers who made their living sneaking Iranian gasoline and other products over the porous frontier. The leader of the group, a charismatic cleric named Mullah Krekar, began imposing rules designed to transform the community, mostly moderate Sunni Muslims, into a fundamentalist, Taliban-like enclave. Sharia, the religious law in Kurdish areas before World War I, was reinstated, and attendance at the mosque soon became mandatory. Music, television, and videos were prohibited, women were required to wear veils, and magazines with photos of women were outlawed. Rule breakers could be flogged in public.

Ansar al-Islam began to accumulate a large quantity of small arms and light artillery, reportedly from Iran. Foxholes and bunkers were dug around the border villages, and the positions facing PUK forces were mined. In the months following my first visit to Biarra, which took place in February 2002, low-intensity warfare dragged on with one or two fighters a week being shot. In the fall of 2002—still six months before the U.S. invasion—Ansar mounted several large attacks on PUK forces, killing dozens. As the war neared, Ansar broadened its tactics to include suicide bombings.

KDP and PUK and other party leaders disagreed on the most effective way to deal with the growing threat. Some officials in the rival KDP regarded it purely as a problem for the PUK, blaming the PUK for inviting the terrorists into the area in the first place. Other parties reacted differently. The public position of Komali Islami (Islamic Society), an armed but legal Islamic party, was neutrality—despite indications of support and solidarity of its members with Ansar.

The Kurdistan Socialist Democratic Party (KSDP) had managed to stay out of the fighting, despite the fact that its front lines abutted those of the militants and despite repeated requests from the PUK for military assistance. The Socialists, a small party with about one thousand members, did not want to fight Ansar and had protested the relocation of the militants from Qandhil Mountain, complaining to the PUK that the fundamentalists were likely to cause trouble. The protest apparently fell on deaf ears. According to one Socialist official, Jalal Talabani had responded at the time, "They have a right—the earth belongs to God."

Socialists

Critics from the PUK said the Socialists had stayed safely on the sidelines only because their leader, Muhammed Haji Mahmoud, was pro-Iranian, and they claimed Iran had warned Ansar not to terrorize his party. The need of the Kurds as a whole to accommodate Iran, their powerful neighbor, was a charge that could have been leveled at many PUK officials as well. When I asked Barham Salih, the PUK prime minister, why the PUK did not attack the villages around Biarra and dislodge Ansar, he answered that one of the reasons was a reluctance to antagonize Iran. (The other was the heavy toll the PUK *peshmerga* would take just at the time their focus was on toppling Saddam.) "If we had an airport or an independent link to the outside world, it might be different," he said, "but we have to *live* here." Indeed, many of the goods that fueled the booming economy in Kurdistan came via Iran, and in the past, Iran had provided weapons to fight the Iraqi regime. Iran also supplied visas to PUK leaders who needed to travel from landlocked Kurdistan to Europe and the United States.

Everyone referred to Muhammed Haji Mahmoud as Kaka Hama. In Kurdish society, "Hama" is a common diminutive of Mohammed, and "Kaka" is a term of respect, like "Sir" or "Mister" in English. Kaka Hama, a barrel-chested man about fifty years old, had been a guerrilla in the mountains most of his life. He told me he had been wounded five times. He said his last injury was sustained in an Iraqi air raid during the 1991 uprising in Kirkuk, and he joked that the shrapnel in his back still set off security buzzers at airports in Europe.

The Socialists had six bases in northern Iraq, including a headquarters at a place called Gulla Hana, and they had their own TV and radio station for broadcasting Kurdish news. The party had garnered only three percent of the vote in the last election, which was in 1992, the year before the big KDP/PUK civil war dissolved the multiparty parliament. The KDP and the PUK had each polled about 40 percent in the election, and some disgruntled Socialists groused that the major parties had rigged the vote. International monitors found only minor irregularities, however, and Kaka Hama himself refused to complain about the results.

Kaka Hama was a writer who had published eight books. He was also an avid reader, and his study was lined with books. His supporters told me that during his years of sleeping on the ground in the mountains, he had written numerous battle accounts by candlelight. Everyone said that Kaka Hama had one of the most complete archives of the Kurdish revolution. He was certainly proud of his writing, but he loved all forms of record keeping. The Socialists now had a full-time cameraman, and the party had a growing library of Kurdish videos and news footage.

Kaka Hama had a thick neck and huge, hamlike hands, hardly the look of a polished politician. A reporter from the *Minneapolis Star Tribune* who met him, a writer named Paul McEnroe, joked that he looked like the comedian Buddy Hackett. Among the Kurds, he had a reputation as a food lover. One of his detractors in the PUK claimed that once he had eaten a whole sheep at a single sitting.

Before breaking with Talabani to establish his own party in 1979, Kaka Hama had been a prominent leader in the PUK fight against the Iraqi military. In 1978, Talabani had dispatched him to Turkey with the legendary Ali Askeri in a doomed bid to buy arms. That was three years after the KDP had given up the fight against the Iraqi army, and PUK defiance of the KDP order to stand down had triggered a civil war between the rebels. Kaka Hama told me that the PUK had eight hundred fighters in Turkey at the time, but they'd come under a withering six-week assault by KDP forces allied with the Turkish and Iranian armies. They were bombed repeatedly by the Turks and Iranians and were forced to engage in almost daily combat on the ground. He handed me a Kurdish *pishtwen* that *peshmerga* use to wrap their waists. "That was Ali's," he said of the old keepsake. "He gave it to me in Turkey, for bravery in battle."

It was the last time he saw Askeri, as Askeri was later captured and executed by KDP forces. Kaka Hama and six other *peshmerga,* the only PUK survivors of the disastrous 1978 campaign, returned to the hills of Gulla Hana by foot, a distance of almost three hundred miles.

Kaka Hama's base at Gulla Hana was a few miles from the Iranian frontier, next to Ansar territory. The first time I went there, Kaka Hama dropped a bombshell: He told me he was receiving money from the CIA to construct a Radio Free Iraq transmitter on a peak behind his mountain redoubt. Everyone suspected the American spy agency of operating in northern Iraq, but Kurdish leaders usually met such questions with coy denials. I was taken aback by his candor.

The Socialists, a minority party in the Kurdish power structure, were visibly pleased that a foreign reporter would have the interest to visit their base—although they expressed concern that an American was so close to Ansar positions. They had prepared a lavish lunch of lamb, chicken, and fish, and they seated me in a place of honor next to Kaka Hama and across from his son, Pishtiwan, a polite and somewhat reserved twenty-two-year-old. The young man, who was dressed in the traditional baggy *peshmerga* clothes, carried a sidearm in a holster on his waist, like many Kurdish leaders. In fact, Pishtiwan had grown up in Sweden, not Kurdistan. After the gas attacks in the late 1980s, Kaka Hama, like many fighters, had sent his family to Europe. The son had grown up in Stockholm listening to stories about his famous father. Pishtiwan had just arrived from Sweden, believing he would be at his father's side for the U.S. attack, the potential turning point in Kurdish history. Tragically, it would not be his destiny to witness the war. Just a few days after our lunch together, he was killed in a gun mishap at home. Reportedly, he said he was cleaning his new pistol in his room late at night when it went off accidentally, but one member of the party told me that the young man, who had not grown up around weapons, had been warned in the past—by more experienced fighters—not to play with the gun. He told me that Pishtiwan died in front of a mirror, "practicing fast draws like American cowboys."

I wanted to see the site the CIA had chosen for the proposed radio station. It took forty-five minutes for a caravan of SUVs and bodyguards to get me to the top of the mountain. From that vantage point, less than a mile from the Iranian border, we could see Biarra and the Ansar base in the distance. Two buildings had already been built on the proposed radio site, and delivery of the transmitter itself—which Kaka Hama said he'd arranged through Iranian territory—was expected presently. So far, he had received only $20,000 of the $600,000 promised for construction. The U.S. Congress had appropriated the money in the Iraq Liberation Act, which was passed during the Clinton administration, but the disbursement was being funneled through the Iraqi National Congress (INC). There were deep divisions between the INC, which was based in London, and resistance groups like the Kurds, those on the ground in Iraq.

Kaka Hama had little time for the INC, the group of Iraqi expatriates headed by Ahmed Chalabi, the Shiite leader and Pentagon favorite. Chalabi had been educated in Chicago, and he spent most of his life outside Iraq. The Socialist leader called INC followers "*peshmerga* in hotels." He said they'd lived abroad in luxury, safely jockeying for future power in a post-Saddam era, but they had paid no dues in the long struggle inside Iraq. He complained that the INC was siphoning off the funds that Washington had earmarked for the transmitter. "The money gets to the INC in London, but it's a bit like *snow*," he said. "When it's passed around, it melts."

The objective of Radio Free Iraq was psychological warfare, to broadcast anti-Saddam propaganda in Arabic to the Iraqi population. Kaka Hama told me the CIA had picked the radio site after showing him satellite photos of the area. He said the CIA had first approached the major parties, the PUK and the KDP, to host the transmitter. Both parties thought it was too much of a provocation and had declined. Not so Kaka Hama. "Let Iraqis try to knock it down," he said proudly. "They never succeeded [before] in getting to us in these mountains."

Komali Islami

Komali Islami, composed primarily of Sunnis, was the largest armed Islamic group in Iraqi Kurdistan, with a force of about a thousand armed *peshmerga*. Some of its members viewed the PUK as apostates, fallen-away believers. Ansar al-Islam had even stronger views. The difference was that Ansar was openly dedicated to killing PUK followers, while Komali was an official component of Kurdish self-government in northern Iraq.

Komali Islami was a legal party. As such, it was entitled to regular allotments from the funds the PUK collected from the local population, primarily from customs taxes on imported goods. The Komali share each month amounted to a reported 2.5 million "old" dinars, about $250,000 U.S. at the exchange rate in use until shortly before the war. The regular subsidy rankled many members of the PUK politburo, the PUK governing council, who believed that Komali Islami was sympathetic to—if not actively supporting—Ansar al-Islam.

PUK intelligence knew of instances where Komali checkpoints had allowed Ansar militants to pass. Komali identity cards had been found on the bodies of the assassins who tried to kill Barham Salih. Now, as the Kurdish government prepared for the U.S.-led effort to topple Saddam, the question was whether Komali merely had rogue elements in its midst or whether the leadership itself represented a fifth column aligned with Ansar. If the groups were actually linked, U.S. soldiers fighting the Iraqis might have an enemy at their backs.

The Halabja area had been a center of Islamic tradition and learning since the 1980s, long before anyone heard the name *al-Qaeda* or thought very much about Islamic extremists. Like most of the Kurdish parties, Komali had conservative, liberal, and radical wings. Like most Kurdish Islamic groups, it had its roots in the IMK, the Islamic Movement in Kurdistan. When the IMK and the PUK were guerrilla armies fighting the Iraqi dictatorship in the 1980s, the parties were allies. In the power struggle that followed the 1991 uprising, however, there was a shooting at a PUK checkpoint near the town of Kalar that triggered a war between the groups. Several IMK *peshmerga* were killed in the incident, which took place in 1993. The PUK said it was an accident, but the IMK branded it an assassination, setting off a feud that cost hundreds of lives and lasted until 1996.

These were Islamic fundamentalists and U.S. advisors directing the Kurds viewed their presence as a red flag. It didn't matter that they had fought the Iraqi army for more than a generation or that they were a legal party with a following, just like the KDP and the PUK. In the political landscape envisioned by U.S. war planners, their time in Kurdistan had expired.

The leader of Komali was a baby-faced Muslim cleric named Ali Bapir. He was a likable, charismatic leader with a beard and a gentle demeanor who enjoyed good relations with the international press. He vociferously denied that he supported Ansar's philosophy or methods. Bapir was a former guerrilla commander in the struggle against Saddam Hussein and was known for both skill and ruthlessness. It was said that he had had his own brother executed, after discovering he was a spy for the regime.

Bapir had an office and dormitory for his men in Sulaimaniah, but his headquarters were an hour to the east in the town of Khurmal, less than a ten-minute drive from socialist Kaka Hama's base at Gulla Hana. Thousands of his followers and their families lived in Khurmal. Most of them were poor, uneducated farmers and manual laborers. In the swirl of changes that Kurdistan was undergoing at the dawn of the new century, Bapir was their leader and loyal spokesman. Khurmal was Bapir's base—the Ansar base was fifteen to twenty miles away—but many of the families of the Ansar lived in Khurmal, and the fighters were known to use back roads to sneak into town for shopping trips and to stay overnight. Their periodic presence made it risky for outsiders, especially Westerners, to visit Khurmal.

The majority of Komali followers were moderate religionists who attended Friday prayers and otherwise went about their business. The PUK's Sulaimaniah, a modern city with luxury cars, home appliances, DVDs of Hollywood movies, alcohol, satellite telephones, and naked bodies on the screens at Internet cafés, was a short drive the northwest. To the east and the south was Ansar-land, a zone of control dedicated to reversing the pro-Western tilt and all the values of "atheist" Sulaimaniah.

The leadership of the PUK was split about what to do about Bapir. The cleric had an honorable record as a *peshmerga* fighting Saddam. Some leaders believed that he was a simple man nurturing a pitiful flock, trying to lead his people out of the wilderness. In that view, he was like the Shiites, who made up at least 60 percent of Iraq and had long suffered religious persecution under the Iraqi dictatorship.

Other officials saw Bapir as a cunning chameleon playing both sides of the Islamic street to broaden his power base. According to that view, Bapir could not be trusted, so attempts at compromise were futile. A PUK military commander on the front lines in the war with Ansar claimed he once heard Bapir preach that all forms of the Muslim mission were the same. "We are all wings, with one beak," the cleric purportedly said.

Most members of the PUK leadership were not religious, but they were Muslims in a cultural sense, attending the mosque—when they did—for ceremonial reasons, such as showing respect at the death of a friend. Whoever and whatever Bapir was, the spread of fundamental Islam represented a major challenge to the

PUK and its pro-American institutions. Now, as an initial step, the PUK would require that for every mosque the Islamic parties wanted to build, a school and health clinic would have to be constructed as well. The government already funded the mosques, and, according to Barham Salih, the PUK would begin revoking licenses from Kurdish imams, Muslim priests, who failed to preach "positive messages." The move was an attempt to keep Kurdish politics and religion separate, he said, denying that the PUK was imposing censorship on rival political parties. "We pay for the salaries and microphones for these guys," he said. "Why should we let them preach hate?"

"This is a fight," Salih declared, "for the soul of Islam."

Forty-three Massacred

Sometime in August 2001, a seasoned Islamic militant from Jordan named Abdul Rahman arrived in the Biarra area. According to PUK intelligence, he was an envoy from Osama bin Laden. On September 1, 2001, Mullah Krekar, the leader of the militants, announced that Jund al-Islam had changed its name to Ansar al-Islam and was dropping armed struggle to pursue political change. The announcement may have been a ruse. Barely three weeks later, Ansar guerrillas massacred forty-three PUK *peshmerga* who had surrendered near Halabja following a firefight. It was clear to officials who examined the bodies of the victims that several had been tortured before being shot. Some had been clubbed to death; a few had been beheaded.

Ansar boasted of the killings on its Web site and circulated a video that displayed gruesome photos of the mutilated victims. Many of the dead came from Sulaimaniah. Even for a population that had experienced two generations of repression by the central government, the graphic pictures were a shock. News of the gruesome killings spread terror throughout the city.

21

Palace Hotel

If you see a fox, it means you are lucky.

—KURDISH PROVERB

Karzan

It was October 2002, six months after the Ansar attack. Karzan Mahmoud, Barham Salih's wounded driver, was still hurting. I watched him limp into the Palace, the upscale hotel owned by Jalal Talabani's PUK. He was walking slowly under the huge glass chandelier that dominated the two-story lobby, past the leatherlike couches where bodyguards sprawled with their AK-47s, drinking tea. He looked as though he was enroute to an important event. He wore a three-piece suit and smelled of cologne, but was dragging his left leg across the marble floor, and the tight expression on his face betrayed his constant pain. It was the first time I'd seen him since the assassination attempt the previous spring. Considering the fact he'd been shot twenty-three times, it was hard to believe he was still alive, much less walking. I was at the front desk at the time, trying to deal with an issue of bad hotel service. I didn't realize at first that he was on a mission to get my help.

When the Iraqis controlled Kurdistan, the Palace Hotel had the look of a dour, Soviet-style dormitory. The PUK renovated it in 2001, awarded it a five-star rating, and proclaimed it "Kurdistan's finest." The grand opening, a late-night gala for PUK members and friends, gave the Palace a reputation as a meeting place for the elite, attesting to the power of the party and the vibrancy of the Kurdish economy. In 2002, before the approaching war drove up the prices, a regular room at the Palace had rented for $30, a large suite for $50. Either would have been a bargain—if the guest didn't know any better. Despite its first-class appearance, the owners had done little to train the clerks, bellboys, maids, and restaurant help. Kurdistan had no tradition of public lodging. Because of the region's political and geographic isolation, few of the workers themselves had ever stayed in a hotel as a guest. The conflict-dominated history of northern Iraq had not prepared the staff for the normal service requests of foreign visitors.

Most of the workers were paid the equivalent of only $50 to $100 a month. They had little experience with strangers—especially high-maintenance guests like journalists, who demand timely room service, message delivery, or faucet repair. The air conditioning was invariably too hot or too cold, a condition that sometimes could be corrected by opening or closing the windows. In one instance, I complained of having hot water in the *toilet bowl,* but none in the tub. Like all the Kurds in the hotel, the repairman was friendly, but despite promises to the contrary, it was two days before the problem was resolved.

Karzan held out his left arm, the one that still worked, and we shook hands. When I'd last seen him, he was a proud black belt in tae kwon do with a prestigious government job, a vital young man in the prime of his life. Now he was a disabled nobody in a Third World country, standing under a crystal chandelier in a hotel for foreigners. He told me his girlfriend had abandoned him soon after the attack, when it appeared he'd never walk again. She'd come to the hospital, and they'd shed tears together. Karzan told her she would have a better life with a partner who wasn't injured. He said he didn't blame her. They cried some more, and then she left.

It was early in my stay—three months before Christmas and six months before the war. I was the only American journalist in the Palace, and I had my own suite. We went to the room and drank a soda from the minibar. I gave Karzan a photo taken of the two of us in the Halabja Valley in March of 2002, a few weeks before he'd been wounded. "You [are my] friend," he said.

Karzan had come to tell me that his family had raised money for him to go to Baghdad to see an Iraqi medical specialist. "Aren't you afraid?' I asked him. "Not afraid of Baghdad," he said. "But my leg . . . ," he said, proceeding to describe in limited English a botched surgery by Turkish doctors at a hospital in Ankara. Then he removed the dressing from the wound. Six months after the surgery, his thigh bore a purple-colored scar about a foot in length. It was oozing pus.

A few weeks later, Karzan showed up again in the lobby of the Palace. He was carrying a large envelope, maybe thirty inches in length, and he immediately proceeded to pull out the X-rays that had been taken in Baghdad. The desk clerks looked over curiously, and an undercover cop got up from his couch and started our way. "Just a minute here," I said, trying to avoid attention. "I'm not a doctor, I can't read these."

We went up to my room, where Karzan recounted his recent trip to Baghdad. Medical care was better there, he said, than in a Kurdish hospital. In the end, however, a specialist had advised him that nothing more could be done for him in Iraq. His only chance, according to the Iraqi doctor, was to get help on "the outside," in Europe or America. He showed me a letter from a Baghdad hospital, written in broken English. It looked official, but it merely described the wounds to Karzan's leg, elbow, forearm, and hands—a routine overview any observer could have written. There was nothing in the letter about seeking treatment abroad.

Karzan surveyed the suite. He made his way to the windows, which overlooked the Salem Street plaza and a huge color mural of Qazi Muhammed, the legendary founder of the Mahabad Republic in Iran. The mural faced four bronze statues of men in uniform, the Kurdish officers in the Iraqi army who defected in 1945 and went to Mahabad as freedom fighters. After the collapse of the short-lived republic, the Iraqi regime lured them home with the promise of amnesty. Upon their return to Baghdad, the four Kurds were arrested as subversives and executed by a firing squad.

It was late afternoon, and the low autumn sunlight above the statues was streaming into the hotel room. I took the first X-ray, a cloudy, dark print of a shattered bone, and taped it to the glass. The X-ray was now superimposed on our view of the Kurdish martyrs, dimming the light from outside. Karzan waited patiently, asking no questions, like someone already familiar with the ad hoc procedure. With my new digital camera, I photographed the first X-ray, the second, and so on, until the envelope was empty.

Karzan took the dressing off his upper leg. The wound was dripping, and it looked more infected than before. I took a picture, then moved on to shots of his crippled fingers and arm. I told him I'd write to a friend for a medical opinion, and that I'd try to send the pictures by e-mail. Karzan had heard of e-mail, but he had never used it. I told him that my friend was a doctor in Boston, but there was probably nothing he could do. Karzan had never heard of Boston. I told him it was a city. "I [am] very happy," he said. "You help me?"

After Karzan left, I went to the Internet parlor and typed a quick e-mail to my friend Mike Brabeck, an internist at the Brigham and Women's, the prestigious teaching hospital in Boston.

"Here is a wild request . . . ," I began.

A few days later, Karzan was back in the hotel. He found me in the restaurant, where I was vainly trying to get some service. From the day I'd first set foot in northern Iraq, I'd sensed the special warmth Kurdish people had toward Americans—and the staff of the Palace restaurant was no exception. Kurdistan, however, lacked the custom of tipping. Like some places I'd traveled in Eastern Europe and Central Asia, no one hustled to attend to the newcomer in the expectation of a later reward. At the point Karzan that showed up, I was hungry, and I wanted to order, but I'd been unable to get the attention of the waiters, who were busy socializing with each other, oblivious of waiting diners.

"*Sah chow!*" I said to one, reciting the common greeting that means, "I see you—I recognize you" (literally, "I have you in my eye").

Sah chow is an expression of respect in Kurdish, indicating that the speaker acknowledges the existence, even the importance, of the other person. *"Sah chow!"* the waiter replied with a smile, as he passed me by with his order pad. A few minutes later, he went by again. *"Sah chow!"* he repeated, this time making a gesture with his hands for me to be patient—and so it went. There were other people he needed to wait on, although some of them had arrived after me. I guessed he'd just gotten rattled and had forgotten my table. Finally, after twenty minutes, a few more *sah chow*'s and gestures to be patient, I stood up and motioned to the waiter, who at that time was leaning on the bar near the kitchen, talking to another worker. When he arrived, I said, "Listen, I know you have me in your *eye*, but where I want to be is on that *pad* of yours!" He smiled and took out his pen.

Karzan was smiling, too, but he'd come for an update on his case, not for lunch. By that time, I'd been to see the PUK prime minister, but Salih hadn't been encouraging about the prospect of getting Karzan a visa. That would take political capital with Washington, Salih had indicated, adding, "If Karzan got help, the other guys who were shot would wonder why they weren't given the same chance."

What that told me was that nothing was going to work without a concrete hospital offer. I wrote back to Boston, urging my friend Mike to pitch Brigham and Women's about the PR value of a "good deed." It was late 2002, a few months before the war and the news was full of stories of victims in Iraq. In one e-mail, I argued that America was living in "Iraq-aware" times, and that Karzan had been "shot by enemies of the United States." Mike wrote back, "I wouldn't know where to start, but am willing to investigate this." After that, whenever I ran into Karzan, I'd made small talk. For the time being, there was no point in getting his hopes up.

Qandhil Mountain

After a few weeks in the Palace, I developed a case of cabin fever and decided to take a trip to the countryside. I hired a four-wheel drive Land Cruiser and drove to the mountains to see the PKK, the Kurdish rebels who dutifully followed Apo Ocalan's orders to abandon Turkey after he was captured in 1999. Now there were about five thousand PKK fighters holed up on Qandhil Mountain, on the Iranian border. At the time of my visit, the guerrillas weren't mounting attacks into Turkey. Locally, they had clashed with Iraqi Kurds, but a cease-fire with the PUK had been in effect for more than a year. Like everyone else in northern Iraq, they were armed, but this time they were reluctant to let me photograph them with weapons. Also, contrary to classic guerrilla strategy, they were no longer on the move. In a shift of direction, they now were busy with development projects. They had mules, chickens, and goats and were planting crops in several dozen small settlements. They had graded the dirt road to the nearest town and had built a water turbine to generate the area's first power. One rebel told me, "All the villages under our flag now have electricity." It was a proven formula for community organization: The Turkish Kurds had come to Iraq to set up a political base.

The most striking indication of PKK permanence was a new cemetery, a seeded, mowed lawn enclosed by an expensive steel fence with the yellow star of the PKK welded over the entry arch. Incredibly, considering its remote location, the burial plot had a flower garden, fountains, and an *electric sprinkler system*. One of the commanders told me the remote graveyard had cost about $40,000, a huge expenditure in local currency.

This was a sacred burial plot for rebel *shahid*s. I counted forty headstones, all made of marble and professionally engraved with PKK flags and carved maps of Greater Kurdistan showing the Kurdish regions of Iraq, Turkey, Iran, and Syria. The inscriptions, attesting to the pan-Kurdish ideology of the movement, listed names of male and female fighters from each of the countries, as well as the name of a Russian Kurd. Most of the dead were between the ages of eighteen and twenty-two, and many of them were from Syria.

Some of the forty may have died in factional fighting with Iraqi Kurds, but I guessed that the PKK, with its premium on Kurdish martyrdom, had carried some of the bodies from afar—even from Turkey—and had reburied them. The creation of the cemetery violated the cardinal rule that a guerrilla army should never try to *hold* territory, but to PKK thinking, the deceased fighters had achieved the highest state of consciousness, the "Kurdistan of the mind." Their remains *were* the homeland.

The Shrine of Martyrs demanded ongoing sacrifice by the living. The remains of the dead had transformed a mountain burial plot in a tiny corner of northern Iraq into a collective shield for the guerrillas. With the PKK political party outlawed in Turkey and their imprisoned leader directing them not to fight, the nearly forgotten rebels had planted their dead on a hillside and stopped to make a stand. "This is Media," one commander told me, referring to the centuries-old kingdom. "This is our *house*, and we will defend it."

A lot had gone on since 1996, when I'd last seen the PKK in the mountains. Now, in 2002, the armed uprising seemed all but dead. The organization was trying to transition to political activities and had changed its name to KADEK. Despite the attempted makeover, the United States and Turkey immediately declared KADEK a terrorist group. The European Union had refused to do so, at least so far, adopting a wait-and-see approach.

Despite its name change, the group seemed frozen in the past, like a stranded Japanese soldier on a Pacific atoll long after the war. Many guerrillas still had

Apo wristwatches, and everyone seemed busy with endless tasks. Satellite TV beamed PKK information from Europe; posters of Apo and dog-eared copies of his old political tracts were everywhere. By now I was familiar with the gruesome rebel allegations of torture by the Turkish army ("Her heart was cut out and hung on the tree"). And the rhetoric was the same ("Turkey is a patient in the hospital, and America keeps donating blood," and, "If it weren't for German tanks and U.S. Cobra helicopters, we would have had a Kurdistan a long time ago"). Once again, I heard the PKK prohibition against sex ("If you were us, would you trade the freedom of your country for sleeping with a woman for one night?"). It seemed like a time warp.

At the start of the twenty-first century, the Kurds in Turkey were still being treated like second-class citizens, with no apparent way to change their lot peacefully. The PKK was still blindly following the failed ideology of one prisoner in the hands of the enemy. With the looming war against Saddam Hussein, attention was focused on Iraqi Kurds, but the greatest concentration of Kurds was in Turkey, and they were still in a lose-lose predicament. Although Apo had sent thousands of teenaged peasants to their deaths against the superior technology of the U.S.-supplied Turkish army, in the first moments of his captivity by Turkish commandos, Apo had reportedly begged for mercy, claiming, "My mother was Turkish!" He spent the days that followed quickly undoing his life's work, calling off the war, pleading for humane treatment for himself, a proverbial tail between his legs. I wondered about those parents I'd met in Turkey and Syria who had given their children so readily to his cause. Their sense of betrayal and anger, I guessed, must run deep.

Still, there was no denying it: Apo had put the Kurds of Turkey on the political map. Nevertheless, he wasn't a Moses, and he would not lead the wandering Kurds out of the wilderness. To his bitter disappointment, he would not join Salahuddin, Qazi Muhammed, and Sheikh Mahmud in the pantheon of Kurdish heroes, at least not any time soon. When it came to honor, the threshold Kurdish virtue that made everyone, high or low, stand up when another Kurd entered the room, Apo had not acted *honorably*. Yet the PKK, the bloody vanguard for Kurdish struggle in Turkey, seemed locked in the past, following his ghost.

In mid-December 2002, Dr. Brabeck approached the department at the Brigham and Women's Hospital in Boston that dealt with international affairs and made a pitch for pro bono surgeries for Karzan Mahmoud, a Kurd from Iraq he'd never seen or spoken to. As Mike recounted later, he was "turned down flat, no reason given." Rather than giving up, he sent Karzan's Baghdad medical reports and my photos of Karzan's X-rays, along with what he called my "functional assessment of Karzan's physical capabilities and limitations," to his cousin, an orthopedic trauma surgeon at Yale–New Haven University Hospital. The surgeon reported back almost immediately that Karzan had "such extensive neurovascular damage that the likelihood of successful reconstruction and rehabilitation was low." He added that his hospital "wouldn't touch the case," being more favorably disposed to consider cases of "innocent little children who need heart operations" than victims of politically inspired violence.

In late December 2002, I received an e-mail from Mike informing me his proposal had been rejected and saying that he thought it was "hopeless" to persist with further efforts. At that point, he told me later, "I was hoping I didn't hear back from you—that you'd let it go." Ten days went by, and I called him from Iraq on my satellite phone, asking if he'd be willing to try a back-door approach, outside of normal channels and protocol. Mike spent a week chewing on unofficial ways to reroute the request, but came up empty-handed. Then, on a Friday, by a stroke of luck, he received a phone call from the office of the president of the hospital. It turned out that the president, who was a physician and a community psychiatrist, had been planning for some time to honor staff doctors who'd volunteered their time at a shelter for homeless veterans in downtown Boston. Brabeck was one of the volunteers—would he join the others for a breakfast with the president and his staff at the shelter the following Tuesday?

Mike, who had already received a written invitation but was not planning to attend the tribute, said "a light suddenly went on" in his head. He phoned his wife, Mary, then a dean at Boston College, who was on a business trip to Milwaukee. Mary realized that her husband now had direct access to a top decision maker at Brigham, a powerful institution with a full time staff of more than sixteen hundred physicians. "This is your first, last, and only chance," she remembered telling him. Over the course of the weekend, e-mails flew back and forth between Boston and Milwaukee as the couple wrote and rewrote their request to the president, outlining why Brigham's involvement might not only be good for Karzan but for the institution as well. At 4:00 P.M. "on a gray Sunday afternoon," after "no fewer than eight revisions of my initial version" and still feeling the chances were "marginal," Brabeck hit the SEND button. At the time, he said later, he held out little hope of a response. Within thirty minutes, however, he had one. The president's reply stated briefly, "Mike, this looks like the right thing to do on humanitarian grounds—let's talk after breakfast Tuesday."

As Dr. Brabeck would later write in a report, Karzan's condition prior to the operations was such that he "had the use only of the index finger and thumb on the left hand, [had] an entirely immobile right hand with an elbow in a fixed position, a badly infected right thigh and a chronically draining sinus on the left thigh, probably attributable to infected hardware." Nevertheless, the hospital was

now ready to proceed with the necessary surgeries, together with intensive physical and occupational therapies—on the condition Karzan could get a valid visa
to the United States.

I was in my room in the hotel when I got the news. I made a beeline for the
home of the PUK prime minister. "Barham," I said, "we have an offer."

22

Al-Qaeda in Kurdistan?

Sulaimaniah is full of atheists.

—A FOLLOWER OF THE KOMALI ISLAMI

In the fall of 2002, Ansar al-Islam overran and briefly captured the famous, ill-fated city of Halabja. The insurgents now controlled the blacktop road to Sulaimaniah, the PUK capital, where I was based. Before long, the one hundred square miles of rich agricultural land between Halabja and the Iranian border was dotted with earthen forts, constructed by Kurdish government bulldozers to defend the besieged area. Seen from my four-wheel drive vehicle on the rutted dirt road I used to reach Halabja, they looked like giant anthills. After decades of battling both Saddam and the rival KDP, the PUK was under attack by Islamic militants, and the fear was apparent at every checkpoint. The United States was planning a regime change in Baghdad sometime in the future, but this isolated backwater of Iraq was already in turmoil.

In mid-November, Ansar attacked the PUK customs post near Halabja, the building where taxes on imported goods (chiefly from Iran) were paid. It was a cold, rainy night—good weather for committed insurgents. Three PUK *peshmerga* were killed and eight wounded. Two of the attackers were killed. Shalaw Askeri drove to the scene with other PUK officials. He later told me that one of the militants was "Arab-looking," and that both of the dead wore tennis shoes with no mud on them. As a former guerrilla, Askeri knew the significance of *that* detail. The attackers, it appeared, had not been forced to slog their way through rain-soaked fields to reach Halabja. They had taken a shortcut by car, which suggested that Komali Islami had permitted the Ansar militants to pass their checkpoints on the local highway.

Following the attack, I toured the ward at the military hospital with Barham Salih, and I interviewed most of the men wounded in the Halabja firefight. Afterward, Salih offered me a lift to my hotel in his heavily guarded caravan. I sat next to him in the back of his SUV and recorded an interview. The attackers were part of the same group that had nearly killed him. He was clearly upset.

"I do feel that this is a group closely linked to the al-Qaeda organization," he said, "and [it is] part and parcel of al-Qaeda international network."

"You outgun them; you have more troops," I said. "Why don't you . . . ?"

"It will take significant firepower that we may not have," he said. "Look at what the U.S. had to deal with at Tora Bora. The terrain is very, very difficult; the geography is even more difficult. And you're talking about a group of hardened terrorists who hide in the mountains. You cannot fight [them] with the type of military capability that we have."

At this point, Kurdish leaders were still being secretive about their behind-the-scenes contact with U.S. spy agencies.

"Has the PUK requested air strikes against Ansar positions?"

Salih deflected the question. "We know that this terrorism is part of an international global phenomenon. This is a global responsibility, also. This is not just unique to Kurdistan. This is part and parcel of the network that has threatened or is threatening peace and stability around the world."

I pretended to accept the answer, if only to maintain the information flow. "Does it look now," I asked, "as if these groups are consolidating?"

"We . . . uh . . . *they tried to kill me awhile back.* And unfortunately, they gunned down five of my bodyguards, but two of the assailants were killed, and the other one was captured."

"And did you find that captured attacker to be of interest in terms of information he provided?"

"Well, he told us that this was elaborate planning to destabilize the situation here. This was an al-Qaeda targeted operation."

"So you definitely feel that *al-Qaeda is present in Kurdistan*—or is that an overstatement?"

"Well, the intelligence speaks very clearly to that effect, to the effect that al-Qaeda is present in this area, and al-Qaeda was planning to set up an alternative base to Afghanistan in anticipation of the fallout from September 11. This group was set up on the first of September 2001. According to intelligence that we have verified from a variety of sources, this was done at the behest of bin Laden's command to establish alternative bases, one of which was here in Iraqi Kurdistan. Apparently they were anticipating what was to come in the aftermath of September 11, and that Afghanistan could become a denied area to them."

Could some of those responsible for sending airplanes into the World Trade Center, I wondered, be *here?* "Are you saying," I asked him, "that those who participated in the September 11 attack have sought refuge in Kurdistan?"

"I'm saying," Salih answered, "that al-Qaeda is a network, and as an organization has sought to establish a base here in Iraqi Kurdistan. A base of logistics and operations and command to be an alternative or part of the alternatives to Afghanistan."

If Ansar was truly linked to al-Qaeda, why was Washington waiting to bomb them? Why was the Bush administration waiting for the war against Saddam to attack Ansar? Already, there were rumors that U.S. agents were secretly operating in Kurdistan, a sign that the invasion was getting closer. Salih got cagey when I asked him whether captured Ansar members, including his own attacker, had been interrogated by the CIA.

"Put it this way—terrorism is a global phenomenon, and there is a global interest in terrorism everywhere in the world these days."

"That sounds like a 'yes,' " I ventured.

"Well," he replied with the hint of a smile, "that is for you to interpret."

A Late-Night Visit

It was a few weeks later, near the end of Ramadan, the holy month of dawn-to-dusk fasting. This was normally a time of family visits, feasting, and gift exchanges. Salih invited me over for a glass a wine. It was something we did every couple of weeks, usually late in the evening when his workload started to taper off. I looked forward to the visits, both for the camaraderie and for the chance to get the latest information.

Since the Ansar attempt on his life, the windows in Salih house had been reinforced with steel grating to make them less vulnerable to gunfire or grenade attack. There were checkpoints at either end of the street, and they were manned twenty-four hours a day. I had an open invitation to Salih's house, which I was careful not to abuse by coming too often. His bodyguards knew me by name and often teased me as I passed with the Kurdish expression *bersee?* (Are you hungry?). Everyone knew Salih had a great cook, and the guards knew I loved good food.

Salih liked reporters. We were friends, but he also used social gatherings at his house to collect or leak information, to trade gossip, or to announce his latest plans for modernizing Kurdistan. From big challenges, like what role the United States should give the Kurds in the impending war, down to his proposals to reduce the growing carnage on local highways by requiring seat belts and driving tests for Kurdish drivers, there was an American can-do spirit about Salih, an optimism that all problems had solutions.

The war was coming, and journalists needed the meetings more than Salih did. The Pentagon was feeding him, but Salih was too sophisticated to let us simply pick his brain. However, he had once vowed privately that he would never deceive me, and I relied on that in evaluating his refusal to answer certain questions.

Salih was an engineer by training, and it may be fair to say that he'd never met

a gadget he didn't like. When I walked in that evening, he was sitting in his favorite spot on the gold couch, next to the end table, where two satellite phones
were charging. He was holding a pair of TV remotes. This was his usual hour for
surfing Arabic channels on the new wide-screen television, and he was hungry, as
always, for the latest news on U.N. inspections in Baghdad and the mushrooming
U.S. troop buildup in Qatar.

I was sitting across the room, as usual, next to the television. Salih's attention
was interrupted periodically by one of the phones ringing. Whenever he answered
a call, I'd take the opportunity to surreptitiously lower the TV volume. Salih had
the news I wanted. I needed a minibreak in the TV chatter to dig offhandedly for
information—I thought of it as playing poker for tidbits—before some new and
compelling visuals reminded him to raise the audio again.

In the middle of the ornate Persian carpet that separated us was a large
wooden tea table with plates of fresh pomegranates, oranges, whole cucumbers,
and pistachio nuts: the seemingly boundless cornucopia of organic fruits and
vegetables that Kurds take for granted.

It was early December 2002. There were rumors of CIA paramilitaries roam-
ing around northern Iraq, measuring old airstrips and taking GPS readings to
target Ansar al-Islam. I had a source who said that Salih himself had been meeting with the agents. "I won't confirm or deny that," he said, with only a hint of a
smile. Salih is happy, I thought, *The war is coming for sure.* The more we talked,
however, the more I realized he was worried about whether the fast-developing
U.S.-Kurdish alliance was being built on shifting sands. Would the U.S. permit
the Kurds to be a real partner in the upcoming war? Would the Kurds preserve
the gains they had made during the invasion or were they being used? And whose
neck was on the line if the Kurds were betrayed—again? Salih wasn't the only
leader with fears that the Kurds could be manipulated again. KDP chief Massoud
Barzani had given me a long interview stressing the refusal of his followers to be
"custom revolutionaries" for a cause in which Kurdish interests did not play a
central role.

Salih was a Pentagon favorite, but his first loyalties were at home, where he reported to a dozen or so of Talabani's most trusted confidantes, the PUK steering
committee. The group was commonly known as the "politburo," but Salih regarded the name as a holdover from the Cold War, and he expressed his displeasure whenever I used the term. In fact, Salih himself was a key politburo member,
and one of his jobs was to interpret American thinking for the Kurdish leadership.
He was expected to draw on his Washington experience to dissect the Bush war
plan for its impact on the Kurds and to predict what Uncle Sam would do after
the war—and his credibility with the Kurdish leadership was on the line. The
politburo valued his access to the corridors of power in the administration, but

given past disappointments, the stakes for blind pro-Americanism were huge. Salih had to be far more than a messenger who delivered U.S. marching orders.

As PUK prime minister, Salih was in regular contact with the Department of Defense in Washington and with CIA headquarters in Langley. The agency had installed a secure telephone in his home, in the room next to the one where I was sitting. It was December 2002, and, though I didn't know it, the invasion was still more than three months away. Still, there seemed little question now of American resolve to proceed with the attack, regardless of the outcome of the U.N. inspections. While the Kurdish leadership didn't dare get pushy with the American planners, the leaders were determined that the *pesh*—as journalists referred to the fighters—take part in the ground assault. According to conventional wisdom, postwar power would not be withheld from those whose blood was spilled to win the freedom.

Barham Salih was no fool. The Kurds and Uncle Sam were not equal partners, and America could be a capricious suitor with a wandering eye. Once the war started, the handshakes and photo ops at the Pentagon might well be a thing of the past. Sitting in Salih's parlor, I realized that the Kurdish leaders had an awesome responsibility to their oft-betrayed constituents. They were supplying the Americans with territory and intelligence, but they were still in the dark about their own role in the American plan after the war. So far, all they'd received from Washington were warnings to restrain the *pesh* (once the U.S. attack began) from rushing to the oil-rich cities of Mosul and Kirkuk. Such a move would anger the Turks. Kurdish leaders had assured the Pentagon they could control their troops.

Salih leaned over the fruit bowl and handed me a glass of wine. I could see he was starting to put on a little weight. "Too many state dinners," he said, laughing and patting a healthy-looking paunch. "And not enough of *that*," he added, gesturing to the new treadmill stashed behind the couch.

Iraq First, Terrorists Second

Despite his connections at the Pentagon, Salih wasn't fully in the loop about the U.S. timetable and he had his own priorities. He favored the overthrow of Saddam, but he believed there was a terrorist militia based in his own territory, and that was a more immediate threat. Salih's would-be assassins had been driven from Ansar camps just sixty miles from his home. He was convinced the camps were a sanctuary for al-Qaeda operatives, perhaps for the notorious Abu al-Zarqawi himself, who, though still unknown to most Americans, was by now a household name in Sulaimaniah. In 2004, a year after the U.S. invasion and a time when Zarqawi was coordinating a wave of suicide attacks throughout Iraq, the Bush administration would place a $25 million bounty on his head. Early in 2003, however, Washington had decided, inexplicably, that bombing the Ansar camps—the place where Salih and other Kurdish leaders believed Zarqawi and his terrorist associates were hiding—would not take place *until* the war on Iraq itself was launched. It is significant that months before March 19, 2003, the day the war began, U.S. satellites already had pinpointed the locations of the camps. Why the administration balked at destroying them when it had the chance isn't clear, but it may have been out of fear that if something went awry in the Ansar attack, it might undermine domestic support in the United States for toppling the regime of Saddam Hussein.

At that point, in any case, the PUK already had three thousand fighters devoted exclusively to the Ansar conflict pinned down in the mountains. They would have to wait for the United States to act. Like other Kurdish leaders, Salih had received only vague promises from the Americans about an "Ansar solution," and he was frustrated.

OK, I asked, is it a deliberate American strategy to keep the Kurds stuck in the Ansar quagmire, to keep them from rushing to the oil fields in Mosul and Kirkuk once the U.S. invasion began? Did a need to appease Turkey figure in the U.S. decision *not* to attack Ansar before launching the war on the Iraqi regime? Salih seemed to bite his tongue, and he didn't answer. Sometimes diplomacy required keeping one's own counsel, especially with the media. There were things he didn't know or wouldn't share. The Kurds had nothing to gain by second-guessing the United States in front of an American reporter.

It was after midnight, a fashionably late hour for dinner in some Kurdish homes. We ate slowly, finishing off a bottle of French wine, a rare treat in Kurdistan. As I started to leave, the prime minister took my arm. "Here is some intelligence," he said. "We have reason to believe that Ansar will try to explode a large bomb in Halabja *tomorrow*."

Girdadrozna

I got the news the next morning at the hotel when I came down for breakfast. It was Eid al-Fatr, the first of the three holidays following Ramadan, an otherwise joyous occasion for Muslim celebration. Ansar had planned an attack, all right. As it turned out, however, it wasn't a bomb.

In the predawn darkness, just four hours after I had left Salih's house, the Islamic militants had overrun the two strongest forts in the Halabja valley. More than fifty PUK fighters were dead or missing, and dozens were wounded. Reports of more executions, beheadings, and mutilation were filtering into the city. Ansar's reputation for hideous brutality would indelibly stain the holiday.

The "Supporters of Islam" had simultaneously attacked two Kurdish government forts located eight miles from Halabja, within sight of the Iranian border. The main focus was a heavily fortified garrison called Girdadrozna—Liar's Hill in English—so named because the flat plateau where the bunkers were positioned could not be seen before reaching the top of the hill.

The first of the injured arrived in Sulaimaniah in the afternoon, and I went to the military hospital to interview them. Women in black chadors were clustered in groups at the hospital gate, searching for information on missing husbands and sons, nervously waiting for the next car or truck to arrive from the front. Inside the building there were scenes of bedlam: dimly lit corridors jammed with the overflow of gurneys carrying wounded government fighters, weeping relatives, nurses and doctors trying to stanch the flow of blood in improvised operating rooms.

The militants had ascended Girdadrozna, inexplicably evading the surrounding minefields and breaching the fort without firing a shot. The terror of the surprise attack on one of the holiest days in the Muslim calendar was compounded by a growing suspicion that Ansar had inside information from PUK sources.

A makeshift morgue was set up at an army base outside Sulaimaniah. A few of the bodies of the dead fighters arrived by ambulance, but most were delivered in the back of pickup trucks. Turbaned volunteers washed the corpses on an outdoor concrete slab while others crouched to cut strips of muslin to tie sheets around the bodies for burial. As the sun began to set, a dozen Kurds knelt on the grass nearby, their hands outstretched in prayer.

Executions

Some of the dead displayed major gunshot or shrapnel wounds. The legs of one fighter had been blown off at the knee, presumably during the barrage of mortars in the opening moments of the surprise attack. A man about twenty-one years of age had a large-caliber bullet hole in his forehead, over which a comrade or first-aid worker had applied a hasty but futile bandage. This young man, I said to myself, had been shot at close range, probably after his surrender and capture.

As his clothing was cut away, the adhesive tape was removed and discarded. His body was cleaned and wrapped and then lifted into a simple pine box, one of ten wooden caskets that were stacked on the concrete. A morgue assistant wrote the name of the deceased on a paper on a clipboard. Another helper cut a cotton strip from a large, ready-made roll. The cloth was green—the official PUK color—and he nailed it to the lid of the wooden box. The men moved quickly, practiced at their work. It was now more than twenty-five years since the PUK had split with the KDP, more than a generation of fighting the Iraqis, other Kurds, and now Ansar. A quarter century of washing young corpses and cutting green strips.

Six pallbearers recruited from a crowd of onlookers carried the coffin to a waiting taxi, a battered orange-and-white Toyota, where it was hoisted onto the roof rack and roped to the door handles. By then it was getting dark. Friends of the young fighter piled into the small car. The loaded taxi disappeared into the night, carrying the body home to his family.

After two hours at the morgue, my satellite phone rang. The ABC news desk in London wanted footage of the attack. By now someone had hung an electric wire with a lightbulb outside to illuminate the blood-soaked slab on which the workers were washing the bodies. A truck arrived with another load of cheap pine caskets. That meant more bodies were expected. Another morgue assistant showed up with a dozen takeout dinners of kebab and rice. He politely handed me the first one. I looked around, realizing I was the only non-Kurd, a special guest at the morgue. We found a dry spot on the slab and sat down to eat, for strength.

Trip to the Front

By the next day, a PUK counteroffensive had regained the forts, driving the Islamic militants back to their mountain caves, behind their mined positions. Barham invited me, as well as the newly arrived reporter from the *New York Times,* to accompany PUK officials to the front. We left Sulaimaniah in an armed caravan of fourteen SUVs and pickup trucks and raced through nearby villages, where children with baskets were going door-to-door collecting gifts and money, joyously celebrating the end of Ramadan.

The main highway to Halabja was still controlled by Komali Islami. No one knew for sure where all of the retreating Ansar fighters had gone. Officials said there was a chance one could be lurking at a Komali checkpoint, so our caravan took the military route. It was a rutted back road used mainly by tractors and shepherds with their flocks of sheep. We saw a few cinderblock farmhouses with roofs made of mud and straw. We crossed a bridge near a water well I had visited a few months earlier. At that time, Ansar fighters had pulled a random farmer off his tractor, killed him, and stuffed his body down the well. I never found out why it had happened, but I knew by now that even this military road was not without risk.

It was a beautiful trip, nonetheless, despite the bone-jarring ride. The Halabja valley is rich farmland known for the production of vegetables and fruits, including the best pomegranates in Kurdistan. Nowadays, though, the country at the base of the snowcapped Surren Mountains along the Iranian frontier, a lovely verdant plateau, belonged to the Supporters of Islam—especially at night.

The arrival of government officials was a clear morale booster for the fighters. The caravan honked its way past checkpoints and sandbagged bunkers, where *peshmerga* in traditional baggy pants, their waists wrapped tightly by long cummerbunds, saluted. The PUK fighters held aloft their AK-47s, rocket launchers, and BKCs, the old Soviet-made machine guns that were popular in Afghanistan a generation ago. They cheered and waved as we passed, visibly buoyed by the pilgrimage to their remote outposts.

The well-planned attack, the largest in the fifteen months since the Islamic guerrillas had relocated from Qandhil Mountain, had been timed for the eve of a major Muslim feast, one comparable to Christmas in the West, and the surprise offensive found a greatly reduced defense force. Half of the Kurdish government troops in the Halabja valley—some fifteen hundred fighters—had been sent home on holiday leave. Now, an official said, the troop strength would be increased to forty-five hundred. The buildup was evident as the caravan passed military trucks headed for the front, including one that was trailing a powerful 120 mm artillery piece.

Salih and other PUK officials attended the funeral of a dead fighter at a mosque near the site of the battle. They joined the mourners in prayer, sitting cross-legged and shoeless on an ornate Persian carpet as the soulful chant of the village mullah filled the cavernous room. An old man searching for his son, who was still missing from the battlefield, wandered about the service, asking questions. At that moment, no one had the heart to tell him that the young man's body already had been found. Instead, one of the mourners escorted the father from the mosque and offered him a glass of tea, delaying the news until after the delegation had departed.

Salih invited Chris Chivers, the *New York Times* reporter, and me to ride with him on the trip back to Sulaimaniah. The prime minister tried to put the best gloss on the devastating attack, but his take on the events was hard to accept. "We routed them," he exclaimed, unconvincingly. "Ansar is in disarray."

In reality, the militants were still as audacious as they were ruthless, and for the moment they had the upper hand. That evening, my translator summed up their advantage. "The *peshmerga* are dreaming about getting married and buying houses and cars," he said. "At the same time, each of the Ansars has already dug his own grave in Biarra."

Foreign Relations Committee

In mid-December 2002, with the Ansar threat at the top of the PUK's agenda, an important delegation arrived from Washington. The group was headed by Senator Joseph Biden (D-DE), and Senator Chuck Hagel (R-NE), senior members of the Senate Foreign Relations Committee. Officially speaking, the Foreign Relations Committee had come to assess for itself how well the rival parties were cooperating. This was the highest-ranking congressional group ever to visit the Kurds, and the presence was another signal to me of an awareness on

Capitol Hill that an attack on Saddam was coming, regardless of the success of U.N. inspections.

The visit took place in Salahuddin, the headquarters of the Kurdistan Democratic Party, but both Kurdish parties hosted it. I wanted to know how the KDP regarded the current threat to its old nemesis, the PUK, so I asked a senior KDP official. He told me privately that he thought the PUK had exaggerated the purported link between Ansar and al-Qaeda to "hook the Americans" prematurely into the war. The remark underscored the depth of suspicion that still existed between the parties—a full five years after rival leaders had signed the U.S.-brokered peace accord in Washington.

It was soon clear that the visiting members of Congress were not buying claims that al-Qaeda had an operational presence in Iraq. In separate interviews, both U.S. senators said that while Ansar and al-Qaeda might share the same ideology, and while al-Qaeda members, in Biden's words, "may have been in and out of this area," the members of the Foreign Relations Committee knew of no sustained al-Qaeda presence in Iraqi Kurdistan.

Senator Biden told me privately that he had seen no evidence supporting claims by the Bush administration of an al-Qaeda connection to Baghdad. On the contrary, he said, "Al-Qaeda may well be *targeting Saddam*." The remark was startling. The polls indicated that about two-thirds of the American public believed White House claims that Saddam was connected to the destruction of the World Trade Center, and many believed that invading Iraq, therefore, would be an act of righteous vengeance. However, Senator Biden, privy to classified intelligence, was saying the opposite. He was particularly blunt in drawing a comparison between the post-9/11 era and the Cold War. "It used to be," he told me, "that when allies wanted money or help from the United States, they'd say, 'The commies are coming!' Now they say, 'Al-Qaeda is coming!'"

Biden's Republican counterpart, Senator Hagel, also was skeptical that al-Qaeda had bases in northern Iraq, although he told me that intelligence he'd seen suggested al-Qaeda operatives had at least visited the area. After the delegation returned to Washington, I telephoned my contacts on the staffs of both senators, who confirmed that neither senator had changed his mind. Despite their skepticism about the alleged connection between Saddam and al-Qaeda, however, both senators accepted the claim by the administration that Iraq had weapons of mass destruction, and both had just voted to give the president the authority to go to war.

Not only did Biden and Hagel believe that Hussein's regime possessed WMD, they were convinced that Iraq would *use* the weapons if cornered. Both senators told me they believed the Kurds—and anyone else in northern Iraq—were particularly vulnerable. Neither could understand why the Kurdish population had not been provided with protective gas masks. Both assured me they would raise the gas-mask issue with the Bush administration when they got home.

The visit by members of the Senate Foreign Relations Committee took place just before Christmas. Six weeks later, in early February 2003, the Bush administration set forth the same argument Salih and the PUK had been making for months, namely that the perpetrators of 9/11 or their accomplices were, in fact, based in northern Iraq and posed an imminent threat to the Kurds and to the United States. U.S. officials buttressed their claim with detailed satellite photos, images that made the Ansar camps look like sitting ducks for missile attack. Oddly, while the "address" of the terrorists was then known to the world, there was no apparent urgency to go after the group until March 19, a full six weeks later. Not until the attack on Baghdad was launched did the United States begin bombing the Ansar camps in Iraqi Kurdistan. Even then, the Pentagon would fail to commit U.S. ground troops to prevent the insurgents' escape to Iran. The failure would be a replay of the debacle at Tora Bora in Afghanistan, when wishful U.S. military planners relied on corrupt warlords to block al-Qaeda trails to Pakistan. The warlords allowed Osama bin Laden and key operatives to escape. In northern Iraq, Ansar militants relied on mountain passes to retreat to Iran. Kurdish *peshmerga,* though not corrupt, could not take the place of U.S. troops, and many Ansar militants survived U.S. bombing, ready to fight another day.

In the end, critics would say that homeland security had yielded to politics: The timing of the Iraq attack had taken precedence over the hot pursuit of terrorists who were in league with those who destroyed the Twin Towers and parts of the Pentagon. In the years following the U.S. invasion, some families in northern Iraq would regard the failure to seize the initiative against Ansar al-Islam with bitterness. The Ansar militants who had escaped the delayed attack in 2003 reestablished themselves after the invasion under the banner Ansar al-Sunnah. In 2004, the group took credit for bombing a U.S. Army mess hall in Mosul, killing twenty-four soldiers, and for a spate of suicide bombings that killed almost two hundred Kurds. In early 2005, several Ansar members were arrested in Europe. Following the coordinated train bombings in London on July 7, 2005, investigators began probing possible links to Ansar.

With months still to go before the war, there was a sense of helplessness and exasperation among many rank-and-file Kurds in Sulaimaniah. For those who had lost a relative or family member, Ansar was a personal, immediate threat, not a policy issue whose significance lay in the potential to connect Saddam to either al-Qaeda or to September 11. As a result, leaders such as Salih, normally supporters of U.S. policy, found themselves facing increasingly alienated constituents who regarded the elimination of Ansar a greater immediate priority than attacking the regime of Saddam Hussein.

The sense of communal resignation in the city was described to me by a hotel reception clerk. It was just after Ramadan, normally a joyous time like Christmas or Chanukah. I asked the man if he had had a good holiday. The answer was no, *not* a good holiday. "In Sulaimaniah," he added darkly, "every family [is] not happy."

23

WMD and Tipsters

I think a lot of people are saying, you know, by gosh, I hope we
don't have a war. I hope this can be done peacefully. It's up to
Saddam, however, to make that choice.

—PRESIDENT GEORGE W. BUSH, "QUOTE OF THE DAY"
THE NEW YORK TIMES, NOVEMBER 1, 2002

War Beats Every Other Story

It was the fall of 2002, and I was in Iraq, eight thousand miles from home. By now, it was clear to almost everyone that an attack was coming. The prospect filled me with an odd mixture of dread and impatience. I felt I was caught up in busywork, filling my days with inconsequential activity, anticipating an event that seemed as terrifying as it did inevitable. At the same time I was tired of waiting, and sometimes I just wanted to get it over with.

Kurdistan was my beat, but it seemed more like a stakeout than a regular assignment for filing stories. Back in the United States, there was little appetite for features on Kurdish agriculture, economy, or politics. The newsrooms of the world were focused on U.N. inspections in Baghdad and war maneuvering in Washington. I could follow those stories, like much of the English-speaking public in the Middle East, on BBC television. For the time being, northern Iraq was being treated by the media as a sideshow—unless or until Saddam pulled a crazy stunt like peremptorily striking us all with weapons of mass destruction.

Some of my days went by in slow motion, like the passage of time in the play *Waiting for Godot*. After weeks in Kurdistan, I felt marooned, a ticketed passenger at the airport waiting for an unscheduled flight. Then on October 11, the U.S. Senate voted 77 to 23 to authorize President Bush to attack Saddam Hussein if he refused to surrender weapons of mass destruction, as required by the United Nations.

Two years later, the Iraq war would be a central debate in the 2004 presidential race, but in 2002, supporters of the war powers measure included presidential candidate Senator John Kerry, who argued at the time that Iraq possessed chemical weapons, "probably including mustard gas, sarin, cyclosarin, and VX," that Iraq was working to develop "airborne vehicles for delivery of biological agents," and that Baghdad "could have a nuclear weapon within one year." On the same day, the House of Representatives voted in favor of the measure 296 to 133. The president praised the joint congressional action, declaring, "America speaks with one voice."

Over the course of the fall, as France, Germany, and Russia successfully campaigned for U.N. inspections, arguments for a deadline for Iraqi compliance— three months hence—began to emerge. In mid-November, the deadline was finally set, but only after contentious debate in the U.N. Security Council. The United States had demanded a shorter deadline, but agreed to go along with the additional time. Despite the tightening inspections, war momentum in the United States seemed unstoppable. U.N. inspectors had been absent from Iraq for four years, and they were facing complicated searches in a large and secretive country. They had had been on the job barely two weeks before an op-ed piece in the *Wall Street Journal*—one of many in U.S. newspapers—criticized Hans Blix, the chief inspector, for going too slowly. More than a year later, after the U.S.-led invasion, both *The New York Times* and *The Washington Post* would apologize to readers for failing to challenge White House assertions about Iraq's weapon's capability, but the posture of most media outlets at this point was not confrontational. Most Americans now believed that Saddam had WMD and that Iraq had played a role in the events of 9/11. War fever was in the air. In many conversations a sense of a "done deal" seemed to lurk just below the surface: not whether the attack would take place, but *when*.

According to a new Security Council resolution, Iraq now had until December 8 to report all WMD to the U.N. By December 23, the weapons inspectors would analyze the submitted data and then they would return to Iraq. After that, the inspectors would have until February 21 to make their final report. The Security Council would argue about what to do next. The run-up to war was beginning to take shape, and I had a reserved seat.

It was November 2002. With the new timetable, I'd be stuck in a hotel in Kurdistan for at least another three months. By now, I had developed a routine: taking walks, running errands, or drinking tea with Kurdish shop owners in the morning, going to lunch with government officials, and having dinner with friends or eating alone in the greasy spoons, where the cooks knew my name and sometimes served me their homemade baklava. As I made my rounds, I frequently stopped at KurdSat, the PUK satellite station that was perched on a mountainside near Sulaimaniah with a commanding view of the city below. My friends Hiwa Rafiq, the resourceful technical director who managed to keep the station on the air—often when parts and trained engineers were scarce—and Azad Sediq, KurdSat's overworked but constantly wisecracking news director, were never too busy to schmooze about local politics and I always enjoyed their company.

All the while, I was trying to drum up news for daily e-mails to the ABC desks, shooting television footage, and periodically filing print stories for the ABC Web site. I was one of many human weather vanes who told New York and London news desks which way the wind was blowing—or whether it was blowing at all—and I was waiting.

No other ABC staffer had succeeded in getting into northern Iraq, and the network satellite dish intended for my area was still sitting in a crate in London. Access to northern Iraq tightened in mid-October after CNN trumpeted its arrival by broadcasting a story of its TV crew crossing the Tigris River with a small flotilla of boats full of equipment. The broadcast reneged on an agreement made with Damascus officials not to air stories about the route, effectively ending all access for journalists through Syria. At the time, hundreds of reporters had applications pending for transit visas sitting at Syrian and Iranian consulates in Europe, but now no one was getting permission.

Kurdistan had become an island.

Elsewhere, it was as if a starter pistol had been fired, and the players were already in motion. U.S. military bases were placed on alert, equipment made ready, leaves canceled. Expecting a bonanza of new orders, defense contractors stepped up production. Some of the arms plants, reportedly, were running twenty-four-hour shifts, and companies such as Boeing and Lockheed had already seen a spike in their stocks. The Pentagon was preparing staging areas from Europe to the Middle East. Thousands of reporters stationed all over the world were gearing up for the coming event, feeding the news cycle with the "Saudi angle" on the war, the "Madrid angle," and the "Tel Aviv angle." The war was a kind of full employment act for reporters including, I had to admit, myself. The war was the big story, and whatever propelled it was news.

Yet it did not feel like a "normal" war, one that starts with a sneak attack or a conflict that ignites after a long border dispute, like the ones between Pakistan and India. The war in Iraq had a strangely *rational* sense to it, like a coming event or an appointment to be entered into your Palm Pilot or a big boxing match, with tickets that could be ordered in advance. There was a steady and progressive sense of anticipation, bringing to mind the long lead-up to the Muhammad Ali/George Foreman fight in Zaire in 1974, the heavily promoted Rumble in the Jungle. For months before the first bombs fell on Baghdad, the slow but inexorable advance of war would dominate the headlines.

Insider Information

If I hadn't had access to the Kurdish leadership, I might have wondered if the United Nations or the widespread public peace marches would derail the war. After all, major U.S. allies favored the inspections, and millions of antiwar protesters were filling the streets of cities around the world. Barham Salih was particularly convincing. Although he revealed little of an explicit nature, his moods were powerful clues, as when he spoke excitedly about the United Nations withdrawing from the country, a clear signal that war was close at hand. He was, he said, "absolutely certain" that Saddam had hidden chemical weapons, that the inspectors wouldn't find them, and that the U.S.-led invasion was imminent.

The thought gnawed at me. If Saddam did have WMD, why *wait* until the weapons were discovered or until the United Nations criticized the regime for not cooperating with inspections? Either event could trigger an attack, so why squander that element of surprise? The United States was capitalizing on the inspection timetable by moving troops into position throughout the region. Why would Saddam wait until the enemy had him cornered?

The nearest Iraqi launchers were only sixty miles away from my hotel in Sulaimaniah. Based on information from paid spies in the Iraqi military, Kurdish intelligence doubted that Saddam had the necessary spray nozzles to arm his Scud missiles with gas, but the truth was, no one really knew. After the 1988 gas attack on the nearby town of Halabja, thousands of frightened survivors had fled to Sulaimaniah. Everyone I spoke to seemed to know—or even be related to—one or more of the Halabja victims. The collective fear of another chemical attack was buried deep in the Kurdish consciousness, and the Iraqi regime was keenly aware of it. In 1991, the Iraqi military had successfully used gypsum powder to help quell the uprising in Kirkuk. All Saddam would have to do, a Kurdish shop owner told me, would be to drop sugar from a helicopter. "Everybody would think it was anthrax," he said. "In a few hours, a million Kurds would be in the mountains again."

Surviving WMD

As I passed my evenings in the hotel room watching the news on BBC, the "buzz" of war talk sounded so far away: The wrangling between the Bush administration and naysayers in the Security Council was a distant argument with little bearing on me, but Sulaimaniah, where I was based, seemed to be in the eye of the storm. My hotel was less than a three-hour drive from the presidential palaces of Saddam Hussein in Tikrit. If the U.S. hit Tikrit, and the regime counterattacked, how would I react in that moment of terror? The question triggered images of fumbling for the chemical weapons suit, the one I'd gotten on the British air base. The bulky nylon outfit, with its protective hood, gas mask, and oversized rubber boots, was still in the original "Survivor" backpack. I had stashed it in the bottom of my closet, hoping the maids—who had no such protection—would not notice it.

The military trainers in England had warned me to remove my glasses before trying to strap on the mask. The mask had its own built-in slots for lenses, and there wasn't enough room for my own frames. There was an optician near my hotel, but I hadn't gotten around to filling my prescription for the lenses. Now I found myself trying to guess where I would be at the time of attack—in a café, on the street, or maybe asleep in my bed. I imagined myself squinting without my glasses, the escape routes a blur of bad choices.

By then, all Kurdistan was talking about the impending war. Predicting a date for the U.S. attack had become a popular pastime. Still, if Iraq retaliated with WMD, it would be a catastrophe for ordinary Kurds, even the ones who talked about tying wet handkerchiefs over their faces and getting to higher ground. Only foreigners and maybe a few government leaders would be protected by gas masks. The others, the have-nots, would have little chance of survival.

The optician knew I was American. If he saw the mask, he'd think I had inside information. I was embarrassed. I didn't want to be taken for "one of the saved." But now, with a probable timetable for the war, I couldn't procrastinate any longer.

Prewar Stories

One of my early ABC stories from northern Iraq focused on a scheme by the Iraqi National Congress (INC), the London-based exile group. The INC had been a major recipient of the $97 million from the Iraq Liberation Act passed by Congress in 1998. The funds were appropriated during the Clinton administration, but the act was the brainchild of a group of neoconservatives that included current Secretary of Defense Donald Rumsfeld, his deputies Douglas Feith and Paul Wolfowitz, and Deputy Secretary of State Richard Armitage. The INC was paying a Kurdish political splinter party to recruit local Arabs for U.S. military training in Eastern Europe. The plan was to use them as advisors with the Northern Front, the U.S. troops expected to sweep down from Turkey. According to rumors, 150 Arabs had gotten cash bonuses, and one recruiter already was driving around in a new Mercedes-Benz, a model the Kurds called the "Jumbo." The unusual part was the background of the guy who was organizing the scheme to round up Arabs for the war effort. Ironically, he was the former general secretary of the Communist Party of Iraq.

One night over dinner, I ran into a tip for a bigger story. A local family invited me to join their friends for *kifta*, a traditional Kurdish specialty consisting of lamb, rice, and raisins. The host told me in advance that one of his guests—a man I'll call Marawan (not his real name)—who was visiting from the city of

Erbil, had special information about Iraqi weapons. Apparently, Marawan knew the wife of an Iraqi scientist in Baghdad who was being detained by the regime to keep him from being interviewed by the U.N. inspectors. The scientist's wife had grown up in the Kurdish region.

Marawan had met the scientist on a business trip to Baghdad a few years earlier. My host said Marawan had mentioned the matter only in passing, one Kurdish friend to another. The offhanded manner gave the tip a measure of credibility. My ears perked up.

After dinner, the guests retired to the parlor for tea and fruit. I chose a moment when the rest of the room was occupied in conversation, and I casually broached the subject with Marawan. He admitted that he knew the scientist's wife, but he seemed too edgy to say much more than that. I decided to leave the matter alone for the time being. The host said he'd persuade Marawan to call me.

The Biggest Story?

By this point, the scientists were considered the central key to proving the existence of weapons of mass destruction, the stated justification for war. Across the world the media carried images of U.N. inspectors racing around Baghdad in their white SUVs, looking for frightened researchers to interview. President Bush himself was talking about the need to debrief the scientists outside the country, beyond the reach of government retaliation. If the regime was *hiding* the scientists, the man Marawan knew could be the proof that Iraq actually still possessed the outlawed weapons.

If that were true, I had stumbled across the biggest story on earth. Right there in sleepy Kurdistan, off the beaten news path.

I knew from experience that Marawan's story might be just a rumor that had run amok, or a scam for money like the faked sightings I encountered in the 1980s when I'd investigated the disappearance of an American in Central America. Back then, I was writing a story for the *Los Angeles Times,* but I had no way of knowing that the missing man, an ex-Marine, was already dead. By the time I got involved, he had been murdered by a military death squad in Guatemala. Before his mother and father found out the truth, they would spend several years posting reward flyers in tourist spots throughout Central America. They were obliged to endure painful contacts from con artists and bounty hunters. Many of the fake sightings sounded promising, at least at first. The callers had a knack for telling the frantic parents what they wanted to hear.

By the time I met Marawan, I had been in Kurdistan long enough to know that the region was swimming in spies: Iraqi, American, Turkish, Syrian, Israeli, Russian, and Iranian. It was common knowledge that some visiting businessmen and tourists were agents for foreign interests and that local Kurds were being recruited to help them obtain information. In some cases, the paid helpers were said to be members of the main Kurdish parties.

Despite the fact that the KDP and the PUK were U.S. allies and sworn enemies of the Iraqi regime, it was well known that they maintained back channels to Saddam's regime, right up until the war started. It was reasonable to believe that some of the Kurdish go-betweens, the ones who made periodic four-hour drives to Baghdad, were, in fact, double agents paid to collect information, on both the Kurds and their foreign visitors.

Given the premium on accurate information, it was not surprising that the spreading of lies—the use of disinformation—was a common tool. As a reporter in a strange culture, it was difficult for me to know whether "tips" were genuine or whether they'd been planted to set me up for a fall. I was baffled, for example, when a Kurd who worked for one of the parties told me, cryptically, "The *Iranians* say that you are not a 'normal journalist.'" The Kurd said a man working in Iran's "interest section" had given him that tip after discovering I had investigated the Kurdish mountaintop site the CIA was scouting to set up a radio transmitter. I could see how an American visiting such a site might raise suspicion with Iranian agents. What I never learned was which of the Kurds who escorted me there had informed on me, and, more important, whether the "tip" would somehow be used to discredit my work as a journalist.

One day, I got a call from an Arab journalist who had fled from Baghdad after one of his stories incurred the wrath of the regime. He told me that Ba'athists had attacked his home and tried to kill him. He said he was away at the time, but the assailants had killed his wife and child. Now he was trying to earn money in Kurdistan as an Arabic/English translator, despite his mediocre grasp of English. The next day, he showed up in the hotel lobby with an unshaven Kurd in his late twenties, who was wearing a black suit without a tie. The Kurdish man was selling something and wanted to speak to me privately, in my room. Getting right to the point, the newcomer said he had a friend in a weapons factory in Baghdad who could sneak materials out. That would *prove* that Saddam had WMD, he said, which would be "big information" for any journalist.

"Radiation Detector"

The tipster showed me a photo of a device that he claimed was a radiation detector used in the factory, and he told me his friend could smuggle out plastic bottles with drawings of skulls and crossbones on their labels. My cost would be "only $50,000." When I asked him why he didn't report the information to the Kurdish government, he said he was afraid he would be arrested and interrogated by the *Zanyari*, the Kurdish intelligence service. He claimed the Kurdish leaders wanted to control all potential channels of communication to the United States.

He got angry when I told him journalists don't buy information, and it wasn't my role to try to broker such deals with my government. "You are an American," he said sarcastically, suggesting that meant I was a "friend" of the Iraqi National Congress (INC), the dissident exile group headed by Ahmed Chalabi. "America wastes millions of dollars on the INC, but the INC has no real intelligence inside Iraq," he said. "So why not spend $50,000 to get *proof?*" The stranger acted angry when I sent him away, and I regretted I'd brought him to my room. Nonetheless, his point was valid. Maybe reward signs weren't posted on every corner, but the word was out: Uncle Sam was looking for information to kick-start the war, and he had a fistful of dollars. The irony was that Marawan, the man I'd met at the dinner party, eventually would be paid $10,000—although not by ABC News— for his own tip about weapons of mass destruction. I would broker the deal, and my network would broadcast his story.

Competition

Few news stories could top the prospect of a U.S. invasion. Reporters were under pressure, and the stakes had been magnified by the suggestion that Iraq was involved in the events of 9/11, the worst foreign attack on America in history. Together, the merging of Iraq and the 9/11 issue guaranteed a constant demand for new information, pictures, and interviews. In the supercharged race for fresh coverage of the war, an item that advanced a U.S. attack could "beat" the competition.

Marawan's tip put me in a quandary. If I could prove scientists actually *had* been abducted, the story would have an incredible scoop for ABC News. If not, or if the piece aired without solid confirmation obtained in Baghdad—hard to get, given regime security—I might only be adding to the war hysteria.

Would breaking this news save the scientists or would it endanger their lives and the lives of their families—who might later be blamed for the "leak"? Would the news hasten a U.S. attack—and possibly Saddam's WMD reprisal—but *save* lives, because the regime would collapse sooner? Or would a lot of people die while I got credit for an exclusive?

The possible outcomes seemed as varied as they were terrifying. My thoughts took me back to my early days as a reporter, to the funeral on the Indian reservation when I'd flinched and put my camera down. I decided to follow the facts where they took me.

24

Ashti Hotel

If Kuwait grew carrots, we wouldn't give a damn.

—LAWRENCE KORB, ASSISTANT SECRETARY OF DEFENSE (1981–1985) IN THE
REAGAN ADMINISTRATION, ON THE IMPENDING U.S. ATTACK ON IRAQ IN 1991

November 2002

In late November I moved to the Ashti, a small, refurbished hotel located a
couple of blocks from the Palace. I had stayed there in 1991, just after the
abortive Kurdish uprising, when the hotel was known as the Salam (peace). Despite the passage of time, my memories of the place were still fresh. In those days
the lobby was dark and cold, the reception area heated by a single kerosene stove
that gave off more fumes than warmth. Men wearing overcoats sat on couches,
drinking sweetened tea and fingering their AK-47s. The hotel electricity seldom
worked, and the only light in the lobby came from the steamed-up windows,
where old masking tape—precautions against shattering glass during shelling by
the Iraqi army—still struck to the glass.

Back in 1991, the reception clerk was a slight fellow with a thin moustache
named Mohammed. It was wintertime, and the Salam was cold and dark. Mohammed was bundled up in a wool scarf and a white London Fog trench coat,
smoking a long, filter-tipped cigarette, and calmly reading some writing on a
scrap of paper illuminated by an oil lamp. He seemed quite at home, impeccably
dressed for someone who had to wear an overcoat to work indoors. With a silver-
streaked, every-hair-in-place look, he struck the pose of a David Niven character
in an old movie, someone who maintained an air of privilege whatever the ad-
versity. He was the only person in the hotel who spoke English, and the rest of the
staff relied on him for the infrequent occasions when a foreign guest showed up.
He seemed like a visitor himself, someone too urbane for such dingy surround-
ings. Indeed, he told me when we first met, he had worked in the better hotels in
both Baghdad and Basra. During my 1991 stay at the Salam, we developed a
cross-cultural exchange. Mohammed was looking for suggestions about how he
and his family might get out of Iraq, especially any information I could provide

about visas to the United States. In return, he was helpful with tips like warning me to double-check bottles of drinking water to make sure the seals were unbroken. The water was particularly dirty since the allied bombing of the treatment plants. Some unscrupulous vendors, he told me, were refilling the blue plastic bottles with ordinary tap water. Northern Iraq in the aftermath of the first Gulf War was not a good place to get sick.

On the wall behind Mohammed, below an Arabic calendar, was the defunct hotel switchboard, which consisted of an antique wooden box, a wind-up crank and pullout cables. Prior to the Gulf War in 1991, the cables had been used to connect calls, by hand, to the rooms above. Nowadays, Mohammed was the chief hotel operator, and he had three separate desk phones in front of him. Two of the phones worked, but only for local calls. The national telephone system had been destroyed in the war, and long-distance service was no longer available. Without linkage between cities, Mohammed said, he could be confident that whenever the telephone rang there would be a Kurd on the other end of the line.

Few of the people who frequented the Salam lobby were actually guests. The hotel had become a link to the world outside of Kurdistan, a place for curious locals to get news and for the Kurdish police to check up on newcomers in town. Until the 1991 uprising drove out the Iraqis, Mohammed said, it had been forbidden to associate with foreigners. In those days the hotel was full of spies.

Mounted over the reception desk was an ornate plaque from the Hotels and Restaurants Association of Iraq awarding the Salam two stars for the year 1987. Considering the ripped carpets, the unheated rooms, and the holes in the wall over my bed, that seemed like a generous rating. In those days, a night's lodging at the hotel cost the equivalent of $55.50 at the official Baghdad exchange rate. But I was paying $1.85 at the black-market rate, which seemed more in line with the quality. The plaque depicted a knife and fork crossed above a wine glass, with a room key dangling in the mouth of the glass. The fancy symbols suggested a bygone lifestyle, one that contrasted with the shadowy figures with machine guns over their backs who passed through the freezing, dimly lit lobby.

I recalled one exchange with Mohammed, a moment when the power returned in the middle of our conversation. The nearby elevator, no longer stuck between floors, started up again. Two fluorescent tubes behind the reception desk buzzed back to life. Mohammed nonchalantly reset the time on the lobby clock and returned to the business at hand, painstakingly attaching food and bar bills to the guest registration sheets by means of straight pins (there were no staples in Kurdistan at the time). Now and then, he would pause to sip from a glass of arak, which he said was a fruit-flavored, high-proof, home brew. He was not tipsy, but I could see he was a little flushed. "Are you Muslim?" I asked him with a straight face. *"Sometimes,"* he said with a laugh, stirring the chunk of ice he had managed to find for his drink.

Now it was 2002, and the name Salam had been changed to Ashti, the Kurdish word for "peace." The PUK owned the hotel and had done extensive renovations. The cost of a room had risen to the equivalent of $30. The PUK would further increase the price as the war approached and space for visiting journalists became a premium.

In early December, more than four months before the U.S. invasion, writer Chris Chivers of the *New York Times* and Chang Lee, a *Times* photographer, arrived. After weeks of lobbying at the Iranian embassy in London, they'd won a ten-day visa to northern Iraq. They viewed it as a one-way trip. As some of the lucky few to get into the country, they had no intention of giving up their hard-won access to the war. "The only way I'm leaving Iraq," vowed Chang, "is through Baghdad."

After a short stint in the swanky Palace, Chris and Chang moved down the street to the informal, friendlier Ashti. A few weeks later, we were joined by Jeff Fleishman of the *Los Angeles Times*, who also had managed to cross the border from Iran. It had been a long time without other reporters around, and I welcomed the company. Over the next few months Chang would ceremoniously chart the passage of time in the Ashti bar, where we gathered for dinner beneath the oil painting of Sheikh Mahmud, the legendary Kurdish insurgent. Smiling, Chang would raise a glass each evening and make the same toast, "Here is to another day closer to home—*alive.*"

Jeff had just been hired as bureau chief for the *Los Angeles Times* in Berlin, following a Neiman fellowship at Harvard and a dozen years at the *Philadelphia Inquirer,* some of it as a war correspondent in the Balkans. Chris had come to the *New York Times* after working at the *Providence Journal,* following a six-year enlistment in the Marines and graduation from Columbia University's School of Journalism. On the morning of September 11, 2001, he had been on a routine assignment for the *Times* in lower Manhattan. For the next forty-eight hours, he filed eyewitness reports from Ground Zero. He and Chang, a gifted, indefatigable "shooter," had covered the war in Afghanistan together. In the months ahead, Chris, Jeff, and I would travel northern Iraq together, covering many of the same stories. Rizgar, one of my translators, nicknamed us the "Irish Lobby"—because all of us had Irish roots—and he joked that Chang, who was born in Korea, was an honorary member of the group.

Chris had grown up fishing and trapping with his father in upstate New York. As far as I could tell, he'd brought only two shirts to cover the war: a red plaid wool hunting shirt and a green plaid wool hunting shirt. Every morning at the hotel when he came downstairs, he'd be wearing one or the other. I remember him in

the breakfast line getting yogurt and olives, a medium-sized guy with a hint of deliberate shoulder slouch that made him seem a little smaller than he was. He may
have understated himself physically for the same reason he shared his news sources
and offered up notes when another reporter missed an interview.

Maybe it was his military training to hold something in reserve. Then one day
it hit me: He was a "stealth" reporter. He was deliberately flying under the radar:
The only thing that mattered to him was that a good story landed in the paper,
not the role of being a pro among colleagues. Other people could get in your
notebook, but nobody could get in your head. That kept strangers off balance,
because it went against the usual competitive instincts. Maybe he figured being
"smaller" would make people underestimate him, like the farmer back home he
had once described who tucked himself into a small box, cut an eye slit in the card-
board, and slowly crept up on a flock of grazing geese. "It took all day," he said, "but
the guy got eleven birds."

Chang was not a country boy. He was a New Yorker with a reputation as a gour-
met food lover. It wasn't surprising that the first Kurdish vocabulary he had learned
were the names of spices and pickles. Chang had spent too much time in French
cafés and Manhattan sushi bars to accept the monotonous Kurdish diet of kebab
and chicken "shish." Over-tipping the waiters at the Ashti and slipping bottles of
scotch to the cooks, he soon had the hotel restaurant serving spicy "African chicken"
and another peppery dish he called "Thai chicken." He also convinced one chef to
prepare freshwater fish "Baghdad style," a slow-cook method using a wood fire.

The Ashti waiters liked Chang. When I revisited the restaurant in 2004, a year
after the U.S. invasion, the first thing they asked me was whether I wanted
"Chang Chicken"—an all-purpose reference to any customized dish that wasn't
on the menu.

Chris's father had gone to the war in Vietnam, and, from what I gathered, he
had come home a quieter man. Chris told us he and his dad liked to throw some
rods and reels in the family skiff and row out to the middle of a lake to talk and
drift and to listen to the silences. Chris said his career goal was to be a wildlife
writer, to leave the *Times* "and work for a nature magazine."

One night Chris managed to get four bottles of Budweiser short necks smuggled in from Baghdad. No one had ever seen Budweiser in Kurdistan, and Chris
wouldn't say how he'd pulled it off. But when he showed up he was grinning like
a rascal. He gave us his trademark frozen-deer-in-the-headlights look, the one
that telegraphed that he was about to say something important. "I never really
cared for Bud," he allowed, "but this is what we drank in the boat."

Jeff was a good reporter but he was also a serious film buff who was stuck in
northern Iraq, where there wasn't a single movie channel or public theater.
"Meryl Streep is the greatest actress of the century," he'd say over dinner.

"What about Vanessa Redgrave?" Cameron Barr, the writer for the *Christian Science Monitor,* would counter.

"Number two, but you're right—it's a close call. Depends on how you felt that morning. Did you see *Sophie's Choice?*"

"The accents were corny."

"I love the accents. Such simmering sexuality just beneath the surface."

Sex

It was Friday, the Kurdish marriage day and the Muslim weekend. The streets were full of wedding caravans, car horns honking, colored scarves, and streamers flying from windows, videographers with modern digital cameras, a bride and groom in Western dress, and attendants in traditional Kurdish clothes.

The times were changing. Most marriages were still arranged by the families, with a negotiated dowry of gold going to the bride—to be returned if the couple broke up later. After the Kurdish "safety zone" was set up in 1991, activist Kurdish women had overturned several family laws that repressed or discriminated against women. The so-called honor killing of unmarried women who were accused of having had premarital sex was outlawed, although the practice still took place occasionally, usually in the outlying villages.

The old Kurdish custom *jinn by jinn* also had been banned, although it, too, still persisted. *Jinn by jinn* was a complicated arrangement in traditional Kurdish society. It allowed a family whose daughter already was married the right to choose a bride from their son-in-law's family for their own son. For reasons I never understood, the fate of both marriages was tied together, like a package deal. If one relationship broke down and that couple divorced, the other marriage, no matter how happy, had to be dissolved as well.

The Kurdish *peshmerga* now included women, although the units were small, female-only troops and were rarely—if at all—used in fighting. The recruiting model, apparently, was the PKK in Turkey, where, unlike Iraqi Kurdistan, women frequently did take part in combat.

Same-sex relationships among the Kurds were said to exist, but homosexuality was considered taboo, and the topic itself was rarely discussed.

In Iraq, as in Turkey, the male-dominated Kurdish culture still ostracized women for engaging in sex before marriage, and teenagers generally were not permitted to date. In Iraq, however, a more public interest in sex, albeit repressed, was clearly evident. While it was rare to hear of women who had had sex for money, there were unconfirmed reports of a Kurdish brothel in Sulaimaniah and Iranian-made condoms were said to be available in local pharmacies. The recent advent of satellite TV and the Internet had introduced pornography to Kurdistan, and, from all appearances, it had a strong following.

There were more than one hundred Internet cafés in northern Iraq. I frequented several different ones for e-mail, depending on which had a working satellite connection on a given day. Computer monitors in many of the cafés were installed in individual booths, like library carrels, which offered private viewing spaces for customers. Many of the patrons were Kurdish males with a curiosity that reflected the isolation of life in northern Iraq, a culture without movie cinemas or cable television. When a newcomer arrived to log on in the booth, the screen sometimes displayed pornographic photos from the last customer. The images were only teases for paid hardcore sites, because there was no way to pay for access to the sites themselves. Full-fledged Internet sex required a credit card, a phenomenon not yet available in Kurdistan.

Reporters joked about going to the cafés to transmit a news story, only to have an explicit pop-up interrupt their e-mail. In some cases there was interest in cyber violence as well as cyber sex. Jeff Fleishman told me he'd been confronted on one visit by photos of naked bodies and dead bodies, side by side. When he'd sat down in the computer booth that day, two Web sites visited by the previous customer were still on the screen. One was pornographic; the other depicted the mutilated corpses of *peshmerga*. The latter site was the work of Ansar al-Islam, the al-Qaeda–linked group that was on everyone's mind.

First Lady of the Press Corps

By the end of her day, the dress shoes Dildar Kittani wore to the office were often muddy from tramping through villages to orient reporters to the Kurdish cause. Dildar was a multitasker, as they say in the West. She was a wife and mother, the family breadwinner, and a symbol of the changing role of Kurdish women. When I met her, she was working sixteen-hour days for the Council of Ministries, the headquarters of the Patriotic Union of Kurdistan. I hired her as a translator for ABC News, but after Chris, Chang, and Jeff arrived in Kurdistan, she helped them as well. As March of 2003 and the start of the war approached, dozens of new reporters arrived, many in need of orientation, so Dildar returned to work for the Council of Ministries.

Iraqi Kurdistan was still a patriarchal society, a place where women worked long days behind the scenes, and men drank tea together in public, discussing the "things of importance." Some women were exceptions, like Normeen Osman, the urbane minister of women's affairs for the PUK, who struggled with limited resources and qualified teachers to raise the level of literacy in Kurdistan (which stood at 27 percent in 2003). Another exception, on the KDP side, was Nasreen Barwari, the Kurdish superstar with an MBA from Harvard, who directed the KDP Ministry of Public Works, a monumental task of reconstruction in a country where more than four thousand villages had been razed by the Iraqi regime.

Dildar was fluent in English. She had spent the decade of the 1990s fighting for—and winning—political asylum in Britain. Before that, she and her husband were armed *peshmerga* in the mountains fighting the soldiers of Saddam Hussein.

Dildar didn't talk much about the 1980s, but one day, when she was translating an interview for me with a victim of an Iraqi gas attack, she happened to describe the *smell* of deadly chemicals. Back in those days, she told me, the Iraqi planes would make two passes over the *peshmerga* positions or over partisan villages suspected of giving food or other help to the guerrillas. The first planes dropped balloons to measure the wind direction. The second wave dropped the chemicals, usually a cocktail of VX, nerve, and mustard gas. "They never hit me directly," she said, "but they killed people I was with." The first whiff of gas, she recalled, was not unpleasant. "It smelled a bit like apples and garlic."

One night Dildar invited me for dinner to her home, where I met her husband, Hamid. He was an educated man with a literature degree, and Dildar said the government wanted to hire him as a deputy minister in one of the departments. Despite the offer of a car and a good salary—at least by local standards—he had decided to decline. Dildar confessed she was disappointed, because the family needed the income.

Dildar and her husband had left the mountains in 1989. She was eight months pregnant at the time, and she told me they walked ninety miles before reaching an Iranian hospital. There were complications during the delivery, but the doctor managed to save the baby. It was a few months before Dildar was well enough to be smuggled from Iran to Europe. After they reached London, she started working in the court system as a Kurdish and Arabic translator, which helped to put Hamid through college.

Now, after ten years of liberation in England, Dildar was back in Kurdistan, a society that expected her to iron and cook after getting home from the office.

The dinner list consisted of seven Kurdish men and me. When I arrived at the house, Hamid was on the couch, reading a book about postmodernity. I tried being polite by asking him something about the contents. Then Dildar came into the room, wearing an apron, with a pair of glasses on a gold-plated chain that made her look more like a matron than a former rebel who was shaping the Kurdish future each day by guiding foreign journalists.

Dildar had come home early to prepare a Kurdish specialty of lamb intestine stuffed with rice and meat. With the U.S. attack still a month away, and new reporters arriving for orientation each day, she seemed to be on the edge of burnout. As she served the special dish to her guests, I noticed that her thirteen-year-old son had joined the all-male guests at the dining room table. Dildar returned to the kitchen, where she ate with a woman friend, out of sight.

The role of women in Iraqi Kurdistan was complicated. Although Kurdistan offered more freedom for women than many Muslim countries, Kurdish society as a whole still retained a traditional view of females as mothers and homemakers. Dildar embodied a bridge from the old to the new ways, and I would see her at other social occasions, away from the home, where the sexes were mixed. Advocates of the impending war spoke of a new age of independence for the country. I wondered what changes were in store for Kurdish women, and whether Dildar's multitasking would continue as before.

Dinner on a Leash

In January of 2003, three months before the U.S. invasion, Chris, Chang, Jeff, and I decided to spend a night on the PUK front lines with the *peshmerga* who were fighting Ansar al-Islam. In Chris's words, it was time to "commit some journalism." The *peshmerga* were dug in on Shinerwe Mountain near Halabja, the site of the famous chemical attack in 1988. It was a cold and lonely outpost, within sight of the Ansar positions.

Chris felt that guests shouldn't arrive empty-handed. Before we left, he bought several sheep in the local market, led them with rope leashes to a rented pickup truck, and carted them to the front. Bringing gifts has a traditional place in Kurdish society, and the fresh mutton was delicious, a welcome change of pace from the fighters' usual staple of rice and tomatoes. Combined with Chris's habit of embracing commanders—a Kurdish custom often reserved for long-time friends—the gesture made us "well sourced," as they say in journalism.

There is nothing like showing up for an interview with a tasty dinner on a leash. "Chow down," Chris joked to his colleagues. "The war will be here soon, and we'll all be eating Crest toothpaste."

For Chris, the overnight outing triggered memories of growing up in a rural area. "I'll tell you what 'normal' was in upstate New York," he said in the jeep on the way back to the hotel. " 'Normal' was my dad with his .357, sitting all day on a boat cushion—*in a tree*. And that was the *second* day of deer season. He wouldn't go hunting on the first day—too many nuts out there.

"In upstate New York, you go to gun shows on Sunday and buy a deer rifle. Then you clean it while you're watching the NFL game. A couple of weeks later, you go to another gun show and sell it back.

"My friends used to get drunk at the Glen Pine Inn, then go out and drive on the frozen lake. One winter, one of their cars went through the ice. They got out in time to see it swirl down, watching transfixed as one headlight went *plunk,* then the other. After that, a jar of tavern pickles floated out the window, and they bobbed to the surface.

"You know, I came *this* close," he said, putting two fingers together, "to being a redneck."

Qais Ibrahim Khadar

"Anyone who was a part of the September 11 attack may be on the blacklist of America, but he'll be on the *white* list of God."

It was three months before the war. Chris and I were visiting the PUK security prison in Sulaimaniah interviewing the would-be assassin of Barham Salih, the man who had shot Karzan and killed several of his friends. Dildar Kittani was translating for us.

The killer's name was Qais Ibrahim Khadar. Despite the notoriety of his crime, everyone—including Salih—referred to him simply as "Qais." He was awaiting execution, and he claimed he was looking forward to the moment. "I have invited my mother to be present," he told me chillingly. "I want her to pass out sweet cakes to the witnesses."

It was Christmas Eve in the West, and Qais's group, Ansar al-Islam, had just uplinked photos of the attack at Girdadrozna to its Web site. Captured PUK fighters had been lined up on the shoulder of a road and executed. Brains were spilling out of their heads. It looked as though they'd been hit with axes.

Emotions in Sulaimaniah against Ansar in general—and Qais in particular—were running high. A friend of one of the slain bodyguards told us, "We have to kill Qais ten times, then bring him back to life ten times and kill him again." Nevertheless, Qais was still alive, and it was unclear whether Salih, the intended target and former member of Amnesty International, would sign the necessary death warrant.

"Why not just take him out of town and shoot him—let 'Kurdish Justice 101' take care of the problem?" Chris wisecracked.

"I'm opposed to the death penalty," Salih said. "The state shouldn't take life. Only God should do that. And I don't think it is a deterrent. But it is a difficult moral dilemma for me. I lost five dear people in the attack. It's hard to remove the personal element when you lose friends.

"I don't think I'll sign the warrant."

Salih said he hoped that President Bush would authorize the attack on the Ansar camps *before* the attack on Saddam.

"My idea of justice is when we see these guys *go up in smoke.*"

"Wouldn't that be the death penalty?" I asked him.

"Well, they'd be combatants then," he said.

Qais was twenty-six, a wiry man with the trademark long beard of the other Ansar prisoners I'd interviewed. Unlike some of the captured militants, however, he had a clear-eyed, self-possessed manner, the near-beatific glow of a monk who takes his strength from a deep, quiet place. Since the attack eighteen months earlier, he'd been in solitary confinement in a small, unheated cell.

Qais admitted killing three PUK bodyguards himself, and calmly described his state of mind as he set out that day to assassinate the prime minister. "My heart was coated with honey," he said matter-of-factly. Sitting just a few feet away, Qais was warming his fingers over a kerosene heater in a jailer's office and exuding a messianic bravado. I was happy his wrists were in handcuffs.

"If I got out of jail tomorrow, I'd try to kill him again," he said softly, fixing me with a perversely gentle smile.

Why did you attack Barham Salih, I asked him, rather than another leader?

Because he was "the biggest infidel," Qais said. Because, he added, the prime minister was being "watered like a plant" by the powers in Washington.

Colonel Wasta Hassan, the warden of the prison, listened carefully. Qais was Colonel Hassan's most famous inmate, and he hung on Qais's every word. Hassan, an ex-*peshmerga*, had a heavy shock of black hair, a large moustache, and a wide-eyed stare so intense it could make a visitor avert his own glance. There had been several attempts on Hassan's life, and he carried a gun in a holster under his black suit jacket and black trench coat. We were on good terms, and he was known to leak "special" information to the "Lobby," like the time he revealed to us that he was hiding suspected terrorists—one PUK official called them Hassan's collection of "antiques"—in a cell block unknown to the International Committee of the Red Cross.

Born a Muslim, the colonel told me he "hated Islam." He was a *qaffer*, a religious apostate, and he often joked about his fallen-away status. He had gone to a "school" in Virginia—presumably at the CIA, although he wouldn't say—to improve his skills in intelligence and interrogation. He had a variety of techniques for getting information, ranging from force to providing cooperative inmates with special visits by family members. That day, he offered Qais a piece of cake. I couldn't tell if the gesture was for Qais's benefit or for ours. Qais may have been hungry, but he declined the offer, accepting tea instead.

Porn Therapy

Qais was the colonel's greatest challenge, but not because he was withholding information. After eighteen months in captivity, Qais had little to offer of any timely importance. While Ansar al-Islam represented the gravest of security threats, Colonel Hassan had a network of other informants throughout the area. Hassan's mission, as he saw it, went beyond conventional interrogation. He viewed Islamic fundamentalism as a *disorder*, and he was determined to reprogram captured jihadists.

He told us he'd been trying, without success, to give Qais alcohol to drink and to get him to watch X-rated films (the colonel told us he had a large collection for such purpose). Qais would have none of it, and he seemed to delight in frustrating Hassan, baiting him at every turn, relishing the intensity of the lawman's stare.

"These men are infidels," he said in a confident tone, gesturing toward Chris and me, "but you, Hassan, you are an *apostate,* which is much worse."

Qais scoffed when I showed him a photo of Abu Musab al-Zarqawi, the Jordanian terrorist who the PUK believed may have given Qais the assassination plan. He did the same at the mention of Osama bin Laden, acting almost insulted. In his own mind, Qais was *just as big and just as important as they were.* Qais was a true warrior, a power unto himself in the holy battle against the infidels. He didn't get orders or inspiration from *them.* Al-Qaeda wasn't a group with bosses and followers. It was a state of mind, an *idea.*

"You cannot kill it," he said calmly.

25

Abducted Scientists

More Americans get their news from ABC than from any other source.

—NETWORK PROMOTIONAL TAGLINE

Keeping One Story Secret

A week after our dinner, Marawan called and asked if he could see me. He was visiting Sulaimaniah, but he refused to meet at the hotel. Instead, he gave me an address on the far side of the city. He insisted I come alone and not tell anyone. The secretiveness was understandable, but I didn't know him, it was already 10:00 P.M., and the call spooked me. For a moment, I had an image of Danny Pearl chasing a hot tip into a blind alley. I put it out of my mind. I couldn't tell the other reporters, but I wrote a note with the address of the building and I placed it on the bed. This time, I took all the cash that I had—about $14,000—and taped it under the bottom drawer of my dresser. I put $300 back in my pocket and hailed a cab in front of the hotel.

The precautions weren't necessary. Marawan apologized for the late hour, saying he was taking advantage of the fact that he had keys to the office of his business partner. He didn't want his Sulaimaniah associate, a man he referred to as "Mr. X," to know we were meeting.

I studied my new source of information. He was a small man with an abbreviated moustache, trim by Kurdish standards. He had darting eyes and a weak, halting voice. I couldn't tell if he was nervous by nature or because of the clandestine meeting and the story of intrigue he was about to reveal. I gave him my word that I would protect him as a confidential informant. The deal meant he was free to back out anytime he wanted. While Saddam was in power, no one would know his identity, not even ABC News, without his express consent. It was guaranteed.

With those assurances, Marawan laid out the story. Fifteen days earlier in Baghdad, the Iraqi intelligence service had abducted a group of weapons scientists. The scientists were being held at a secret location to prevent the U.N. inspectors from interviewing them. There were as many as ten in the group. Marawan said he had the names of two. He had met one scientist in 1998 through the man's wife and brother-in-law, who were Kurds. Marawan referred to the scientist's brother-in-law as "Mr. Y." Over the years, Marawan and his partner, Mr. X, had bought electronics in Baghdad through Mr. Y and resold them in Kurdistan. Mr. Y, the scientist's brother-in-law, was the source of information about him and the other missing scientists.

Marawan said that all the families of the Iraqi scientists were terrified. The families lived together in a special apartment building, which was guarded by the secret police. No one was permitted to leave the building unless accompanied by one of Saddam's agents. Food and other necessities were supplied by the regime, and the telephone lines were monitored. Marawan said he was worried that if the names of the scientists were made public, they might be killed. If Marawan's own involvement was suspected, his relatives in Baghdad or Kirkuk could be arrested.

Selling Information

Before agreeing to go deeper into the story, Marawan wanted money—"maybe a lot"—as well as a promise of protection. He also demanded that ABC News transport his partner, Mr. X, and and both their families out of Iraq. I told him I'd get back to him after I'd spoken with my editors.

ABC assigned my story to the Investigative Unit, the special projects division for deep background and undercover cases. Money was available, but the information couldn't be purchased. If Marawan were telling the truth, he'd become a paid consultant for *World News Tonight*, but first the names of the scientists and other details had to be verified. Marawan was still a stranger to me, but the network would not make a deal until I could vouch for his story 100 percent.

The next time Marawan came to town we met in a crowded teahouse. The windows in the place were steamed up from a portable propane heater, and guests at the tables around us were smoking water pipes, what the Kurds call "nergla," filling the air with the smell of apple and cinnamon-flavored tobacco. Some of the patrons were watching a wall-mounted TV, which was airing an Arabic-language news story about U.N. inspectors in Baghdad searching for scientists. Marawan began his pitch by tracing circles and squares on the plastic tabletop, his way of being precise about what he had to offer and how much he wanted for it. His fingers were thin and delicate, and he repeated each stroke for emphasis. "Fifty thousand dollars, cash," he said, drawing an invisible circle around the money. "And we all get taken to an English-speaking country."

That was the starting point. He insisted he would not divulge the names until he had received the money. Over the next few weeks, we met a number of times, usually at random cafés in Erbil and Sulaimaniah. I informed him that ABC was willing to meet some of his conditions, but his price was out of the question. As I gradually gained his trust, more details began to emerge.

Marawan said he first met the scientist in 1998, when the Iraqi was working as a professor of physics at the University of Baghdad. The academic position was a cover, Marawan said, for the Iraqi's real job as a researcher in the top-secret WMD program. Marawan said the *mukhabarat* required all the scientists to sign two statements. The first document said they would cooperate with the United Nations and reveal all that they knew. That was to please the inspectors. The second one went to the police. That was a pledge of secrecy, which they signed under penalty of execution.

The scientist said he was convinced he was "dead either way," so he made plans to escape from Iraq. In 1997 his brother-in-law, Mr. Y, put him in touch with Marawan and Mr. X and their network of Kurdish contacts and profit-making schemes. When the partners returned to northern Iraq and proposed the idea of escape to Kurdish officials, they were told that "money is no problem." After that, the partners hatched a scheme to drive the scientist across the border into Kurdish-controlled territory. They planned to tell the Iraqi border guards they were on a short trip to retrieve the scientist's car, which they would claim had been stolen in Baghdad. On the appointed night, only a few miles before the checkpoint, Mr. Y lost his nerve and turned around. Marawan waited on his side of the border "until the sunshine." By then, it was clear the plan had failed.

That was five years earlier. Now, Marawan had a list of demands, including a bid for ABC to guarantee him higher education abroad. I listened, and I said I'd look into it.

Nuclear Device for Sale

Another week went by. Marawan showed me some grainy video footage of a steel tube that he said contained "red mercury," purportedly a nuclear fusion device produced in Russia. The tube had some printing in English, but all I could make out was the word DANGER.

He claimed the Russian mafia had tried unsuccessfully to sell the mercury, along with "five and a half grams of uranium," to Hussein Kamel, Saddam's notorious son-in-law. Kamel had been in charge of Iraq's unconventional weapons program until he defected to Jordan in 1995. He was later lured back to Iraq, where he was murdered by Saddam's henchmen. Marawan claimed that the mercury/uranium package was currently for sale on the black market in Iraq, and that intermediaries had provided him with the videotape. "Maybe al-Qaeda will buy it," Marawan said in an apparent effort to boost my interest.

To me, the story sounded far-fetched. By way of bolstering its credibility, Marawan told me that he had shown the same video to an unnamed Westerner who worked at the United Nations in Baghdad. Marawan said the man was an engineer, and that he'd given him the same information about the Iraqi scientist and the aborted escape attempt. The Westerner had reacted as if he recognized the scientist's name. Soon thereafter, he slipped Marawan a typed list of nineteen questions to pass on to the scientist's wife.

Australian Spy?

Marawan showed me the list. The inquiries, which were written in precise, educated English, focused on the Tuwaitha Nuclear Research Center near Baghdad and a facility he called the Tahaddi Scientific Center. Marawan said the stranger promised him "a lot of money," as well as relocation to Europe.

At first, Marawan recounted, he'd given the man documents about "V-gas," a Russian-made nerve agent allegedly stockpiled in Iraq, but later he became distrustful of the man, deciding not to reveal to him the latest development, the news about the missing scientists. "I believe his nationality was Australian," Marawan said. "I thought he was some kind of spy—and I became afraid of him."

A foreign agent chasing the same information? I wondered whether Marawan had told my competition about me. Either the plot had thickened, I thought to myself, or I was being leveraged in an effort to drive up the price. It was true that Marawan was Kurdish, but he did not fit the Western image of a downtrodden minority endangered by a brutal regime. He had exploited his Kurdish connections for money in an effort to liberate a threatened scientist, flirted with war profiteers in a police state, and now he was showing videos to hawk WMD components. I pictured him doing his business in Baghdad, sitting across from the Australian, tracing dollar signs on tablecloths, trying to make a deal. Marawan was not an attractive personality, but I tried to keep in mind that I was after facts, not friendships.

The only question was whether the scientists were actually missing. If I could spirit Marawan out of Iraq, the ABC Investigative Unit might be able to confirm his account with current or former U.N. inspectors.

ABC was eager to do the story. The network execs thought Marawan could headline *World News Tonight with Peter Jennings*. First though, additional details in my source's account had to be cross-checked. ABC wanted Marawan to drive to Baghdad again—under the pretense of buying more electronics—to talk directly to the wife of the missing scientist, but Marawan felt the trip was too risky. Her apartment was being watched, and her brother, Mr. Y, who lived separately, was also under surveillance. Marawan said Mr. Y sometimes called from a Baghdad phone booth.

We had no choice but to wait. "Be patient," he said.

Meanwhile, ABC researchers in New York had located ex-U.N. inspectors, ones who had worked in Iraq prior to 1998, to try to get information. They also interviewed Khidhir Hamza, a former Iraqi scientist and member of Saddam's inner circle, whose cloak-and-dagger defection to the United States in 1994 became the basis of his spy thriller, *Saddam's Bombmaker.* The results of all the interviews were inconclusive, but the inspectors did confirm the regime's past practice of segregating scientists and their families.

The ABC bureau in Baghdad tried without luck to match up the scientist with physics professors who might be "on sabbatical" at the University of Baghdad. The investigation in Baghdad was hampered by the constant presence of Iraqi minders who were under orders to report all movement of foreign journalists. Despite restrictions, ABC was able to confirm the location of the apartment building that Marawan maintained was housing the scientists and their families. Marawan had told me it was across the street from the Sheraton Hotel in Baghdad. His description of entrances, staircases, and other details matched what our people could see from a distance without arousing suspicion.

The ABC office in New York obtained satellite pictures of the scouted building and forwarded them to me by e-mail. I had a close call in the Internet parlor when my nosy translator surprised me just as I was printing the pictures. Luckily, I was able to pass them off as an unrelated ABC story a colleague had broadcast the week before. Later, Marawan looked at the photos, reconfirming the building and the location.

I wanted more information about the Australian engineer at the United Nations. Over the next few weeks, I managed to get Marawan to reveal personal details, such as the man's age and hair color and the specific office where he worked. I didn't tell Marawan, but I had my own contact at the United Nations. My contact gave me the name of the engineer who was responsible for projects in Erbil. The engineer was Australian, a fact that struck me as more than a coincidence. One evening, when Marawan and I were having dinner in an Erbil restaurant, I dropped the man's name out of the blue. Marawan seemed genuinely shocked and wanted to know the source of my information. I told him I'd reveal that as soon as he revealed the name of the scientists. "No," he said, "not until after I'm safely in Europe or America."

Marawan called near the end of December. His partner, Mr. X, had just returned from a road trip to Baghdad. The news was bad. Mr. Y, the scientist's brother-in-law, was in jail. The police had picked him up at the battery factory where he worked. More ominously, one of the scientist's colleagues, another weapons researcher, had just been killed in a mysterious car crash. The scientist's second brother-in-law—Marawan referred to him as "Mr. Z"—was the new source for information. Everyone in the scientist's family was frightened. The car accident was probably a warning. The next step could be worse. The regime might turn the scientists over to the U.N. inspectors but keep their entire *families* hostage. Mr. Z demanded that Marawan break off all efforts to communicate.

I couldn't tell whether Marawan's partner, Mr. X, was an innocent conduit for the Baghdad update or whether Marawan was plotting to cut him in on the ABC profits, but it didn't matter. A few days later, Marawan told me that he'd received a telephone call from Mr. Y in Baghdad. Mr. Y was out of jail. His family had sold some personal belongings, raising enough money to buy his freedom.

Notwithstanding the danger, Marawan claimed Mr. Y still wanted him to "do something" to help the scientists. I had gone as far as I could to confirm Marawan's story. After three months of trying, I had been unable to trip him up on the tiniest of details, no matter how many times he repeated them. He had even given me the actual checkpoint pass that Kurdish intelligence had provided in 1998, the night he tried to smuggle the scientist into Kurdistan. The decision to go ahead boiled down to the fact that both parties—Marawan and ABC—had aces in the hole. Marawan would not divulge the names until he was out of the country, and ABC would not pay him until the names were confirmed.

Out of Iraq

It was time to get Marawan out of Iraq, and he was ready to leave the country. My only surprise was his decision to drop the demand to relocate Mr. X, his business partner from Sulaimaniah, and to leave his own wife and children behind in Erbil. Marawan said he was afraid that, in the West, "my children would not be under [my] control." The decision made my own logistics simpler, although his stated reason was less than convincing. It didn't make sense that a person in Marawan's position would trade a life with his family for the lonely future of an immigrant in Europe or America. However, his roots in the tight community bolstered his credibility. He knew I had good access to Kurdish leaders. If he took money under false pretenses and then tried to return to Kurdistan, he could be in jeopardy with the local authorities.

In the end, the ABC office in New York promised that Marawan would receive $10,000 as a news consultant, plus expenses, relocation, and help with a job in a new country. The question of getting Marawan an exit visa fell to me. Passports were for sale in the Kurdish bazaar, both "good fakes" and "bad fakes," depending on the price. I ordered a "good fake," which ended up costing a whopping $2,900, including special "taxes" for the KDP at the Turkish frontier. Another $500 had to be paid to a Turkmen on the Kurdish side of the border. The Turkmen's job was to carry the passport over the bridge the day before departure for preapproval by the Turkish border guards.

As it turned out, Turkish immigration spotted a defect in the lamination on Marawan's photo. Luckily, our forger had guaranteed the passport, and he agreed to fix it for nothing, but that delayed the crossing another few days. In the mean-time, I bought two Turkish cell phones. They had a twenty-mile coverage in northern Iraq and could be used to keep track of Marawan once he crossed into Turkey. I gave Marawan Turkish cab fare and instructed him to wear a red scarf when he arrived at the designated pickup spot, a new hotel in Diyarbakir. An ABC crew would meet him in the lobby, drive him directly to the Diyarbakir air-port, and give him a prepaid ticket to Istanbul. Marawan told me that this would be his first ride on an airplane.

Marawan was afraid of both Iraqi *and* Kurdish agents. We spent the final nights in separate hotels near the border, hoping that no one knew what we were up to, while we met after dark in a designated tea shop, another den for smoking water pipes and trying to act natural. It turned out that Marawan's most difficult demand—a visa to travel to other countries—was beyond the ability of ABC to provide. The network could make him the promise in writing, but in the end, ABC had to rely on a U.S. government contact, someone who had supplied a visa a year earlier for a source in a similar situation. The only thing the ABC Inves-tigative Unit would tell me over the phone was that the provider was not one of the "alphabet groups," i.e., the FBI, CIA, or the DEA. Whatever agency it was, it wouldn't give him a U.S. visa until he was debriefed, "to make sure he wasn't a terrorist." The debriefing would take place as soon as ABC filmed the interview. The situation was getting complicated.

Helping Colin Powell

On February 10, 2003, ABC's *World News Tonight* broadcast Marawan's story. The anchor, Peter Jennings, began by citing the latest *Washington Post*/ABC poll, which said that 66 percent of the American public now favored a U.S. military action in Iraq. He segued from the poll to a failure of U.N. inspectors to convince Iraqi scientists to talk. ABC, he said, had gotten "unusual access to what some of the scientists think and fear." With that, he turned the story over to investigative reporter Brian Ross, who presented an interview with Marawan, shot in silhou-ette to protect his identity. Ross called Marawan a "defector" and said by then he'd already told his story to the U.N. inspectors. Moreover, Ross said, Secretary of State Colin Powell had used Marawan's story in the case for war he'd made to the United Nations on February 5, five days earlier. That was news to me.

The February 5 U.N. address took place just six weeks before the U.S. attack. According to Powell, Iraqi scientists at the time were assembling "mobile produc-tion facilities for biological agents" that allowed Saddam Hussein's regime to pro-duce anthrax "on demand." The secretary of state estimated that Iraq already had stockpiles of "between one hundred and five hundred tons of chemical weapons agents . . . enough to fill sixteen thousand battlefield rockets. Saddam Hussein," he continued "had all Iraqi scientists warned of the serious consequences that they and their families would face if they revealed any sensitive information to the inspectors." Powell said that according to his sources, "A dozen experts have been placed under house arrest . . . at one of Saddam Hussein's guest houses."

Powell's speech was aimed at swaying world leaders who were still unconvinced about the need to confront Saddam Hussein militarily. President Bush would later maintain that he himself had not made the decision to invade Iraq until he heard the secretary of state's dramatic charges. More than a year later, Powell would admit that the alleged evidence about Iraqi weapons he submitted to the U.N. Security Council was false. The dramatic—but misleading—argument for war would come to haunt his legacy and later he would refer to the unproven assertions of Saddam Hussein's WMD arsenal as a "blot" on his record. Following the re-election of President George W. Bush in 2004, Powell resigned from the administration. One national commentator called him "a casualty of war." At the time of the U.N. speech, however, I took the secretary's graphic claim of anthrax-filled rockets *personally,* and I couldn't help visualizing the deadly chemicals being loaded into launchers within range of my hotel.

The use of Marawan to buttress Powell's justification caught me by surprise. My source did have important—albeit unconfirmed—evidence that Iraqi scientists were missing, but he had not *seen* the scientist in question for five years—since 1998—and his knowledge of the pivotal issue was secondhand.

Marawan had gathered his information from *other* people. If Powell's U.N. argument was based even in part on Marawan's secondhand accounts, the secretary of state was using what lawyers call "totem-pole hearsay." It was twice-removed information that, as such, would never have been allowed in a court of law.

Of course, the hearsay may have been accurate—I had no doubt that Marawan believed what he heard in the telephone call from Baghdad. None of us at the network, however, had independent corroboration *from any other source* that the scientists were missing. Accordingly, it would have been legitimate to say that Marawan had *heard* that they were missing and even to state that one of them was rumored to have had died in a mysterious car accident. Given the climate at the time, the feverish run-up to war, Marawan's introduction, together with his appearance in silhouette, gave the viewer the impression he had *direct* knowledge of abduction and murder by the Iraqi regime—right on the eve of the U.S. invasion.

Faustian Pact?

Marawan's demand for relocation to a country beyond Turkey had produced unintended consequences, and now U.S intelligence was involved. Perhaps I was naïve to believe that once he crossed the border I retained any control over the story—and naïve to believe that the visa interview would be limited to a background check for terrorism. Or maybe I rationalized that the safety of the scientists and the presence of WMD in Iraq was an emergency exception to mandates for journalistic objectivity. In the end, I realized that ABC and I had formed a partnership with the U.S. government to coproduce the story for *World News Tonight*. That left me to wonder whether I'd crossed the line—whether to save lives or to boost ratings—and had played a part, albeit minor, in bringing on the war.

In the end the government, not ABC, paid Marawan his fee. The story ended with a whimper, not a bang. Three weeks after his clandestine trip to Turkey, Marawn was back in northern Iraq, and we bumped into each other on the street. We went to a teahouse to talk and I found out, to my surprise, that he'd decided not to relocate to another country. He told me about the ABC interview, his "VIP treatment," and the three "representatives of the U.S.A." he'd met at the Hilton Hotel in Istanbul. One of them was an Arab-American sent from Washington, who asked hard questions and acted, Marawan said, like a "tough man."

The friendliest of the three was "Steve," a tall, broad-shouldered American who peeled off $10,000 in crisp $100 bills, promising Marawan that if he returned to northern Iraq "there might be more where that came from." Marawan recounted the meeting confidently, using his forefinger to trace dollar signs on the plastic tablecloth. Marawan said that when he departed Istanbul for his return trip to Kurdistan, Steve had kissed him on both cheeks.

26

Kurds Reign in the Press

You can't always refill a jug from the stream and bring it back safely.

—KURDISH PROVERB

Sergat

Up until the February 5, 2003, speech at the United Nations, the Bush administration's case for war had met remarkably little resistance from Congress or the Washington press corps. Reporters already on assignment in Iraq did not, for the most part, challenge assertions that Saddam Hussein still possessed WMD or that his regime was connected to al-Qaeda. However, when Colin Powell informed the U.N. Security Council that there was a "poison lab" in northern Iraq in a village called Khurmal, a place he said was controlled by Ansar al-Islam and connected to the Baghdad regime, the focus of the world shifted to a remote area in Kurdistan—and that was my beat.

At the time of the U.N. speech, the name Ansar al-Islam was barely known outside of Kurdistan, but its notoriety would soon expand. After the U.S. invasion, Ansar al-Islam would morph into Ansar al-Sunnah. Under its new name, the terror group would claim responsibility for a string of suicidal bombings, including a double explosion on February 1, 2004, in the provincial capital of Erbil. The coordinated two-pronged attack, which targeted KDP celebrations marking the end of Ramadan, claimed the lives of more than one hundred Kurds. Then, after more than a year of relative calm in northern Iraq, Ansar would strike again, this time at a police recruitment center in Erbil. The new suicide bombing took place May 4, 2005, just one week after the installation of a new Iraqi government with a Shiite as prime minister and a Kurd as president. The explosion killed 60 and wounded 170. Hours later, a notice posted on the insurgents' Web site claimed the attack was retribution for the Kurds' cooperation with the U.S.-led occupation.

Contrary to Secretary Powell's U.N. statement, the alleged poison lab was located in Sergat, not in Khurmal. Sergat, a thirty-minute drive from Khurmal, was a sparsely populated hamlet. By contrast, Khurmal was a sizeable village of about fifteen hundred Kurds. Not surprisingly, the mislabeling frightened Khurmal residents into believing *their* homes were targets for U.S. missiles.

Until now, it had been considered almost suicidal for Western journalists to attempt a visit to Ansar territory, but once the administration asserted that the Sergat site represented a key justification for the war, we had to find a way to get there—without being killed. For that, we turned to Komali Islami, the legal but increasingly controversial party of Ali Bapir, the enigmatic Muslim leader who made his headquarters in Khurmal. Bapir had a motive to help, because the PUK-led government, with U.S. direction, was pressuring him to relocate his followers from Khurmal to a site one hundred miles to the north. Bapir, who claimed the PUK was exploiting the Ansar threat "to get more money from the U.S.A." had refused to relocate, but now that Powell had singled out Khurmal, Ali Bapir warned his followers that a bloody war was coming.

The militants didn't live full-time in Khurmal, but many of their families did. Bapir claimed that when the Ansar fighters came to town to visit, they left their weapons behind in Sergat and the other camps. Reporters, nonetheless, were wary of setting foot in Khurmal, so Bapir agreed to contact the Ansar leadership. On February 8, three days after Powell's dramatic speech, Ansar "invited" us to come to Sergat. On the appointed day, Chris, Chang, Jeff, and I set out for Bapir's base in Khurmal. By then, word of the trip had leaked, and we were joined by a dozen other reporters. When we reached Komali headquarters, Bapir served us a lavish banquet and assured us his own fighters would accompany us to Sergat to guarantee our safe return. The arrangement seemed beneficial to everyone concerned. The luncheon for the foreign press would raise the public profile of Komali Islami, a minority party in a region otherwise dominated by the PUK. In return, we'd get an armed escort, protection—as one reporter put it—to visit "Indian country."

In the end, we succeeded in getting safely in and out of Sergat, but our face-to-face encounter with Ansar easily could have gone the other way. None of us was naïve enough to believe that the terrorists respected the media's objectivity. We were all nervous, but Chris had special reason for concern. He had a large Marine Corps tattoo on his shoulder, a drawing of an eagle with the words USMC: DEATH BEFORE DISHONOR.

The other reporters and their translators took their own Land Cruisers, but I chose to ride in one of the two gun trucks Ali Bapir sent along to guard us. Riding with the armed fighters in the back of the pickup gave me a chance to get good footage for ABC. I also figured that if we were ambushed on the way up the mountain, the firepower might give me a better chance for survival.

A group of militants met us in their own pickups at a crossroads called Girdi

Go. Moments after our arrival, an inexperienced reporter from the *Guardian* in London set a bizarre tone for the day by draping a friendly arm around a bearded militant. "So, are we the *first* foreign journalists you have met?" he asked giddily, massaging the stranger's back as he peppered him with questions. "Are you the emir of Ansar al-Islam? Just tell us a bit about Ansar—you have a bad reputation in the West as a sort of bad organization. Is that right? Tell us—." Jim Muir, a seasoned BBC reporter with a long history of reporting from the Middle East, interrupted, trying to end the nonsense. "Should we try and organize what we're going to do, before we start gangbanging him?"

We got back in our vehicles and followed the militants up a twisting, rutted road toward the snowcapped Iranian frontier. A half hour later, we saw Ansar's black flags fluttering from trees and a compound of several buildings matching Powell's satellite photo came into view. It was Sergat.

The site consisted of seven small houses, two towers, earthen bunkers, and a fort with a sandbagged entrance. There was a small generator, but most of the buildings had neither heat nor electricity. The visit lasted less than an hour, during which time we were closely monitored by bearded men with AK-47s, most of them fiercely unwilling to engage in conversation. Two leaders would talk to us, but the overall tour amounted to a typical dog-and-pony show, with spokesmen denying the presence of a poison lab, encouraging us to "search" for ourselves, and claiming their group had only Kurdish membership and no foreign fighters. In fact, there was no way for the visit to achieve success. We weren't trained inspectors: If the lab was there, they weren't about to showcase it to the foreign press. All we could ascertain for ourselves was the primitive nature of the camp.

The Ansar representatives were unprepared for verbal confrontation from strangers, and before long our hasty and ill-conceived visit turned edgy. It was already noontime in Britain, and the *Guardian* writer was nervous. "We're on deadline, and you're *not*," he snapped at a TV reporter who was interviewing an Ansar spokesman. Then, turning to the militant, he demanded, "Has this place been used for the manufacture of chemicals?"

Within a few minutes, he was pressing for answers about purported links between Ansar and Baghdad and the alleged presence of "Arab fighters."

"We haven't got them," the militant responded defensively in English.

"I don't *believe* him!" the reporter shot back, argumentatively.

A few minutes later, another reporter asked the militant a leading question, "Does Ansar admire Osama bin Laden?"

"We admire and love all Muslims, because they are our brothers," the militant replied in English.

If that's true, the reporter countered, why did the Ansar Web site showcase "videotape of you [people] playing with PUK corpses?"

The prosecutorial tone of the questions was beginning to blow my mind. Had he forgotten where we were? This wasn't a normal press conference, where "superior facts" had a chance of trumping a blowhard. We were on a remote mountain on the Iraq-Iran border, a burrow beyond rescue or assistance. Nearby, in preparation for battle with "infidels" like us, our hosts had already dug their own graves. This was no time to argue with men who had repeatedly demonstrated a willingness to die to prove their ideology was right. Under the circumstances, cross-examination and insults might well succeed in provoking a juicy quote, but our captors had a nasty habit of splitting open the heads of their captives with pickaxes, so none of us might be alive to print or broadcast the remarks.

A few minutes later, the two leaders, visibly upset, bolted from the room to confer with one another. The press briefing was over.

Behind the buildings, on a high spot above the camp, an angry militant with an AK-47 was yelling in Arabic about the pushy visitors. He shouted to an associate to bring him a BKC, the large rapid-fire machine gun mounted on a tripod nearby. My translator said the gunman was enraged because a photographer had strayed from the camp tour and was attempting to get an overhead shot of the hamlet. Referring to us, the militant began to yell, "I want to kill them all!"

We tried to leave, but Ayub Afghani blocked the way. Also known as the Bombmaker, Ayub was a Kurd from the city of Erbil who'd gotten the name *Afghani* in the 1980s as a U.S.-trained jihadist fighting the Russians. He had his own video camera, and now it was time to turn the tables on the media. Before we were allowed to leave, several reporters were forced to give video testimonials denying the presence of a poison lab in Sergat. Luckily, I was not among those chosen.

We made our way down the mountain, past Girdi Go, the place we'd first encountered the Ansar escorts. Three hours later in Girdi Go, an Ansar hit squad assassinated a leading delegate of the Kurdish parliament. The victim's name was Shawkat Haji Mushir, a member of the PUK leadership committee and one of the founders of the party in the 1970s. Mushir, a powerful and wealthy man with a strong following, was the most prominent Ansar victim to date. He had been lured to his death by a trick: the promise that two hostages would be released and that large numbers of Ansar militants wanted to defect; reportedly, his killers robbed him of $50,000 in cash from the PUK, a payment that was to have been part of the exchange. Two civilians, one of them a nine-year-old girl, also died from wounds suffered in the attack. I visited the child in the hospital a day before she was taken off life support. The Ansar planners had been busy during our visit to the mountain.

I sent the Sergat story to New York by satellite. As it turned out, Colin Powell was a scheduled guest the next morning on ABC's *This Week,* where he was quizzed about my footage. Insisting that Ansar was tied to Saddam and that chemicals were being made at the location I'd filmed, Powell asserted the obvious: "Anything that the owners of that camp did not want reporters to see, reporters did not see." The moderator asked the secretary, "Why didn't you just take the terrorist camp out if you *knew* they had activity there?"

At this point, the U.N. inspections were running their course, but the attack on Saddam was still six weeks away. Regardless of the presence of terrorists, the United States had determined there would be no military action in Iraq—not even in the Kurdish region—until Baghdad itself was attacked.

In April 2003, following the rout of Ansar—a full eight weeks *after* Powell warned the United Nations about the alleged "poison lab" in northern Iraq—reporters returned, with Special Forces, to Sergat. Only days earlier, the buildings we'd visited following Powell's speech in early February had been leveled.

During the simultaneous U.S. bombing of Baghdad and the Ansar positions in Iraqi Kurdistan, many of the militants escaped to Iran. Afterwards, despite the damage to the area, military inspectors found conventional bomb making material, printed documents about chemicals and biotoxins, and some rudimentary poisons, including a cyanide-based body lotion. Most of the discoveries, however, were garden variety compounds like those in bug spray—many of them available in a high school chemistry lab—and no evidence was discovered of a mechanism for the insurgents to "weaponize" the poisons. Like Saddam Hussein, they may have wanted WMD. However, neither party apparently possessed the weapons.

At the end of ABC's *This Week,* the moderator pressed Colin Powell to explain U.S. reluctance to attack a known terrorist site. "Why didn't you destroy it [the Sergat camp]?"

The secretary of state replied, "I am not going to discuss why we did or did not do a particular military action in public."

Unembedded and Unpopular

The visit of journalists to Sergat concerned—and annoyed—the leaders of the PUK. From a personal standpoint, they thought the trip was dangerous and they were concerned for our welfare. However, such adventures also posed political risks for war plans in Washington, which by then were in their final stages. Here, reporters were running around a conflicted area with no government supervision, interviewing an enemy, and drawing their own conclusions about sensitive facts. Had a large number of foreign journalists been killed in a part of Iraq *not* controlled by Saddam Hussein, the fallout could have impacted public support for the impending invasion. The lack of press control represented a throwback to lax government control of reporters during the Vietnam War. In the eyes of officials, some of us had become a problem.

Meanwhile, Pentagon plans to send large numbers of U.S. troops to attack Iraq from the north fell through when the Turkish Parliament voted not to allow deployment from Turkish territory. The Turkish rebuff seemed to take the Bush administration by surprise, sparking public recriminations and a postinvasion cooling of U.S.-Turkish relations. Kurdish leaders were ecstatic, however, as they feared that allied forces would have included Turkish soldiers, a presence they believed would threaten their autonomy. A "northern front" would certainly have affected the press. Had a ground invasion come from Turkey, the Kurdish region would have been militarized by coalition troops, at least for a period of time, and it is likely the freewheeling behavior of the media would have been curtailed.

VIP's No More

In the 1990s, when little attention was paid to the Kurds, the occasional foreign reporter in Iraqi Kurdistan was given VIP treatment and afforded almost unlimited access to government officials. As the war approached, however, the sensitivities changed. After I did a stand-up report for ABC on a deserted airstrip, which I predicted would be used to land American troops, Hoshyar Zebari, the spokesman for the KDP (he became Iraq's interim foreign minister in 2004), sent me an e-mail saying that such conduct might prompt his party to discontinue cooperation with me and with ABC News. It was unclear whether the termination of cooperation would prevent my access to areas controlled by the KDP or only to certain party officials. In either case, the threatened sanction was intended to cramp my ability and that of ABC to gather news.

Chris Chivers ran into a similar problem on a *Times* story in KDP territory when he tried to travel without a party minder and received a tongue-lashing from another KDP spokesman. The same official reminded me on a different occasion that reporters based in the rival PUK area of Kurdistan were forbidden to operate in the KDP region without hiring KDP translators (i.e., a PUK Kurd was not allowed to translate the words of a KDP Kurd). He warned me that a violation of the rule could negatively affect a reporter's "rating" with the party. "You want to stay on the A-list, don't you?" he asked rhetorically. There was also a KDP rule against bringing a PUK bodyguard into KDP territory, although the opposite was permitted, and I once used an armed KDP driver in the PUK region.

Lockdown

We were starting to see disguised CIA paramilitaries and Special Forces on the roads (sometimes conspicuously riding in brand new SUV's). They were dressed in *peshmerga* outfits, complete with Kurdish headdress and *shirwal*, the traditional balloon pants. We called them "the rabbits" because they were hard to spot and even harder to catch. U.S. news outlets were clamoring for pictures of the

American agents, but the Kurds were keeping them at a low profile. Jalal Talabani had given his thirty-year-old son Bafel, an Oxford-educated Kurd with a reputation as a playboy, the position of liaison. His duties included preventing photographers from getting shots of the undercover agents. One day, as we were leaving a Kurdish military compound, we spotted five big Land Cruisers with tinted windows. The SUVs were new luxury editions with the buxom fenders, the high-end models the Kurds call Monicas. "My people like fleshy women," my translator Rizgar observed wryly. "And 60 percent of Monica Lewinsky is fleshy."

It was the *rabbits*. Four of the cars moved out quickly from the parking lot. The fifth one stopped. Out stepped Bafel Talabani, dressed in a pressed worsted wool *peshmerga* outfit. He was carrying a 9 mm automatic in a shoulder holster and wearing sunglasses, the Ray-Bans favored by his new companions in the Monicas. "Look at that," Chris said from a safe distance, his eyes widening as he pretended to grab an imaginary tow bar, "Bafel's really up and waterskiing now."

It was funny, and I laughed, but Bafel was part of the royal family, and we would soon collide with his authority.

Bafel was the commander of the Special *Peshmerga* "Cobra Force." One evening, a few weeks before the war, he and a group of his Cobra guards suddenly blew into the Ashti, shut off access to the hotel, and herded U.S. journalists into the dining room. He was wearing an American-style baseball cap, and he quickly introduced himself as the director of counterterrorism for the PUK. "You have been targeted by the Iraqis for immediate assassination," he declared haltingly, "on the grounds that [you] are CIA operatives working in the region collecting intelligence to bring about the downfall of Saddam Hussein." He announced that all of us were going to be moved to what he called a "secure location" in "a more controllable area." Henceforth, he told the stunned group of reporters, "I think it's very important that we know exactly *who* you're seeing and *who* you're meeting."

Bafel said he could not divulge the source of the purported threat, but claimed it had come from "a very, very reliable" contact, stressing that the potential danger did not concern Ansar al-Islam. "This is a threat directly from the government-controlled Iraqi regime," he said. In view of the unfolding emergency, he said, "the main objective is to get you all to safety, where we can regroup, and then talk about possible developments we can discuss step by step. In the future," he added, "we will be providing you with security to assist you in your travels."

Reporters from both the Palace and the Ashti, we were told, were the targets of the planned killing, and security buses were standing by to take everyone to a guarded motel on the outskirts of the city. Chris Chivers and I looked at each other. With the outbreak of war only a hair trigger away, something in this picture of emergency escape didn't seem right.

I turned to Bafel. "Doesn't it seem like the *wrong time*," I inquired, "for Saddam to be threatening Americans?" Bafel said he agreed. "But then again," he quickly added, "we have had supposed peace for years, and yet every time an American plane flies over an Iraqi position, they are fired upon—obviously, you could argue the same point there."

Chris, Jeff, Chang, and I went to my room to talk. As the other reporters boarded the buses to be taken away, we sent out word we would stay put in the Ashti Hotel. If Bafel was truly afraid for our welfare, he could assign extra guards to the hotel. What was the worst punishment for disobedience under the circumstances? We sat around a table and tried to make light of our options. At this point, the authorities could kill us, arrest us, blacklist or restrict our movements. Or they could wait a week, rethink Bafel's gambit, and have a good laugh.

By the next afternoon, the reporters at the "secure location" had mutinied and were back in their own hotel rooms. No overnight guards had been assigned to protect the four "refuseniks" at the Ashti. We concluded that the issue had more to do with news management than safety. Press control was a phenomenon practiced in many civilized countries. The Kurds were coming of age.

The First Hole

More and more journalists were arriving, and Dildar's press office was getting swamped with requests to accompany the visitors to Halabja.

"Halabja is the first hole on the golf course [for newcomers]," Jeff Fleishman cracked. "I'm glad I got here two months ago."

Indeed, it was no wonder. The gassing of five thousand Kurds at Halabja was Exhibit A in the litany of horrors perpetuated by the Iraqi regime. Now, with a U.S. attack all but certain, the revived interest in the Halabja tragedy underscored a renewed urgency to stop Saddam Hussein from another use of weapons of mass destruction.

In many papers back home, the fifteen-year-old tragedy of Halabja was getting the attention it had deserved in 1988. The impact of fresh stories on public opinion in 2003, however, was—wittingly or not—predictable. With the drum beating for war, the portraits of death and deformity at Halabja in 1988 seemed even more heart wrenching, producing new outrage for the old crimes.

Never before had the medical staff at the Halabja hospital seen so many foreigners. The old and dilapidated building was besieged by reporters and photographers searching for patients with illnesses tied to the 1988 chemical attack, and they were all on deadline. Some of the personnel simply noted the competition for patients, but others took offense. Dr. Baktiar Faiq Hama, a young physician I'd met in 2002, told me he was fatigued by the media hounding and claimed he had no time left over for medical work. He complained that less-photogenic victims of the gas attack were being passed over by the press. "The photographers all ask for burn cases or patients with visual ailments like cleft palates and other birth defects," he lamented. "They are not interested in cancer victims, because it doesn't make a good picture."

The interest in the 1988 tragedy was overdue, but some of it seemed ghoulish. I recalled a Halabja victim I'd visited in the spring of 2002, almost a year before the war, a time when proactive TV companies were already gearing up for the Iraq story. A PBS producer asked me to shoot footage of a man dying of testicular cancer, and I accompanied her to visit the victim in the hospital. She was producing one segment on chemical weapons for a multipart series on weapons of mass destruction. A second segment would be devoted to biological weapons, and she was keen to secure interviews that would also land her a producer's role on the follow-up program. The problem with including Iraq in that segment was the inconvenient fact that there had been no confirmed use of biological weapons by Saddam Hussein's regime. To get around that obstacle, she repeatedly asked doctors if they would care to speculate about Saddam's *possible* use of biological weapons.

The patient was moaning. He had just come out of surgery and his prospects for survival, according the surgeon, were slim. The doctor showed us a jar of formaldehyde containing the man's testicles. A relative sobbed nearby, tears streaming down her cheeks. The producer crossed the room, whispering excitedly for me to film the jar and then zoom in on the woman's face. It was the kind of shot to cap a sequence before the fade to black.

Pressure

It wasn't as if there was a directive on the bulletin boards of newsrooms telling reporters to serve up stories of past horrors or to sensationalize the suspicion that WMD were present in Iraq. Given the climate, however, the incentive to do so seemed to be in the air. When an unexploded artillery shell was found in a bomb crater near a government bunker in the Halabja Valley, a young BBC radio reporter asked colleagues if he should break out his gas mask and chemical suit to examine it. Someone had noticed a strange smell near the crater, he said, speculating that Ansar might have launched chemical weapons in Kurdistan. If it were true, it would have been the first use of a chemical weapon in Iraq in a generation and the first in the region by a terrorist group. Such a discovery on the eve of the war would be an enormous scoop.

The radio reporter had no way to test the ordinance, no evidence beyond his own imagination to evaluate reports of a strange smell. Chris and Jeff tried to dissuade him from donning the suit and mask in public. Without more to go on, the spectacle of a foreigner jumping into a crater—in a full-body hazards suit—seemed irresponsible. Considering what the Kurds of Halabja had experienced in actual gas attacks, the maneuver could trigger a panic. The young correspondent went ahead anyway. His subsequent broadcast provided a gratuitous disclaimer: There was no *proof* that the shell in question contained chemicals.

Ali Bapir

Ali Bapir's time was up. Two weeks before the war, he met with his top deputy in Khurmal to discuss mounting pressures from the PUK to relocate his Komali Islami party and their followers. A few hours later, the deputy and four of his associates were shot to death at a PUK checkpoint. Chris, Chang, and I arrived at the checkpoint, the small village of Taslogeh near Sulaimaniah, just in time to see the deputy's body dragged away from a bullet-riddled Land Cruiser and dumped on to the bed of a Toyota pickup. A few minutes later, Bafel Talabani, son of the future president of Iraq, arrived on the scene. By now, the area was crowded with reporters and *peshmerga*. Bafel was speaking English to his cousin and other armed men—which seemed surprising, because their first language was Kurdish. These were the men, we learned later, who had given chase to the Land Cruiser. "If they shoot at *you*," Bafel announced in a voice loud enough to be heard by the reporters, "you have every right to *return* fire."

Talabani told reporters that the victims were Ansar militants who had refused to stop at the roadblock. We rushed to the morgue and examined the bodies, where they had been dumped on the floor between the autopsy tables. The men were bearded, and all had suffered multiple wounds to the face and body. To get a wide-angle shot, I climbed on top of one of the tables and began filming. Unfortunately, I hadn't noticed the slow-turning electric fan overhead. A moment later, one of the dull metal blades clipped me on the back of the head, sending me sprawling on top of one of the blood-spattered corpses below. I picked myself up, more stunned by the macabre encounter than physically hurt. On the ride back to the hotel, we speculated about the killings. At one point the conversation descended into gallows humor. In a dark attempt to make sense out of the mysterious incident, someone joked that this was a case of "driving while bearded."

The initial and official position of the PUK matched Bafel's account: The Land Cruiser had been fired upon only *after* it tried to run the checkpoint. Unknown to authorities, however, a French cameraman happened to be passing the checkpoint at the time, and he had videotaped the Land Cruiser parked for several minutes *before* the attack on the car. He did not want to incur the wrath of officials by publicizing the tape, though, fearing a possible backlash might impact his ability to report the looming war. As it turned out, his room was across the hall from mine at the Ashti Hotel, and he let me make my own copy of the footage. Chris, Chang, Jeff, and I showed the footage to several of the top PUK leaders, carefully gauging their reaction. The leaders watched the scene in silence.

It was clear that the Komali Islami men had not been killed, as first reported, because their Land Cruiser failed to stop. Something had gone terribly wrong at the checkpoint—by accident or on purpose.

Two weeks later, a day after U.S. bombing began in Baghdad, a battery of cruise missiles destroyed Ansar targets, including the compound we had visited at Sergat. It was only the beginning. Two nights later, U.S. missiles wiped out Ali Bapir's headquarters in Khurmal, the site of the earlier banquet for reporters. Forty-five of Bapir's *peshmerga*, most of them sleeping in an adjacent building, were killed in the attack. Bapir, who was in a nearby house at the time, escaped and immediately went into hiding. He later joined fifteen hundred of his followers who had been relocated near Qandhil Mountain, one hundred miles to the north.

A few months after the fall of the regime, Bapir was invited to lunch at a U.S. Army garrison in northern Iraq. En route with a small retinue of bodyguards, his caravan was intercepted by U.S. commandos. He was handcuffed and a hood put over his head. He was transferred to a desert prison near Basra in the south of Iraq, the same area, ironically, used by the former Iraqi regime for the internal exile of dissident Kurds.

A message had been sent about Islamic fundamentalism in Iraq, at least in the region controlled by the U.S.-allied Kurds: Armed Islamic groups, regardless of their history as fighters against Saddam Hussein, were a thing of the past.

27

End Game

You are invited to the storm before the storm.

—INVITATION TO NBC PARTY AT THE PALACE HOTEL,
A WEEK BEFORE THE IRAQ WAR

"Bullet Tax"

In the last few days before the war, Jaff Abid, my driver, sent his wife and children to the mountains. He said he hoped they would be safe with relatives until the war was over. Jaff had seen war, but what lay ahead made him nervous. One day he asked me for a raise, "in case our Land Cruiser gets hit with a rocket-propelled grenade." I agreed—and I began paying him $550 a month, three times his usual salary. He was worth it. I'd had a good feeling about him from the first day of work, when we were surrounded by a Kurdish "antiterrorist squad" at the local airstrip, where the CIA Special Ops teams were supposed to be landing supplies.

The favorite tactic used by security forces in many countries is to threaten the journalist's driver or translator. The thinking is that the locals have to live there after the reporters leave, making them more vulnerable to pressure. We didn't see any Americans on the airfield that day, but the Kurdish guards really hassled Jaff. I learned later that Jaff was an "old" *peshmerga* who had suffered in the mountains in the eighties. He was not one of the young guys who'd never had to eat grass for supper or dodge gas attacks from Russian-made MiGs and the experience had given him grace under pressure.

Jaff didn't flinch easily. He had guts, not bravado, and being my driver wasn't just a matter of making good money. He had personal reasons, as I later learned, for wanting to see the end of the dictatorship. In 1986, Iraqi agents had come to his house and arrested his brother, who was a member of an underground Kurdish cell. After two years of imprisonment and torture, the brother was executed. Jaff went to Baghdad and visited him before he died. After the young man's death, the family had to scrape together seventy-five dinars—about $225 at the time—to retrieve his body for burial. The money, according to the prison guards, was a "bullet tax" to pay for the execution.

Driver Training

The two young Kurdish translators Chris hired were medical doctors. He paid them $1,000 a month, four times what they could make at the Sulaimaniah hospital. Unlike the other reporters, who had stashed gas masks in their rooms and who sometimes shared their anxieties about chemical attacks over drinks at night, Chris wasn't unduly concerned about exposure to nerve gas. He had been a U.S. Marine captain in Kuwait during the Gulf War, however, and he was concerned about bullet injuries and the loss of blood.

"The price for these guys [the doctors] in a zip code like this is worth it," he cracked. "They might have to tie off my leg."

Chris sent his doctors to scour the bazaar for bulletproof vests. They bought ten used flak jackets and painted TV in large white letters on the fronts and backs. Chris, Jeff, Chang, and I had brought our own vests from the States. Now there were enough vests for all our drivers and translators. The doctors also managed to buy a mishmash of U.S., British, and Israeli gas masks, plus an old Iraqi one that needed some caulking. We laid everything out on the floor of Chang's room at the Ashti. Chris started the orientation course by talking about the need for everyone to shave his beard each day once the war had started. The seals on the masks had to be skintight. Then he moved on to the issue of equipment allocation.

"Every car will have the same number of blankets, helmets, flaks, and first-aid kits," he said. "It will be the responsibility of each driver every morning to tape a fresh chemical sensor to the windshield. We are not soldiers, but if we drive by mistake into a cloud or we're covering a hospital where there are victims, we could get cross-contaminated from a stretcher or an ambulance. Whatever happens, you'll all have the same stuff." That was one of the things about people who worked for Chris: Equal risk meant equal protection.

Still No Masks

As the prospect of a U.S. attack on Iraq increased, the Red Cross prepared tents for evacuees in the mountains, and Kurds began stockpiling food and drinking water. The lines at the gas pumps in the cities started to lengthen, and refugees began streaming out of Kurdish villages that abutted the strongholds of Ansar al-Islam.

The war was about to start. Saddam's arsenal of WMD was an accepted belief, but still the United States had not equipped the Kurds with gas masks. In a public letter to President Bush, party leaders Massoud Barzani and Jalal Talabani complained they "have yet to receive any of the protective equipment promised by your officials to deal with the very real risk of chemical or biological weapons attacks on the cities of Iraqi Kurdistan."

Some of the anxiety in Kurdistan was mixed with anger. Herokhan Talabani, the wife of PUK chief Jalal Talabani, told me, "If the U.S. wants war, it has the responsibility to protect the Kurds."

Hero, as Mrs. Talabani was known, was a former *peshmerga*. She told me she had filmed victims of Saddam's gas attacks in the mountains in the 1980s. "No one was interested in my videos of gas attacks at that time," she lamented. Now that the West had turned against Saddam, she said, "still no one will protect the Kurds." Referring bitterly to a recent Reuters wire story about the availability of pet-friendly gas masks in Jerusalem, she said, "The Kurds are still alone."

A week before the war, the NBC News bureau in Suly threw a party at the Palace Hotel. Invitations to the shindig called it "the storm before the storm." An hour into the party, an Australian TV reporter, someone I'd helped gain entry to Kurdistan, beckoned me to the side of the room. He had four auto injectors of atropine in his hand. "This is what you asked for in your e-mail," he said with a grin. Now my driver, translator, and I had antidotes to nerve gas.

On March 17, Karzan came to the Ashti Hotel to say good-bye. He was wearing new shoes for the big trip to America. His parents had bought him an Iranian-made three-piece suit at the local bazaar. "Here is a *deeari* [gift]," he said, handing me a package. It was a very large bottle of cologne, at least a pint's worth. He'd bought it in the open market.

"*Supaz,*" he said, quietly. "Thank you."

On March 19, 2003, the first bombs fell on Baghdad. As Turkey prepared to close the border with Iraq, Karzan Mahmoud limped across the international bridge, leaving Iraq and beginning his journey to an operating room in Boston, Massachusetts.

28

Friendly Fire on an April Morning

War is sweet for those who haven't tasted it.

—ERASMUS

The war began when forty Tomahawk missiles and several two-thousand pound satellite-guided bombs struck a crowded Baghdad restaurant where the Pentagon believed Saddam Hussein and his sons were meeting. There were diners in the restaurant at the time, but it turned out Saddam and his sons were not among them. Chris Chivers, Jeff Fleishman, and I went to Barham Salih's house and watched the BBC replays of the strikes and their aftermath. Several PUK leaders were present, gathered around Salih's television set, mesmerized by a London news anchor describing an attack that was only two hundred miles away. Spirits visibly high, they clasped each other's hands. The long awaited war had begun.

Looking back on the first two weeks of the war, the dates of April 2 and April 6 stand out. On April 2, Iraqi soldiers abandoned fortified positions on the southern edge of Kurdistan, and journalists rushed into Iraqi territory. Kaveh Golestan, a cameraman working for the BBC, stepped out of his SUV to film a deserted bunker near the town of Kifri. A buried land mine exploded, killing him instantly. Kaveh was an award-winning photographer from Iran who had covered war for a generation. We had made the hair-raising trip to the Ansar camp together. I liked him and I respected his work.

April 6 is memorable because that was the day I was nearly the victim of a U.S. air strike.

It was a friendly fire bombing by F-14 Tomcats in Iraqi territory, about forty kilometers from Kirkuk, between the villages of Pirdowd and Debaja. For the previous five days, the area had been the scene of fierce ground fighting and intense aerial bombardment. Just the evening before, I was stuck on a dirt road nearby with other journalists, watching the U.S. jets scream overhead and listening to the bombing in the distance. We were trying to get over the last hill for a peek at the fighting, but KDP *peshmerga* blocked the way. They said it was too dangerous and told us they had orders to keep reporters away from the front.

I made plans to return to the same area that morning. Then, in the middle of breakfast, I suddenly got the idea to tap an old connection to get me to the front. I drove to the office of Wagea Barzani, the younger brother of KDP leader Massoud Barzani. Wagea was a senior KDP *peshmerga* commander, and his last name alone was enough to cut most red tape.

I knew Wagea from the year before, when he'd invited me to film a training exercise. The experience made me appreciate why the Kurdish military wanted U.S. help so badly. The exercise consisted of a parade of outdated armored personnel carriers (APCs) captured from the Iraqis, as well as a single Russian-made T-62 tank that had a bad clutch. The tank was belching diesel smoke, and it looked as if its fighting days were numbered. One of the APCs had a heavy machine gun on a tripod mounted on the top, and Wagea offered to let me fire a few bursts at a target on the hillside. Without thinking, I accepted the invitation.

Wagea and his fighters watched with approval or pity—it's always hard to know in those situations—as I climbed with my cameras to the top of the tracked vehicle. My performance was spotty. Afterward, he politely joked that perhaps I ought to stick to photography and writing. Then he climbed up next to me and someone used my camera to take a picture of the two of us. He was sporting a bright red beret that day, the kind the KDP commandos wear. Before I left Santa Barbara, I'd had the picture enlarged, and this seemed like a perfect time to deliver a copy. Not incidentally, I hoped he would give me a letter to pass the checkpoints.

I was too late. Wagea had just left his office. He had been asked to escort army Humvees with U.S. Special Forces and several SUVs carrying VIP Kurds to the same front lines I wanted to visit. A BBC television team with political connections had managed to join the caravan at the last minute.

I left Wagea's office and quickly drove to the nearby town of Salahuddin. There, I hoped to get a similar letter from General Ali, the commander I'd met at the end of the first Gulf War, the man who told me he had been trained by the CIA during the 1975 Kurdish revolution. I had printed a photo for him as well. When I arrived at KDP headquarters, U.S. Special Forces officers were inside the large complex trying to iron out disagreements between Wagea's brother, Massoud Barzani, and Jalal Talabani.

Now that American soldiers were on the ground in northern Iraq, rival Kurdish factions had put aside most, but not all, of their differences. I struck up a conversation in the parking lot with a Special Forces sergeant, the driver of a U.S.

colonel who was mediating inside. The sergeant, who introduced himself only as Gary from Lincoln, Nebraska, told me, "There's quite a tiff going on in there." Suddenly, Massoud Barzani rushed out of the meeting. He was whisked away by bodyguards. General Ali emerged from the building and gave me the news: U.S. planes had struck Wagea Barzani's caravan by mistake.

Eighteen Kurds were killed in the friendly fire incident, and forty-five were injured. Several Special Forces soldiers were wounded but, according to U.S. Army spokesmen, none had been killed. Wagea Barzani was airlifted by U.S. helicopter to Harir, a Kurdish air field, and then by fixed-wing aircraft to Germany. He had sustained permanent head wounds. Also wounded, although not seriously, was Masrour Barzani, the thirty-three-year-old son of KDP leader Massoud Barzani and the youngest member of the KDP politburo.

The area where the incident occurred, about thirty-five kilometers from Erbil, had been captured from the Iraqi army in the previous twenty-four hours. At the time of the incident, the *peshmerga* and the Iraqis had been fighting over a key bridge. The *peshmerga* had disabled an Iraqi tank, which the Iraqis then abandoned. The opposing forces were a few miles apart. No one seemed to know why U.S. jets had bombed the convoy.

Later, I learned that the mixed convoy of VIP Kurds, Special Forces, and reporters had stopped next to the disabled tank. A Kurdish driver who witnessed the attack told me he saw *peshmerga* in uniforms with red berets celebrating on top of the tank. That night at the hotel, the BBC cameraman told me he'd just shut off his camera when he saw the F-14 drop the bomb. "It was white with a red tip," he said, recalling how he watched, transfixed, as it floated toward the earth. When he turned his camera on again, the lens was covered with blood.

U.S. Special Forces riding in the Humvees ordered the air strike, according to Tom Giles, a BBC producer. "The bomb may have been intended for a group of Iraqi tanks that were in the valley, but they were at least seven kilometers away," he told me. Giles was slightly wounded by shrapnel. His SUV, parked between the blast point and the spot on which he was standing, had shielded him.

A twenty-three-year-old Kurd translating for the BBC, who was standing in the open only a few yards from Giles, was killed by shrapnel. His name was Kamaran Abdurazaq Muhamed. He was the only breadwinner from a large family in Erbil. He had majored in English in college, and his language teacher had introduced him to news companies looking for translators. He had been with the BBC for only twenty days.

I caught up with Giles later in the day at the Towers Hotel, where each of us had a room. For the past few nights, the windows in the hotel had been rattled by the thunder of B-52 bombers. Giles, who saw the Special Forces who called in the air strike, said the soldiers were "stunned and embarrassed" by their error. "Iraq doesn't have an air force," Giles said, "so I immediately knew it had to be 'friendly fire.'"

It was Giles's birthday. He told me he'd used the convoy's stop at the abandoned tank to telephone his mother in England on his satellite phone. He was talking to her when he heard the roar of the F-14 warplane overhead. "That's the sound of freedom," he said he told his mother just before the bombs hit.

The blast made him drop the phone. "Everyone was screaming," he said. "There were arms and legs all over the ground." Several minutes went by before he picked up the phone again. His mother was still on the line. She was in shock. She had heard everything.

American Casualties?

The KDP quickly swung into action with damage control. Photographers who tried to get shots of American military arriving at the hospital to visit the Special Forces victims were blocked and threatened by KDP guards. One guard grabbed my video camera, but I managed to wrestle it away. It was clear that the days of Kurdish passivity toward the press were over. At a hastily convened press conference at the Chwar Charra Hotel, KDP spokesman Hoshyar Zebari confirmed that eighteen Kurds had been killed and forty-five wounded. He told a room of about one hundred journalists that he had no information on U.S. casualties. The tragic incident, he stressed, should not deflect attention from the fact that America had come to liberate the Kurds.

An official Pentagon statement mirrored Zebari's claim of no dead Americans. I certainly recognized that few things in war had more potential for mission embarrassment than a friendly fire incident, but despite all the secrecy at the hospital, I guessed it would be hard to hide evidence of dead Americans. Then I ran into Moklis Faroq Hassan, a thirty-four-year-old KDP official who was wounded slightly by shrapnel in the attack.

Hassan was the cousin of my 1991 contact, General Ali, the man who first told me about the friendly fire. The day after the incident, I went to Ali's house for lunch, and he talked to me about his relative. Then Ali took me to Hassan's home, where the family had just slaughtered a sheep for a thanksgiving dinner in honor of Hassan's survival. My translator was with us, and I recorded a short interview on video.

The wounded man insisted that American Special Forces troops *had* been killed in the attack. He said he personally loaded two bodies "in a good way"— meaning respectfully—into a pickup truck. He said one American had been killed by head injuries and the other from a wound to the chest. "I took care of two of them by myself," he said. "But my friends counted a total of four [American] dead." I played the devil's advocate, suggesting otherwise, but Hassan clung to his account. He said he had pleaded with a translator in the caravan to talk to other U.S. soldiers, apparently to prevent another attack. Everything at the scene was "nervous and confused," but the soldiers said, "We don't have any equipment to contact the plane."

Hassan was at a loss to explain the mistake, especially because the U.S. Humvees were flying oversized American flags from their bumpers, which he assumed were visible from the air. He told me he was glad to be alive, but saddened that several of his friends were among the dead. I asked him if he was angry. No, he emphasized, he was not, but he did want an accounting. "This accident must not go so easy," he said. "There must be an investigation, because we look up to America as a great country and America is a technology state [sic]."

I was baffled by the account. There didn't seem any reason for Hassan to lie, and General Ali, a member of the KDP politburo, had acted against party interest in connecting me to the story. However, there was a war going on, and the events of each day were overtaking those of the day before. The importance of the contradictions would soon recede.

29

The War in Kurdistan

Too long a sacrifice can make a stone of the heart.

—W. B. YEATS

Halabja Valley

I was taking a break in my hotel in Suly, following a week of watching U.S. planes bomb the strongholds of Ansar al-Islam. It was a chance to shop for toothpaste, to scrape the mud off my only pair of shoes, and to wash the clothes I'd slept in for a week

The aerial bombardment in the Halabja Valley had scattered the Ansar militants, but they were still a lethal threat. As B-52 bombs and F-16 missiles rained down on their camps along the Iraq-Iran border, the insurgents took their revenge on civilians. The first attack was a suicide car bomb near a crossroads at Girdi Go, which wounded twenty-four and killed five. The dead included Paul Moran, an Australian cameraman who was filming refugees fleeing the war zone.

The day of the attack, my daughter Caitrin was at home in Santa Barbara, watching CNN, when she saw a streaming news bulletin that an ABC journalist had died in a suicide bombing in northern Iraq. Fearing her father had been killed, she called the ABC office in New York, but did not identify herself. A "nice guy at the news desk," she later told me, took the seemingly random call in stride. He told her matter-of-factly that the dead newsman worked for the Australian Broadcasting Company, not the American Broadcasting Company.

I had been traveling that morning with Chris, Chang, and Jeff, but I had lingered in the Halabja hospital to film war wounded, while they went to the checkpoint at Girdi Go, ten miles down the road. They had just finished interviewing a group of refugees when an Ansar bomber drove up in a car that had been painted to look like a taxi and blew himself up at the checkpoint. When the bomb went off, Chang told me later, the three of them were only one hundred yards away, and the force of the blast rocked their vehicle. When he turned around with his camera, Chang saw a fireball shooting into the air. He managed to get off a shot for the *Times* before he and the others jumped in their car and sped away. Karl Vick, a reporter from the *Washington Post*, was headed in the opposite direction at the time. The bomb blew out the back window of his Land Cruiser, but the flying glass did not hit anyone. His driver stepped on the gas, and they quickly evacuated the area. When I arrived with a video camera, the checkpoint was strewn with vehicle debris, and Kurdish police were wandering about with stunned expressions on their faces. A bystander ran up to my car, beckoning me in the direction of the blast site. I followed the stranger to some nearby bushes. The leaves of one bush were smeared with blood and human tissue. A moment later, Rizgar, my translator, caught up with me, visibly upset. "Let's get out of here," he implored. "Suicide bombers come in *pairs*."

Three days later, I was filming another exodus of refugees near the same checkpoint at Girdi Go. U.S. jets had just appeared overhead, and I could feel the thunder of falling bombs on the valley floor. Shepherds in a nearby field suddenly had ringside seats for a war. For a moment, they stopped shaking sticks at a flock of sheep, and one of them pointed to a plume of smoke rising from a bomb crater. We looked on, united as spectators in a common event, like an audience of strangers watching fireworks on July 4. The smoke drifted toward the snow-capped mountains in the distance.

It was early in the morning, but the highway where I'd placed my tripod was busier than I'd ever seen it before. Hay wagons crammed with families poured out of the war zone, while trucks full of cheering *peshmerga* bound for the front raced by in the opposite direction. Refugees were fleeing any way they could, some on horseback, some on foot with rice sacks full of goods on their shoulders. A woman passed me with her cow on a rope lead.

Suddenly, I heard small-arms fire and an explosion from the direction of Girdi Go. It was another suicide attack by an Ansar militant at the same checkpoint. My driver, translator, and I jumped in the SUV and raced to the scene. This time, only the bomber was dead. He had been shot before he could detonate his TNT-packed car. When we arrived, he was lying faceup on the potholed highway, a few yards from his thirty-year-old Land Cruiser. He'd tried to throw a grenade at security forces. They'd shot him to death just as he'd pulled the pin, and his right hand was blown off completely. The grenade pin lay on the asphalt in a pool of blood near the body. The roof rack of the old Land Cruiser still held the old mattresses and household goods the attacker had placed there in hopes of blending into the caravan of fleeing refugees. In the back of the car were eight plastic jerry cans filled with explosive powder, surrounded by five-gallon cans of gasoline. For some reason, the huge bomb had failed to go off.

A group of *peshmerga*, the intended victims of the would-be bomber, milled around the corpse, recounting their reactions to the threat of the bomb-laden Land Cruiser hurtling toward their checkpoint. I studied the dead man closely, looking for clues to his purpose or motivation, but I drew a blank. He appeared to be a Kurd in his early thirties who had recently shaved his telltale Ansar beard. Other than that, he looked a lot like people I saw every day. I thought of the bearded Ayub Afghani, the Ansar leader known also as the Bombmaker, the Kurd who'd forced the visiting reporters to give video testimonials before they left the Ansar base. If the suicide car was one of Ayub's concoctions, it had missed its target.

Inside the Perimeter

After the death of the Australian journalist, the Kurdish government set up a cordon around the valley in an effort to keep out reporters. I was already inside the perimeter, ensconced with a good vantage point at Kaka Hama's, and I decided to stay. For several nights, I slept on the floor in a *peshmerga* compound. After dark, the fighters sat around barefoot on carpets, drinking sugared tea, clicking their prayer beads, and trading news about the war on their doorstep. When there was electricity, we watched a Baghdad television station as the Iraqi regime reran images of a downed Apache helicopter and a captured American crew. Outside, on the mountaintops above us, we could see the muzzle flashes from Ansar cannons as they traded fire with a U.S. AC-130, the armored gunship that flies so slowly it practically loiters in position. Each morning, just after dawn, the B-52 bombers arrived, rattling the windows in the compound and rousting the sleepers. Then came the cruise missiles, fired from distant battleships.

I spent three nights with the family of a *peshmerga* in a farm village called Qadifari, awakening each day to the sound of roosters and bombs. We were about two miles from the nearest air strikes, but I knew from experience that targeting mistakes were possible. Jokingly, I told my translator that I hoped that some twenty-two-year-old at the keyboard of a faraway computer, a soldier and fellow countryman, "didn't reach for his pizza at the wrong time."

The roofs of many of the houses in Qadifari were made of mud and straw. The few villagers who had all-concrete houses climbed wooden ladders to get on their rooftops, straining to catch a glimpse of the high-altitude bombers. It was strange for me—during the first six months in Kurdistan I hadn't seen or heard an airplane. Now there were dozens of bombers overhead every day. The sound of the warplanes, oddly, renewed my connection to the West.

I was a stranger but the family treated me well. The men of the house served me food on the customary plastic tablecloth on the floor, and the women giggled at me, darting behind doors to avert my gaze. A *peshmerga* slept next to me at night with his AK-47 rifle. My daytime in the house was spent in the company of children. They were curious and playful, sitting on my lap, the little ones babbling baby Kurdish, the older ones trying on my helmet and bulletproof vest or taking inventory of my camera gear. A big stranger had landed in their midst, and they were in wonder, too young to be afraid.

The villagers may not have known it, but there were only about 125 U.S. Special Forces deployed in the valley, not including an indeterminable number of CIA paramilitaries. I had already seen Special Forces teams on hilltops using laser-sighting devices to call in air strikes on Ansar positions. Some of my new neighbors had caught glimpses of the undercover foreigners, the Americans in baggy *peshmerga* clothing with Russian-made AK-47s, but the locals were confused why one of their own was hosting me. My presence was interpreted as a threat after I made the mistake of going outdoors to call the ABC desk in New York on my satellite phone. I had pointed the antenna of the sat phone to the sky to capture a signal. I was trying to be quiet, but someone heard me talking in English. The eavesdropper warned the host that if he allowed me to remain, "a missile might come down on [our] houses." I was sorry to leave town, but I understood. When you can see the bombs exploding from the roof of your home, you have a right to be afraid.

By the end of the week, the official PUK casualty count for the *peshmerga* was twenty-three dead and seventy-four wounded. PUK officials said that three hundred Ansar fighters had been killed. Few in the press corps believed that figure, but the freezer at the morgue in Sulaimaniah was crowded with Ansar corpses, and reporters were given access to the ghoulish scene of bearded, frozen bodies stacked on one another. More were on the way, and, when I returned to the Halabja Valley for the clean-up operation, I passed a garbage truck with part of a militant's body hanging off the back.

U.S. commanders had placed Kurdish *peshmerga* on the front lines, and the fighters had done the best they could to prevent insurgents from escaping to Iran. As in Tora Bora in Afghanistan, the better-trained and -equipped U.S. forces remained in the rear echelon and were not deployed to the snowy mountain passes to block the retreat. The proxy strategy may have contributed to the apparent success of the enemy retreat: An estimated five hundred Ansar militants made it across the international border. Of those, two hundred reportedly were arrested by the Iranian Revolutionary Guard, including the Bombmaker, Ayub Afghani. Later, the Iranian border guards were reported to have released their prisoners. Western intelligence experts believe that many of the Ansar militants subsequently returned to Iraq, where they reinvented themselves as the terror group Ansar al-Sunnah. Among them was Ayub Afghani, who was implicated in a series of bombings (in 2004, he was captured by government forces in the provincial capital of Erbil, his hometown).

Biarra

Traveling a rutted dirt road in a four-wheel drive, I was able to reach Biarra, the former command center of Ansar al-Islam. The militants had fled from Biarra the day before, after controlling the remote village for more than twenty months. U.S. Special Forces and *peshmerga* were conducting mop-up operations and clearing booby traps left behind in shops. It was a springlike day in the exquisite Switzerland-like setting, and the river was full of melted mountain snow. The *peshmerga* who had led the attack looked exhausted. Several told me they were relieved that the Ansar nightmare now appeared to be over.

I was traveling with a reporter from the *Boston Globe* that day. On one building we were greeted by a sign in Kurdish: GOD BLESSES THOSE WHO FIGHT IN HIS NAME AND WHO STAND TOGETHER LIKE BRICKS IN A STRONG WALL. Below the inscription were the words ANSAR MILITARY CORPS: FATAH BATTALION. We visited the damaged mosque, its minarets outlined against the snowpacked mountains. The mosque had been hit a day earlier by a U.S. missile, but much of the baroque structure had survived.

We spent some time poring over Ansar documents and photos left behind in the hasty retreat. Some of the papers referred to bomb making, others described ways to extract confessions from prisoners by torture. One prisoner had been executed before the insurgents escaped. His body was lying faceup on the side of the road when we arrived. One of the villagers told me the victim was only eighteen years old. There was a bullet hole in his outstretched hand, which was frozen in death. It looked as though he had thrust his palm toward the killer in a futile attempt to protect himself. His mother had just found his body. She was kneeling by her son, cupping her hands to his cheeks, wailing.

By the end of the week, I was getting forgetful about little as well as big things. At one point, we drove to Halabja to fix a tire puncture. A few hours after we left the town, I realized I'd forgotten my expensive satellite phone at the tire repair shop. The phone was worth almost $1,000. I'd last seen it on the mechanic's table, next to a stand where a vendor was selling gasoline from plastic jugs. We quickly backtracked to Halabja. It was dark and the shop was closed, but before long a man emerged from a run-down house nearby. He was the gas vendor, and the satellite phone was in his hand. He invited my translator and me into his house, where we had tea with his wife and eight children. There were other kids in the house, some of them belonging to a relative, a woman who had fled an Ansar-controlled village shortly after the first missiles struck.

The man, whose name was Abdullah, said that one of his neighbors had warned him not to get near the phone, saying it might be wired with explosives. Another advised him not to give the phone back, that he would be rich if he sold it. Abdullah had decided to return it, he said, "because foreigners use these things to help the Kurds." In the meantime, he told us, he had turned the phone off, thinking he was saving the owner money. "If I couldn't find you this night," he said, "I would not sleep."

We sat around for a couple of hours, drinking tea and eating a box of European candy that Rizgar, my translator, had been saving as a present for his cousin. I told the family I'd come from a place called California. Abdullah said he had watched us getting our tire fixed. He'd yelled at me as the car sped away from the repair shop, but he'd gotten only a wave in return. "I knew you lived in some far-away land," he said, "and your family would be waiting for your call."

30

Road to Tikrit and Home

I and the public know
What all schoolchildren learn
Those to whom evil is done
Do evil in return.

—W. H. AUDEN

When the shooting started, I was standing outside the car near the Arab village of Ramal. My first instinct was to get behind the front fender, to use the heavy engine block as a shield, but everyone was screaming, *"Go, go!"* in Kurdish and English. The doors of our SUV were open, but my driver, Jaff already had the car in gear, and it was moving.

Looting in Kirkuk had subsided the day before, and now a caravan of reporters and translators was en route to Tikrit, Saddam Hussein's hometown and former power base, sixty miles away. Tikrit had just fallen to U.S. troops, but the road from the Kurdish area to Arab villages near Tikrit had not been secured.

It was a lonely stretch of farmland between villages, and we had pulled over by an oil station two miles from Ramal. The Arab tribes in the outlying areas were up in arms, literally, after days of looting by Kurds following the liberation of Kirkuk. We were looking for a tribal escort to give us a safe conduct pass to Tikrit. A magazine reporter went down a dirt road to find the local sheik.

After the fall of Kirkuk, we had heard ugly stories of reverse ethnic cleansing— Arab families being forcibly evicted by Kurdish *peshmerga* (or at least Kurds in *peshmerga* uniforms) claiming official authority. Numerous gun attacks and at least two rapes of Arab women had been reported in the last few days. The Kurdish regional government had hotly denied the charges, but at least some of the reports seemed to be true.

Many of the tribes near Tikrit had been treated well by the Iraqi regime and they were fiercely loyal to Saddam Hussein. The border of Kurdistan was behind us, and now we were in the midst of conflicted territory: Kurd versus Sunni Arab. Scores were being settled, and it was hard to tell who was on which side.

We were north of Tikrit, and gunmen were rumored to be on the highway ahead. U.S. Marines had punched through Iraqi lines from the south, and, according to reports, they controlled Tikrit. We could not tell whether the armed civilians in between were fedayeen, Saddam's militia in retreat from the Marines, or just frightened Arabs trying to protect their property from common thieves.

The shooting began after a pickup truck with a Gulf Oil decal pulled up next to my SUV at the gas station. The driver was wearing a white gown and *qafiya*. We needed a high-profile guide for the short ride to Tikrit, and I'd offered to pay the man for his willingness to be seated, conspicuously, in our front seat. He thanked me for the offer, but he said he had to stay to guard the oil depot.

Just then three cars full of armed Kurds pulled in. They got out, without their guns, to ask if there was any gas. An Arab man asked them politely to leave. The newcomers pretended not to hear. At that point a white pickup and a Toyota sedan appeared on the dirt road from the village. I didn't notice the cars, but Jaff saw them, and he started the engine of our SUV.

Later that day, my translator, Rizgar, would say that seven to eight Arabs in the cars had fired in our direction. Chris would recall "twenty to thirty gunshots." Rizgar would downplay the volley as a mere "warning." I would remind him that he had flattened himself on the floor of the car at the time.

Our SUVs careened along the shoulder and onto the highway. We stopped a mile to the south, out of range. Unfortunately, it was an exposed spot, next to an abandoned Iraqi ammunition dump. A truckload of Kurds had just pulled off the highway, and men in *peshmerga* uniforms were looting weapons from the dump. Jaff said the license plate on the truck indicated that the vehicle belonged to the PUK *fermandi* (army base).

Our caravan advanced another mile and pulled over again. Reporters who had yet to do so put on their flak jackets and helmets. Out came the candy bars for adrenaline, and satellite phones for the news of the road ahead. Chris got a call from a British TV team for ITN that was twenty minutes behind us, and he advised them to turn back. ITN had already lost reporters in the war. "I told them the risks at this stage just weren't proportionate to the rewards."

After thirty minutes, the magazine reporter returned. There would be no Arab escort. The men were needed to defend the village from the Kurds.

A few miles north of Tikrit, we were stopped on the highway by gunmen in ankle-length *dishdashas*. They were Sunnis, presumably loyalists of Saddam, and they turned angry when they saw my camera. A teenager in a soccer jersey stuck his rifle in my window, demanded my press credential, and warned me not to film. After a few minutes, they let us pass. A mile ahead, hundreds of other Arabs blocked the highway. The tape deck in our SUV was playing Kurdish music. Jaff turned it off.

These gunmen were friendly. Two teenagers on a motorcycle carrying AK-47s smiled at my video camera as we passed. A bystander asked us for bottled water. A man without a gun approached me. "Where are the Americans?" he pleaded in English. "We need them here," he said. "We have no food. Our villages aren't safe. You are free to go, but if any Kurds come here, we will kill them."

The bridge into Tikrit was blocked by U.S. tanks and coils of barbed wire. The Marines were searching cars and frisking pedestrians. As we crossed the Tigris River into the city, an oil fire blackened the sky to the west. We continued on to Saddam's presidential palace. By then, the ornate building had been gutted by U.S. missiles.

Behind us lay the lonely highway back to the Kurdish area, with hints of what lay ahead for the country as a whole: a fight for oil, civil unrest, and rising conflict over the wrongs of the past.

Leaving Iraq

U.S. troops raced across the border from Kuwait, reaching Baghdad in less than a week. Kirkuk and Mosul fell soon after, and Kurds and Arabs danced together in the street. It was the end of April, and the war seemed to be over. I telephoned my wife and children. It was time, finally, to leave. Over the course of the long assignment I had missed Thanksgiving, Christmas, Easter, the Super Bowl, and family birthdays. I hadn't walked the dog, gone to a basketball game, listened to rock 'n' roll, watched the *Sopranos*, or used an ATM. I'd all but forgotten the smell of the ocean, the sound of airport gate announcements, and the roar at my son's basketball games. I had been in northern Iraq for seven months. I was ready to go home.

Most of the media attention had focused on the quick and easy capture of Baghdad. Like the rest of the world, Kurdistan had watched the bombing of the capital and the early, triumphant arrival of U.S. troops on television. Journalists assigned to northern Iraq had expected to see large numbers of American soldiers, and when Turkey barred the deployment of U.S. troops from its territory, some reporters felt cheated. "When I get back to London, I'm having T-shirts printed and I'll send you one," a CBS producer joked. "They're going to say, 'I covered the war in Iraq, and all I got was *friendly fire!*' "

Jaff and Rizgar drove me to Baghdad, where I spent my last night in Iraq. Most of the "lobby" was there, and we got together to say good-bye. Chang made a final toast: "To one day closer to home—*alive!*" Jeff was headed back to his family in Berlin, where he'd soon report on possible links between Ansar and information picked up in al-Qaeda phone intercepts in Europe. Chris was still in the north. He had gone back to Sergat, to follow a new lead about Ansar and documents found earlier in a Taliban safehouse in Afghanistan. At this point, the notion of insurgency—a phenomenon we had become accustomed to in northern

Iraq—was still a "sleeper story" with the rest of the country, overshadowed by TV replays of Saddam's statue being pulled down in a Baghdad square. The Islamic militants, however, had a narrow, focused agenda, and it wouldn't be long before their attacks would dominate the headlines.

Jeff and I hired a Chevy Suburban to take us across the desert to Jordan. As I threw my luggage and souvenir Kurdish carpets in the back of the SUV, I looked at the heavy backpack marked SURVIVOR—the one with the unused gas mask, chemical suit, and bottles of Rad Block inside. I had to admit something, at least to myself: I had taken the scare about weapons of mass destruction seriously—and personally. Once the bombing began, I'd been extra sure each night to put my gas mask and breathing canister next to the bed, within easy reach. Now, in the glow of the happily completed assignment, the bright yellow SURVIVOR stitching on the flap of the backpack seemed to spell *overreaction*. Suddenly, the gear seemed like excess baggage, full of artifacts and hyperbole. I felt like a worrywart. Maybe the next time somebody cried, "WMD!" I'd be less gullible.

The driver wanted to get an early start, to avoid the Ali Babas on the highway. We left Baghdad at 7:00 A.M., stopping for gas west of the city. I had been saving a small packet of Folgers instant coffee from the Ashti Hotel. The station attendant, a Sunni Arab dressed in a *dishdasha,* was kind enough to heat a cup of water on the propane burner in his office. He said the town was called Fallouja, but the name didn't ring a bell at the time.

Ahead of us were hours of desert to gaze upon, most of it would be flashing by at one hundred miles an hour. There were no Ali Babas to intrude on my thoughts, and fears of survival were mostly a thing of the past. Fate had hitched the Kurdish future to the U.S. bandwagon, however, and I couldn't help wondering again about U.S. intentions before the invasion. I remembered what Hero Talabani, the wife of Jalal Talabani, Iraq's future president, had told me on the eve of the war. She maintained there was a *reason* the Kurds had not received WMD protection. The reason, she insisted, was that the West just didn't care. I had to agree that the Kurds had presented an easy target for Saddam, but I also wanted to believe that their welfare had been a genuine concern to war planners. The alternate scenario was just too disturbing: that the Pentagon knew all along that the Kurds, an exposed population of almost four million, had no need for masks. Was that a possibility? Could the White House have conducted the war with *actual knowledge* that there were no WMD in Iraq? Was that why no one saw fit to protect the Kurds?

BOOK IV

Victory

31

One Year Later: Return to Iraq

The snake that doesn't bite me: Let him live a thousand years.

—TURKISH PROVERB

In the spring of 2004, I returned to Iraqi Kurdistan. Saddam Hussein had been arrested a few months earlier, his hideout discovered after a tip from the Kurds. Saddam's sons, Uday and Qusay, were dead, killed by U.S. troops in a raid in the northern city of Mosul, reportedly with the help of another Kurdish tipster. By now, most of the Iraqi leadership had been captured. Preparations were underway for war crimes trials, and the Kurds were expected to have front-row seats. Some news stories sounded hopeful. One headline in the business section of the *Los Angeles Times*, spoke to investors. "Could Hussein's Capture Provide a Market Boost?"

At least 270 mass graves had been discovered in Iraq, attesting to the scope of atrocities committed by the former regime. Human rights observers suspected that Saddam and his henchmen would mount vigorous trial defenses, including the argument that even in the face of its publicized use of WMD, the regime had received widespread international support. The ploy was unlikely to save big fish like Saddam and his notorious cousin, Ali Hassan al-Majid, better known as "Chemical Ali." When it came to isolating blame for the monumental crimes, the old CIA claim that Iran, not Iraq, was responsible for gassing the Kurds was expected to muddy the waters.

It had been a year since President Bush's declaration about "the end of major combat operations in Iraq." It might have been a moment of unity and victory for the West and a time of clear accountability for the enemies of America, but, in fact, the reasons for the war were becoming less clear, and questions were being raised about the predicted ease of postregime reconstruction. No WMD had been found, the administration had begun to back away from the claim that Saddam was connected to the events of 9/11, and U.N. Secretary General Kofi Annan was criticizing the war itself as "illegal."

Already, the controversial occupation had taken the lives of 800 American soldiers. Another 500 would be dead by the end of the year and, by the end of 2005, the number would exceed 2,000. So far, at least 25,000 Iraqi civilians had been killed; within a few months, a controversial study in the *Lancet,* the respected British medical journal, would estimate civilian deaths at 100,000.

The headlines continued to be dominated by bombings, hostage taking, and grizzly reports of severed heads. A fierce debate was underway about the pornographic torture of Iraqi prisoners in the prison at Abu Ghraib. Some of the inmates had been set upon by dogs, creatures reviled in the Muslim world as the dirtiest of animals.

The U.S. presidential campaign was underway, but it remained to be seen how Iraq issues would affect the election. Voters might be excused if the lessons of dictatorship and occupation lacked the moral clarity of simpler times.

It had been twelve months since I'd been in the Middle East, a full year of Kurdish leaders saying, at least officially, that the Kurds were "Iraqis first." I had followed the overall Kurdish story for nearly a generation. It was time for closure, time to try to figure out what I'd learned, time for a final trip. The Iraq occupation was falling apart, and some sections of the country already were no-go areas for American soldiers. In the United States, some moderate critics were, for the first time, using the "W" word—withdrawal of American troops—an unthinkable solution only months earlier. The alternatives weren't attractive, and the proposal still seemed like a devastating admission of failure, as well as an unacceptable blow to U.S. credibility abroad. The U.S. occupation was fueling the insurgency but, paradoxically, an American withdrawal seemed a surefire recipe for civil war.

Iraqi factions had a history of uniting to oppose foreign intervention and then succumbing to accept autocratic rule, often with a local face propped up by outside powers. The British learned hard lessons about Iraqi abhorrence of occupation forces after World War I. What united disparate clans and villages was hatred of the intruder. As T. E. Lawrence had put it, "They were fighting to get rid of empire, not to win it." It was tempting to see parallels between the new insurgency in Iraq and the Arab-Kurdish resistance to colonial rule in the 1930s.

This time in Iraq, however, the Kurds were on the side of the foreigner. That was the good news for U.S. interests. The bad news for U.S. policy was that ordinary Kurds in northern Iraq felt even more estranged from other Iraqis than they had before the invasion. Contrary to the wishes of war planners, this was an enclave that increasingly wanted nothing to do with Iraq's Arab majority or the growing anarchy in the rest of the country.

U.S. misfortune in Iraq had propelled the Kurds politically, if only by contrast.

For the moment, at least, their unofficial ministate appeared to be a shining example of democratic self-government. In the fourteen months since the fall of Saddam, not a single American had been killed in Kurdish-controlled Iraq. By now, Kurdistan—the "K" word that had so delighted Barham Salih when a U.S. magazine first used it to refer to northern Iraq—had achieved a high level of public recognition. It was not yet a household word, and if Americans did mention "Kurdistan," it was likely they were referring to a region of *Iraq*. In fact, with a population of only five million, the Iraqi Kurds still made up less than 20 percent of the total Kurdish population in the Middle East.

Still, the twists of fate of the post-9/11 world now made them the vanguard for a scattered, disjointed people. In the Kurdistans of Iran, Turkey, and Syria, all eyes were fixed on northern Iraq.

The Kurds were moving from the shadows to the stage.

No English

I returned to Iraqi Kurdistan in April 2004. My friend Mike Brabeck, the doctor who had arranged the operations at the Boston hospital for my one-time driver, Karzan Mahmoud, decided to come with me. We had known each other since we were teenagers, and I was glad to have him along for the trip. He was just as curious as I was about what had happened to the Kurds since the start of the war. He had a special interest in seeing Karzan and evaluating his progress since the surgeries.

It had been more than a year since Karzan had flown to Washington, D.C., where someone from the local PUK office debriefed him and put him on the Amtrak train for New England. When Karzan limped off the train at the station in Boston, Mike and his wife Mary were waiting anxiously and they greeted him like a long lost relative. From the first moments on the station platform, however, it was clear their new houseguest had extensive injuries. His right arm and fingers were so badly mangled from the gunshot injuries that he couldn't shake hands. His left thigh needed immediate medical attention. Steel pins had been inserted to shore up bones broken by the assassin's bullets, but the procedure had not gone well. The leg was badly infected and at risk of amputation if left unattended. Karzan looked like a "crooked little man" that day, Mike said later. He had a fever and was having trouble supporting himself physically. He seemed both "chronically ill and chronically depressed."

Karzan had a ten-word English vocabulary, at best, and his hosts knew no Kurdish at all, but everyone managed to communicate. As Karzan waited for surgery, Dr. Brabeck acted as his primary physician, treating him for anemia and for rashes that developed from prescribed medicines. The Brabeck home became an infirmary, where the Boston couple drew up a schedule to change Karzan's bags of intravenous antibiotics every six hours around the clock. For four months, beginning in March of 2003, the Brabecks ministered to the wounded stranger, leaving their offices in the middle of the day to change his IV bags or to ferry him to doctor and rehab appointments. Mary, who was then a dean at Boston College, arranged for ESL teachers and introduced Karzan to the Internet, and she set him up at BC with his first e-mail account. Mike, a busy internist with his own caseload of patients, cajoled hospital administrators and surgeons to line up the delicate, high-tech operations. Together with an intensive regimen of antibiotics and subsequent occupational therapy, the value of the pro bono surgeries would exceed $200,000.

When Mike could find the time, he drove Karzan to a volume discount store called Job Lot, where the wide-eyed visitor bought gifts for Kurdish friends, and to Best Buy, his favorite electronics store. In the meantime, Kurdish immigrants in Boston, a small, closely knit diaspora primarily from Iraq and Turkey, came together to support Karzan. They also adopted the Brabecks, tutoring them in Kurdish history and culture, inviting the busy couple to their own homes for traditional meals of stuffed grape leaves, kebab, and *kifta*.

The Neighbors

When Mike and I first discussed the trip to Iraqi Kurdistan, we assumed we'd travel via Syria, the safest and easiest route, at least prior to the war. Now, however, Syria was part of President Bush's "Axis of Evil." Citing the movement of anti-U.S. insurgents into Iraq, the administration was on the verge of imposing a new trade embargo on Syria. Within weeks, the embargo would ban U.S. exports to Syria, restrict banking, freeze a number of Syrian assets, and prohibit the takeoff or landing of Syrian aircraft in the United States.

The Kurds had played a part in the souring of U.S.-Syrian relations. In March 2004, a month before our trip, a dispute between Arab and Kurdish soccer fans in Syria turned violent. The incident occurred in northern Syria near the Tigris, where the famous river divides Syrian Kurdistan from Iraqi Kurdistan. Two days of rioting ensued, leaving at least thirty-six people dead, including policemen. A harsh government crackdown followed, and an estimated one thousand Kurds were arrested. Soon after, Kurdish political parties were banned in Syria.

Discrimination against Kurds in Syria had been a fact of life for generations, but until the incident in the soccer stadium in 2004, there had been no official protest from Washington. Now, in the wake of the regime change in Iraq, U.S. officials were quick to respond. The State Department immediately condemned the arrests, claiming Syrian authorities had "clamped down hard on normal life in cities where there's a Kurdish majority." Spokesman Adam Ereli said, "Citizens of Kurdish descent had [only] been protesting the lack of equal rights." The dramatic and sudden concern for the rights of Syrian Kurds stood in sharp contrast to the hands-off approach by U.S. officials during more severe crackdowns on the Kurds in Iraq and Turkey during the 1980s and 1990s.

The outbreak of Kurdish unrest in Syria was not without irony. For several years, Damascus had done its best to bring the old policy of supporting Kurdish revolution—in Turkey, that is—in line with U.S. demands. In 1999, Syria had terminated PKK leader Apo Ocalan's sanctuary in Damascus and had expelled him from the country, setting off a chain of events that ended with his capture and the collapse of a fifteen-year Kurdish uprising in Turkey. In the eight months before the riot by Syrian Kurds in 2004, the Damascus government had intensified efforts to improve relations with Ankara, sharing intelligence on Kurdish militants and even turning over some thirty-seven PKK suspects to Turkish authorities. In the end, attempts to mollify Turkey had distracted the Syrian government from the issue of Kurdish dissatisfaction at home.

The root of the problem was poverty and discrimination in the underdeveloped Kurdish region of northern Syria and the government's second-class treatment of its own Kurds. The disquiet in Syrian Kurdistan had been fueled by the Kurdish uprising in nearby Turkey. The riot erupted in an area where Kurdish farmers planted their fields along the tense frontier between Turkey and Syria, often in sight of the Turkish guard towers. In the 1980s and 1990s, thousands of their sons and daughters had answered a call to fight repression on the other side of the border. Many of the would-be warriors never came home alive.

The riot broke out in the city of Qamishli, my former stepping-off point for travels to northern Iraq. In years past, I had managed to obtain tourist visas from a Syrian consulate in the Orange County strip mall. Once I landed in Damascus on a tourist visa, I'd relied on Kurdish connections to the Syrian *mukhabarat* for permission to slip across the border to Iraq—but that was before the war.

A lot had changed in the year I'd been away, and Syria no longer permitted Americans to cross the river to Iraqi Kurdistan. As an alternative, we considered traveling to Iran. Since the invasion of Iraq, the status of the Kurds—now American allies—had risen, and Iran was paying close attention to northern Iraq. Tehran had launched a series of aid initiatives, including the revamping of the antiquated electrical system used by the Kurds. At least fifty projects in Iraqi Kurdistan now enjoyed sponsorship from Iranian companies. Every day, hundreds of Iranian trucks filled with foodstuffs, mineral water, soft drinks, home appliances, ceramics, carpets, blankets, and tiles were crossing the border. In just the first three months of 2004, according to a Tehran newspaper, Iran had exported $60 million in goods to northern Iraq.

The problem for us was political: Iran was increasingly afraid that the growing freedoms of Iraqi Kurds would embolden its own restive Kurdish population. In

March of 2004, when the Iraqi interim constitution temporarily granted Iraqi
Kurds the right to form their own government, Iranian police clamped down on
Iranian Kurds after their demonstrations of solidarity turned into riots. Nearly
one hundred Iranian Kurds were arrested. Now Tehran had begun to militarize
Kurdish areas along its western frontier.

My contacts in Iran were weak, and I guessed that travel access might be a
problem. To reach Iraqi Kurdistan from Iran, we would have to pass through the
Kurdish region in western Iran. I had heard reports that the Iranian army was
initiating a network of village guards similar to the controversial system employed in Turkish Kurdistan during the 1990s. In light of growing sensitivities
about the Kurds, gaining permission for two Americans to transit the area could
be difficult.

I didn't relish a couple of weeks cooling my heels in visa offices, breathing
Tehran's famously brown air. In all likelihood, it would be a protracted period of
"torture by tea" with government officials. In the end, we decided to look for another route to northern Iraq.

Turkey offered an alternative, as long as Mike—a nonjournalist—could obtain permission to cross into Iraq from Turkish territory. A trip through Turkey
would give me an opportunity for an update on the status of the Kurds and the
government's continuing efforts to gain admission to the European Union. Legal
reforms were finally underway in Turkey, and Ankara recently had received positive feedback from the European Union on its longstanding application for
membership. Treatment of the Kurds, the old bugaboo, remained an obstacle.
Turkey's efforts to subsume Kurdish identity for the sake of national unity continued to set it apart from Iraq. Even under the brutal dictator Saddam Hussein,
ironically, the Kurds of Iraq had enjoyed greater liberties in clothing, language,
broadcasting, and education than their cousins in Turkey.

For years, the European Union had bluntly warned Turkey to eliminate ar-
chaic language taboos. Hard-liners still argued that such rights would encourage
Kurdish terrorism, but moderate voices were beginning to emerge. In 2004,
Turkey finally legalized the teaching of Kurdish, albeit on a restricted basis for
private schools. Broadcasts in the long-suppressed tongue also were legalized, although the government was limiting Kurdish radio and television to a few hours
a day. The Kurds had not been officially designated as "Mountain Turks" since
1991. Now, for the first time, parents would be allowed to give their children
Kurdish names. In practice, however, the government still outlawed the use of
certain letters unique to the Kurdish alphabet—and essential for many of the
names.

It was a beginning, and the changes were long overdue. What remained to be
seen was whether Turkey would make good on promises to compensate victims

whose property was destroyed by the state during the uprising. As many as one million Kurdish villagers had lost their homes, and a bill to provide reparations was awaiting a vote in parliament.

According to Amnesty International, the Turkish government in 2004 was still harassing Kurdish politicians and human rights violations were still rampant, including routine torture at police stations, but in the last year, the numbers of reported cases had diminished. Turkey's long quest to buy $2 billion worth of U.S.-made Cobra attack helicopters, a deal once stalled by human rights concerns that the gunships would be used against the Kurds, was now moving ahead.

There were rumors that Ankara would soon find a face-saving way to free four Kurdish members of the Turkish parliament who had served ten years of a fifteen-year prison sentence for alleged separatist activity. One of the four was Leyla Zana, the first Kurdish woman elected to the Turkish parliament, who by now had achieved a near–Joan of Arc status among Kurds in Turkey's southeast.

Despite the improvements in Turkey, E.U. admission seemed a long way off. After all this time, the real power in the country still remained with the army. Shortly before my trip to Iraq with Mike Brabeck, the *Los Angeles Times* carried a story about Turkish military intelligence that confirmed the army's ongoing meddling in the country's domestic affairs. The report was based on a document leaked from the Turkish General Staff that ordered local officials to spy on "pro-European Union and pro-Americans, rich kids, ethnic minorities, Satanists, magicians, and people who practice meditation." It seemed doubtful that Europe would soon welcome a country where the generals played so heavy a watchdog role over civilians.

The immediate issue for us was ease of travel in and out of Turkey. From what I was hearing, journalists could apply in Ankara for permission to cross the Iraq border from Turkey. That meant I'd be OK, but I couldn't confirm that Mike would be permitted to enter Iraq from Turkish territory. As much as I wanted to see for myself how the new changes were affecting Turkish Kurds, I was afraid that travel via Turkey might delay or prevent us from reaching Iraqi Kurdistan, our primary destination. After talking it over, Mike and I decided only one viable choice remained: Jordan.

In the year I'd been away, Iraq had gone from the chaotic state of postwar looting with occasional potshots at occupying troops to an organized resistance with widespread guerrilla attacks. The threat of suicide bombers had thinned the usually crowded streets of Baghdad, often transforming a simple trip to buy food at a neighborhood shop into a life-or-death ordeal.

The first hint of Iraq's altered reality surfaced on the flight from New York to Amman, not a route ordinarily popular with Westerners. About a dozen American military contractors boarded the plane at JFK. Most of them were ex-commandos or former members of Special Forces, and all were en route to Baghdad. One told Mike he was from North Carolina, but wouldn't identify his security firm. We guessed it was Blackwater USA, the Pentagon contractor based in North Carolina. Four armed Blackwater guards had been killed in Fallouja the month before, and two of their charred bodies had been hung from a bridge over the Tigris River. During the long flight I bumped into an ex-Ranger who was getting a drink in the galley. His specialty was training American convoy drivers how to steer their trucks and fire weapons at the same time. The biggest challenge, he told me, was avoiding roadside bombs. His best advice? "Don't be the first vehicle on the road in the morning."

We spent two days in Jordan visiting the Roman ruins at Petra and Jaresh, watching Brad Pitt in *Troy* (with Arabic subtitles), and listening to the unsolicited advice of cab drivers. "America will lose in Iraq," said one. "History says that armies cannot win wars in civilian areas."

Then we flew from Jordan to Baghdad, where we boarded a small prop plane for the forty-five-minute trip to the Kurdish region. The passenger across the aisle on the final flight, a tattooed security guard with a ponytail, told me he worked for an American nongovernmental organization (NGO) in northern Iraq. His one personal carry-on in the overhead compartment was his flak jacket.

Iraqi airspace in a time of war was a travel experience like no other. Our pilot was a South African who had flown in Angola and Afghanistan and other conflicted areas. He informed the passengers that during the approach to Baghdad, the plane would need to *dive*, military style, and he warned us to look straight ahead without moving our heads, to prevent nausea. As soon as we saw the airport runways, three miles directly below, the pilot put the plane into a sharp downward spiral. He held the aircraft inside a tight, half-mile circle, and we could see the runways all the way to the ground.

I was sitting by the window. The Gs—the downward pressure during the rapid descent—were so great I had trouble lifting my hands from my lap. Still, I noticed my palms were wet. The cockpit door was open, but all I could see through the pilot's windshield was a rainy blur: The clouds were spinning by like slots in a Las Vegas casino. The last bank was hard to the left, which felt as if we were flying sideways. Just when I thought the wing would scrape the runway, the aircraft straightened out and we touched down.

There was good reason for the evasive action. Several months earlier, insurgents had succeeded in hitting a DHL cargo plane with a rocket as it took off from Baghdad, forcing the plane to make an emergency landing. Once we were safely on the ground, our pilot told us we had been within range of Sam-7s during the final approach, but he said the tight spirals made it difficult for a missile or rocket—had one been fired—to follow our sharp turns. He said the aircraft had been hit on a recent run, "but only by a bullet." He hadn't noticed the damage until he had flown back to Jordan, and he shrugged it off. "It was just a small hole in the flap," he said.

Erbil

Prior to the first Gulf War, Saddam's air force had made regular use of the Erbil airfield, but it had been unattended since 1991. When I last saw it, in 2003, the potholed and weed-choked strip resembled the lot of an abandoned drive-in movie theater.

Before the 2003 war, when reporters were speculating on likely landing spots for U.S. troops and equipment, I'd driven onto the airfield in a battered taxi and used the cab's odometer to measure the length of the runway. Back then, the notion of Americans actually landing on Iraqi fields had an edgy, clandestine feel to it. The Pentagon was being secretive about the location, as well as the date, of first landing. As far as I could tell, the Kurds weren't in the loop. There was a lot of competition in the press corps to get the first shot of American military uniforms in Iraq. Reporters were lurking near the likely airstrips, and several already had been detained by the CIA paramilitaries and their Kurdish guards. In one such case Chang Lee, the *Times* photographer, and I spotted several Special Forces disguised as *pesh,* and we proceeded to photograph them as they climbed into their sport utility vehicles. Suddenly, we found ourselves surrounded by Bafel Talabani and a half dozen of his armed Cobra guards. They angrily confiscated Chang's compact flash card and my ABC News videotape. The next day, after we lodged a protest with PUK officials, the videotape and flash card were delivered to our hotel, along with a surprisingly polite, handwritten apology from Talabani. The images of the American soldiers, however, had been erased.

In the last few weeks before the war, Chang Lee and I talked to a cooperative Kurdish source who revealed to us that U.S. forces were planning a night landing near Sulaimaniah. Believing we had received inside information, we located a hiding spot on a rooftop overlooking the airstrip, but no American soldiers landed. After two sleepless nights in the March cold, we abandoned efforts to get the scoop.

That was then. Now the airfield had been resurfaced with fresh asphalt and lengthened to accommodate U.S. fighter jets and C-130 cargo planes. The first commercial carrier, Royal Jordanian, now had scheduled flights to Erbil, and plans were in the works for a direct link to European cities. It was a reality unimaginable only twelve months earlier.

We walked across the tarmac, past a four-story tower that was under construction, and entered a small terminal made of prefabricated siding. The floor of the terminal was covered with shiny, marblelike tiles. In a room off to one

side, two Kurds in camouflage uniforms sat at a computer by a sign that read
GROUND CONTROL. Cables from the computer ran to a large truck battery on the
floor. It was a backup system to keep airport electricity steady during the occupation's increasingly frequent blackouts.

On the opposite side of the terminal, a baggage handler was weighing suit-
cases on a bathroom scale. Next to him was a second computer terminal, where a
Kurd was reading a Microsoft 98 user's manual. The manual, which consisted of
twelve pages of instructions, had been translated from Microsoft English into
Microsoft Kurdish—a first as far as I knew. I pointed to a random sentence in
Kurdish, and asked the man for the translation. The Kurdish directions said,
"Right click to change password into English."

The airport cafeteria had a single lunch counter and a sign that advertised
MENERAL WATER [sic]. The friendly waiter, a student of English at the local university, promised "beer next month." I had been away only a year, but the notion of a
Kurdish airport continued to astonish me. I felt a bit like Rip Van Winkle awakening from a long nap. "What's next?" I joked with Mike. "A Kurdish *air force?*"

In the middle of the modest terminal we found a desk for Kurdish customs
and immigration. Seated there was a striking-looking young woman wearing
heavy mascara and lipstick. On her wrists were gold bracelets. She was dressed in
a khaki military uniform, with a yellow star on each epaulette. Her long black
hair was dyed blond, except for the roots, and it fell below her waist. She was gap-
toothed, and she smiled broadly at arriving passengers, including me.

The woman had a 9 mm pistol in a hip holster, but her heavy-looking ammunition belt lay on the customs table. "Why did you join the police?" I asked her,
trying to strike up a conversation. She didn't speak English, but her fellow officer,
a middle-aged Kurd who said he'd fled to Norway in the 1990s, did know English. He was eager to tease her. "To attract a husband!" he volunteered, grinning as
he told his colleague what he'd said. The woman smiled. I looked at the European-
style sunglasses that hung from a loop on her uniform. I thought for a moment
how isolated northern Iraq had once been and of the novelty of foreigners now being able to arrive by airplane. I asked her, Was the other immigration officer serious? "Maybe yes," she replied, laughing.

The Abu Sana

My friend Azad Sabir asked us to meet him at the Abu Sana, a smoky, dimly lit
restaurant in Sulaimaniah frequented by politicians and business leaders. The
Abu Sana was known for serving heaping platters of lamb and chicken and lots
of booze. Azad was the PUK stalwart I'd met two years earlier, when he had
worked as a personal assistant to Barham Salih, the prime minister. His brother,
Mohammed Sabir, currently held Barham's old position, the key post of PUK

representative in Washington, D.C. Now that Saddam was gone, there was talk Mohammed might become Iraq's new ambassador to France, and Azad was hoping that the PUK would send him to the Paris embassy at the same time. Maybe party affiliation would give him what it had given his brother—a ticket to the First World. (As it turned out, his brother would soon become the new Iraqi ambassador to China.)

The back lot of the Abu Sana was full of BMWs and Mercedes, about the way I remembered it. Now, though, barrels of concrete blocked the front entrance to ward off suicide bombers—a new feature since Americans had arrived in town.

Azad was a natty dresser, invariably attired in a perfect blue suit, with a pair of eyeglasses perched on the bridge of his nose. He was good-natured with an easy sense of humor. He was always open for ribbing about being a PUK government man or his ongoing—and valiant—efforts to learn proper English. Like most Iraqis, he had learned English from British-trained teachers, and his accent made *no* sound like *new*, which was a constant source of joking between us.

Azad was only thirty, but he directed a program for removing land mines, which was important work to the Kurds, and he was rising quickly through the PUK ranks. Saddam may have been gone, but vast minefields planted in the 1980s, during the Iraq-Iran war, still threatened the population. Like many politicians in the Middle East, Azad mixed politics with business. He was the sales representative for Hitachi, and he used his trips to Dubai and Jordan to import Japanese-made electronics for the family store. Like so many others in his party, he was riding the economic boom in Kurdistan, hoping the semiautonomous enclave could seal out the mounting chaos in the rest of Iraq. At the same time, the Kurds still looked to the outside for help. "My mother is sick," Azad said when he learned that Mike was a doctor. "Would you come to our house to examine her?"

32

Karzan at Home

Life is short, so live it as a rooster.

—KURDISH PROVERB

Karzan strolled into the lobby of the Ashti Hotel grinning as if he owned the place. Since his visit to Santa Barbara the year before, he had gained a few pounds, and his clothing appeared more Californian than Kurdish.

"Look!" Mike exclaimed. "He's not limping!"

More than two years had passed since Karzan had been shot. His days as a tae kwon do black belt were clearly gone, but his improbable recovery from the twenty-three bullet wounds continued to amaze me. He gave us each a hug, the American-style embrace that seemed to be catching on in Kurdistan. He was the same happy-go-lucky Karzan, the small-framed Kurd with the self-deprecating wisecracks, the little guy with a twinkle in his eye who joked about being a "big man."

When I'd last seen Karzan, his U.S. visa was about to expire, and we had visited my congresswoman in Santa Barbara. She liked Karzan immediately, and she promised to get the visa extended. The extension, however, depended on his decision to proceed with the third and final operation, which Mike had arranged without cost at the Boston hospital. The surgeons were ready to graft tendons to the fingers of Karzan's right hand. It would be a painful procedure, and there would be a long period of rehabilitation afterward, with no guarantee of full recovery. By then, Karzan had undergone two major surgeries in just four months. Despite the Brabecks' hospitality, he was homesick for Kurdistan. In the end, he decided to go back.

Now Karzan wanted his parents to meet "Dr. Mike" and to see me again. We were soon on the way to their home, bumping along in his 1986 Volkswagen Passat. The Passat may not be a pretty car, but it is still one of the most common models in the country, and the Kurds swear by its reliability. There was a reason, Karzan told us in his much-improved English, that the roads in Kurdistan were still crowded with old Passats. In 1981, when the war between Iraq and Iran had just begun, Saddam was trying to acquire the Soviet-made T-72 tanks, which were capable of withstanding direct hits by rocket-propelled grenades. At that time, Brazil was a trading partner with the Soviets, and the utilitarian Passats were being built at plants in Rio de Janeiro. As part of a deal negotiated by Saddam, Brazil got cheap oil, and the Iraqi army got tanks.

The Arabs and the Kurds got the VW Passat.

It was Friday, the weekend, and it was drizzling rain, but at picnic sites along the road, traditional music was blaring from boom boxes on the tops of parked cars. Entire families dressed in brightly colored costumes were dancing in big circles, twirling in celebration. It was springtime in Kurdistan.

The windshield wipers on the Passat were broken, but everything else on the old VW seemed to work. It occurred to me that Karzan was lucky to have an automatic transmission. He could not have chauffeured his visitors in a car with a stick shift. The gunshot injuries prevented his fingers from closing around a gearshift knob. The third surgery—the one he had elected not to have—might have given his right hand an additional bit of movement.

Rush Hour in Kurdistan

When I had first visited Sulaimaniah in 1991, the region was suffering from a gasoline embargo imposed by the regime. Many cars had been destroyed in the recent uprising, and it was common in those days to see farm tractors and horse-drawn carts making their way through the city. By 2004, such scenes were largely a thing of the past. The increase in traffic in just the year I'd been away was dramatic. With gas at only six cents a gallon, the roads were choked with freight trucks, bright yellow "Sunny" taxicabs made by Nissan, and Coaster brand buses newly imported from Japan. Since the overthrow of the dictatorship, tens of thousands of private cars had appeared on the narrow streets of Kurdistan, including many looted from government authorities during the chaotic aftermath of the U.S. attacks.

For the first time, the Kurds were experiencing the phenomenon of rush hour, a taste of the horn-blowing gridlock of other countries, albeit on a smaller scale. Few Kurds seemed to mind. The proliferation of new vehicles, many of them luxury cars with European license plates, gave the city a hint of wealth and the feel of progress. The changes were mixed with a heady air of Kurdish nationalism, which only served to increase the sense of separation from Arab Iraq. Outdoor murals on Salem Street still depicted both heroic freedom fighters and handcuffed Kurds being tortured in Iraqi jails. Unlike the rest of the country, there wasn't an Iraqi flag in sight, but we passed dozens of Kurdish flags, many of them flying on Mme. Mitterrand Street and at a Col. Muammar al-Qaddafi Traffic Circle. The street was named for Mme. Mitterrand, the wife of the former president of France, long an advocate of Kurdish independence. Mme. Mitterrand had actively supported the Kurds following the first Gulf War, when few European notables risked visiting northern Iraq—she had survived an assassination attempt during one of her trips—and such advocacy had put the former first lady permanently in the hearts of the Iraqi Kurds. The circle was named in honor of the maverick Libyan leader who took up the cause of the Kurds in the 1980s, an unpopular act for an Arab at the time.

Gazing out of Karzan's car, I saw bulldozers clearing lots and workers raising scaffolding for new buildings. A steamroller was flattening a new highway, and the smell of fresh tar was in the air. In another sign of postwar construction, Karzan told us, expatriate Kurds from Germany and England were investing heavily in commercial real estate, and the market for residential properties, reportedly, was just as hot. Property values had begun to rise with the end of the Kurdish civil war in 1997, but now there was a real estate *boom,* and investors were talking about a "golden era of the Kurds." With Saddam gone, it appeared that times were about to become even more golden. The economic upswing reflected an optimism unmatched in the rest of Iraq, where suicide bombings had become almost a daily ritual and where the economy and the population seemed paralyzed by growing terror.

It was clear that Kurdistan, unlike much of mayhem-ridden Iraq, was evolving in directions unrelated to war or security. We passed the former Iraqi Security Building, which I'd first visited in Sulaimaniah in 1991 following the liberation of the city. In those days, the infamous gulag and torture center was just an abandoned, trashed collection of cellblocks. The building had been transformed into a new museum of the Kurdish uprising, with audio-visual exhibits, photographs, and guided tours. Farther along, we passed a dazzling glass and steel structure, which Karzan said was the new city library, and then we drove by the PUK Council of Ministries, where I had often visited Barham Salih. Later, we would visit the Council and view an architect's model for the Kurdish Performing Arts Center, which was scheduled for groundbreaking by the end of the year.

Karzan's Family

We headed to the poor side of town, where the roads were unpaved, and discarded garbage floated in a runoff from a swollen creek. Karzan's parents had just bought a cinder-block house on a muddy street in a development. Karzan was helping to pay for the house, thanks in part to his job with a U.S. company that provided security for the Coalition Provisional Authority (CPA) in Sulaimaniah. Like most unmarried Kurds, regardless of age, he lived with his parents and contributed to the maintenance of the family dwelling.

Karzan's mother opened the door. She was a small woman with shoulder-length black hair, and she was wearing a royal blue velvet dress that fell to the floor, almost covering her bare feet. We took off our shoes in the vestibule and followed her into the neat but austere-looking home.

On the wall of the living room above a vase of plastic roses was a photo of her brother, Karzan's uncle. It was a memorial, a keepsake common in many Kurdish homes: a grainy and out-of-focus portrait of a smiling young man with a large, black moustache. Like so many Kurds, the young man had been a *peshmerga* in the 1980s. He had been killed in a clash with Iraqi troops near Sulaimaniah. "He is a *shahid*," she said, using the present tense to define her brother's status as a martyr in the Kurdish struggle.

Karzan's father was a long-distance truck driver who had made runs to Basra and Kuwait during the time of Saddam. The roads were too dangerous now, and he was unemployed. He was only fifty-seven, but his lined face and bald head made him look more like seventy. The hyperaging process may have run in the family, at least on the male side. Karzan's brother, Kosak, who was also on hand to greet us, was only twenty-two, but he had Karzan's receding hairline. Like his brother and father, he looked much older.

The youngest sister, Sanza, was eleven, and she was excited to meet her first Americans. Finally there was Heshu, now eighteen, Karzan's disabled sister, the one who had been accidentally run over in 1991 as the family raced to Iran to escape the Iraqi army. Her head was permanently cocked to one side, and she was trembling. Occasionally during our visit she would cry out, screaming like the toddler she was in 1991. Then Karzan's father would bend down by her wheelchair, whispering and kissing her on the cheek. Like Karzan, she wore her misfortune on her body, a badge of Kurdish history, one chapter in a shared odyssey of grief.

Almost every family I met in Kurdistan had a personal story of tragedy, usually about a spouse or parent, child or sibling who had been imprisoned, killed, wounded, or "disappeared." Like Cambodia in the 1970s or the Soviet Union in the time of Stalin, the catastrophe seemed to have touched everyone. The memories were still alive—some of them literally imprinted on the survivors.

Before leaving the room, Karzan's mother served us tea in steaming glasses. When she returned a few minutes later, she was wearing eye makeup—something rare for Kurdish women—and a new brightly colored dress. "Every day I thank God for what you did for Karzan and for us," she said. Her eyes moved toward the ceiling at the mention of "Allah," the word for God in both Arabic and Kurdish. "*Sah Chow!*" she exclaimed, placing her hand over her heart in my favorite Kurdish gesture. *I have you in my eye.*

"Having Karzan in our home was a gift for both Mary and me," Mike replied graciously. "Because of him, we were given the chance to learn something about Kurdish culture, and now we have Kurdish friends in America."

On our way to lunch in the next room, we passed an unfinished staircase, which climbed steeply to the second floor. Steel rebars, some of them two feet in length, protruded like spikes from the rough concrete steps. Karzan's father had been building the house piecemeal, as time and budget permitted. In the meantime, the exposed rebar was an "attractive nuisance," as lawyers like to say, ready to impale the unlucky climber who slipped. The casual danger reminded me of workers I often passed on Kurdish construction sites, guys smashing rocks with sledgehammers, without goggles to protect their eyes from flying chips. The Kurds had made rapid social progress since breaking away from Iraqi control in 1991, but at some level they were still dealing with basic priorities like survival. Safety standards in the Kurdish construction industry were a luxury that would have to wait.

Most Kurdish families eat their meals sitting cross-legged on the floor, the food laid out on a simple plastic cloth, but Karzan's mother wanted her guests to be as comfortable as possible, so she served the meal at a table, American style. Much of the conversation was about Karzan and the help he had gotten in America. Our meal consisted of a huge spread of mixed meats, soup, and rice. It was a feast, a Kurdish thanksgiving.

Later, we took photos of family members, and they took photos of us. Heshu was upset and did not want to be included in the photos. Karzan's father gently insisted. Karzan still had the digital camera he'd used to take pictures at Old Spanish Days in Santa Barbara.

When it came time for us to go, Karzan's parents brought out the gifts they'd been saving for each of us: identical carpets with images of Jesus Christ bathed in a glowing halo. They were the stiff, bulky carpets that are made by the thousands in Iranian factories and sold on street corners throughout the region. They were touching, cross-cultural gifts, no doubt planned long in advance of our visit. For Muslim Kurds with a limited income, the Jesus rugs represented an expensive investment, a perceived gesture of religious respect for the Americans who had helped their injured son.

Old Friends

I hadn't seen Jaff since he'd driven me to Baghdad the year before, when I was headed home after seven months in the country. The war had been good to him. He had saved his ABC salary—including bonuses for driving during the opening days of the U.S. attack, when he nervously kept his gas mask on the dashboard within easy reach—to buy a new taxi. Before I left, I'd given him a new Honda generator that I had bought in case of emergency during the war. The generator now powered his house in blackouts.

Hiwa Rafiq, the technical director of KurdSat TV who had uplinked my ABC footage to London at all hours of the day and night, now had his own satellite company. During the war he had worked for the government-owned station, sometimes putting in one hundred-hour weeks servicing foreign reporters on deadline who needed to send their reports. In post-Saddam Iraq, the satellite market was booming, and Hiwa had a growing list of private clients. I exchanged gifts with him and his wife: T-shirts with images of the Santa Barbara beach for his children and Kurdish jewelry and other presents for my own children.

Azad Sediq, the acerbic former news director of KurdSat, now had a part-time job for the *Los Angeles Times,* and he sometimes worked with my old colleague Jeff Fleishman. The heavy-set Azad, fluent and witty as always, got right to the point. "Why are we even *part* of Iraq?" he asked rhetorically. "Our language is different, our land is different—this is our time to separate."

"Let's not be Muslims anymore!" he exclaimed half seriously, with typical overstatement.

"The Arabs say the United States wants to make Kurds the 'new Israelis,' " he said. "Well, I think that's a good idea." The Kurds should break away from the rest of Iraq, he argued. "Let's give the United States access to the oil fields of Kirkuk in exchange for a fifty-year security agreement."

Despite his pro-Western exuberance, Azad was galled by what he saw as ongoing U.S. ignorance and insensitivity about the Kurds, especially what he had seen from Paul Bremer, the American proconsul. He had recently covered Bremer's first visit to the Kurdish region as a stringer for the *Los Angeles Times,* and he recounted a story of Bremer entering the headquarters of the Kurdistan Democratic Party to meet KDP leader Massoud Barzani. Bremer reportedly swept through one parlor in his blue suit and trademark L.L. Bean hunting boots, stopping briefly to inquire about the identity of a Kurdish fighter in a mural. "Who's that?" Bremer inquired. "They had to tell him it was the legendary Mullah Mustafa Barzani, the founder of the revolution, the most recognized name in Kurdish history!" Azad said. "And this guy is supposed to understand the Kurds?"

Shalaw Hussein

It was Friday, the Kurdish weekend, a day for families, weddings, and for paying respects to the dead. Shalaw Hussein, Barham Salih's twenty-eight-year-old assistant, asked me to join him in the cemetery. The year before, just a few months after the toppling of Saddam, his beloved older brother, Mohammed, had been shot to death in an ambush by Ansar al-Islam. Mohammed, a close friend of Salih since boyhood, had risen to become second in command of police security in Sulaimaniah. At the time of his death, he was trying to negotiate the surrender of three militants in a house near the Ashti Hotel. The Ansar trio was killed in the ensuing shoot-out, and a young girl had died in the crossfire.

The last time I'd seen Mohammed, we had eaten dinner together in the Abu Sana restaurant. As we climbed the hillside toward his brother's grave, it was hot in the cemetery, and Shalaw removed his suit coat, revealing the .45 Glock automatic pistol in his shoulder holster. When we reached the grave, a lone mourner was sitting by the tomb, and cut flowers lay beneath an image of the deceased engraved on the headstone. The stranger told me he came every Friday to pay his respects. He also visited on Tuesday evenings, he said, "along with twenty to thirty friends," the same group that had gotten together on Tuesdays when Mohammed was alive. "That was the time of the week," the visitor said softly, "when Mohammed took time to play."

A few yards from Mohammed's grave was a large crypt, where a faded Kurdish tricolor fluttered in the light breeze. "That is the burial place of Awla Sees Karaman, our most famous *peshmerga*," Shalaw said proudly. He translated the dead man's Kurdish name as "Awla the Skinny Hero" and proceeded to recount the circumstances of his death in British-occupied Sulaimaniah in 1930, as if it were only yesterday. "He is a good man, very brave," Shalaw said, employing the present tense to describe the comrade who'd been dead for seventy years, a man he never knew. "They ambushed him with a machine gun when he was shopping in the bazaar," he said. "Twenty civilians died, too."

New in Kurdistan

Some of the changes since I'd left in 2003 popped up now like random snapshots: cases of Miller High Life stuffed in the trunk of an old Toyota Corona, a woman with dyed hair shopping in the bazaar with her friend covered head to toe in a black chador, a beggar at a traffic light, underwear ads on a high definition TV set, a visiting expatriate talking about the availability of Viagra.

Near Sulaimaniah, an international airport was under construction, and flights to Europe were expected by late 2006. The PUK had built a U.S.-style dollar store in Sulaimaniah (similar to one constructed by the KDP in the city of Dohuk), where Kurds could shop and consumer feedback was welcome (the store displayed a "complain [sic] and suggestion box"). Both political parties had established military academies to train professional soldiers. In the future, Kurdish officers graduating from the two-year curriculum were less likely to be dismissed as "irregular militia."

The first American school had opened in Sulaimaniah. Now Kurdish parents—those who could afford the tuition—could prepare their children for success with a Western-style education, much like their counterparts in Cairo or Beirut.

At the University of Sulaimaniah, conflict resolution workshops were under-way, sponsored jointly by Boston University, Columbia University, and American University. Over breakfast at the Ashti Hotel, I overheard a group of American nurses talking about the course they'd been teaching in sexuality to Kurdish nurses. "Yesterday," one American remarked, "the Kurdish women listened *so carefully.*"

The dean of the local medical school, Dr. Ali Said, was elated. "So much has changed since Operation Iraqi Freedom, and we owe everything to the U.S.A.," he said exuberantly. For one thing, salaries had more than doubled in the post-Saddam era, he said, citing the example of a full professor who had made $250 a month before the fall of the regime and who now earned $550 a month. "There will be economic stability," he predicted. "People feel safe now," he said. The only problem, he added without elaboration, was whether the Kurds would be al-lowed a federal state, one based on ethnicity.

"We are unlucky in geography and unlucky in our religion. If we were Chris-tian, we would have had our own country by now."

Dr. Said expressed gratitude to the East Tennessee State medical school, which had taken on the job of developing an electronic medical library in Sulaimaniah. The Tennessee medical school, which specialized in rural education, had recently installed twenty brand-new computers and had connected them to the Galaxy System, giving local hospitals a window to the scientific progress from which they had been isolated for so long. Now for the first time, Kurdish doctors and medical students had quick access to a worldwide library of medical journals and other information. "We hope Americans will stay here forever," Dr. Said told us. "You can take all our oil," he added with a wink, "and just leave the tar!"

Abu Ghraib

News of the scandal at Abu Ghraib, the prison near Baghdad, had broken, and Secretary of Defense Donald Rumsfeld was en route to the Iraqi capital for dam-age control. During Saddam's regime, Abu Ghraib had been notorious for wide-spread torture, murder, and animal-like living conditions, a hellhole where tens of thousands of Arabs and Kurds languished in despair, forgotten. Now it was a U.S. military prison, and news was breaking that American soldiers had tortured naked detainees.

Diyar Kareem, Karzan's Kurdish friend from Boston, was visiting the Ashti Hotel. We listened to a TV commentator speculate whether Rumsfeld would be forced to resign in the wake of photos showing prostrate Iraqis with dog leashes around their necks. The otherwise soft-spoken Diyar, like many Kurds, was livid at the television images of Abu Ghraib, castigating the commentator's remarks and mocking the reports as anti-American.

"Someone got $1 million dollars for those photos," he remarked with quiet sarcasm.

Diyar had deserted the Iraqi army in 1989, two years before Saddam invaded Kuwait. He told me he had spent the two years hiding in a basement in the Kurdish region and then used the commotion of the first Gulf War to escape from the country. He had earned a green card in the United States, and his friend Karzan was eager to duplicate his success. Diyar, in turn, had tried to warn Karzan that the downside of U.S. life could be "ten-hour shifts in a pizza parlor."

Diyar's father had immigrated to America, but he disliked the immigrant experience, finding the new society cold and impersonal by Kurdish standards. A civil engineer by trade, he had given up his chance to become an American and had returned to Sulaimaniah, where he now had a job on one of Salih's booming construction projects.

"If I crash a car," Diyar asked rhetorically, "should they punish my father?"

"What do you mean?" I asked.

"It's all lies," he replied. "Saddam killed thousands of people in Abu Ghraib, and this is just an excuse to beat up on America because of a few bad apples."

I was wary of the "Saddam-Hussein-was-worse-than-America" argument. Surely, there was a better comparison to illustrate who Americans were as a people. The rationale was a slippery slope, especially in light of the West's record of support for the dictatorship. The Abu Ghraib scandal seemed like a powerful setback. There was no evidence that a single American life had been saved by information from abused prisoners, and reports of the torture had alienated a large segment of the Iraqi people, whose support for the U.S. occupation was crucial. The larger issue went beyond Iraq and defined American character: the need to respect the Geneva Convention and international law. Wasn't it important to ensure that so-called rogue elements at the bottom of the Pentagon got a proper message from the top? I asked Diyar if the secretary of defense should be held accountable.

"Every Kurd knows that Rumsfeld helped Saddam with WMD, but that is no reason for him to resign now," Diyar said emphatically. "What George Bush did was bigger than that," he added, referring to the invasion. "And that is why all the Kurds here and in America support him."

Kurd in an Apache

How much had changed? A half century earlier, in their fight for independence from the Iraqi regime, Kurdish leaders had stood side by side with communists and socialists. During the Cold War, the Barzani family had taken refuge in the Soviet Union, and Jalal Talabani had based himself in Syria and allied the Kurdish struggle with pro-Soviet groups. Now, at the dawn of the twenty-first century, with only one superpower remaining, many Kurdish leaders were sounding not only like Americans, but also like *Republicans*. One, my respected friend Barham Salih, would temporarily become the deputy prime minister of all Iraqis, setting up office in the Green Zone in Baghdad and shuttling back and forth to Sulaimaniah in an Apache helicopter. Like most of the Kurdish leadership, he would support the reelection of George W. Bush, the man whose policies had rid them, finally, of the tyrant Saddam Hussein.

Nevertheless, Saddam had had many allies. I wondered if the pending war crimes trials would set history straight or merely assign the blame selectively. I couldn't help thinking about the international collusion with Iraq's genocidal regime. Many governments, including the United States, had allied themselves with Saddam to advance their own interests, and weapons companies had profited from supplying the dictatorship with arms. Now a U.S. army of occupation was ensconced in the Green Zone in Saddam's palace, the very place where visiting dignitaries like Donald Rumsfeld once had walked on the dictator's handwoven Kurdish carpets. Barely twenty years before, Donald Rumsfeld had come to drink *chi* with the Butcher of Baghdad, as well as with Tariq Aziz, Iraq's former foreign minister, who was also accused of war crimes.

The taxi driver in Jordan was right: It's hard to win a guerrilla war in the middle of a civilian population, an environment where victory is not determined by firepower alone. Even if the Abu Ghraib abuse was not a moral problem, it was a practical one. It was likely that hearts and minds, not superior technology, would tip the balance in Iraq. I recalled what that young American corporal told me in 1991 on my first trip to Istanbul. He was fighting terrorists back then, long before the word was in most of our vocabularies. Now the terrorists seemed to be everywhere.

That corporal was helping to suppress a violent Kurdish uprising back in 1991. There was little media coverage about the Kurds in Turkey at the time; neither he nor the American public in general knew much about the legitimate grievances of the Kurds in Turkey. I also recalled Ian, the British ex-commando who helped teach me WMD survivor skills on the eve of the war. He maintained that a military strategy that failed to address political root causes, especially collective humiliation, was doomed to failure. Despite the fact that suicide bombers had killed hundreds of innocent civilians, many Iraqis continued to blame America for their woes. The use of torture at Abu Ghraib was part of the problem, and it had handed a major political victory to U.S. enemies. Later, the growing insurgency would exploit TV footage of a Marine shooting a wounded, unarmed prisoner in Fallouja. Reports of sexual torture and desecration of the Koran at the U.S. detention center at Guantanamo Bay, Cuba, would further inflame anti-Americanism around the world, undoubtedly buoying the hopes of jihadist recruiters.

However, the Kurds of Iraq had crossed the Rubicon, and they would hear none of it. Like other U.S. allies, they now had friends in Congress, paid lobbyists on Capitol Hill, and leverage in the media. Confident that U.S. betrayals were a thing of the past, they regarded the torture reports as nothing more than anti-American propaganda. The Kurds had cast their lot with the giant and, right or wrong, they would shield him from criticism. Iraqi Kurds believed that they shared a common ideology with the Americans. To borrow a term of affection from the PKK, they were now *hevats*: they were both "going the same way."

"Because of the Iraq war, the Kurds and the U.S.A. have the same friends and the same enemies," Diyar said quietly. "You are with us or you are against us." It was a familiar refrain in a post-9/11 world, and I had heard it before. Still, Diyar was right about the new alliance, even if he failed to address the implications for the rest of civilization: the thorny issue of defending freedom by breaking the law.

In the months to come, in Sunni Arab strongholds in Fallouja, Mosul, and elsewhere, U.S. forces would enlist the famous fighting skills of the *peshmerga* to combat the largely Sunni uprising. The predominantly secular Kurds would help the American military achieve short-term victories against the Arab insurgents—but not without the risk of inciting sectarian reprisals, further undermining U.S. hopes for a unified Iraq.

Much later, I would recall watching television with Diyar that day in the Ashti Hotel. "Every single person on the street wants independence," he told me then in his Kurdish-Boston accent. "These two nations, Kurd and Arab, have blood between them—they can never live together."

33

Kirkuk and Civil War

In Lakota, the Black Hills mean "the heart of everything that is."
We were created and spread out from the Black Hills.

—CHARLOTTE BLACK ELK, OGLALA SIOUX ELDER

Kirkuk is the heart of Kurdistan and we are ready to wage a war
in order to preserve its identity.

—MASSOUD BARZANI, KURDISTAN DEMOCRATIC PARTY LEADER

Powder Keg

In March of 2003, a few weeks before the liberation of Kirkuk, a tailor took my measurements and sewed a Kurdish outfit for me. It was just a precaution. If remnants of the Iraqi military still remained after the city fell, I didn't want to stand out.

On April 9, 2003, the dictatorship collapsed, and the Iraqi army melted away without firing a shot. For a time, Kirkuk had the feel of a New Year's Eve party, as strangers greeted each other with *"Piroz bet!"* (congratulations) and exchanged hugs. Graffiti on walls said THANK YOU, BOSH AND BLEAR [*sic*], and people were dancing in the streets. Jubilant crowds pulled down a statue of Saddam in a Kirkuk square and beat it to pieces for the news cameras. There was no need for a disguise.

The celebration was short-lived. In the year I'd been away, a wave of bloodletting had descended on Kirkuk. Dozens of Kurds, Arabs, and Turkmen had been killed, and saboteurs had repeatedly blown up the oil pipelines. A few months earlier, a Kurdish friend of mine who'd been working for ABC News as a cameraman was shot in Kirkuk during a street protest. ABC had flown him to Germany for a series of operations, and now, in May 2004, he was recuperating in Sulaimaniah. He told me to be careful when I visited. Like the disputed cities of Kosovo and Sarajevo, Kirkuk had become a tinderbox of ethnic tension.

The stakes in Kirkuk had always been high. Iraq had the second-largest supply of proven oil reserves in the world, and Kirkuk's fields produced one out of every five barrels of oil. Bubbling beneath the city and its outskirts were an estimated seven billion barrels of the black gold, roughly the same amount as Prudhoe Bay during the Alaskan oil rush of the 1970s. Future control of the oil fields depended on the long-contested issue of which of Kirkuk's discordant ethnic groups could prove it had the greatest population.

In the 1920s, when British Petroleum made the first oil strikes in Kirkuk, the British estimated that the Kurds held the majority. The last official census, conducted in 1957, found 48 percent Kurd, 28 percent Arab, 21 percent Turkmen, and 3 percent Christian. However, a half century of Arabization in Kirkuk by successive Iraqi regimes had left a legacy of ethnic cleansing and manipulated census figures. The Kurds claimed that 800,000 Kurds had been displaced by the regime, 150,000 alone from Kirkuk. According to the Kurdistan Regional Government, all the refugees had the right of return. Arabs maintained they were being intimidated to leave the city, and an especially nasty dispute was building between Kurds and Turkmen. "Saddam tried to Arabize the city," said Yousef Kemal Yaschili, a Turkmen member of the city council, "and now the Kurds are trying to *Kurdicize* it."

Assassination

On the morning Karzan drove us to Kirkuk, a city councilman named Hiwa Najib Mohammed Amin was headed to his office with his wife. As they emerged from their home, they were met with a fusillade of bullets. Amin's wife survived, but Amin and his bodyguard died instantly. The four killers escaped in a new yellow taxi. Amin was the second Arab member of the Kirkuk council gunned down in three weeks. It was 8:00 A.M.

The Kirkuk mayor, Abdul Rahman Mustafa, had invited Mike and me to visit the council. Had we come a day earlier, it is likely we would have met Amin. Instead, we drove to the cemetery, where hundreds of Kurds, Arabs, and Turkmen hastily gathered in the hot sun for his funeral. Amin's body, wrapped in a simple white sheet, arrived in the back of an old Datsun pickup. He had only been dead for four hours, but the windshields of the truck and other vehicles in the cortege were already plastered with leaflets proclaiming him a martyr. Arab mourners carried the corpse over their heads, laying it in the freshly dug grave on a dusty hillside. They covered the body with rocks, for protection, and filled the hole.

It was noontime, but already the temperature was almost one hundred degrees, and the mourners were sweating. The crowd pressed forward, trampling other graves to hear the speakers. The Kurdish mayor gave a long and impassioned eulogy for his Arab colleague. I watched a man nearby me sink slowly to his knees from shock or heat exhaustion, steadying himself on an old tombstone. A woman next to me thrust her hands to the sky, alternately shrieking and pulling hair from her head.

City Council

That afternoon, we visited the mayor and Kirkuk council. The Kurds held thirteen of the forty seats on the governing body. The remaining seats were divided among Arabs, Turkmen, and Christians. The city hall was far from the kind of approachable municipal center in the States, where residents bring zoning issues or complaints about barking dogs. Visitors in Kirkuk entered a compound fortified by blast walls, sandbags, and concertina wire. The offices functioned in a bubble of intense security, surrounded by U.S. troops, tanks, and Bradley Fighting Vehicles. It was hard to avoid the sense of a besieged local government surviving at the will of occupation forces.

When we arrived, the mayor was watching an al-Jazeera news report of a suicide bombing that had taken place that morning in Baghdad. The attack, which had killed several, prompted him to discuss what he saw as the central drawback of the American attempt to install democracy in the new Iraq. "The biggest mistake the U.S. made," he said, "was to allow the media to be free. The media highlights the *bad*," he added. "When people see shooting on television, it encourages more attacks."

I asked him who was responsible for Amin's murder. "Maybe Arabs," he said. "Maybe Turkmen."

The assistant mayor, Hassib Rozbayani, a Turkmen, had an even broader theory. "Maybe Ba'athists," he said. "Maybe terrorists, maybe Kurds."

Ishmael al-Hadidi, an Arab member of the council, tried to dodge the question altogether, provoking laughter from his colleagues. He said the killers were "Not Turkmen, not Kurdish, and not Arab."

"Well," I said jokingly, "Maybe the *Irish* are to blame. Some people say they've done a lot of killing!" Everyone laughed again.

The Turkmen Front, the most radical of the Turkmen parties, held eight Turkmen seats on the council. The Kurds claim the Front is funded by Turkish intelligence. On July 4, 2003, a few months after the toppling of the Iraqi regime, the U.S. Army incurred Ankara's wrath by arresting a dozen Turkish army officers who were suspected of supplying weapons to the Turkmen Front in Kirkuk, a charge the Front denied. The Turkish officers—fellow NATO colleagues—were handcuffed, hooded, and taken to a prison in Baghdad. Soon after, they were deported to Turkey, where news of their treatment provoked anti-American protests.

Ali Melidi Sadik, a Front member on the council, displayed a sign in English in his office. It read, WITHOUT RIGHTS FOR THE TURKMEN, WE REJECT THE CONSTITUTION. Sadik told me that Turkmen make up more than 50 percent of Kirkuk's one million residents. He expressed anger at American occupiers, whom he blamed for the underrepresentation of Turkmen on the council.

Sadik claimed that during the 1940s the British hired "90 percent Turkmen" to work in the oil fields and that nonresident Kurdish workers were imported from other locations. "Look at the names of the roads and the streets," he said. "They're in Turkish." I really couldn't follow Sadik's suggestion—not, at least, in any scientific way—any more than I could count all the Kurdish names on cemetery tombstones before 1957, the year of the last official census, a suggestion proposed by a local Kurd.

Sadik said that the Kurds were trying to delay a new census in Kirkuk to buy time for the Internally Displaced Persons (IDPs) to return, which would skew the population count in their favor. A Kurdish councilman, Ahmad Askari, agreed that the Kurds intended to count as many IDPs as possible. Askari claimed that three hundred thousand Kurds had been forced out of Kirkuk since 1968, twice the estimate offered by the Kurdistan Regional Government. He said the Iraqi regime had done an unofficial census in 1997. "After all the ethnic cleansing, the city was 41 percent Arab, 37 percent Kurd, and 21 percent Turkmen."

Askari conceded the Turkmen population had seen a rise in 1998, but he attributed the increase to Turkey's offer of food at that time to Turkmen in Kirkuk suffering from international sanctions against Iraq. "The free food was a Turkish trick," he said. "A lot of people wrote 'Turkmen' on the forms only because they were hungry." A reliable census could not be conducted in Iraq, he said, until the "anarchy" subsided. Meanwhile, he said, the IDPs were streaming back to Kirkuk, which he referred to as "the Jerusalem of Kurdistan."

It seemed that the only thing the Kirkuk politicians agreed on was criticism of the occupation. Abdul Rahman Mustafa predicted that the United States would fail to duplicate American-style democracy in Iraq. "The Iraqis have lived under dictatorship so long," he said, "that they don't know what they want." He compared the people to a wounded bird. "They have been in prison for thirty-five years—how can you expect them to come out and fly right away? A different solution [other than democracy] is needed here."

Tahsin Kahya, a moderate Turkmen and chairman of the Kirkuk council, was angered by the recent U.S. decision to give key military posts to ex-Ba'athists. He mentioned the name of an Iraqi commander the coalition had just removed after learning of his record of abuse under the regime. "This was not a clean hand," Kahya said. "It was a dirty hand, so the U.S.A. had to change him." The problem, he argued, was the lack of any postinvasion plan. "They came here without details of Iraqi life," he said. "The U.S.A. is working in Iraq like a *training field*, doing trial and error."

It was time to go. One of the Turkmen gave me a business card with his e-mail. I noticed the address began with *cankerkuk.* In Turkish, that means "the heart of Kirkuk."

Ahmad Askari, the Kurdish councilman, invited us to accompany him on a visit of the oil fields outside of town. On the way, we passed an overflowing trash dumpster with a sign in Kurdish that said PUT YOUR GARBAGE HERE. Askari told us the Turkmen Front was encouraging followers to throw trash on the ground whenever they saw signs in Kurdish. I had no way of knowing whether the story was true or false. Either way, it was a snapshot of the mutual distrust in Kirkuk.

E-mail addresses and litter signs were just symptoms. This was a fight that went beyond language or identity: Kirkuk was about resources and power.

Oil and Refugees

On the way back to town, we stopped at the former Saddam Hussein Soccer Stadium. Hundreds of IDP families were camped inside the huge sports arena, their wash hung on seats and their cook fires glowing in the early evening. Across from the stadium, hundreds more squatters made their homes in tents in a garbage-strewn field. Children were playing by an open sewer, and they flocked to us as we walked in from the road. A few belonged to Hassiba Abdullah and his wife. They had ten kids, and the large family had lived in a tent for the past seven years. When Abdullah learned our nationality, he said, "Thank you, America. You brought us home to our land."

One Kurd introduced himself as Fagradhin Abdullah. He acted as if he knew me. The refugee and his family had abandoned their house during the Kirkuk uprising in 1991. He said he had been twenty-eight at the time. When they returned, their home had been taken by a *jash,* a Kurdish collaborator. "Don't you remember me?" he finally asked. No, I apologized, I did not. "You came to our tent in Penjuin, in the mountains, in 1991 a few weeks after the uprising," he said. "You took photos of my mother," he added. "She is a *shahid* now."

The Penjuin visit was thirteen years in the past, but they were still refugees. I could hardly believe the coincidence of meeting him again.

Another Kurd, a man whose name was Hamih Fatah, told us he had four children, but he had a heart condition and earned only $20 a week as a part-time laborer. "But this is my town," he said. "My father and my grandfather are buried here."

It was getting dark, and the refugees were tending to the final chores of the day. We watched a woman smoking a hand-rolled cigarette as she made dinner for her kids. I recognized the harsh, yellow Iraqi tobacco, a favorite of poor Kurds and Arabs. One of the children in her tent, a teenaged boy, had a skull injury from an accident. She told me she needed money to take him to a brain specialist. The injury happened a few months earlier, the day Saddam was captured. People in Kirkuk were celebrating, firing their guns in the air. She said, "a bullet from the sky" had fallen on his head. It seemed like another heartache in a squalid camp.

The squatters' environment—their *home*—provided a stark contrast between people and resources. The tents sat on top of one of the world's most coveted prizes: oil, a source of conflict and profit for Iraqis and foreigners for almost a century. The oil derricks themselves were less than a mile away. We could see them silhouetted against the night sky, fire leaping from the top of the rigs, the natural gas that never stopped burning.

It made me wonder what the future had in store for the refugees and for the wandering Kurds in general. Iraq's "eternal flame," as everyone called it, was bright, and it held out such promise for so many. Near and far, they all wanted a share of its wealth.

34

Spies and Blame

When the wolf is hungry, you don't know what he will do.

—KURDISH PROVERB

It was May 3, 2004, the sixteenth anniversary of the gas attack on Goktapa. My friend Shalaw Askeri sent bodyguards and an SUV to the Ashti Hotel to pick up Mike and me for a memorial ceremony. The car was a big Chevy Suburban that had belonged to Iraqi intelligence before the war. Shalaw said he'd bought it cheap at a Baghdad auction after the fall of the regime. "I wondered how many prisoners had ridden inside," he said. "The first thing I did was to check the carpets for bloodstains."

According to Dr. Fuad Baban, a British-trained internist from Sulaimaniah, Goktapa was one of some 280 sites where chemical weapons had been used against the Kurds. An estimated five thousand people died at Halabja. Some four hundred people were killed at Goktapa.

About two hundred local Kurds attended the ceremony in the rocky grave-yard, which sits on a plateau above the mud village and a nearby slow-moving river. The graves of the victims, many of them children, were marked with jagged pieces of upturned shale. A weathered alabaster sculpture about fifteen feet high stood at one end of the graveyard. It was the giant face of a man twisted in pain, a mouth agape, the muted cries of agony unheard. Below the alabaster face were sculptures of dead villagers, a cow, a sheep, birds, and a snake. Shalaw said he had lobbied to have the memorial built. He spoke of the tragedy as if it had just happened. "The date was May 3, 1989," he said. "It was a sunny spring morning, and they died in a heap."

Residents of lesser-known venues where chemical attacks occurred are sensitive to the international attention that Halabja received in the run-up to the U.S. invasion. Some Goktapa locals told me they were angry that no top PUK officials were on hand for the 2004 anniversary as they had been in previous years.

By the time the invited guests had spoken, a storm had gathered and it was raining lightly. The mourners thinned out, leaving a few Kurdish women in the cemetery. One of them—I was told she was the mother of a six-year-old boy who had died in the attack—lingered at a small mound of dirt. The wind picked up, and she and the others wrapped black shawls around their shoulders and wound their way down a dirt path to the village.

Shalaw has a country home in Goktapa, a renovated horse stable overlooking the river. We followed him there for lunch, kicking off our shoes in the concrete vestibule and joining the male guests sitting cross-legged on the floor. The women and children ate elsewhere, according to custom, and the bodyguards kept watch in the rain outside, where several Land Cruisers were parked.

Shalaw drove us back to our hotel in the former police SUV. As we rode along the highway, the main artery between Kirkuk and Sulaimaniah, I was reminded how the Kurdish movement since World War I sometimes seems like *Groundhog Day*, with repeating scenes of struggle and betrayal. In the 1930s, during the British occupation of Iraq, Sheikh Mahmud, the legendary Kurdish rebel, was ambushed and wounded by Crown forces on the same road. Some say the attack came after informers supplied his whereabouts.

In 1993, Shalaw himself was ambushed on this road by rival KDP fighters. He showed us the spot where attackers fired from their hiding place, wounding him and several other PUK members in his car. That brought up the subject of the earlier factional clashes between Kurdish groups in Iraq. He spoke again about his famous father, Ali Askeri, a leader of the nascent PUK in the 1970s, who was executed by the KDP.

When I had seen him in 2003, Shalaw had the post of PUK minister of agriculture. He was a rising star in the party, a favorite of leaders like Barham Salih and PUK founder Jalal Talabani. Just recently, however, he had quit Kurdish politics. I asked him why. The answer came as a shock: His famous family, the Askeris, had been accused of collaboration with the Baghdad regime back in the 1970s. The charges surfaced after the invasion, when the Kurds obtained Iraqi police files. Shalaw said the accusations were false, but that PUK leader Talabani had chosen not to defend him. Back in the 1970s, Shalaw would have been a teenager or preteen, presumably too young to have been guilty of such acts—had they occurred. I was curious whether any of the intelligence files were more recent, but I didn't have the heart to press the matter. He said he had resigned from the party in disgust.

Over the years I had seen people and movements betray each other, but I also knew of instances where false accusations were used as political weapons. The charges against my friend Shalaw saddened me. There was no way I could evaluate them. What I didn't realize was that I was in for an even bigger shock from someone else.

Kaka Hama

The next day we were invited to a lavish lunch hosted by Kaka Hama and his Kurdistan Socialist Party. The meal was held at his mountain redoubt at Gulla Hana, the verdant valley near the Iranian border. I found myself seated at the same table where I'd dined in 2002 with the Socialist leader and Pishtiwan, his twenty-two-year-old son, a few days before the young man died from an accidental, self-inflicted gunshot. Gulla Hana had been my vantage point in the war for the massive U.S. bombing of Ansar al-Islam and the final assault on militants by Kurdish *peshmerga* and Special Forces. I used to sit there on a concrete wall, listening to BBC reports of the B-52s taking off from England. We knew from experience that seven or so hours after the bombers' takeoff, the windows at Gulla Hana would rattle and the earth around us shake.

Kaka Hama welcomed my return, pointing through a window to a nearby hillside, which was ablaze with *nergis,* the yellow wildflowers that are depicted in the center of the Kurdish flag. I recalled the winter of 2003, when the nearby snowcapped mountains gave the spot the look of a picture postcard from the Alps. In the past, Kaka Hama had joked about my retiring someday to Kurdistan, offering to let me build a dream house on the site.

"It is still waiting for you," he said with a smile.

After lunch, Mike and I followed Kaka Hama to a small parlor for a private talk over tea and fruit. I noted the lack of ashtrays in the room. Recently, the Socialists had banned smoking in their offices. It was the first such prohibition I'd seen in Kurdistan.

I had come to talk. I had heard painful rumors about Rizgar, an ex-official of the Socialist party whom I'd hired at ABC as my translator and fixer during the war. Rizgar had an independent perspective, one that was outside of the two-party system in Kurdistan, and I liked him. Some of his English wasn't all that good—including words such as *horny* and *lousy,* which he'd picked up from TV—but his connections and political analysis were great. Reporters Chris Chivers and Jeff Fleishman had also relied on him as a source, and Rizgar, who coined the name "Irish Lobby," was often privy to meetings in our hotel rooms. After the regime fell, as I was preparing to return to the States, Rizgar gave me a special going-away gift, a pair of *kalash,* the famous handmade Kurdish shoes.

Rizgar's family often invited me for home-cooked meals, and I was in a position to know his background better than other reporters. We had traveled many hundreds of miles together, sleeping next to each other on drafty floors of random buildings and eating the same food on the tailgate of our Land Cruiser. We shared interviews, documents, and most—but not all—sources. I hadn't shared with him my ABC story on the Iraqi scientists, but we had been through a lot together. We'd been shot at on a road near Kirkuk and we'd recoiled together at the sight of body parts after suicide bombings near Halabja.

The last time I'd seen Rizgar was in Tikrit, after American troops captured Saddam's presidential palace. I had photographed him in front of the dictator's ornate home, next to three U.S. soldiers posing with their M-16s. The picture captured an early moment of American triumph in Iraq. I had enlarged a copy for Rizgar and brought it back for him as a souvenir. The palaces were off-limits to visitors nowadays, and I expected he'd be pleased with the memento.

Kaka Hama was fingering his prayer beads with one hand. He stirred a tiny glass of tea with the other. "Rizgar was a *jasus* [spy]," he announced softly. "I was angry when I found out, but I told him I wouldn't kill him. Even when we were in the mountains, I was against executing a *jasus*. I always believed they could be changed."

Before the war, the Iraqi *mukhabarat* were said to have had a network of 450,000 agents and informers throughout the country. I knew the secret agency kept meticulous records on its victims, as well as on the "helpers"—even those who had provided little or no information. In one police station captured during the war, I had seen files on some individuals with as few as one or two entries.

But *Rizgar?* How could he have helped the dictatorship at all?

I couldn't believe it. This time, I wanted proof.

Kaka Hama said that after the fall of the regime, each of the political parties had received several boxes of police documents pertaining to its own members. "It was a big shock to people. Sometimes wives and husbands didn't know about each other. Sometimes one informed on the other."

"Come to Sulaimaniah tomorrow," he said. "We have the files."

The next afternoon I went to his office, but he was busy with constituents. A delegation had just arrived from Khanikin, an oil-rich city whose control—like that of Kirkuk—had become a bone of contention between Kurds and Arabs. The visitors were sitting around a large Persian carpet in the reception room, drinking Diet Pepsi and voicing complaints about the occupation. They were angry with the PUK, the controlling party, for not allowing the IDPs—internally displaced persons—to reclaim their houses from Arab families. By now, some Arab families had lived in Khanikin for more than a generation, but the Americans were pressuring the Kurdish authorities to keep the IDPs from returning to Khanikin and Kirkuk until a census could be updated. Adequate housing and jobs were needed for returning refugees, as well as funds to relocate Arab families.

Kaka Hama praised those displaced residents who rushed back after the toppling of Saddam to retake their homes. "You must teach your children that the little we have for ourselves today is because of the blood of our people," he said. "We want no more than the Arabs or Turkmen or Iranians—only what is rightfully ours. The days ahead will be hard, and you must teach your children not just Kurdish history and poetry, but exactly where their lands are."

"We are allies of the U.S.A." he said, "and America's only true friend in the region. But we don't know if the U.S.A. really regards us as allies." To underscore his point, he cited a letter from a U.S. Army colonel demanding that the Socialists give up their weapons. Kaka Hama said he had refused to relinquish the arms, but had agreed to talk with the American officer. "I told him that the PUK and the KDP were not the only Kurdish parties and that the Socialists had fought for twenty-seven years. Saddam's plan was to clean the Kurds from the map. I don't understand how [America] can come here without knowing our history."

"Look at what happened to the Transitional Administrative Law," he continued. He was referring to the 2004 act that gave the Kurds—or any three other Iraqi governates—a joint veto over proposed legislation in the country. The Kurds had argued that it was a way to prevent "tyranny by the majority"—a reference to the Shiites—and the United States had supported the act. However, the veto power was temporarily dropped after the Grand Ayatollah Ali al-Sistani, the Shiite cleric, pressured occupation powers.

Kaka Hama favored a binational state, Kurdish and Arabic. He was worried that the Kurds could lose autonomy in the new Iraq. "Kurdish land is different from Sunni or Shia land. The economy is different here and our race is different. The areas must be separated."

What Kaka Hama was preaching was the diametric opposite of the official position of the major Kurdish parties. Regardless of private misgivings, the KDP and the PUK officials had declared their support for being, as they said, "Iraqis first," and they were doing their best to downplay loose talk of separation. Turkey wouldn't permit such discussion without the threat of invasion. The Kurds needed to stay in the good graces of their protector, the United States.

"We want federalism," Kaka Hama continued, "but our friend America won't support us. During *Newroz*, the Kurdish New Year, the U.S. made us take down the Kurdish flag." I understood his position, but by then I had seen so many Kurdish flags flying that any attempt to reduce their display seemed like a lost cause, even if it provoked the Turks to invade or led to a civil war. The word on the Kurdish street was independence.

The constituents were taking their time, and my mind returned to Rizgar. I thought of his father, a quiet man who taught English at a local elementary school. Despite his job title, the man had a poor command of the language, and our conversation in English was stuck at the "How are you?" level. According to Rizgar, he received only a small salary for his efforts, not enough to feed the family. Rizgar's younger brother worked as a "de-miner" for one of the NGOs, clearing land mines in Kurdistan. It was dangerous work, but he was the main breadwinner in the house, and everyone looked up to him. He made $180 a month, good pay locally, although he sometimes complained that the United Nations paid the local contractor $600 a month for the same services.

Rizgar had an older sister who years before had dreamed of going to Rome to start a career. I remember his telling me of the difficult time she had getting out of Iraq, but it had all turned out well. Now she had a good job in Italy, and every month she sent money home to the family. Rizgar seemed to have a special bond with her, and his facial expression softened when he mentioned her name.

When the visitors left, Kaka Hama brought out two dog-eared files. He laid them on a desk in the reception room, spreading out a dozen documents. The information was in Arabic, but the telltale eagle of Saddam's regime was stamped on every sheet. Rizgar's photo was there, all right, along with receipts for money, as well as copies of his sister's Iraqi passport with the visa giving her permission to leave for Italy.

I felt the hair stand up on the back of my neck.

"A Little Dirty"

I photographed the files. The next day, I called the mobile phone I'd given Rizgar as a gift when I'd left the country the year before. It was a Friday, family day, and everyone in his house was just leaving for the countryside. The family would love to see me again. Could I join them for a picnic?

No, I said, but I did need to talk. The next morning, Rizgar came to the Ashti Hotel.

It was distasteful stuff, and I'd feared he might deny everything or explode in rage, thinking, correctly, that he'd been lowered in my eyes.

"Why did you quit the Socialists?' I asked him.

"You might say I was 'backing the wrong horse,' " he said, using a colloquialism.

"Saddam?"

"No, the Socialists."

If he was ashamed, he handled it well. "I am not the only one," he said calmly. "Maybe Kaka Hama didn't know everything I was doing, but his advisors did. I went to Baghdad secretly, but I was an official representative of our party. All the Kurdish parties played the same game. They tried to get ahead of each other by making secret contacts in Baghdad. Every one of them kept a back channel to the regime, right up until the end. The Socialists got money from Saddam, just the way the PUK and the KDP did at other times. Don't forget that Saddam supported Talabani against the KDP, when the KDP was stronger. Then in 1996, when the PUK was stronger, the KDP invited Saddam's troops to Erbil, and they helped Barzani get the city back from the PUK."

Rizgar told me he had taken steps to protect himself before he left the Socialists. He said he had photocopied material implicating top members of his party, although not Kaka Hama. "If they want to make something out of this, I have my own files."

Rizgar said he was studying accounting now, hoping for better opportunities "with democracy in the new Iraq." Now that Saddam was gone, he said, "Everyone was pretending, smiling as if nothing had ever happened." In his view, Saddam could not have exerted his appalling brand of control without a lot of cooperation—at home and abroad. He said many of the new smiles looked a little rotten—"like the face of a fish that has been dead too long."

"We were all a little dirty," he said.

Rizgar left the hotel, and I remained at the table, stunned and saddened by the conversation. I had wanted to ask my old translator whether he had ever passed on information about ABC News or me to the Iraqi police, but the question was irrelevant now, and would only have exaggerated my importance.

Instead, Rizgar's rationalization sent me careening into the quagmire of collective responsibility. Who was primarily to blame for the enormity of evil represented by the Iraqi regime? Certainly, Saddam Hussein had killed untold tens, if not hundreds, of thousands. His sons Uday and Qusay had committed more than their share of heinous crimes, as well. Undoubtedly the dictator and his major accomplices would receive their just desserts at trial, but what about low-ranking guards in the prisons, the ones who tortured Iraqi citizens suspected of conspiring against the regime? If the guards who directly administered electrodes to the tongues, breasts, or genitals of prisoners were unambiguously "dirty," what of the informants who assisted the police in bringing those unlucky people to torture? What about Iraqis who had a chance to resist in some small and safe way, but chose not to get involved? What of the prisoners who weakened under the beatings, strangulations, electrocutions, and the like, whose testimony led to the deaths of their co-conspirators? Were they, too, at least partly accountable for the tyranny that reigned in Iraq—or did the threat of torture absolve them of responsibility for supplying information?

In the past, I'd always had the luxury to believe that a spy was a spy and an informer was an informer. It may have been an easy position to hold in a morally elevated society like the United States, where few are faced with such stark choices. Yet the potential for "passive citizenship"—the determination at all costs not to rock the boat—was not confined to totalitarian states. Wasn't it possible in a democracy to betray the community, albeit in a quieter and less dramatic way, by failing to actively engage in issues crucial to the common good? How often were citizens in the West faced with an official but misdirected policy that called for them to choose between their conscience and complicity with wrongful acts?

Say, for example, when their taxes went to prop up an antidemocratic regime like Iraq or to support weapons makers who enriched themselves by doing business with autocratic governments? In Saddam's Iraq, only a miniscule percentage of people dared to resist, understandably, by word or action. In a democracy, where there should be no such fear of speaking out, it is often the case that only a relative few are willing to do so. In both instances, whether out of fear or apathy, it may be easier simply to look the other way.

Rizgar was "a little dirty," all right. But his self-serving behavior paled by comparison to the actions of scores of international corporations that profited from contracts with Saddam Hussein. Might the makers of the weapons used to kill the Kurds and others bear at least partial responsibility for what took place in Iraq? What about President Jacques Chirac of France, who had helped Saddam build nuclear reactors, the Italians who exported plutonium-separation equipment to Iraq, or the Russians who'd traded arms for oil? What about precedent-setting Churchill's advocacy of using "poison gas against uncivilised tribes" in Iraqi Kurdistan? What about the Reagan-Bush administration that opposed imposing trade sanctions against Iraq after the Kurds were gassed in 1988? What about European arms merchants who smuggled weapons to Iraq even *after* the U.N. embargo in 1991? What about Halliburton and other U.S. companies that made billions in the 1990s by trading with the enemy? And what about Bechtel envoy Donald Rumsfeld, who befriended Saddam Hussein in the early 1980s in the hopes of striking a deal for an oil pipeline across Iraq?

Were they all "a little dirty," too?

The evil acts in Iraq seemed complex and ambiguous, but there was little doubt their existence depended on massive international collaboration. As the war crimes tribunals geared up, with hopes for a cathartic wiping clean of the moral slate, the lessons of the recent past cried out for attention. Prosecutors said that Saddam Hussein's crimes had cost the lives of two million people. Atrocities like those committed against the Kurds and others, however, were likely to be repeated elsewhere, by and against others, if the wider context for these crimes—including the key question of aiders and abettors—was ignored. Hussein's victims deserved a full accounting of what had taken place in Iraq, and citizens of western democracies needed to learn the truth about assistance given the regime in their name. Would the tribunals pursue that wider inquiry, or would they seek to punish Saddam Hussein and his immediate accomplices, while they absolved everyone else?

35

The Dodger

He went away all broken up, and he came back
looking like . . . a gentleman.

—NIZAR, A PUK OFFICIAL ON KARZAN MAHMOUD

Driving in 2004

All week long Karzan had been buying us meals and small gifts, acting as our official guide, and chauffeuring us around in his old VW Passat. Now, when we needed a four-wheel drive car to go Halabja, he decided that was his responsibility, too.

Karzan hadn't driven for Barham Salih since the assassination attempt. The week of our visit, Salih was away in Washington for talks. The United States was preparing to hand sovereignty to the Iraqis, and the Kurds were assured high-profile jobs in the new government in Baghdad. Hoshyar Zebari, the KDP official I'd tangled with over my footage of the secret airfield, would represent the Kurds at the United Nations. Barham, the amiable Kurdish populist with the British accent, would soon be sworn in as deputy prime minister in Iraq's transitional government. When that appointment expired, he would become Iraq's minister of reconstruction, an enormous challenge in a country that continued to bleed from the war. Much had changed since our late-night visits for wine and political talk in the anxious run-up to the U.S. invasion, but Salih had taken time to drop me an e-mail from Washington, and I suspected he was the reason that Karzan showed up one day in a new Toyota Land Cruiser, a car usually driven by Salih's bodyguards.

Now Karzan was back at the wheel of the boss's car, and we were underway, just like the old days. We headed to Halabja on the paved road, a route I'd been unable to take during my seven months in northern Iraq the year before, due to attacks by Ansar al-Islam. There were still government roadblocks on the highway, but the *peshmerga* recognized the new SUV with the smoked windows and waved us around the checkpoints. Karzan loved it. He beeped the horn as he bypassed the queues of waiting cars, joking with charm and bravado that he was a big man once again.

I was in the front of the SUV in the passenger seat, riding shotgun. The last bodyguard to use the car had left a MP5 9 mm submachine gun on the floor, and occasionally I could feel it bouncing around by my feet. The MP5, according to its maker, Heckler and Koch, is the "weapon of choice for antiterrorist teams . . . a highly accurate weapon, ideal for close combat situations." The U.S. Marines use the MP5 for their Security Force Battalions, and the FBI equips its Hostage Rescue Team with the same weapon.

It was now more than two years since Karzan had been wounded. In the meantime, PUK security had been revamped. A second dormitory for body-guards had been built next door, and the streets, the ones in front of and behind the house, had been closed. Barham's security details had upgraded their arsenal. These days, they carried MP5s like the one that lay at my feet. Despite a hefty price tag—$1,000 each—the MP5s gave the Kurdish guards weapons parity with their European and American counterparts.

The SUV smelled of Karzan's favorite brand of cologne, a French knockoff smuggled in from Iran and sold in the local market. Karzan sat at the controls of the Land Cruiser, smiling and clearly satisfied. His American friends had needed a car, and this was his treat, a small but meaningful way to repay the dramatic U.S. visit that had restored so much of his health. Karzan had been smitten with the experience, and his new affinity for things American was obvious from his wardrobe. Gone was the shiny three-piece suit he had worn almost daily on his first trip to the States. Now he was decked out in a blue jean jacket and Dock-ers chinos, a brand only recently available in Kurdistan. He sported silk socks imported from China and a pair of oversized wingtips from the local market that he called his "Popeye" shoes. "Where is my *spinach?*" he asked, grinning.

The Kurds, I thought to myself, might be the only clear winner in the chaos of post-Saddam Iraq, at least in the short run. I glanced at our happy driver, notic-ing for the first time his pink Italian shirt with the manufacturer's monogram on the pocket. It was a copy of one I'd seen worn by a program director in the coali-tion office where Karzan worked as a part-time driver. With his new wraparound sunglasses and a baseball cap that said "Triple Canopy," the private security firm hired by the coalition, Karzan had taken on the rigorously casual look of the Americans, his new associates.

Triple Canopy and Guns for Hire

Karzan's employer, Triple Canopy, was based in Chicago (at that time), but the security firm had upwards of one thousand armed guards under contract in Iraq. According to its Web site, the company provided "legal, moral, and ethical Special Operations services consistent with U.S. National Security interests." Triple

Canopy was one of dozens of firms that had received multimillion dollar contracts in a burgeoning private security business, underwritten in part by Congress's passage of the $87 billion Iraq Reconstruction Act. Some of the companies were start-ups, but many already had a lucrative list of established government and private clients. A year after the stated end of major hostilities, they were capitalizing on the dangerous—and spreading—chaos. In the words of a *New York Times* story, they had "struck gold in the lawless frontier of Iraq."

Some companies required their personnel to have military experience, including the London-based firm Pilgrims, the outfit ABC News hired to guard staffers in Baghdad. ABC paid Pilgrims $5,000 a day for five guards. The company, in turn, paid the guards, all former SAS commandos in the British army, $500 to $800 each per day.

The security costs were in addition to paying for the five armored SUVs ABC kept inside its two-block, heavily guarded compound. Pilgrims had modified the cars, adding high-performance tires, bulletproof windows, and other equipment. Each month, the company arranged to have the vehicles spray painted with a new, dull color that did not attract attention. The aim, according to one bodyguard, was "to keep the opposition guessing."

Lex, one of the Pilgrims' security men who guarded me in Baghdad in the spring of 2004, told me that most of his colleagues were veterans of the war with the IRA. He claimed the job similarities between Belfast and Baghdad outweighed the differences ("same meat, different gravy," he said). I knew something of the risks and conflict in Northern Ireland. But I had to believe that he was downplaying—for the sake of his clients—the far greater dangers of working in Iraq.

In March 2004, the so-called risk management firms in Iraq made front-page news when four employees of Blackwater USA were killed in Fallouja and their bodies defiled. The Pentagon wouldn't say how many private guards had been hired to provide security in Iraq, but the number was mushrooming, and some estimates exceeded twenty thousand—more than twice the number of regular troops contributed by Britain to the U.S.-led coalition. Critics complained that hiring these modern soldiers of fortune came at a price to American taxpayers. While it saved the government from paying pensions and other benefits, the outsourcing of security lacked accountability for potential crimes committed abroad by private contractors. Unlike soldiers, the gun-toting guards were not subject to court martial or other forms of military justice. In one publicized incident a few years earlier in Somalia, an American security guard who was a suspect in a rape investigation had avoided detention by local authorities when his U.S. firm simply put him on a plane and shipped him back to the States.

Indians in Iraq

Six weeks after the killings in Fallouja, Mike and I landed at the Baghdad air-port, a facility guarded by a different security firm. After deplaning, we crossed the hot tarmac to the Babylon terminal, a glistening but nearly empty building, where two Iraqis with U.S. security badges were mopping and remopping the floor.

A private American guard wearing sunglasses and a baseball cap and carrying an MP5 approached us, asking for our identification. We told him we were mak-ing connections to the Kurdish area in northern Iraq and showed him our pass-ports. The guard's pant legs were stuffed into combat boots, army style, and he wore a blue golf shirt with CUSTER BATTLES stitched in white letters. The logo conjured up images of familiar—but long-forgotten—conflicts with Native Amer-icans. At first, I guessed that "Custer Battles" was just an unfortunate moniker, not one designed to resonate with Indian history.

I was wrong.

The company founders, according to the airport guard, were two Americans named Custer and Battles. They had met as cadets at West Point. Custer, said the man in the sunglasses, was a relative of another West Pointer, George Armstrong Custer. It seemed astonishing. The founder of Custer Battles, the company con-tracted by the Pentagon to guard the besieged Baghdad airport, was directly re-lated to the famous general killed in 1876 at the Battle of the Little Bighorn—the man the Lakota called "Yellow Hair," probably the most reviled figure in Ameri-can Indian history.

It made me stop and think.

The so-called Indian Wars took place a century or more before scandals like My Lai, Abu Ghraib, and Guantanamo. The Geneva Conventions did not apply. There was no recognized code of conduct to investigate the alleged distribution of smallpox-infected blankets—a crude form of biological warfare—by soldiers. Nor were there accepted doctrines of human rights to judge the Trail of Tears, the massacres at Sand Creek and Wounded Knee, or abuses committed in small Dakota villages by Custer's men as they guided gold miners into the Black Hills, a territory Congress had set aside by treaty for exclusive Indian use.

By the same token, there were no accepted rules in place to evaluate war crimes committed by Native Americans. Had the word "terrorist" been a part of the lexi-con at the time, reporters probably would have applied it to brutal acts of Indian resistance. A derogatory term for Indian people in those days was "savages," and reporters frequently used it, without apology, to describe the U.S. enemy. The us-age was entirely unremarkable. The founding documents of the republic itself re-flected the same language, if not the same viewpoint. A hundred years before Custer's time, the expression "Indian Savages" had been enshrined in the Declaration of Independence: ". . . merciless Indian Savages, whose known rule of warfare is an undistinguished destruction of all ages, sexes, and conditions . . ."

The defiling of the Blackwater securitymen's corpses at Fallouja, Iraq, was shocking but hardly without precedent.

During efforts to subdue American Indians, scalping and severing body parts was a common practice—on both sides. After the defeat of the Seventh Cavalry at the Little Bighorn in 1876, Sioux and Arapaho women, among others, went onto the battlefield to cut up the dead and to loot their belongings. The women pierced eardrums of the fallen with sewing needles, darkly suggesting it might "improve" their hearing about treaty demands. The mutilation of soldiers' bodies was widely publicized, and news accounts of the battle employed the epithet "savages" to refer to Indians. In 2004, some news stories used the word "terrorists" to describe the insurgents who burned the bodies of military contractors at Fallouja.

William Faulkner was right when he wrote, "The past is never dead. It's not even past." Iraqi insurgents were by no means modern-day Indians—except perhaps to some U.S. soldiers on the front lines. In Najaf, during the 2004 Shiite uprising, U.S. Marines set up a forward operating base (FOB) only a few hundred yards from the Shia holy shrine, naming their outpost "the Apache Hilton." In Karbala, where I was embedded at the time with the U.S. Army, I heard soldiers use the term "Indians" to refer to the armed followers of the rebel cleric Muktada al-Sadr.

The references may have merely been an extension of American sports culture, where teams like the Washington Redskins use pretend Indians as mascots on the sidelines and the fans of the Atlanta Braves make chopping gestures with rubber tomahawks. It is tempting to dismiss such labeling as loose talk signifying nothing, and to reject the notion that a modern and sophisticated society like America is still wrestling with the contradictions of policies that dispossessed the first Americans, but it may be just as tempting to gloss over such contradictions and to treat the history of the American West as a self-serving myth.

Arriving in Baghdad, I was struck by how conscious U.S. weapons makers had become of Indian heritage. During the Vietnam War, the army had used helicopters like the Sioux Scout (Bell) and the Shawnee (Boeing). Today, Tomahawk missiles were just one part of a new and expanded generation of battle equipment named for Native Americans. Parked at Baghdad's gargantuan airport were dozens of Black Hawks. The helicopters were used to ferry troops to and from Camp Victory, the huge American outpost on nearby Route 8, the road from the airport to the city so famous for bomb attacks that the U.S. military dubbed it the "Highway of Death."

Kiowa Warrior observation helicopters and Longbow Apache gunships were landing and taking off from the airport every few minutes. A big Chinook, the transport chopper named for the Indian tribe on the Columbia River in northern Oregon, was parked near the terminal. Only the fearsome, long-anticipated Comanche gunship was missing. A couple of months earlier, the Pentagon had scrapped a high-tech stealth prototype of the Comanche, after billions of dollars and twenty years of research by the Sikorsky corporation. Until then, the Comanche had been touted by the manufacturer as "the world's most advanced helicopter and the cornerstone of the U.S. Army's aviation modernization plan."

I wondered why Indian names were more popular with arms dealers than, say, the names of *other* minorities or nationalities, and why Indian mythology in far-away Iraq still retained a romantic—albeit distorted—grip on the American imagination. The fascination went well beyond sports mascots and mimicked battle whoops. Indian symbols had been deliberately incorporated into modern warfare—even if the enterprise itself was now impersonal and antiseptic. In the late nineteenth century, during the height of the Indian Wars, which drove Native Americans from their lands, many Indian warriors fought with bows and arrows; much of their skill was physical: riding, running, crawling, and hand-to-hand combat. Today's fighters were a different breed, and battles were no longer won by being up close and personal. The soldiers in the Apache helicopters rarely saw the face of the enemy. They were twenty-first-century technicians, targeting foes at a computer screen with the push of a button. In the mythic reality of modern conflict, the Apache gunship itself was a *warrior* in the tradition of Geronimo and the Apache tribe, a people whose fierce resistance to occupation, paradoxically, had long ago been crushed.

In Custer's day the issue was gold, not oil. General Custer came to prominence after the Civil War, during Reconstruction, when times were lean. He made a name for himself in the Dakotas, unlawfully spearheading a gold rush on protected treaty lands. His exploits were popular, justified in the minds of many Americans by Manifest Destiny and a belief that God was on their side. He had hoped to use his victories against the Indians for political gain, and he had planned to attend the 1876 Democratic Convention in St. Louis. Some said he was thinking of running for president.

Custer's legacy was alive today in Iraq, 128 years after his death. Baghdad may have been a long way from the Black Hills of South Dakota, but Custer Battles had cleverly marketed the name of the notorious general to obtain lucrative Pentagon business. In just eighteen months, the colorful start-up had captured $100 million in taxpayer contracts. In early 2004, however, unbeknown to its flamboyant founders, Custer Battles came under investigation for war profiteering. Late that year, the company's luck finally ran out. The U.S. military suspended Custer Battles for fraud and overbilling, including the alleged use of sham companies in Lebanon and the Cayman Islands. Criminal indictments followed, and trials were expected. The namesake of General George Armstrong Custer was faced with his own Battle of the Little Bighorn.

Riding with Karzan

There were things that bothered Karzan about Triple Canopy. Some of the guards had southern accents, which were difficult for him to understand. He didn't like the guys with tattoos "who always say those words" (obscenities). He didn't like being forced to drive aggressively in town, especially when Triple Canopy pressured him to edge other Kurdish drivers to the side of the road. It was easy to be with the guards in the chandeliered lobby of the Palace Hotel, where they hung out drinking cappuccino with wires in their ears and weapons in their laps, but the guards referred to the simplest errand outside the hotel as a "mission," and even trips of a few blocks seemed filled with stress.

The new job, however, had advantages. Triple Canopy paid Karzan $5 a day to chauffeur the foreigners and their weapons. That was good money in Iraq, and working for a group that protected Americans gave him an added measure of prestige with his Kurdish friends. He was using his new connections to try to get out of the country. Karzan's English was still limited, but his boss had written him a strong letter of reference to the U.S. embassy in Jordan, extolling his work as "a movement coordinator for Triple Canopy's Close Protection Team." The letter generously referred to Karzan as a "translator."

For his role as a movement coordinator, Triple Canopy assigned Karzan an air-conditioned Chevy Suburban with blackened windows. Unfortunately, the SUV was "thin skinned"—not armored—so it was a big and vulnerable target. Triple Canopy provided its American staff with Individual Protective Equipment, or IPEs, but the road to Baghdad was littered with Improvised Explosive Devices, popularly known as IEDs. Karzan had no body armor, neither flak jacket nor helmet.

Karzan's most frequent out-of-town destination was the Kirkuk airport, a trip of one hundred miles on a narrow road of patched asphalt, a little more than an hour away at the speeds he drove. The job was dangerous, but it provided access that few Kurds in Iraq enjoyed. Karzan now had an official ID from the Coalition Provisional Authority (CPA). The credential hung from his neck in a see-through pouch, giving him the run of the American-built terminal in Kirkuk. The visits sometimes triggered memories of his trip to the United States. There was a new McDonald's in the fortified compound, the first such franchise in the country. Karzan's eyes lit up when he talked about the "real cheeseburgers."

Dodging

The roads to Kirkuk and Baghdad, which Karzan drove for money, seemed like high-speed gauntlets. When he was alone in the Suburban, his only lifeline was the car's two-way radio, which he used to keep in touch with his base in Sulai-maniah. After a month or so, the Triple Canopy dispatcher, a contractor everybody called the Deuce, gave Karzan a nickname. He christened him the Dodger. The new handle, according to the Deuce, was meant "for security" in radio talk. In any case, the moniker stuck, and after that everyone used it. Karzan liked being the Dodger, and he liked the way the Triple Canopy guys sometimes brought up his story in front of strangers. Unlike most of the security guards, he had had an actual face-to-face encounter with terrorists. In their eyes, Karzan had dodged death.

Triple Canopy sent Karzan to Kirkuk once or twice a week to drop off or pick up bodyguards and periodically dispatched him to Baghdad. After a recent trip to the capital, he brought home a photo of himself standing next to Paul Bremer, the American proconsul. In the photo Karzan and Bremer are standing elbow to elbow, both dressed in tailored blue suits with red neckties. "Karzan big man," he said, proudly handing me the picture. I knew that politicians liked photo ops, but it had never occurred to me that Karzan would find them useful. My friend was learning fast.

When I'd last seen Karzan, he was bidding good-bye to friends in the United States. Just before he left for Iraq, a Kurdish woman in Washington, D.C., gave him $700 cash to deliver to her family in Sulaimaniah. Karzan's trip, however, soon turned into a nightmare—because of his Kurdish ethnicity—and he ended up having to spend her money to get home. His itinerary had called for him to fly to Istanbul and then to take a bus across Turkey to the Iraq border, but when he landed in Istanbul, the Turkish police detained Karzan in the airport, interrogated him for twenty-four hours about Kurdish-related issues, then deported him back to New York. His American visa had expired with his recent departure from the United States and authorities at JFK refused to let him reenter the country.

The prepaid return ticket to Turkey was now worthless and Karzan had little money of his own, so he decided to use the $700 he'd been entrusted with to buy a one-way ticket to Jordan, with a connection onward to Syria. When he landed in Damascus, his plans to travel overland to Iraq were thwarted when he made the mistake of telling an airport policeman that his final destination was *Kurdis-tan*. The officer slapped him across the face, angrily insisting that there was "no such place in the world called 'Kurdistan.'"

Karzan spent another twenty-four hours in the Damascus airport, sometimes drinking cups of "bad color" tea that had far too little sugar for his Kurdish palate. "I do not like tea in Syria," he told me, dwelling more on the unpalatable beverage than on the physical assault.

Syrian police finally decided to return him to Jordan. The member of the *mukhabarat* assigned to accompany him on the plane demanded *baksheesh*, but by that time, Karzan had no money for a bribe. The policeman warned Karzan what awaited him in Jordan: "In two hours, you will go back to the U.S.A. again." When Karzan was turned over to authorities in Amman, his luck suddenly changed. Within an hour, he had convinced the big boss of immigration to give him a transit visa so he could travel by crosscountry bus to Iraq. Did Kurdish ingenuity do the trick? Karzan just laughed. "I am *Dodger*," he said, citing his new nickname.

I began to realize that Karzan had developed the touch of a con man, a skill no doubt honed by a drive to get ahead in spite of his disability. Dodger seemed to fit him perfectly. When he talked about returning to America for more surgery, he dismissed the fact that Mike no longer worked at the Boston hospital where the first operations had been performed. It didn't bother Karzan. He was too busy plotting his grand return to the United States, and he laughed off questions about where additional surgery would take place or who would pay for it. He was resilient, with the new luck of the Kurds, and America was on his side.

Karzan had a charming ability to win over people to his cause—in this case, abandoning a dangerous job and pursuing the American dream. With his puckish grin and the sly way he was able to size up new situations, he resembled a character from Dickens. If this were *Oliver Twist*, Karzan would be our Artful Dodger.

One day, out of the blue, Karzan said, "I [do] not like Saddam's picture in passport." He handed me the fake Iraqi travel document bought in the local bazaar the year before. That reminded me of what had *not* changed in Iraq. Ninety-nine percent of the people in the country still did not have valid passports, much less visas. For them, there was no way out of Iraq. They were trapped. After a full year of independence, the only passports in use—even the ones in the hands of prominent Kurds—were counterfeit. Embossed with the ugly green eagle of the fallen regime, they had been meticulously crafted by Kurdish forgers. Sometimes they worked; sometimes they didn't.

"I want *green card*," Karzan boldly announced to Mike and me. "You get me green card?"

It was hard to tell whether he was joking. I recalled one of Mike's anecdotes from Karzan's visit to Boston. During the time he was recovering from surgery in 2003, Karzan had broken a latch on his Kodak Easy Share, rendering it inoperable. When Best Buy, the store where he'd bought the camera, wouldn't accept it as a return, Karzan replicated a stratagem he'd observed in Iraq. He bought a second, identical Kodak, switched the broken part, and returned the new camera. The unsuspecting clerk confirmed the serial number on the second camera— which now had the broken latch—and gave Karzan back his money. Thereafter, Mike would refer affectionately to his houseguest as the Bad Boy of Best Buy.

One of the many who called Karzan the Dodger was John Lister, a career official from the U.S. State Department who was stationed in Sulaimaniah. Lister was the deputy chief of the Coalition Provisional Authority (the CPA, mindful of the latent rivalry between the Kurdish parties, had a separate office in the KDP area). His security, like other CPA personnel, was the responsibility of Karzan's new employer, Triple Canopy, which was located in the same building.

The CPA office manager turned out to be none other than Dildar Kittani, the first translator I had hired when I set up the base for ABC News six months before the war. Dildar was a talented administrator, a good find for Americans trying to navigate the new culture, but her first loyalty was to the Kurds, especially to Barham Salih, the man she affectionately called, "His Excellency." She was one of the few women in a position of influence in the PUK who had also carried a gun in the mountains against Iraqi troops. The CPA paid her salary, but the Kurdish leadership relied on her for what took place in the office of the visiting Americans. It would have been remiss of Dildar not to pass on what she saw and heard.

Barham Salih's assistant, Nizar, also worked in the CPA office. Nizar had grown up with Salih in Sulaimaniah. In the 1970s, he had immigrated to the United States, where he became a citizen and, eventually, the manager of an Alamo car rental agency in Maryland. In 2002, when the Kurds were getting ready for the U.S. attack, Salih asked him to return to Kurdistan. "I was at Dr. Barham's house," Nizar told me, "the night that Karzan came back from America. All the bodyguards were crying, and everyone was kissing him."

"He went away all broken up"—Nizar made a contorted motion with his arm, mimicking Karzan's injuries—"and he came back . . . looking like a *gentleman*." Nizar straightened up in his chair when he said the word "gentleman."

"He was only one person, but he gave all of us hope."

Since my last trip to Kurdistan, Karzan had become a minor celebrity, even with the State Department officials. "Everyone likes the Dodger," Lister said with a grin. Lister added that he was writing a letter of reference to a State Department contact in Jordan, so Karzan could get a U.S. visa to for additional medical care. A new visa "wouldn't be a slam dunk," Lister said, "but I think he'll get it."

Lister, I found out incidentally, had a connection to the little-covered issue of Kurdish repression in Turkey. He was married to Aliza Marcus, a courageous reporter I'd met in Turkey in the 1990s. Aliza had been a resident correspondent for Reuters News Service during the Kurdish uprising, and she had reported the burning of Kurdish villages by the Turkish army. The reports violated the unstated—but understood—press policy of ignoring such stories. She was accused by the Turkish government of inciting racial hatred, and she had been threatened with prison. The incident caused an international furor. Walter Cronkite and others publicized her case, and the charges subsequently were dropped, but Aliza never reported again in Turkey.

The U.S. handover of sovereignty to the Iraqis was only a month away—the end of June 2004—and Karzan was about to lose his job. Lister's CPA office would close, but the private security business as a whole was expanding because of the increasing chaos in Iraq. Companies like Triple Canopy had plenty of other clients in the country. The ex-commandos at Pilgrims, the company that guarded ABC News, regarded the rapid expansion of security firms with a combination of alarm and contempt. One of the Pilgrims was the friendly Englishman who had picked me up at the Baghdad airport after my visit to the Kurdish north. En route to the city in an ABC armored jeep, he talked about the lure of easy money—$250,000 U.S. a year for guards in some cases. He said the high salaries were attracting the "wrong sort of bloke" to Iraq. The lure of fast dollars had given rise, he said, to a raft of fly-by-night companies in London, fortune hunters who didn't appreciate that good security was a function of keeping a low profile. Some applicants who answered ads, he said, seemed eager for confrontation, including a few who listed experience as barroom bouncers as a job qualification.

"The guards are always brandishing those guns," a Kurdish-American assistant to the prime minister said about Triple Canopy. According to the assistant, who wished to remain anonymous, the U.S. security contactors had no understanding of Kurdistan, the place of their assignment. "They have no tact," he maintained. "They're cowboys." He said they had recently incurred the wrath of Omar Fatah, a well-known member of the PUK politburo, by barging into his private home and searching it without permission prior to the arrival of Lister and other CPA officials for lunch. Apparently, the guards had no idea that, at the time, Fatah was the PUK's equivalent of J. Edgar Hoover. He was in charge of the *Zanyari*, the Kurdish secret police. In all likelihood, he had files on each of them.

According to the assistant, Fatah was fit to be tied. "Don't they realize they are in *Kurdistan!*" he reportedly yelled when he learned of the clumsy search. "Who do they think provides *their* security when they are inside the Palace Hotel?"

The Road to Halabja

Along for the ride that day was Saman Shali, a Kurdish businessman from California. Born in Sulaimaniah, Shali had fought as a *peshmerga* in the mountains in the 1970s. After what he called the "betrayal of the revolution" in 1975, he had immigrated to the States, earned a Ph.D. in chemistry and, for a few years, worked as a professor at Penn State. Now he split his time between a telecommunications company he'd founded in Orange County and his duties as president of the Kurdish National Congress (KNC), the nonprofit organization that represents the Kurdish diaspora in the United States and Canada.

In March 2003, on the eve of the U.S. attack on Iraq, Shali had been part of a delegation of Iraqi opposition leaders invited to the White House to meet senior members of the Bush administration. During the meeting, he recalled, "I advised [Vice President] Cheney and [Secretary of Defense] Rumsfeld that Iraqi Arabs would not welcome the U.S.A. as *liberators.*" After that, Shali told me, he was isolated by the White House. "They labeled me a Kurdish nationalist," he said.

Shali's KNC was backing a local referendum for a ballot initiative on Kurdish independence. The referendum, which had collected almost two million signatures in Kurdistan in just the year I'd been away, ran counter to U.S. views that the Kurds were Iraqis first and that the country should not be split up. Kurdish leaders, sensitive to the implied threats of their neighbors—Turkey in particular—were holding publicly to the U.S. line that they were Iraqis first. However, television and radio stations owned by the major Kurdish parties were giving referendum backers free time to make their case. The Kurds, who by this time held posts in the central government, including foreign minister and deputy prime minister, seemed to be flirting with forbidden fruit.

It was no wonder. More than half of the Iraqi Kurds were under twenty-five, too young to remember the schools of the regime and their mandatory teaching of Arabic. The older Kurds, ones who could still speak Arabic, rarely did so, as they associated the language with the overall repression they'd suffered. Most Kurds looked to their political parties, not to Baghdad, for leadership. Many told me they feared that an Iran-style theocracy—a government dominated by the Shiite majority—would emerge in Iraq. The Kurds had governed themselves for thirteen years. What, most referendum signers asked, did they have in common with the chaos and bloodshed that was sweeping the rest of the country?

The Internet did not reach northern Iraq until 1999, when Shali opened the first café connecting the Kurds to the world of cyberspace. Now Shali was back in the country to visit relatives, to check on his burgeoning business interests, and, like so many Kurds abroad, to take the pulse of the fast-evolving political scene.

I had met Shali in California a few years earlier through his friend Rashid Karadaghi, the man who had first introduced me to the Kurds. By now, Rashid had finished writing his Kurdish-English dictionary, a Herculean task that had taken thirty-three years. To save money and increase accuracy, the huge dictionary was being published in Kurdistan, and the first edition was expected by 2006. Meanwhile, a local Kurd was laboriously typing Rashid's sixty-five thousand final, handwritten entries into Kurdish. In 2003, Shali had smuggled Rashid's original dictionary entries through Turkey in the crate of a satellite dish addressed to one of his Internet centers in northern Iraq.

The immense manuscript of Kurdish words and translations had escaped detection in Turkey, the final leg of a long journey. A new century with new hope had begun. Rashid, the Kurdish-American Ph.D., was about to realize the dream of building a bridge between his two cultures. I thought of my father and recalled one of his favorite expressions: "What is bred in the bone will out."

36

After Halabja

The greatest treason is to do the right thing for the wrong reason.

—T. S. ELIOT

September 11 taught America how to feel; they saw what
the Kurds had already seen: the hand of terror.

—IBRAHIM HAWRAHMANI, DIRECTOR, HALABJA MEMORIAL

The $3 million Halabja Memorial had been completed in the fall of 2003. The memorial had a base made of local marble, which was positioned under a massive cone-shaped framework of steel that rose sixteen meters into the air, symbolizing March 16, the day of the 1988 gas attack. The names of the five thousand Kurdish victims were engraved in the marble, and a sculpture of the Kurdish flag formed the top of the cone. Next to the flag were sixteen steel hands, the planet Earth, and four electric candles, which symbolized the Kurdistans of Iraq, Turkey, Iran, and Syria. The fingers of the hands were made of different thicknesses, representing the size of Kurdish populations in the respective countries. The thickest fingers belonged to Turkey, the thinnest to Syria. Behind the memorial was a landscaped area with fountains and a manicured lawn. A gardener was cutting the grass with an electric power mower, the first such machine I'd seen in Kurdistan.

A large sign hung from the front gate, a message to the party of Saddam Hussein: IT IS NOT ALLOWED FOR BA'ATHS TO ENTER HERE.

Inside the memorial were a 240-seat theater, rooms for seminars, and an extensive photo exhibit documenting the aftermath of the Iraqi attack. The memorial director, Ibrahim Hawrahmani, ushered us into the reception area, where a thirty-six-inch TV screen was replaying footage of corpses in the streets of Halabja, the famous close-ups of anguished parents cradling their gas-stricken infants at the moment of death.

Hawrahmani was a Halabja native, a middle-aged Kurd with heavy eyes and a quiet but firm voice. He had witnessed the 1988 attack from a nearby mountain, and he recounted for us the events of the fateful day. "At first, I thought it was only napalm," he recalled, chain-smoking Pleasure cigarettes, an inexpensive local brand, as he spoke. He said he lost friends and relatives, but his mother was the only member of his immediate family to be hurt, and the injuries were not serious. Her only scar from the attack, he said, was a chemical burn on her nose.

We were the only guests in the museum, and Kurdish teenagers in waiter uniforms stood idly in the distance, studying us. Hawrahmani summoned one and asked him to bring us tea and a plate of cakes. The conversation turned to Abu Ghraib, the news topic of the day.

"I oppose what happened at the prison," he said, his voice rising, "but what about the Kurds? Did you know that 287 companies got contracts for the chemical weapons that were used against us and that we were tortured for years?" In those days, he continued, "You news people didn't come here to do reports."

"I saw [U.S. Secretary of Defense] Rumsfeld on television yesterday apologizing to Iraqi prisoners at Abu Ghraib," he said pointedly, "but no one ever has apologized to *us*."

Hawrahmani was present when Colin Powell and Paul Bremer came to Halabja to dedicate the memorial in September of 2003. "They were crying tears of guilt," he said bitterly. "But neither one would mention the word *Kurd*. We are all supposed to be 'Iraqis' now. Yet we sacrificed more than the others to get rid of Saddam."

"But didn't thousands of Shiites die in the swamps of southern Iraq?" I asked.

"Most of the Iraqi army itself was Shia," Hawrahmani replied. "Why didn't they desert the army and join the Kurds?" He was suggesting the Shiites had failed to do enough under the awful regime. I was back in the swamp of pinpointing blame. This was not an argument that I would win or one that I wanted to pursue.

"What should be done to Saddam?" I asked, steering the exchange in another direction. Hawrahmani responded that he opposed execution. "Saddam should be tried by the people of Halabja," he said, adding that he'd like to see the former dictator "kept in a cage" at the entry to the city, perhaps as a sort of living annex to the memorial. "Whatever he fed our prisoners, I will feed him in his cage."

Residue

For several years, a small American organization called the Washington Kurdish Institute (WKI), a non-profit agency with the motto "For Kurdish People Worldwide," had been working to aid the victims of the Halabja attack. According to its Web site, "WKI amplifies informed, independent perspectives of issues which affect Kurds and bear directly on regional stability and U.S. national interests." The Washington Kurdish Institute was founded in 1991 by Najmaldin Karim, an Iraqi

Kurdish-American brain surgeon in Washington, D.C., who had deep roots in the Kurdish liberation movement. Upon graduating from medical school in 1973, Karim had abandoned a residency in Kirkuk to join Kurdish rebels in the mountains. It was there that he later became the family physician for KDP chieftain Mullah Mustafa Barzani. The executive director of the WKI in 2004 was Mike Amitay, who worked with a small staff and some volunteers in a two-story office located near the Capitol. Amitay, an American Jew who is married to a Japanese immigrant, has had a long and keen interest in the "Kurdish holocaust."

Halabja, the best known of Saddam's chemical targets, had a population of 80,000 prior to the 1988 bombings. The WKI estimates that as many as 5,000 to 7,000 Kurds died immediately and 20,000 to 30,000 others were injured, many severely. According to Amitay, as many as 250,000 people in the immediate region may have been affected at some level, making the Kurds "the largest civilian population ever exposed to chemical and biological weapons." The WKI had taken it upon itself to conduct public seminars, organize witnesses for testimony before Congress, and to educate interested journalists.

According to initial studies by the institute, 52 percent of those living in Halabja today were exposed at the time of the attack. Dr. Fuad Baban, the Kurdish internist, lost several relatives in the Halabja attack. He told me, "Up to 40 percent of the surface area of Kurdistan was exposed to chemical—and possibly, biological—weapons." Fuad said that the victims responded to the gas exposure in different ways. Some spurted blood from their ears, some vomited, and others fell down laughing. Because of the varied reactions, he believes that different Iraqi planes dropped different poisons: mustard gas, sarin nerve gas, VX gas, and, possibly, biological agents. The reason no one knows for sure, he said, is because no tests were ever conducted. As a result, he argues, scientists should work backward, starting with the prevalent skin and lung afflictions of survivors. So far, he lamented, "there hasn't been the interest."

The only military eyewitness to the Halabja bombing I ever met was a man named Qasem Hussein Mohammed, an Iraqi double agent whom I interviewed in a Kurdish jail in 2002. He said he was an Iraqi military officer at the time of the aerial attack and had monitored developments from a hillside overlooking the city. Just before the airplanes appeared, Mohammed told me, he heard three words on his radio: "Gas! Gas! Gas!" He and his men immediately put on their protective masks. After the attack, another radio transmission gave the signal that it was safe to remove the gas masks. That day, the code for "all clear," he noted chillingly, was *salam*, the Arabic word for peace.

I visited Halabja in 1991 and 1992. Ten years went by before I visited again, in February of 2002, when I attended a town meeting at the office of the mayor. It was more than a year before the U.S. invasion would take place. The meeting had been called by survivors to lobby the Kurdish government to set up a compensation fund for victims. There was little money to distribute and a myriad of sensitive questions about how to do so fairly. Should those who were the sickest be the priority? Should injured who had jobs get in line behind the jobless? And so on.

When I took more testimony from witnesses, I was struck by a low-key testiness, which seemed out of character for Kurds in their exchanges with foreigners. I was the only reporter in Halabja that day, but over the years they had seen many of us, beginning in the early 1990s. Three of the victims were women dressed completely in black. They had been young when they incurred the chemical exposure, and now they were in their late thirties. Since the time of the attack, each woman had undergone multiple operations for cancer. "Look," one of them said, "the journalists always come here and tell us they will get help, but nothing ever happens—what is the use of talking to them?"

At that point, fourteen years had passed since the gas attack. Regime change in Iraq was under discussion in Washington at the time, and Mike Amitay just had received a grant from the State Department to study war crimes in Iraqi Kurdistan. He was using the funds for a preliminary survey of the elevated levels of cancer and heart disease in the region. He and an English doctor, Christine Gosden, were submitting their research for publication in the *Lancet*. What was missing and sorely needed, Amitay said, was a full-blown environmental assessment with control groups, toxicity studies, and radiation monitors.

The ill-equipped Halabja hospital continued to try to diagnose late-blooming tumors and other residual illnesses, but in most cases there was little local doctors could do for the victims. Amitay said the patients who were tested showed a higher than normal incidence of cleft palates, gastroenteritis, and chronic diarrhea, with additional ailments in children and infants. He said it was likely that survivors' DNA had been damaged, but no medical group had conducted a study to confirm those suspicions. Some Halabja residents had received private donations, but only a few victims had benefited from surgeries in Europe, and the unequal treatment had triggered recrimination among the survivors.

It was sad, but not surprising. After the 9/11 attacks in New York, I got a taste of post-disaster resentments when I visited a friend in Tribeca, the Manhattan neighborhood near the World Trade Center. My friend's high-rise was so close to the WTC that at night the lit skyscrapers fully illuminated the living room of her eighteenth-floor apartment. When I visited New York six months after 9/11, there were two vertical shafts of light shooting into the night where the Twin Towers had stood. The skyline looked amputated. My friend said there were "a lot of people in the neighborhood who received FEMA grants [Federal Emergency Management Agency] and Red Cross handouts who didn't deserve them." The doorman in the high-rise gave me a copy of the Tribeca community paper.

Inside, there was a letter to the editor complaining that one recipient had used his "free money" to buy a new car.

Forgetting the Past

By 2004, the Washington Kurdish Institute had completed a survey of twenty thousand Kurdish households. Using Geiger counters and other devices, WKI researchers had, according to Amitay, documented "widespread environmental contamination" in the Halabja area. WKI, he said, was in the process of "trying to lay the incidence of illnesses in grids over dozens of attack sites," and the institute hoped to "conduct biological testing with informed consent." Early results of the research suggested that the 1988 attacks had produced significant DNA damage in the population, and that the presence of contaminants in Halabja represented "an ongoing health hazard."

Two developments soon occurred: Amitay's prewar grant ran out (the State Department decided not to renew it) and construction began in Halabja on two new schools, funded by a $1 million U.S. grant that had been announced by Secretary of State Colin Powell at the dedication of the Halabja memorial. (The grant was part of $87 billion, the first congressional appropriation for the reconstruction of Iraq and Afghanistan.)

Amitay's organization had already identified the new school sites as probably contaminated. He was horrified. "Halabja was used to justify the war, and now no one will pay for a simple soil or water sample," he complained. "With the war crimes trials coming up," he added, "Halabja will be the centerpiece of the big cases, but no one is examining the earth for clues to the crime—information that could also help these victims. It's mind-boggling."

Amitay maintained that U.S. soldiers who served in the Halabja valley during the Ansar campaign could be at risk, and he speculated that the failure to confront the issue might be rooted in the fear of lawsuits, either against the U.S. government or some of the companies that had supplied WMD components to the Iraqi regime.

"It's a political minefield," he said, "just like the refusal to look at Agent Orange after the Vietnam War." Amitay said the prospect of exposing a new generation of Kurdish schoolchildren to harmful toxins from the 1980s was a "grotesque irony."

He complained, "You can't just sweep this under the rug like a part of history you want to forget."

Genocides

The attack against the Kurds of Iraq is one of many genocides documented by the Institute of Holocaust and Genocide in Jerusalem. Other genocides chronicled by the institute include those in Armenia, Bangladesh, Burundi, Cambodia,

East Timor, Indonesia, Rwanda, South Africa, and the Ukraine, as well as the Jewish Holocaust of World War II. Topping the death toll is the genocide of American Indians. According to Israel W. Charny, the director, an estimated fifteen million Native Americans perished due to genocide following the arrival of Europeans in 1492.

A few weeks after Mike and I made our visit to the Halabja memorial, a surprise editorial appeared in the *New York Times*. The editorial called for the passage of a proposal directing the federal government to issue an official apology to American Indians for the "violence, maltreatment, and neglect" inflicted on them for centuries. The resolution referred to wounds still open in American society caused by genocide, and it urged President Bush to "bring healing to this land" by acknowledging the government's offensive history.

Apologizing to Indians in the twenty-first century? The prospect may have caused some newspaper readers to roll their eyes in apathy or disbelief: *Wasn't all that behind us?*

The *Times* noted a range of reaction from Indian leaders, from wariness ("words on paper") to modest approval ("a good first step"). By coincidence, the editorial appeared on the same day the United States handed over sovereignty to the Iraqis, and it prompted me to wonder what would be learned from the pending war crimes trials in Iraq.

In Halabja, it was clear that a health emergency still existed. But sixteen years after the 1988 crime, there still was no agency equivalent to the Red Cross or FEMA, no systematic analysis, and no treatment plan for victims. Not a single government in the world had offered help. "Wind and water carry the toxins," Mike Amitay said, "and food could still be affected." However, no scientist or lab tech even had taken a simple soil sample from the rich farmlands of the Halabja valley, where so many of the fruits and vegetables eaten by the Kurds were grown. Initial analysis would cost only $5,000, but no local group could afford it. "If you maintain that Saddam Hussein is guilty of using WMD, you have to face up to the fact that long-term health hazards have been created," Amitay said.

Poisoned Snakes

One of my translators in Halabja was a Kurd named Ayub. Ayub was self-taught, and his English was excellent. (After the war he ended up in Baghdad, translating for the BBC.) He was a short guy with one bowed leg, the result of an Iraqi artillery attack near Halabja when he was four years old. His entire family had fled the area just prior to the 1988 chemical bombing, but his parents returned and they live there today. He told me that no one he knew could comprehend the residual dangers in Halabja. Still, many people believed the risks were still a threat.

Ayub said that in 1996 his cousin died instantly after being bitten by a poisonous snake, one of several such fatalities reported in the area. The doctor told Ayub's family that the bodies of many of the 1988 victims had lain in the sun for several days. The snake that killed Ayub's cousin, he said, repeating the grotesque folklore of a still-terrified population, had probably feasted on their flesh.

Amitay believed his institute had to "maintain a strict nonpartisanship and uncompromised support for international human rights standards." However, it was clear he had strong feelings, and I wanted to draw him out. What was the matter with *Halabja* becoming a household word? Wasn't it good, I asked him, that the Iraq war was shedding light on the issue of weapons of mass destruction?

It would be wrong, he answered carefully, for the Kurdish tragedy to have been used to rally support for the war "without a broad-based commitment" to reconstruct the lives of the victims and their descendants and to bring to justice those responsible "directly and indirectly" for the tragedy. "It is astonishing that no government agency has ever studied Halabja," he said. "The fingerprints of the weapons are still on these people."

Setting History Right

It may be a long time before newspapers call for governments to apologize to the Kurds. When and if the time comes, the gesture will be significant. Both American Indian and Kurdish histories offer an opportunity to learn from mistakes. Regardless of events at Wounded Knee, Halabja, or Abu Ghraib, few would argue that for every wrong there is a redress. Yet historical self-examination serves a vital purpose in democracies. Apologies may not change the past, but they may help to redeem the future. That was a lesson of the truth commissions in Guatemala and South Africa and the international tribunal in Rwanda.

Part of what those tragedies revealed was that evil acts often require accomplices. Soon, many Kurds, Shiites, and other victims of more than a quarter century of madness would confront their tormenters in the dock of justice. However, if the parties who armed the killing machine escape reckoning—if none is required to make even a pro forma apology—a snake full of poison will still be loose.

How then could anyone say, "*Never again*"?

Epilogue

The future is not clean, but it smells good.

—DIYAR KAREEM, EXPATRIATE KURD IN BOSTON

October 2005

As Iraq inched its way toward civil war, I returned to the Pine Ridge Indian Reservation in South Dakota. My son Seamus, a history major in college, came along and the two of us ended up one morning in the tiny hamlet of Wounded Knee. The only other tourists there were an elderly white couple who were parked in front of the historical marker, reading the account of the 115-year-old killings through the windshield of their rental car. The same sign had been there in 1973 when I'd come to the reservation as a reporter, but back then it said "*Battle* of Wounded Knee." In the meantime, someone had printed "Massacre" on a neatly cut piece of plywood and nailed it over the word "Battle." The text of another sign, which commemorated the victory at the Little Bighorn by the Lakota chief Crazy Horse, also had been altered, although not as neatly. A reference to the Indians as "hostiles" had been scratched out, and someone had scrawled the words "Free People" in the space above.

Not long after we arrived, a Lakota woman in her midthirties showed up, hoping to sell a beaded necklace, and she spotted us up at the mass grave where the soldiers had buried the bodies in 1890. Bypassing the couple, she briskly climbed a low hill to the mesa where the simple cemetery spreads out in front of a log church. There was a new chain link fence around the acre-size grave, setting most of it off from the private burial plots, and we were leaning over the fence trying to read the inscriptions on the weathered tombstone.

The woman told us her daughter was buried in the cemetery, and she led us to a child's grave. She said the girl had been killed in 1995, when she was seven years old, by a bookmobile that was doing outreach for a library in nearby Nebraska. A photo of the little girl was affixed to her headstone and a copy of the same image was attached to a village traffic sign where she was struck down, appealing to motorists to watch out for children. During the armed takeover of her famous village in 1973, the mother had been just a child, but she volunteered what she knew about the ten-week siege, and then she relayed the stories she had heard from her relatives about Wounded Knee, 1890.

A few yards away were reminders of the bloody conflict that convulsed the tribe in the 1970s. There, the grave of Buddy Lamont, the Vietnam vet I'd seen die in a Wounded Knee firefight with federal agents, lay near the grave of Glen Three Stars, a Bureau of Indian Affairs (BIA) policeman who had opposed the occupation and who had died, of natural causes, a few years afterwards.

While the shooting in Indian country had stopped, the memories of both 1973 and 1890 were still strong. The log church behind the cemetery was new since my time on the reservation, but I still had an image in my mind of its pre-decessor: a stark white structure with a narrow steeple and gabled roof—and a couple of Indian riflemen crouched in the bell tower. It had been built in 1913, using the Gothic revival style common to prairie churches erected by immigrants from northern Europe. A couple of months after the 1973 occupation, vandals burned it to the ground. Everything else was much as I remembered it from the 1970s, including the historical signs marking the nearby Big Foot Trail. That was the route Chief Big Foot and some three hundred believers in the outlawed Ghost Dance had taken in sub-zero weather on December 28, 1890, the day before their deaths. A few miles from Wounded Knee, they were captured by a reorganized unit of General Custer's Seventh Cavalry, which Crazy Horse and his allies had wiped out at the Little Bighorn fourteen years earlier.

The names of Big Foot and other Lakota prisoners were still readable on the face of the big tombstone, and we noticed that mourners had put an eagle feather, some sage, and other sacred objects near the base of the monument. The mourners, followers of Indian religion, had also placed tobacco offerings on the mass grave, wrapped in tiny bundles of red and yellow prayer cloth. The colors were still bright, indicating the offerings were recent. We stood there thinking about mourners, modern day pilgrims who pray for kinfolk a century after their deaths, as we talked about culture, the grip of the past, and—in Seamus's words—"how some things never seem to get over."

It was mid-October, and the dead in Iraq were also being remembered. The first of Saddam Hussein's war crimes trials was about to begin, and voters had just ratified the controversial Iraq constitution amid another wave of suicide bombings. The charter was still opposed by many Sunni Arabs, who charged that Kurds and Shiites had awarded themselves semiautonomous zones in the north and south while they were left with desert and farmland in the center of the country and no guaranteed access to the country's oil riches. To the Sunnis, the constitution was not a compact for national unity but, rather, a recipe for the break-up of Iraq.

The military situation in Iraq was not going well, and the Kurds were closely watching U.S. leaders for signs of political wavering. Two thousand American soldiers had been killed since the war began in March 2003. A comparable number of U.S.-trained Iraqi soldiers had been slain in the first nine months of 2005 alone, and countless numbers of Iraqi civilians had been blown up by suicide bombers during the same period. Although the death toll in the Kurdish region was only a fraction of the overall total, the insurgency in the rest of the country was rapidly expanding. Increasingly home grown—at least nine out of every ten insurgents were now thought to be Iraqi nationals—it was clear that sealing the country's borders, even if that were possible, would not put an end to the insurgency. In the United States, an AP poll just released said that 67 percent of the public now "disapprove of the way George W. Bush is handling the situation in Iraq" and 60 percent now believe "the United States made a mistake in sending troops to Iraq." Three weeks earlier, 100,000 antiwar protesters had demonstrated in Washington, and the "Out of Iraq" caucus on Capitol Hill now had sixty-eight members, all Democrats. In the wake of devastation from hurricanes Katrina and Rita, the fraud and money laundering indictments of Rep. Tom De Lay, the House Majority leader, and the fact that some gas prices were hitting $4 a gallon, Republicans were looking nervous, eyeing midyear elections in 2006, worried that the increasingly unpopular war would hurt the party.

Karzan

Karzan, my friend and one-time driver, didn't get to relocate in America after all. But he came close. In 2004, the U.S. embassy in Jordan rejected his request for a medical visa when he could not produce documentation for additional treatment at a U.S. hospital. He returned to Iraq, where he worked for a year in Baghdad as a driver for Barham Salih, Jalal Talabani, and other Kurdish leaders in the Green Zone. Then PUK officials, apparently believing that Karzan had been exposed to enough danger for one lifetime, arranged for him to join the staff of the Iraqi embassy in Canada, where the new ambassador was a Kurd and long-time member of the PUK.

Karzan arrived in Ottawa in the spring of 2005. It was a relief not to have to carry guns for protection, but the overall transition from Baghdad wasn't as smooth as he'd hoped. After a few weeks in the Canadian capital, he was complaining about a former Baa'thist on the embassy staff and he told me he was homesick for Sulaimaniah. By midsummer, his life had improved dramatically. By then he had a new girlfriend, an Iranian-born woman he'd met through a dating service, he was living in a new apartment on the twentieth floor of a building overlooking the city, and he was making payments on a used Mercedes he'd bought from the Chinese embassy. He had gotten to know other expatriates in Ottawa's small Kurdish community, and he had even become friendly with the Ba'athist, the lone Arab who worked in the embassy. The Iraqi ambassador had expressed confidence that Canadian surgeons would provide the final operation on his arm and hand, and Karzan had registered for college, where he hoped to study journalism. Best of all, Canada had given the Dodger a diplomatic passport, enabling him to visit his Kurdish friends in Boston and Washington, D.C. Karzan had taken to signing off phone calls with "Have a nice day!" He was joking about being a "big man" again, and he was happy.

In the meantime, our mutual friend Mike Brabeck had moved to New York City, where he was working as an internist at Bellevue Hospital. Over the summer Mike flew to Ottawa and spent a weekend with Karzan. When he returned, he told me a story about a day he picked up his wife Mary from work at NYU's Steinhardt School of Education, where she was now the dean. The Brabecks walked home through lower Manhattan, stopping at a place called Raymond's Café on Seventh Avenue. They sat down at a sidewalk table and began to reminisce about the "crooked little man" who'd come into their lives at the beginning of the Iraq war. Mike described the thrilling moment, a year after the Boston surgeries, when he'd seen Karzan gallop a full block to catch up with a friend. "You know," he told me, recounting his conversation in the café, "the pure essence is that a lot of people came together and gave Karzan his life back."

"So Mary and I are sitting out there under this awning having a beer, and I'm telling her about Karzan running, and I break down and start crying. And I just couldn't shut it off."

Homeland

In the end, Kurds and American Indians did have a number of things in common—an ancient civilization, a land base, kinship bands, a history of repression, and a struggle to preserve culture and language—but the differences were immense. The Kurds had come to prominence, if not power, for two reasons: because Iraq invaded Kuwait in 1991 and because the U.S. invaded Iraq in 2003. However, if the U.S. occupation of Iraq had succeeded as planned, Washington might have insisted—as it had initially—that all militias in Iraq, including the *peshmerga*, be disbanded. Without the *peshmerga*, the Homeland Security of the Kurds, the dream of federalism—of separateness—might have been postponed. The Americans, like the Ba'athists and British before them, had sought to mix disparate peoples under a single umbrella, but the Kurds no more wanted the mixture than Native Americans wanted to see assimilation through the termination of their remaining reservations. U.S. hopes for an American-style melting pot, a new secular state in the Middle East, one nation of Arabs, Kurds, Turkmen, and Christians, no longer seemed to be in the cards. The Kurds, like American Indians, seemed to prefer a "stew" to a melting pot, and the fallout from a failed Iraq policy had given them the chance for permanent separation.

One of the world's oldest peoples, Kurds in Iraq now had independence in all but name. The talk of "Iraqis first" would remain a fiction for outside consumption, a necessary means to an end, and the Kurds would go along with it a while longer as they tried to navigate a would-be ship of state in a sea of regional powers.

The emblems of quasi-sovereignty were everywhere: President Jalal Talabani addressing the United Nations last month in Kurdish, a first for the U.N.; a Kurdish language version of Iraq's official presidential Web site; voter registration cards in Kurdish; the new, direct flights from Europe via Kurdistan Airways, with no need for risky connections in Baghdad; people using cell phones called Kurdistell and watching a widening selection of Kurdish TV stations; the absence of Iraqi flags and the fact that Arabic was no longer spoken in the three Kurdish provinces; an economic boom featuring the construction of a twenty-five-story luxury hotel in Sulaimaniah; the announcement that passports of visitors entering northern Iraq henceforth would be stamped "Iraqi Kurdistan"; and a new law passed by the Kurdistan Parliament forbidding Iraqi troops from entering the Kurdish region without a special vote of Kurdish lawmakers.

Seemingly overnight, the Kurds had become key to the stability of the Middle East. Now they were America's best (and perhaps only) friend in Iraq. Still, the undisguised yearning for Kurdish independence—public pronouncements of some Kurdish leaders notwithstanding—ran counter to U.S. plans for a *unified* country. If Iraqi Kurds moved rashly to formalize independence, they risked the loss of U.S. protection from hostile neighbors like Turkey. And yet, a de facto partition of Iraq had already emerged and Kurdish intentions could not have been more apparent. In September 2005, Massoud Barzani, President of the Kurdistan Regional Government, delivered a speech in the Kurdish city of Dohuk in which he appealed to Turkey, Iran, and Syria to change their attitudes toward the Kurds. "These are new days, not only for the Kurds but also for the countries that have Kurds," he told his listeners amid bursts of applause. "Whether they like it or not, we are a nation."

The Kurds, it was clear, believed they already had a homeland.

Now they would have to defend it.

Notes

BOOK I: THE STAGE IS SET

1. Viva la Fiesta

Pages 10–11 History of the Medes: Mehrdad Izady, "Are Kurds Descended from the Medes?" (www.kurdistanica.com, March 1994), in http://www.kurdistanica.com/english/history/articles-his/his-articles-08.html, accessed 20 May 2005.

Page 11 RAF ordered to bomb: David Omissi, *Air Power and Colonial Control: The Royal Air Force 1919–1939* (Manchester: Manchester University Press, 1990), 242.

Page 11 British troops fired: Kerim Yildiz, *The Kurds in Iraq: The Past, Present and Future* (London: Pluto Press, 2004), 13.

Page 11 Short-lived Kurdish republic: William Eagleton, *The Kurdish Republic of 1946* (London: Oxford University Press, 1963), 95–99.

Page 12 Kissinger Information: U.S. House Select Committee on Intelligence Report (Pike Committee), 94th Congress, 1st session, 1975, 2nd session, 1976 as published in *CIA: The Pike Report* (Nottingham, England: Spokesman Books, 1977), 26–94.

2. 1991: Secret Nation or Forgotten Enclave?

Page 15 Quote from Kenneth Hale was cited in *The Economist,* November 3, 2001.

Page 15 The Spenser quote is from *A View of the Present State of Ireland.*

Page 18 Simku information: McDowall, *A Modern History of the Kurds,* 214–22. (London, England: I. B. Tauris, 2004), 214–222.

3. A Second Visit to Kurdistan

Page 25 Churchill quote: Geoff Simons, *Iraq: From Sumer to Saddam,* 2nd ed. (New York: St. Martin's Press, 1996), 213.

Page 28   Turkish Kurdistan: Kendal Nezan, "Kurdistan in Turkey," in *A People Without a Country*, edited by Gerard Chaliand (New York: Interlink Publishing Group, 1993), 38–94, 238–47; Aliza Marcus, "Turkey's Kurds After the Gulf War: A Report from the Southeast."

Page 29   Human rights abuses: Amnesty International, "Turkey: Systematic Torture Continues in Early 2002" (Amnesty.org, September 2002), in web.amnesty.org/library/Index/engEUR440402002?OpenDocument&of=COUNTRIES%5CTURKEY, accessed 15 November 2004.

Page 30   The Kurds have no friends but the mountains: McDowall, *A Modern History of the Kurds*, 21–37.

Page 31   President Woodrow Wilson's Fourteen Points were delivered January 8, 1918.

Page 31   British feared Turks on their border: From a letter to author from scholar David McDowall.

Pages 31–32 Sheikh Mahmud Barzinji history: McDowall, *A Modern History of the Kurds*, 155–163.

Page 32   RAF casualties, Lionel Charlton and "Bomber" Harris: Omissi, *The Guardian*, 19 January 1991, in http://www.cambridgeclarion.org/e/omissi_graun_19jan 1991.html, accessed 3 May 2004.

Page 32   Kurdistan as weapons lab: Simons, *Iraq: From Sumer to Saddam*, 214; C. Townshend, "Civilization and Frightfulness," 148, Wg/Cdr to CAS, 19 February 1920, Trenchard Papers MFC 76/1/36; Martin Gilbert, *Winston S. Churchill*, IV (London: Heinemann, 1975), 494, 810; Companion IV, ii, 1066–7, 1083, 1170; quoted in Omissi, 160.

Page 32   "Excellent moral effect": Omissi, *The Guardian*, 19 January 1991, in http://www .cambridgeclarion.org/e/omissi_graun_19jan1991.html, accessed 3 May 2004.

Page 32   Quote regarding Churchill: Simons, 213.

Page 33   Churchill's quotes regarding gas: Sir Winston Churchill, "Prime Minister's Personal Minute, Serial No. D. 217/4." Source: Photographic copy of original four-page memo, in Guenther W. Gellermann, *Der Krieg, der nicht stattfand* (Munich: Bernard & Graefe Verlag, 1986), 249–251, July 2004, in www.global research.ca/articles/CHU407A.html, accessed 25 May 2005.

Page 33   Barzinji friends and detractors: This information is from a letter to the author by Kurdish scholar David McDowall.

4. Atrocities

Page 37   4,000 villages: Human Rights Watch, *Genocide in Iraq: The Anfal Campaign Against the Kurds* (New York, Human Rights Watch, 1993), in http://www .hrw.org/reports/1993/iraqanfal/, accessed 15 November 2004.

Pages 37–38 Saddam Hussein quote appeared in Iraq's state-run newspaper *Al-Iraq*, 13 September 1983, reprinted in Human Rights Watch Web site at http://hrw.org/reports/1993/iraqanfal/ANFAL1.htm, accessed 5 December 2004.

Page 38   Declaration of the Kingdom of Iraq, 30 May 1932, Chapter 1, Article 5 in http://www.solami.com/a3a.htm, accessed 12 June 2005.

Page 38   Forced collectives: Peter Galbraith, *Kurdistan in the Time of Saddam Hussein— A Staff Report to the Committee on Foreign Relations of the United States*

Senate (Washington, D.C.: U.S. Government Printing Office, November 1991), 13–14.

Page 38   Unquiet graves: Middle East Watch and Physicians for Human Rights, "Unquiet Graves: The Search for the Disappeared in Iraqi Kurdistan" (February 1992), in http://www.hrw.org/reports/1992/iraq/iraq0292.pdf, accessed 10 September 2003.

Page 39   U.N. report: U.N. Special Rapporteur's report, concluded in 1992 (U.N. Doc E/CN.4/1992/31, para. 154), in http://www.firethistime.org/feariraqgovt.htm, accessed 5 September 2004.

Page 40   U.S. collaboration: Douglas Frantz and Murray Waas, "Bush Secret Effort Helped Iraq Build Its War Machine," *Los Angeles Times,* 23 February 1992, A1.

5. The Leadership

Page 50   Barzani RAF bombings, Barzani to Iran: Christiane Bird, *A Thousand Signs, A Thousand Revolts* (New York: Random House, 2004), 186.

Page 51   "Komala opened chapters": Archie Roosevelt, "The Kurdish Republic of Mahabad," in Chaliand, 122–38.

Page 51   Kurdistan People's Government: Ibid., 128–29.

Page 51   Quote re Qazi Mohammed: Ibid., 132.

Page 56   Pike Committee report, 88.

Page 56   Kissinger's "covert action" quote: H. R. Haldeman, *The Haldeman Diaries: Inside the Nixon Diaries* (New York: Putnam, 1994), 672.

Page 56   Kissinger's "distortions" quote: Daniel Schorr, "1975: Background to Betrayal: How Kissinger, Nixon and the Shah Rallied—Then Shrugged Off—an Uprising," *The Washington Post,* 7 April 1991, D3.

Page 56   Ailing Barzani quote: William Safire, "Son of a Secret Sell-Out," *The New York Times,* 12 February 1976, 30.

Pages 58–59   Schorr threatened with jail: Schorr, ibid.

Page 59   Kurdistan offered as 51st state: Schorr, ibid.

6. Illusory Borders, Part I

Page 63   The Walter Scott quote is from *Rob Roy.*

Page 66   Quote from Kemal's essay: Yasar Kemal, "Turkey's War of Words," *The New York Times,* 6 May 1995, 19.

Page 76   Fingerless Askik, the painter: Ramazan Yavuz, "From the Mountains to the Gallery," *Hurriyet,* 24 June 2004, 26.

7. Illusory Borders, Part II

Page 77   The Tennyson quote is from the poem "The Charge of the Light Brigade."

Page 78   Yazidi membership figures: According to Lazgin Khalid Barany, University of Mosul, Iraq. John Daniszewski, "[Yazidi] Ancient Faith is a Reminder of Iraq's Diversity," *Los Angeles Times,* 10 March 2005, A5.

Page 78   Yazidi minority religion: Yildiz, 9.

Page 81   One hundred Black Hawk helicopters: Tamar Gabelnick, William D. Hartung, and Jennifer Washburn, *Arming Repression: U.S. Arms Sales to Turkey during the Clinton Administration, A Joint Report of the World Policy Institute and the*

Federation of American Scientists, October 1999, in www.fas.org/asmp/library/reports/turkeyrep.htm, accessed 10 September 2003.

Page 82   Black Hawk sale same day as El Salvador massacre: John Tirman, *The Spoils of War* (New York, Free Press, 1996), 152–63.

Page 84   "Stick a fork in him . . .": "Avoidable Error," *ABC Primetime Live,* 8 March 1995.

BOOK II: WAR IN TURKEY

8. Passing Down Revolution

Page 89   Quotation from the poet Namik Kemal: Masami Arai, *Turkish Nationalism in the Young Turk Era* (Leiden, Netherlands: E. J. Brill, 1992), 3.

Page 89   The Einstein quote is from his 1921 essay, "The World As I See It."

Page 89   White House proclamation about Ataturk, 1981: In http://www.Reagan.utexas.edu/archives/speeches/1991/40281d.htm, accessed 20 September 2005.

Page 90   Treaty of Sèvres: Andrew Mango, *Ataturk* (London, John Murray, 1999), 131–37.

Page 90–91   Ataturk as "Saviour of Kurdistan": Kendal Nezan, 46.

Page 91   "National and social rights of the Kurds": McDowall, *A Modern History of the Kurds,* 125–28, 184–211; Kendal Nezan, 46–47.

Page 92   According to historian McDowall: David McDowall, *The Kurds: A Nation Denied* (London: Minority Rights Publications, 1992), 36.

Page 92   The state was "indivisible": Article 8 passed by the Turkish Parliament reads, "Written or oral propaganda, along with meetings, demonstrations, and marches, that have the goal of destroying the indivisible unity of the state with its territory and nation of the Republic of Turkey cannot be conducted." From http://hrw.org/press98 /feb/fe-turk.htm.

Page 93   Mahmud's uprisings against British control: McDowall, *A Modern History of the Kurds,* 156–63.

Page 93   Permanent border proposal accepted: McDowall, *A Modern History of the Kurds,* 142–46.

Page 93   Said hanging: McDowall, *A Modern History of the Kurds,* 194–96.

Page 93   Settlement law: Kemal Kirisci and Gareth M. Winrow, *The Kurdish Question and Turkey: An Example of a Trans-state Ethnic Conflict* (Abingdon, UK: Frank Cass, 1997), 98–99.

Page 94   Crude social engineering: McDowall, *A Modern History of the Kurds,* 207.

Page 94   Pleas by Seyt Riza: McDowall, *A Modern History of the Kurds,* 208.

Page 94   Devastation of Dersim: Kendal Nezan, 57–58; Martin van Bruinessen, "The Suppression of the Dersim Rebellion in Turkey (1937–1938)" in http://www.let.uu.nl/~martin.vanbruinessen/personal/publications/Dersim.pdf, n.d.

Page 95   Seyt grabbed noose: Paul J. White, *Primitive Rebels or Revolutionary Modernisers? The Kurdish Movement in Turkey* (London: Zed Books, 2001), 82–83.

Page 95   Mustafa Kemal dies: Mango, 518–528.

9. Turkey, 1993

Page 99   300,000 security forces: Jennifer Washburn, "Don't Sell Weapons to Turkey," 2 February 1997, in http://kurdistan.org/Washington/washburn2.html, accessed 18 November 2004.

Page 99–100   Legend of Dehak: Mark Campbell, "Kawa and the Story of Newroz," n.d. in http://www.newrozfilms.com/the_legend_of_newroz.htm, accessed 13 May 2005.

11. The Business of Killing

Page 117 $134 billion in 1980s and increase in 1990s: Dr. Victor W. Sidel, "The International Arms Trade and Its Impact on Health," *British Medical Journal,* 23 December 1995, in http://www.ippnw.org/MGS/V3Sidel.html, accessed 15 September 2005.

Page 117   73 percent of weapons trade to the Third World: "World Military Expenditures and Arms Transfers, 1983–1993," United States Arms Control and Disarmament Agency, May 1995, 24th edition. Washington, D.C., in http://ssdc.ucsd .edu/ssdc/icp06516.html, accessed 18 September 2003.

Page 118   U.S. weapons in use in 39 of world's 48 conflicts: Hartung, "The Role of U.S. Arms Transfers in Human Rights Violations: Rhetoric versus Reality," Testimony before the Subcommittee on International Operations and Human Rights, House International Relations Committee, 7 March 2001, in http:// www.worldpolicy.org/projects/arms/reports/testimony030701.htm, accessed 5 December 2003.

Page 118   Estimated 85% of American arms exports to regimes: Sidel.

Page 120   Report ordered by Congress: U.S. Department of State, "Report on Allegations of Human Rights Abuses by the Turkish Military and on the Situation in Cyprus," 1 June, 1995, in http://www.fas.org/asmp/profiles/turkey_cyprus_ 1995.txt, accessed 19 May 2005.

Page 120   State Department report quote: Ibid.

Page 122   GM Hughes sold sixty helicopters: Mark Phythian, *Arming Iraq: How the U.S. and Britain Secretly Built Saddam's War Machine* (Boston: Northeastern University Press, 1996), 37–38.

Page 122   "International air-to-air weapon of choice": Federation of American Scientists, "U.S. Military Aid and Arms Sales to Turkey," in http://www.fas.org/ asmp/pro-files/turkey_weapons.htm, accessed 16 September 2003.

Page 122   Santa Barbara Research (SBR), the industry leader: SBR is the old name for a company now called Santa Barbara Remote Sensing.

Page 123   152 Lockheed F-16s made in Turkey: Gabelnick, et. al.

Page 123   Human rights groups documented civilian fatalities: Human Rights Watch, *Weapons Transfers and Violations of the Laws of War in Turkey* (New York: Human Rights Watch, 1995), in http://hrw.org/reports/1995/Turkey.htm, accessed 16 September 2003.

12. 60 Minutes

Pages 126–27   Securing Kurdish rights in Syria: Mustafa Nazadar, "The Kurds in Syria," in *A People Without a Country,* edited by Gerard Chaliand, 194–202.

Page 128   GAP figures come from the Turkish Embassy's Web site for the Southeastern Anatolia Project Regional Development Administration (GAP), n.d. http://www .gap.gov.tr/gap-eng.php?sayfa=English/Ggbilgi/gnedir.html, accessed 20 September 2005.

Page 128   Information on the Turkey-Israeli relationship in the 1990s: Robert Olson, *Turkey's Relations with Iran, Syria, Israel, and Russia, 1991–2000* (Costa Mesa, California: Mazda Publishers, 2001).

Page 128   Israeli military assistance: The Military Training and Cooperation Agreement (MTCA), the pact Turkey and Israel signed in 1996, followed several years of joint military cooperation between the two countries, which included Israel's providing of arms and expertise during the mid-1990s, the height of the Kurdish rebellion.

13. PKK Visit, 1996

Page 139   The Yeats quote is from the poem "Easter, 1916."

Page 159   PKK committed widespread abuses during fifteen-year uprising: Human Rights Watch, *World Report 1999: Turkey,* in http://www.hrw.org/worldreport99/europe/ turkey.html, accessed 19 September 2003; and "Turkey: Forced Displacement of Ethnic Kurds from Southeastern Turkey," Human Rights Watch Helsinki. New York: Vol 6, No. 12, October 1994, 21–23.

14. Well-Founded Fear of Persecution

Page 166   Leyla Zana nominated for Nobel Peace Prize: Amnesty International, "Leyla Zana, Prisoner of Conscience," n.d., in http://www.amnestyusa.org/action/ special/zana.html, accessed 18 May 2005.

BOOK III: WAR IN IRAQ

15. 2002: Northern Iraq

Page 171   U.S. intelligence tracked Ocalan: Jane Hunter, "Ocalan's Odyssey," *Covert Action,* n.d., in http://covertaction.org//content/view/90/75/, accessed 13 May 2005.

Page 171   Fifteen-year rebellion over: BBC, "Ocalan File: Timeline," 12 March 2003, in http://news.bbc.co.uk/2/hi/europe/281302.stm, accessed 16 November 2004.

Page 176 $5 billion goods blocked by U.S.: Joy Gordon, "Cool War," *Harper's Magazine,* November 2002, 43, in http://www.scn.org/ccpi/HarpersJoyGordonNov02.html, accessed 24 May 2005.

Page 180   Turkish press and Turkmen minority: Cuneyt Arcayurek, "Turkey, the U.S., and Northern Iraq," 17 October 2002, in http://home.cogeco.ca/~konews/17-10-02-tky-us-kurdistan.html, accessed 16 November 2004.

Pages 180–81 *Newsweek* cite: Owen Matthews, "Welcome to Kurdistan," *Newsweek,* U.S. edition, 25 March 2002, 22–23.

16. Stranger in My Cab

Page 186   CIA report regarding mustard gas in arsenal: Six months after the taxi ride, Stephen Pelletiere, a CIA senior political analyst on Iraq during the Iran-Iraq war, made the same argument about Iran's culpability, in a *New York Times* op-ed titled "A War Crime or an Act of War?" (31 January 2003), A29.

Page 186   Purported link of Saddam Hussein to al-Qaeda: Jeffrey Goldberg, "The Great Terror," *The New Yorker,* 25 March 2002, 52–75.

Page 187   Open letter to presidential advisor Karl Rove: Jude Wanniski, "Bush and Cheney Are Misinformed," 25 March 2002, in http://wanniski.com/showarticle.asp? articleid=1920, accessed 3 June 2005.

17. Fall 2002: Six Months Before the War

Page 189   The Robert Frost quote is from the poem "Mowing."

Page 189   President Bush live television address: From a speech given on October 7, 2002 in Cincinnati, Ohio.

Page 189   "The absence of evidence": Donald Rumsfeld, "Press Conference," NATO Speeches, 7 June 2002, in http://www.nato.int/docu/speech/2002/s020606g.htm, accessed 25 May 2005.

Page 190   Administration removed Iraq from list of state sponsors of terrorism: Phythian, 37–38.

Page 190   Envoy for Bechtel Corporation: Joyce Battle, editor, *Shaking Hands with Saddam Hussein: The U.S. Tilts Toward Iraq: 1980–1984*, National Security Archive Electronic Briefing Book, No. 82, 25 February 2003, in http://www. gwu.edu/~nsarchiv/NSAEBB/NSAEBB82/, accessed 13 May 2005.

Page 191   Dana Priest, "Rumsfeld Visited Iraq in 1984 to Reassure Iraqis, Documents Show," *The Washington Post,* 19 December 2003.

Page 191   New U.S.-Iraqi relationship "useful" quote: Jeremy Scahill, "The Saddam in Rumsfeld's Closet," CommonDreams.com, 2 August 2002, in http://www.commondreams.org/views02/0802–01.htm, accessed 12 September 2003.

Page 191   *The New York Times* story, 29 March 1984: Quoted in Scahill, accessed 12 September 2003.

Page 192   Cocktails of mustard gas, sarin, and VX gas on Kurdish villages: Said K. Aburish, *A Brutal Friendship: The West and the Arab Elite* (London, Victor Gollancz, 1997), 99. "It was an American company, Pfaulder Corporation of Rochester, New York, that supplied the Iraqis in 1975 with a blueprint that enabled them to build their first chemical warfare plant. With this in hand, Saddam used the repatriated scientists and engineers to buy the components for the plant piecemeal from different countries and assembled it himself. The site of Saddam's first chemical warfare plant was at Akhashat in northwestern Iraq, and the cost was $38 million for the plant and $40 million for the safety equipment."

Page 192   "Groundwork for U.S. biological shipments": Michael Barletta and Christina Ellington, "Iraq's Biological Weapons Program," Center for Nonproliferation Studies, Monterey Institute for International Studies, November 1998, in http://cns.miis.edu/research/wmdme/flow/iraq/seed.htm, accessed 20 May 2005.

Page 192   "American Type Culture Collection": Mike Toner, "Germ Sharing a Necessary Risk? CDC Exported Shipments to Fight Diseases," *Atlanta Journal-Constitution,* 2 October 2002, A4.

Page 192   Jonathan Tucker, former U.N. weapons inspector quote: Philip Shenon, "Iraq Links Germs for Weapons to U.S. and France," *The New York Times,* 16 March 2003, sec. 1, p. 16.

Page 192   Dual-use exports: Tony Paterson, "Leaked Report Says German and U.S. Firms Supplied Arms to Saddam," *The Independent,* 18 December 2002; and Andy Oppenheimer, "Who Armed Iraq?" *Jane's Chem-BioWeb,* 17 April 2003, in http://www.janes.com/defence/news/jcbw/jcbw030417_1_n.shtml, accessed 20 May 2005.

Page 192   CIA supplying intelligence on Iranian troop deployments: Patrick E. Tyler, "Officers Say U.S. Aided Iraq in War Despite Use of Gas," *The New York Times,* 18 August 2002, sec. 1, p. 1.

Page 192   U.S. jets aiding Iraq: John Barry and Roger Charles, "Sea of Lies," *Newsweek*, 13 July 1992, 29–39.

Page 192   U.S. Department of Agriculture financing: Alan Friedman, "Warning Forced Bechtel out of Iraq Chemical Project," *Financial Times*, 21 February 1991.

18. Suly: October 2002

Page 200   Potassium iodide quote from U.S. Department of Homeland Security at http://www.ready.gov, accessed 20 September 2005.

Page 200   "Winds of war" reference: according to the once-secret Downing Street Memo, which chronicled a July 2002 meeting between U.S. and British officials to discuss war plans, "the intelligence and the facts were (already) being fixed around the policy."

Page 200   "Softened up for war": Michael Smith, *London Times* (Sunday) 29 May 2005, 2. In a story entitled "RAF Bombing Raids Tried to Goad Saddam into War" the *Times* reported, "The RAF and U.S. aircraft doubled the rate at which they were dropping bombs on Iraq in 2002 in an attempt to provoke Saddam Hussein into giving the allies an excuse for war." The paper cited statistics from the British Defense Ministry showing, "the Allies dropped twice as many bombs on Iraq in the second half of 2002 as they did during the whole of 2001." According to the *Times*, "a full air offensive" was underway six months before the allied invasion officially began.

Page 203   Kurdistan as "the fifty-first state": Jim Hoagland, "The Kurdish Example," *The Washington Post*, 27 July 2003, B7.

19. A Sheikh in a Suit

Page 205   The quotation is from the essay "Of Revenge" by Francis Bacon.

Page 206   Kurds' insistence that they control Kirkuk oil fields: Human Rights Watch, *Genocide in Iraq: The Anfal Campaign Against the Kurds* (New York: Human Rights Watch, 1993), in http://www.hrw.org/reports/1993/iraqanfal/, accessed 13 September 2005.

22. Al-Qaeda in Kurdistan?

Page 239   U.S. buttressed claim with satellite photos: These accusations appeared prominently in Colin Powell's 5 February 2003 address before the United Nations Security Council.

23. WMD and Tipsters

Page 242   Presidential candidate Kerry argued that Iraq possessed chemical weapons: These quotes come from a speech John Kerry gave on the Senate floor in support of the Iraq War Resolution on 9 October 2002.

Page 242   Criticism of Hans Blix: From *The Wall Street Journal* editorials. Gary Milhollin, "Hans the Timid," 26 November 2002, A24.

Page 245   Iraqi National Congress: By January 2001, according to the *Washington Post* writer John Lancaster, the U.S. government had distributed only $6 million of the allotted $97 million from the Iraq Liberation Act. Of this $6 million, the INC received $4 million. John Lancaster, "U.S. Gives Go-Ahead to Iraq Opposition," *The Washington Post*, 14 January 2001, A1.

26. Kurds Reign in the Press

Page 279   Capture of Ali Bapir: two years later, Babir was released from a U.S.-run detention center. He expressed resentment in an interview for having been jailed with Ba'athists, "men he had fought against most of (his) life" and he claimed he had been tortured, but he would not provide details. Bapir declared that he opposed terrorism and advocated ties with the West and that he now hoped to convince the West of mistakes it had made with the Islamic world (Michael Howard, "Kurd Chief Who Taught Mercy to Saddam's Men," *The Guardian*, May 27, 2005, 14).

29. The War in Kurdistan

Page 288   The Yeats line is from the poem "Easter, 1916."

30. Road to Tikrit and Home

Page 294   The Auden quote is from the poem "September 1, 1939."

BOOK IV: VICTORY
31. One Year Later: Return to Iraq

Page 301   Economic Boost for Iraq: "Could Hussein's Capture Provide a Market Boost?" Josh Friedman, *Los Angeles Times*, 15 December 2003, D1.

Page 302   Twenty-five thousand Iraqi civilians killed; estimates several months later of 100,000: Les Roberts, Riyadh Lafta, Richard Garfield, Jamal Khudhairi, and Gilbert Burnham, "Mortality Before and After the 2003 Invasion of Iraq: Cluster Sample Survey," *The Lancet*, no. 9448, 29 October 2005, 364.

Page 302   Lawrence quote: Lawrence, T. E., *Seven Pillars of Wisdom: A Triumph* (New York: Garden City Publishing Company, Inc., 1938), 422.

Page 304   Quote from spokesman Adam Ereli: Mr. Ereli made these remarks during the 17 March 2004 State Department noon briefing.

Page 304   Kurdish parties banned in Syria: Gary C. Gambill, "The Kurdish Reawakening in Syria," *Middle East Intelligence Bulletin*, April 2004, in http://www.meib.org/articles/0404_s1.htm, accessed 25 May 2005.

Page 306   Parents allowed to give their children Kurdish names: Canada, Research Directorate, Immigration and Refugee Board, Ottawa, "Country of Origin Research: Turkey," 25 August 2004, in http://www.irb-cisr.gc.ca/en/research/ndp/ref/?action=view&doc=tur42658e, accessed 24 May 2005.

Page 307   Turkish government still harassing Kurdish politicians: Amnesty International, "2005 Country Report: Turkey," in http://www.amnestyusa.org/countries/turkey/document.do?id=ar&yr=2005, accessed 20 May 2005.

Page 307   Document leaked from Turkish General Staff: Amberin Zaman, "Spying Order from Turkish Generals Sparks Wide Protests," *Los Angeles Times*, 12 March 2004, A8.

33. Kirkuk and Civil War

Page 324   Official 1957 census: Nouri Talabany, "Kirkuk, Past and Present," 9 March 2003, in http://www.ksma.org/en/articles/articles-009.html, accessed 22 May 2005.

Page 325   Turkish officers taken prisoner and deported: Soli Ozel, "Which Way Is West for

Turkey?," *Project Syndicate,* October 2004, in http://www.project-syndicate .org/commentary/ozel2, accessed 3 May 2005.

35. The Dodger

Page 338   MP5 manufactured by Heckler and Koch: See: http://www.hk94.com/ hecklerkoch-mp5.html.

Page 339   "Struck gold in lawless frontier" quote: James Glanz, "Modern Mercenaries on the Iraqi Frontier," *The New York Times,* 4 April 2004, 4.5.

Page 339   Estimated 20,000 private security guards: This figure appeared in assorted publications. For example, see "Private Contractors in Iraq" in the 7 April 2004 edition of *The Economist,* 22–23.

Page 340   Derogatory term: One example was the use of "savages" in a *New York Times* editorial, 12 July 1876.

Page 341   The Faulkner quote is from *Requiem for a Nun,* Act I, Scene 3.

Page 342   Stealth prototype of the Comanche helicopter: Renae Merle, "Army Scraps $39 Billion Helicopter," *The Washington Post,* 24 February 2004, A6.

Page 342   Custer Battles security firm: Matt Kelley, "Contractor Accused of Overbilling in Iraq," Associated Press, 8 October 2004 in http://www.msnbc.msn.com/ id/6208744/, accessed 20 September 2005; Erik Eckholm, *The New York Times,* "Whistle Blower Suit May Set Course in Iraq Fraud Case," 22 May 2005, 1.14.

36. After Halabja

Page 350   The Eliot quote is from the play *Murder in the Cathedral.*

Page 352   Washington Kurdish Institute estimates of deaths from 1988 bombings: Halabja Post-Graduate Medical Institute, http://www.kurd.org/halabja/.

Page 355   *The New York Times,* "The Long Trail to Apology," 28 June 2004, A18.

Sources

Aburish, Said K. *A Brutal Friendship: The West and the Arab Elite*. London: Victor Gollancz, 1997.

Ambrose, Stephen E. *Crazy Horse and Custer: The Parallel Lives of Two American Warriors*. New York: Doubleday, 1975.

Amnesty International. "2005 Country Report: Turkey." http://www.amnestyusa.org/countries/turkey/document.do?id=ar&yr=2005 (accessed 20 May 2005).

Amnesty International. "Turkey: Systematic Torture Continues in Early 2002." Amnesty.org, September 2002. http://web.amnesty.org/library/Index/engEUR440402002?OpenDocument&of=COUNTRIES%5CTURKEY (accessed 18 November 2004).

Amnesty International. "Leyla Zana, Prisoner of Conscience," n.d. http://www.amnestyusa.org/action/special/zana.html (accessed 18 May 2005).

Arai, Masami. *Turkish Nationalism in the Young Turk Era*. Leiden, Netherlands: E. J. Brill, 1992.

Barletta, Michael and Christina Ellington. "Iraq's Biological Weapons Program: Flowchart." Center for Nonproliferation Studies, Monterey Institute for International Studies, November, 1998. http://cns.miis.edu/research/wmdme/flow/iraq/seed.htm (accessed 5 May 2005).

Barry, John, and Roger Charles. "Sea of Lies." *Newsweek*, 13 July 1992, 28–39.

Battle, Joyce, ed. "Shaking Hands with Saddam Hussein: The U.S. Tilts Toward Iraq: 1980–1984." *National Security Archive Electronic Briefing Book*, no. 82. 25 Feb. 2003. http://www.gwu.edu/~nsarchiv/NSAEBB/NSAEBB82/ (accessed 17 Nov. 2004).

Bird, Christiane. *A Thousand Sighs, a Thousand Revolts*. New York: Random House, 2004, 186.

British Broadcasting Corporation (BBC), "Ocalan File: Timeline." 12 March 2003. http://news.bbc.co.uk/2/hi/europe/281302.stm (accessed 16 November 2004).

Campbell, Mark. "Kawa and the Story of Newroz." n.d. http://www.newrozfilms.com/the_legend_of_newroz.htm (accessed 16 November 2004).

Canada, Research Directorate, Immigration and Refugee Board, Ottawa, "Country of Origin Research: Turkey." 25 August 2004. http://www.irbcisr.gc.ca/en/research/ndp/ref/?action=view&doc=tur42658e (accessed 24 May 2005).

Chaliand, Gerard, ed. *A People Without a Country: The Kurds and Kurdistan.* London: Zed Books Ltd., 1993.

Churchill, Winston. "Prime Minister's Personal Minute, Serial No. D. 217/4." Photographic copy of original four-page memo, in *Der Krieg, der nicht stattfand,* edited by Guenther W. Gellermann. Munich: Bernard and Graefe Verlag, 1986. 249–251. www.globalresearch.ca/articles/ CHU407A.html (accessed 16 November 2004).

Constitution/Turkiye Cumhuriyeti Anayasas (No. 2709 November 7, 1982). "List of Turkish Laws Violating Free Expression." http://hrw.org/press98/feb/fe-turk.htm (accessed 21 September 2005).

Daniszewski, John. "[Yazidi] Ancient Faith Is a Reminder of Iraq's Diversity." *Los Angeles Times,* 10 March 2004, A5.

Eagleton, William. *The Kurdish Republic of 1946.* London: Oxford University Press, 1963.

Eckholm, Erik. "Whistle Blower Suit May Set Course in Iraq Fraud Case." *The New York Times,* 22 May 2005, 1.14.

Economist, The. Editorial, "Dangerous Work; Private Security Firms in Iraq." 10 April 2004. U.S. edition, p. 22–23.

Elphinston W. G. "The Kurdish Question." *International Affairs (Royal Institute of International Affairs)* 22, no. 1 (January 1946), 91–103.

Entessar, Nader. *Kurdish Ethnonationalism.* Boulder, Colo.: Lynne Rienner, 1992.

Federation of American Scientists. "U.S. Military Aid and Arms Sales to Turkey." http://www.fas.org/asmp/profiles/turkey_weapons.htm (accessed 16 September 2003).

Frantz, Douglas and Murray Waas. "Bush Secret Effort Helped Iraq Build Its War Machine Persian Gulf: Documents Show That Nine Months Before Hussein's Invasion of Kuwait the President Approved $1 Billion in Aid." *Los Angeles Times,* 23 February 1992, A1.

Friedman, Alan. "Warning Forced Bechtel out of Iraq Chemical Project." *Financial Times,* 21 February 1991.

Friedman, Josh. "Could Hussein's Capture Provide a Market Boost?" *Los Angeles Times,* 15 December 2003.

Gabelnick, Tamar, William D. Hartung, and Jennifer Washburn. *Arming Repression: U.S. Arms Sales to Turkey During the Clinton Administration. A Joint Report of the World Policy Institute and the Federation of American Scientists.* New York: 1999. http://www.fas.org/asmp/library/reports/turkeyrep.htm (accessed 6 December 2003).

Galbraith, Peter. *Kurdistan in the Time of Saddam Hussein—A Staff Report to the Committee on Foreign Relations of the United States Senate.* Washington, D.C.: U.S. Government Printing Office, November 1991.

Gambill, Gary C. "The Kurdish Reawakening in Syria." *Middle East Intelligence Bulletin.* April 2004. http://www.meib.org/articles/0404_s1.htm (accessed 7 May 2005).

Gellermann, Guenther W. *Der Krieg, der nicht stattfand.* Munich: Bernard & Graefe Verlag, ed., 1986, 249–51. www.globalresearch.ca/articles/CHU407A.html (accessed 16 November 2004).

Glanz, James. "Modern Mercenaries on the Iraqi Frontier." *The New York Times,* 4 April 2004. Sec. 4, 5.

Gilbert, Martin. *Winston S. Churchill.* IV, Heinemann, London, 1975, 494, 810; Companion IV ii, 1066–7, 1083, 1170; quoted in Omissi, 160.

Goldberg, Jeffrey. "The Great Terror." *The New Yorker,* 25 March 2002.

Goodman, Amy. "Halabja: How Bush Sr. Continued to Support Saddam After the 1988 Gassing of Thousands and Bush Jr. Used It As a Pretext for War 15 Years Later." Democracy Now. 29 September 2003. http://www.democracynow.org/article.pl?sid=03/09/29/155243# transcript (accessed 14 November 2004).

Gordon, Joy. "Cool War." *Harper's Magazine,* November 2002. http://www.scn.org/ccpi/ HarpersJoyGordonNov02.html (accessed 17 May 2005).

Hartung, William D. *And Weapons for All.* New York: HarperCollins, 1994.

Hartung, William D. "The Role of U.S. Arms Transfers in Human Rights Violations: Rhetoric Versus Reality." Testimony before the Subcommittee on International Operations and Human Rights, House International Relations Committee, 7 March 2001. http://www.worldpolicy .org/projects/arms/reports/testimony030701.htm (accessed 4 August 2004).

Hoagland, Jim. "The Kurdish Example." *The Washington Post,* 27 July 2003, B7.

Howard, Michael. "Kurd Chief Who Taught Mercy to Saddam's Men." *The Guardian,* 27 May 2005.

Human Rights Watch Helsinki. "Turkey: Forced Displacement of Ethnic Kurds from Southeastern Turkey." New York: Vol. 6, No. 12, October 1994.

Human Rights Watch. *Genocide in Iraq: The Anfal Campaign Against the Kurds.* Human Rights Watch. New York: 1993. http://www.hrw.org/reports/1993/iraqanfal/ (accessed 13 September 2003).

———. *Weapons Transfers and Violations of the Laws of War in Turkey.* New York: 1995. http://hrw.org/reports/1995/Turkey.htm (accessed 9 September 2003).

———. *World Report 1999: Turkey.* New York: 1999. http://www.hrw.org/worldreport99/ europe/turkey.html (accessed 16 November 2004).

Hunter, Jane. "Ocalan's Odyssey." *Covert Action,* Issue 67, 20 October 2004. http://covertaction .org//content/view/90/0/ (accessed 20 September 2005).

Izady, Mehrdad. "Are Kurds Descended from the Medes?" *Kurdish Life,* 10 March 1994. http://www.kurdistanica.com/english/history/articles-his/his-articles-08.html (accessed 20 May 2005).

Kelley, Matt. "Contractor Accused of Overbilling in Iraq." Associated Press, 8 October 2004. http://www.msnbc.msn.com/id/6208744/ (accessed 20 September 2005).

Kemal, Yasar. "Turkey's War of Words." *The New York Times,* 6 May 1995, 19.

Kendal (Nezan). "Kurdistan in Turkey." In *A People Without a Country: The Kurds and Kurdistan.* Chaliand, Gerard, ed. London: Zed Books Ltd., 1993, 38–94.

Kerry, John. United States Senate speech, Washington, D.C., 9 October 2002.

Kirisci, Kemal and Gareth M. Winrow. *The Kurdish Question and Turkey: An Example of a Trans-state Ethnic Conflict.* London: Portland, Or.: Frank Cass, 1997.

Kurdish Parliament Article 8. http://hrw.org/press98/feb/fe-turk.htm (accessed 1 June 2005).

Lancaster, John. "U.S. Gives Go-Ahead to Iraqi Opposition." *The Washington Post,* 14 January 2001, A1.

Lawrence, T. E., *Seven Pillars of Wisdom: A Triumph.* New York: Garden City Publishing, Inc., 1938.

Mango, Andrew. *Atatürk: The Biography of the Founder of Modern Turkey.* Woodstock, New York: The Overlook Press, Peter Meyer Publishers, Inc., 2000.

Marcus, Aliza. "Turkey's Kurds After the Gulf War: A Report from the Southeast." In *A People*

Without a Country: The Kurds and Kurdistan. Chaliand, Gerard, ed. London: Zed Books Ltd., 1993, 238–43.

Matthews, Owen. "Welcome to Kurdistan." *Newsweek*, U.S. edition, 25 March 2002.

McDowall, David. *The Kurds: A Nation Denied.* London: Minority Rights Group Publications, 1992.

———. *A Modern History of the Kurds.* London: I. B. Tauris, 2004.

Merle, Renae. "Army Scraps $39 Billion Helicopter." *The Washington Post*, 24 February 2004, A1.

Middle East Watch and Physicians for Human Rights. "Unquiet Graves: The Search for the Disappeared in Iraqi Kurdistan." February 1992. http://www.hrw.org/reports/1992/iraq/iraq0292.pdf (accessed 22 September 2003).

Milhollin, Gary. "Hans the Timid." *The Wall Street Journal*, 26 November 2002.

Nazadar, Mustafa. "The Kurds in Syria," in *A People Without a Country: The Kurds and Kurdistan.* Chaliand, Gerard, ed., London: Zed Books Ltd., 1993, 194–202.

New York Times. Editorial. "The Long Trail to Apology." 28 June 2004.

Olson, Robert W. *Turkey's Relations with Iran, Syria, Israel, and Russia, 1991–2000.* Costa Mesa, California: Mazda Publishers, 2001.

Omissi, David. *Air Power and Colonial Control: The Royal Air Force 1919–1939.* Manchester University Press, 1990.

———. "Baghdad and British Bombers: Iraq Is No Stranger to British Aerial Bombardment." *The Guardian*, 19 January 1991.

Oppenheimer, Andy. "Who Armed Iraq?" *Jane's Chem-BioWeb.* 17 April 2003. http://www.janes.com/defence/news/jcbw/jcbw030417_1_n.shtml (accessed 19 May 2005).

Ozel, Soli. "Which Way Is West for Turkey?" Project Syndicate. October 2004. http://www.project-syndicate.org/commentary/ozel2 (accessed 12 May 2005).

Paterson, Tony. "Leaked Report Says German and U.S. Firms Supplied Arms to Saddam." *The Independent,* 18 December 2002.

Pelletiere, Stephen C. *The Kurds: An Unstable Element in the Gulf.* Boulder, Colo.: Westview Press, 1984.

Phythian, Mark. *Arming Iraq: How the U.S. and Britain Secretly Built Saddam's War Machine* (Northeastern Series in Transnational Crime). Boston: Northeastern University Press, 1996.

Priest, Dana. "Rumsfeld Visited Baghdad in 1984 to Reassure Iraqis, Documents Show." *The Washington Post,* 19 December 2003.

Roberts, Les, Riyadh Lafta, Richard Garfield, Jamal Khudhairi, and Gilbert Burnham. "Mortality Before and After the 2003 Invasion of Iraq: Cluster Sample Survey." *The Lancet* 364: 9448, 20 November 2004, 1857–1864.

Roosevelt, Archie. "The Kurdish Republic of Mahabad," in *A People Without a Country: The Kurds and Kurdistan.* Chaliand, Gerard, ed. London: Zed Books Ltd., 122–138.

Rumsfeld, Donald. Press Conference. 7 June 2002. http://www.nato.int/docu/speech/2002/s020606g.htm (accessed 25 May 2005).

Safire, William. "Son of Secret Sell-Out." *The New York Times,* 12 February 1976, 30.

Scahill, Jeremy. "The Saddam in Rumsfeld's Closet." CommonDreams.com: 2 August 2002. http://www.commondreams.org/views02/0802-01.htm (accessed 13 November 2004).

Schorr, Daniel. "1975: Background to Betrayal: How Kissinger, Nixon and the Shah Rallied—Then Shrugged Off—an Uprising," *The Washington Post,* 7 April 1991, D3.

Shenon, Philip. "Iraq Links Germs for Weapons to U.S. and France." *The New York Times*, 16 March 2003.

Sidel, Dr. Victor W. "The International Arms Trade and Its Impact on Health." *British Medical Journal*, 23 December 1995. http://www.ippnw.org/MGS/V3Sidel.html (accessed 15 September 2005).

Simons, Geoff. *Iraq: From Sumer to Saddam*, 2nd ed. New York: St. Martin's Press, 1996.

Smith, Michael. "RAF Bombing Raids Tried to Goad Saddam into War." *The* [London] *Times*, 29 May 2005, 2.

Southeastern Anatolia Project Regional Development Administration, GAP. Website of the Turkish Embassy. http://www.gap.gov.tr/gap_end.php?sayfa=English/Ggbilgi/gnedir.html (accessed 20 September 2005).

Tirman, John. *Spoils of War*. New York: Free Press, 1997.

Toner, Mike. "Germ Sharing a Necessary Risk? CDC Exported Shipments to Fight Diseases." *The Atlanta Journal-Constitution*, 2 October 2002.

Townshend, C. "Civilization and Frightfulness." 148, Wg/Cdr to CAS, 19 February 1920, Trenchard Papers MFC 76/1/36.

Tyler, Patrick E. "Officers Say U.S. Aided Iraq in War Despite Use of Gas." *The New York Times*, 18 August 2002, 1.1.

United Nations Special Rapporteur's report, concluded in 1992 (UN Doc E/CN.4/1992/31, para. 154). New York: U.N., 1992.

United States Arms Control and Disarmament Agency. "World Military Expenditures and Arms Transfers, 1983–1993," May 1995, 24th edition. Washington, D.C. http://ssdc.ucsd.edu/ssdc/icp06516.html (accessed 18 September 2003).

U.S. Department of State. "Report on Allegations of Human Rights Abuses by the Turkish Military and on the Situation in Cyprus." June 1, 1995. http://www.fas.org/asmp/profiles/turkey_cyprus_1995.txt (accessed 19 May 2005).

U.S. House Select Committee on Intelligence Report (Pike Committee), 94th Congress, 1st session, 1975, 2nd session, 1976 as published in *CIA: The Pike Report*. Nottingham, England: Spokesman Books, 1977.

Vali, Abbas, ed. *Essays on the Origins of Kurdish Nationalism*. Costa Mesa, CA: Mazda Publishers, 2003.

Vallette, Jim, Steve Kretzmann, and Daphne Wysham. "Crude Vision: How Oil Interests Obscured U.S. Government Focus on Chemical Weapons Use by Saddam Hussein." 2nd edition. Washington, D.C.: Sustainable Energy and Economy Network/Institute for Policy Studies, 2003. http://www.seen.org/PDFs/Crude_Vision2.pdf (accessed 8 December 2003).

van Bruinessen, Martin. "The Suppression of the Dersim Rebellion in Turkey (1937–1938)." n.d. http://www.let.uu.nl/~martin.vanbruinessen/personal/publications/Dersim.pdf (accessed 14 September 2003). In "Genocide in Kurdistan? The Suppression of the Dersim Rebellion in Turkey (1937–1938) and the Chemical War Against the Iraqi Kurds (1988)," in *Conceptual and Historical Dimensions of Genocide*, edited by George J. Andreopoulos. Philadelphia: University of Pennsylvania Press, 1994. 141–70.

———. "Uprising in Kurdistan." *A Democratic Future for the Kurds of Turkey. Proceedings of the International Conference on North West Kurdistan (South East Turkey), March 1–13, 1994, Brussels*. London: Kurdistan Human Rights Project, 1994, 32–36.

Wanniski, Jude. "Bush and Cheney Are Misinformed." 25 March 2002. http://wanniski.com/showarticle.asp?articleid=1920 (accessed 3 June 2005).

Washburn, Jennifer. "Don't Sell Weapons to Turkey." 2 February 1997. http://kurdistan.org/Washington/washburn2.html (accessed 18 November 2004).

"White House Statement About the Centennial Anniversary of the Birth of Mustafa Kemal Atatürk of Turkey," in "The Public Papers of President Ronald W. Reagan." Ronald Reagan Presidential Library. http://www.reagan.utexas.edu/archives/speeches/1981/40281d.htm (accessed 18 May 2005).

White, Paul. *Primitive Rebels or Revolutionary Modernisers?: The Kurdish Movement in Turkey.* London: Zed Books, 2001.

Yavuz, Ramazan. "From the Mountains to the Gallery." *Hurriyet,* 24 June 2004.

Yildiz, Kerim. *The Kurds in Iraq: The Past, Present and Future.* London. Pluto Press, 2004.

Zaman, Amberin. "Spying Order from Turkish Generals Sparks Wide Protests." *Los Angeles Times,* 12 March 2004.

Index